Parish Nursing
Healthcare Ministry within the Church

Parish Nursing
Healthcare Ministry within the Church

Mary Elizabeth O'Brien
SFCC, PhD, MTS, RN, FAAN
The Catholic University of America School of Nursing

JONES AND BARTLETT PUBLISHERS
Sudbury, Massachusetts
BOSTON   TORONTO   LONDON   SINGAPORE

World Headquarters
Jones and Bartlett Publishers
40 Tall Pine Drive
Sudbury, MA 01776
978-443-5000
info@jbpub.com
www.jbpub.com

Jones and Bartlett Publishers
Canada
2406 Nikanna Road
Mississauga, ON L5C 2W6
CANADA

Jones and Bartlett Publishers
International
Barb House, Barb Mews
London W6 7PA
UK

Library of Congress Cataloging-in-Publication Data

O'Brien, Mary Elizabeth.
  Parish nursing : healthcare ministry within the church / Mary Elizabeth O'Brien.
    p. cm.
  Includes bibliographical references and index.
  ISBN 0-7637-2389-4
    1. Parish nursing. I. Title.

  RT120.P37O27 2003
  610.73'43—dc21

                                                                              2002043429

Acquisitions Editor: Kevin Sullivan
Production Manager: Amy Rose
Associate Editor: Karen Zuck
Associate Production Editor: Karen C. Ferreira
Production Assistant: Jenny L. McIsaac
Associate Marketing Manager: Joy Stark-Vancs
Marketing Associate: Jennifer Killam-Zambrano
Manufacturing and Inventory Coordinator: Amy Bacus
Composition: Chiron, Inc.
Cover Design: Kristin Ohlin
Printing and Binding: Malloy Inc.
Cover Printing: Malloy Inc.

Printed in the United States of America
07 06 05 04 03   10 9 8 7 6 5 4 3 2 1

This book is lovingly dedicated to parish nurses, past, present, and future, who proclaim the gospel message of Jesus in the caring and compassionate carrying out of their healthcare ministries.

CONTENTS

Chapter 3   The Parish Nursing Role: Spiritual Companion in Health and Illness   49

Chapter 4 Education for Parish Nursing Practice   75

Chapter 5 Conceptual Models of Parish Nursing Practice: A Middle-Range Theory of Spiritual Well-Being in Illness   99

Chapter 6 Initiating a Parish Nursing/Health Ministry Program   117

Chapter 7   The Spirituality of Parish Nursing   151

Chapter 8   Parish Nursing Ministry with Diverse Populations   175

Chapter 10 Parish Nursing Ministry in Contemporary Congregations: The Lived Experience   285

Appendices   305

PREFACE

This book, describing parish nurses' healthcare ministry, has been written in my heart for a very long time. Almost 30 years ago, as I was developing my doctoral dissertation research, which explored the relationship between social support and physical and psychosocial coping among persons with chronic renal failure (CRF), I began to think about patients' spiritual needs. Although most of my study questions were to be focused on broader issues of social support, such as relationships with family and friends, I asked my dissertation committee for permission to include two questions examining the place of personal religious faith in coping with renal failure and maintenance hemodialysis; they acquiesced.

The questions, one quantitative and one qualitative, asked whether and/or how a CRF patient's personal faith impacted coping with his or her illness and treatment regimen. The responses, from the 126 study participants, were overwhelmingly positive in terms of the value they placed on religious faith in helping them cope with their conditions. From then on, I began including some exploration of patients' spiritual needs in all of my research efforts. Ultimately, I decided to study theology so that I could focus my nursing research, writing, and practice on the spiritual and religious needs of those who are ill or disabled.

Almost a decade ago, I became interested in parish nursing. My first interview with a parish nurse, who had ministered in a Lutheran congregation for over five years, took place in 1995. At that time, the "parish nursing education" that the nurse described consisted of a weekend workshop at the conclusion of which she was commissioned as a parish nurse. Following that interview, I started to read more about the specialty of parish nursing and to ask questions of parish nurses, both formally and informally. In 1998, I began work on a research proposal to identify and describe the activities of parish nurses and the impact of parish nursing intervention on the recipients of the ministry. The study proposal was submitted to the Our Sunday Visitor Institute in late fall 1999 and was funded the following spring. The project titled "An

Experiment in Parish Nursing: The Gift of Faith in Chronic Illness" was concluded in the summer of 2001; much of the data included in that report is presented in Chapter 9 of this book. In the spring of 2001, I also was blessed to be commissioned as a parish nurse, after completing a Nurses Christian Fellowship parish nursing education course. This course is described in Chapter 4, which discusses education for parish nursing practice.

The following pages contain many anecdotes describing the creative and innovative nursing and pastoral care interventions carried out by contemporary parish nurses ministering within a variety of Christian denominations. Most importantly, data obtained through the formal research process reveal that parish nursing does indeed have a positive impact on the spiritual well-being and quality of life of chronically ill parishioners. Parish nursing's emphasis on health promotion and holistic health is reflected, also, in the increased sense of hope and life satisfaction described by study participants following the parish nurses' intervention. In presenting the research data, descriptive of instances in which either parish nurses or those to whom they ministered are "named," pseudonyms are used to protect confidentiality; the only exception occurs in one interview with a parish nurse leader who gave permission for her name and credentials to be shared in order to validate the information presented.

Although I must admit that this book is written for Christian parish nurses, as it is Christian theology that guides and inspires my work, I hope that nurses whose personal spirituality is supported by a different ethic might also find meaning and inspiration in the poignant examples of parish nursing care and commitment represented here. In support of the Christian theological undergirding of the book, the chapters are based in scripture, both Old and New Testament; each chapter begins with a biblically-based parish nurse's "meditation," and scripture references are interspersed liberally throughout the text. The book's appendices conclude with a compendium of biblically-based parish nurse's prayers, which may be used as presented or modified for use within a particular church setting.

A careful attempt was made to include an overview of the current state of parish nursing in the contents of the text. Chapter 1 explores the spiritual call to parish nursing ministry, including discussions of the Church as a center of health ministry and the theology of parish nursing. In Chapter 2, a spiritual history of parish nursing is presented, from the time of Jesus' healing the sick and calling all to wholeness on a Gallilean hillside, to the contemporary work of the International Parish Nurse Resource Center, under the aegis of Deaconess Parish Nurse Ministries in St. Louis, Missouri. Chapter 3 explores the role of the parish nurse as "spiritual companion" in health and illness; and Chapter 4 describes the present state of parish nursing education, including a discussion of the "credentialing" issue. In Chapter 5, several grand theories of parish nursing are described, and my development of a middle-range theory of spiritual well-being in illness is presented. Chapter 6 details the activities involved in initiating a parish nursing/health ministry program within a faith community; and Chapter 7 explores the parish nurse's personal spirituality. Chapter 8 gives examples of the ministry needs of diverse populations, such as the homebound adult and the hospitalized parishioner. Chapter 9 includes methodology and both quantitative and qualitative study findings for the project, "An Experiment in Parish Nursing: The Gift of Faith in Chronic Illness." And, in Chapter 10, the lived experiences of parish nurses serving within a variety of faith traditions and settings are presented. The appendices, as well as including parish nurses' prayers, also contain a Parish Health Assessment Profile, a Parish Health Needs Assessment Form, and other assorted parish nursing report forms that may provide helpful models for parish nurses initiating parish nursing/health ministry programs in their churches.

ACKNOWLEDGMENTS

Finally, it is most important to acknowledge that "it takes a village" to produce a book such as this; thus, there are many people and institutions to be thanked for completion of the work. First, I am deeply indebted to the Our Sunday Visitor Institute for financial support of the study "An Experiment in Parish Nursing: The Gift of Faith in Chronic Illness" and to the institute's executive director, Thomas J. Blee, Esq., for his personal interest in the project. The Nurses Christian Fellowship parish nursing education program, "Parish Nursing: Connecting Faith and Health," under the leadership of Judith Allen Shelly, RN, DMin, and Marabel Kersey, MSN, taught me much about the biblical basis of parish nursing and provided wonderful grounding for interpretation of study findings in light of contemporary Christian parish nursing.

I am very grateful to Norma R. Small, PhD, CRNP, consultant and educator for Parish Nursing and Health Ministries, Johnstown, Pennsylvania, consultant for the *Scope and Standards of Parish Nursing Practice*, and historian and archivist for the Health Ministries Association (HMA), for granting me a personal interview in which she explained the history and development of the HMA, as well as gave permission for me to cite extensively from her article, "Professional Credentialing for Parish Nurses." Deep thanks go to Rev. Deborah L. Patterson, MDiv, MHA, Executive Director, and Alvyne Rethemeyer, RN, MSN, Director of Parish Nursing, International Parish Nurse Resource Center (IPNRC), Deaconess Parish Nurse Ministries, for permission to cite the description of the IPNRC transition from two issues of *Parish Nurse Perspectives*. Special appreciation also to Rev. Deborah Patterson for her careful review of selected chapters of the manuscript.

Much gratitude is extended to Geraldine H. McDaniel, RN, CNA, CRRN, coordinator, Woman's Missionary Union of Virginia, Roanoke Valley Baptist Association, co-coordinator of the Virginia Parish Nurse Education Program (VPNEP), for permission to describe the VPNEP's biblically based distance-learning program. And, last, I am very much indebted to the many anonymous parish nurses who willingly shared their experiences in the hope of helping others who might one day walk a similar path.

Thanks are extended to the administrators of two healthcare system–based parish nursing/health ministry programs, who granted permission to cite materials and to reprint selected items from their unpublished program documents; they are Robert Short, Director of Parish Based Health Ministry, a pastoral outreach of the Caritas Christi Health System, and Lorraine Carrano, RN, MBA, Corporate Vice President for Mission Services, St. Vincent's Medical Center.

My very deep and heartfelt gratitude goes to Judy Shelly, RN, MAR, MDiv, editor of the *Journal of Christian Nursing*, for her prayerful and meticulous review of the entire manuscript; as always, Judy's suggestions contributed significantly to the final outcome of my work. I am also most appreciative of the caring and commitment of my editorial, production, and marketing team members at Jones and Bartlett Publishers, including Penny Glynn, PhD, RN; Karen Zuck, BA; Karen Ferreira, BA; and Joy Stark-Vancs, BA.

And, finally, my deepest gratitude is given to God, the source of my joy, the center of my life, and the true author of this book; to the Father, who gives me strength to "walk and not grow faint," even when I get very tired; to His Son, Our Lord Jesus, who inspires me with the passion to share His gospel message in my work; and to the Holy Spirit of wisdom and understanding, without whose guidance the words in this book would never have been written.

CREDITS

NRSV: For use of scripture citations from the *New Revised Standard Version Bible.*

St. Vincent's Medical Center: For description of program (citing from unpublished brochure) and reprinting of program materials: "Parish Nurse (Activity) Report" and "Newsletter Submission Form."

Caritas Christi Health System Parish-Based Health Ministry: For description of program (citing from unpublished brochure) and reprinting of "Health Assessment Profile" (Sections 1, 2, and 3).

Our Sunday Visitor Institute: For permission to publish OSV study data from the research project "An Experiment in Parish Nursing: The Gift of Faith in Chronic Illness."

Norma Small, PhD, CRNP: For permission to cite from her Health Ministries Association newsletter article, "Professional Credentialling for Parish Nurses."

Judith Allen Shelly, RN, DMin: For permission to cite from an editorial in the *Journal of Christian Nursing,* Summer 2002; and the Nurses Christian Fellowship, for permission to cite from the unpublished brochure "Parish Nursing: Connecting Faith and Health."

Virginia Parish Nurse Education Program: For permission to cite from the unpublished brochure "Virginia Parish Nursing Education Program."

Deaconess Parish Nurse Ministries: For permission to cite from two issues of the newsletter *Parish Nurse Perspectives.*

Jones and Bartlett Publishers: For permission to reprint several items from *Prayer in Nursing* and *Spirituality in Nursing: Standing on Holy Ground* (2nd ed.).

CHAPTER 1

THE GOSPEL CALL TO PARISH NURSING

For I was . . . sick and you took care of me.
—*Matthew 25:36*

Lord, When Did I Care for You?
A Parish Nurse's Meditation

Dear Lord,
"I beg your help," You said to me; "so many
    of my children are in need.
They're sick, and they're anxious and
    they're lonely; and there's no one
        to care for them.
The harvest is plentiful but the laborers are few
                        (*Luke 10:2*).
    Won't you become one of my laborers?;
      and care for Me?"

"I don't have time, right now," Dear Lord,
    I answered at first.
"Couldn't you ask someone else? I have so
    much 'business' to attend to,"

             (*Matthew 22:5*).

And, needing another defense, I added:
  "All of Your commandments 'I have
    kept since my youth';
                    (Mark 10:20).
  Isn't that enough?"

But then, You looked at me, Lord, with that
    look; the one that said you
        'loved me'; and it rent my
            heart.
    "Come follow me."
            (Mark 10:21) You whispered
  gently, and I was helpless.

And so, I followed You, Dearest Lord;
    I became Your laborer.
I have cared for Your children: those who
        were sick, and those who were anxious,
            and those who were lonely,
                but when,
                my Lord and my God,
                did I care for You?

Jesus replied:
  "When you fed a frail parishioner
        so the family could rest,
            you gave Me food.

"When you got a drink of water for a
    parishioner's sick child,
        you gave Me drink.

"When you invited a new parishioner
    to tell you her needs,
        you welcomed Me.

"When you brought a warm sweater to a
    wheelchair-bound parishioner,
        you clothed Me.

"When you counseled a parishioner
    diagnosed with cancer,
        you cared for Me."

And,

"When you prayed with a parishioner
        confined to a nursing home,
            you visited Me.

"In all of your ministries to these, my 'little ones,'
        Dear parish nurse," the Lord replied:
            "You cared for Me."

"And so," He added: "I shall, one day have another
        invitation for you, which I will issue
                with great joy":
        "Come, you that are blessed by my Father.
        Inherit the kingdom prepared for
                you from the foundation of
                    the world."

(Matthew 25:34).

"And You Cared For Me"

A Parable of Parish Nursing

The weather was bone-chillingly damp that late-fall Sunday morning; a harbinger, it seemed, of the winter that was just around the corner. This was the first cold snap of the season, and I really, really didn't want to get out of bed. I was just recovering from a busy and stressful workweek and the persistent buzzing of the alarm clock was a nasty intruder invading the warm, cozy cocoon of my bedcovers. I tried to hide my head under the pillow but, like the "Energizer Bunny," the alarm just kept going and going and going. Of course, I have to admit that I had set it the evening before to do precisely that. Then, however, my adrenalin had been flowing much better than it was this morning, and I was excited about my first day as the parish nurse team leader of our church's newly created Parish Health Ministry program. My planned health care ministry for the day was to bring Communion to one of our elderly and disabled parishioners, after morning worship, and to spend some time visiting with her and assessing her holistic health needs.

Mrs. O'Callahan was 78 years old and had been a parishioner of my church for over 50 of those years; she had a long history of service to the parish as a member of the Altar Society, as well as having belonged to a variety of ad hoc groups to which she had devoted many hours. She had lost her beloved husband over a decade ago, and their two sons were now married and living in another state. The sons worried a lot about their mother, alone in her small apartment, but Mrs. O'Callahan was adamant about not being ready for a nursing home; and she was not about to, in her words, "foist herself" upon her children and their families. Actually, up until a few weeks ago, "Mrs. O," as a lot of parishioners called her, had been able to get out and about quite well on her own. Unfortunately, a fall from a small stepladder had shattered one ankle and left her quite fragile in terms of walking or even driving, at least for the immediate future. Mrs. O'Callahan desperately missed the worship services and volunteer church activities around which her life had come to revolve in recent years. My parish nursing assignment to visit Mrs. O was decidedly daunting, considering her highly regarded position in our parish coupled with the fact that this was to be my first pastoral visit.

I had prayed a lot about the ministry visit but still arrived at Mrs. O'Callahan's door feeling shy and insecure; she quickly took care of that. I soon realized that I was in the presence of a holy, and a loving, and a very understanding woman. Before the visit even began, she told me what a special gift my coming to see her was; how she knew that it was hard to "get moving" on a Sunday morning, after working all week, and how it was especially difficult "when the weather is as nasty out" as it was that day. She asked about me: how my health was; how my nursing was going; how my patients were. I began to relax and feel myself being cared for and ministered to; I who had come, somewhat hesitantly, to be a caregiver and a minister.

As our visit progressed, Mrs. O and I prayed together, we laughed together and we even cried a little together over the many sufferings in our world. And Mrs. O'Callahan shared her own insecurities and concerns, now that it seemed her health was beginning to fail; her greatest fear was that she might one day become a burden on her family or friends. Mrs. O allowed me the privilege of listening to her worries, of learning her needs, of ministering to her: the reason for which I had come. As I said, she was a very holy and a very wise woman. We said a final prayer together, hugged warmly, and I took my leave.

As I got in the car and glanced at my watch, I was shocked to see that I had stayed with Mrs. O'Callahan for almost three hours; the time seemed to have flown by. I thought, when preparing for this ministry, that an hour would be an "appropriate" time in which to conduct a health ministry visit; that, of course, was leaving out the intervention of the Holy Spririt, who, I have learned, never allows things to happen exactly the way we plan. That would make life much too predictable!

I was also surprised at how energized I felt. Usually, Sunday afternoon is, for me, a time to "let down," a kind of relaxed, sleepy time. But not this Sunday. As I was driving home, I began to reflect on why I felt so light and so peaceful and yet so full of energy and joy. And suddenly the scripture, the beautiful and powerful passage from the Gospel of Matthew, which guides parish health ministry, filled my heart and my spirit: "For I was ill . . . and you cared for me" (Matthew 25:35). This was the gospel message that had inspired my desire to undertake the work of parish nursing; today, I experienced the very ministry which Jesus, Himself, urged His followers to embrace over 2000 years ago. And I realized that in caring for Mrs. O'Callahan in her illness, I had indeed cared for Him. This is the treasure of parish nursing; this is the blessing of parish health ministry. This is the gift for the parish nurse.

Today, chronically ill people live longer than ever, many remaining in their own homes even as multiple physical and psychosocial complications associated with the aging process escalate. Healthcare systems, nevertheless, mandate abbreviated hospital stays for those who require periods of intensive medical services; thus, the role of long-term care for a number of these persons falls to families or friends. In some cases, such home care is supplemented by volunteers from an ill person's church. Never before has Jesus' gospel mandate to care for each other, carried out in terms of a parish or congregational health ministry, been so critical for frail or disabled individuals in our society; this is true not only for homebound persons, but also for those residing in long-term care facilities where no spiritual support is provided by the institution. Pastoral care provided by parish nurses and health ministers can be vitally important in helping such ill church members cope with their illnesses and disabilities. And, in this era of health-system flux, the health promotion activities of parish nurses are essential to filling the gaps existing in health education and support.

As I began to explore contemporary parish nursing and parish health ministry in the literature, I also reviewed Internet sites for references to the topics; much to my surprise, my first search documented over 43,000 sites under the parish health ministry listing. I visited the first 750 websites. Many were websites created by individual congregations to publicize their programs of health ministry. Some of the ministries were well organized, with structured "health cabinets" or "health and welfare committees" providing oversight and one or more parish nurses leading a ministry team. Other churches described only the role of their "parish nurse"; and a few congregations admitted that they had not yet begun a program but were hoping to initiate parish health ministry and were seeking interested volunteers. A variety of religious denominations were represented on the parish nursing and health ministry websites. Some of the faith traditions included Lutheran, Episcopalian, Baptist, Roman Catholic, Presbyterian, Methodist, Evangelical, Adventist, United Church of Christ, Reformed Church, and Church of the Nazarene. Most of the sites identified some basic roles of the parish nurse; a point emphasized was the fact that a parish nursing or health ministry program was not to be considered a substitute for the existing healthcare system. The health ministry team, rather, consisted of members of a faith community who felt called to provide support and assistance in negotiating the system or in supplementing health and pastoral care needs of parishioners in an informal manner; these activities were carried out in a way consistent with the directions of the pastor and the church's parish council or health cabinet.

Several churches identified their parishes' health ministry programs as falling under the umbrella of "social ministries" within the congregations, although for the most part, health ministry programs stood alone. The majority of ministries appeared to be operating on an all-volunteer basis, including the activities of the parish nurse. In churches where the parish nurse role was formalized as a staff position, the nurse's official office hours were generally scheduled for three to four hours, once or twice a week. During this time, phone calls requesting home visits were accepted, as well as walk-in consultations. A number of churches also held "Health Ministry Sundays" on which health promotion activities, such as blood pressure screening, were carried out following worship services.

Virtually all of the congregations that described parish health ministry programs supported by their churches identified the charism or philosophy of the program as derived from the example and teachings of Jesus, as related in Christian scripture. Thus, while parish health ministry, or congregational health ministry as it is called by some churches, is a new and developing area of pastoral care within today's faith communities, it is also a very old ministry, with roots firmly entrenched in the healing ministry of Jesus and his followers in the early Christian Church.

I visited several hundred of the 57,400 parish nursing websites on the Internet. These websites described such topics as educational programs to prepare nurses for parish nursing ministry, the sharing of individual congregations' parish nursing experiences, the description of the parish nursing role, the philosophy of parish nursing, and the scriptural call to parish nursing. As with the health ministry sites, the parish nursing websites represented a variety of faith traditions within the Christian community.

The bottom line of my research, both in the literature (cited later in this book) and on the Internet, was a conclusion that the concepts of parish nursing and parish health ministry are gaining significant interest and attention among contemporary faith communities. In writing a chapter on parish nursing only a couple of years ago, I introduced the topic by citing an anecdote related by a parish nurse in which a group of Christian pastors, after hearing a presentation on parish nursing, came away still not understanding what the concept really entailed (O'Brien, 2003, p. 291). At a recent discussion with a group of parish nurses from local churches, one nurse shared with us the fact that her pastor, learning that she was about to retire, had come to *her* and said: "*I need a parish nurse!*" This is quite a reversal from the many reports of parish nurses who have described having to advocate aggressively to convince a pastor or church leadership group of the need for and the worth of parish nursing and of developing a health ministry program for the congregation.

The Scriptural Call to Parish Nursing

In looking at the classic gospel passage in which Matthew (25:35–36) captures Jesus' teaching to those disciples who would one day be called "blessed" by His Father, it is possible to see clearly how a parish nurse's role responds to the Lord's teaching. Jesus pointed out that those who would "inherit the kingdom" had cared for Him in caring for brothers and sisters in need; He explained: "For I was hungry and you gave me food"—parish nurses assist homebound parishioners with shopping or even feeding, if involved in respite care for very ill parishioners; "I was thirsty and you gave me something to drink"—parish

"For I was hungry and you gave me food, I was thirsty and you gave me something to drink, I was a stranger and you welcomed me, I was naked and you gave me clothing, I was sick and you took care of me, I was in prison and you visited me"
—*Matthew 25:35–36*

nurses assist frail elders or acutely ill patients in getting a drink of water or juice when visiting; "a stranger and you welcomed me"—an ill parishioner may well be a "stranger" to a parish nurse on a first pastoral visit, yet, through the ministry, the parishioner is welcomed into a new dimension of parish life; "naked and you gave me clothing"—parish health ministry programs often have a "loan closet" or "clothing shop" of slightly used but serviceable items that may be shared with those who are financially compromised because of illness and disability; "sick and you took care of me"—while the parish nurse does not carry out invasive health care procedures, there are many physical, psychosocial, and spiritual comfort care procedures involved in pastoral ministry visits; and "in prison and you visited me"—many parishioners who are restricted to their homes or to health care facilities feel that they are imprisoned by their illness or disability, and the visit from a parish nurse can provide a caring interaction that greatly alleviates their loneliness and isolation.

> *"Jesus went throughout Galilee, teaching in their synagogues and proclaiming the good news of the kingdom, and curing every disease and every sickness among the people"* —*Matthew 4:23*
>
> *"Many crowds followed him and he cured all of them"* —*Matthew 12:15*
>
> *"As the sun was setting, all those who had any who were sick with various kinds of diseases brought them to him; and he laid his hands on each of them and cured them"* —*Luke 4:40*

As well as the preceding cited passage from Matthew's gospel, there are also a number of scripture narratives describing Jesus' healing activities that support the health care dimension of parish nursing. Some of these include group healings: "Jesus went throughout Galilee, teaching in their synagogues and proclaiming the good news of the kingdom, and curing every disease and every sickness among the people" (Matthew 4:23); "Many crowds followed him and he cured all of them" (Matthew 12:15); and "As the sun was setting, all those who had any who were sick with various kinds of diseases brought them to him; and he laid his hands on each of them and cured them" (Luke 4:40). Jesus' ministry of caring involved numerous individual healings as well: "Simon's mother-in-law was suffering from a severe fever, and they asked him about her. Then he stood over her, and rebuked the fever, and it left her. Immediately, she got up and began to serve them" (Luke 4:38–39); "Then Jesus stretched out his hand, touched [the leper] and said . . . 'Be made clean.' Immediately the leprosy left him" (Luke 5:13); "He said to the one who was paralyzed, 'I say to you, stand up and take your bed and go to your home.' Immediately, he stood up before them, took

> *"Simon's mother-in-law was suffering from a severe fever, and they asked him about her. Then he stood over her, and rebuked the fever, and it left her. Immediately, she got up and began to serve them"* —*Luke 4:38–39*
>
> *"Then Jesus stretched out his hand, touched [the leper] and said . . . 'Be made clean.' Immediately the leprosy left him"* —*Luke 5:13*

what he had been lying on, and went to his home glorifying God" (Luke 5:24–25); "He took [Jairus's daughter] by the hand and called out: 'child get up!' Her spirit returned, and she got up at once" (Luke 8:54); "He took the blind man by the hand and led him out of the village; and when he had put saliva on his eyes and laid his hands on him . . . his sight was restored and he saw everything clearly" (Mark 8:23–25); "He cried with a loud voice: 'Lazarus, come out!' The dead man came out, his hands and feet bound . . . Jesus said . . . 'Unbind him and let him go'" (John 11:43–44). In all of these gospel passages, the health care dimension of Jesus' ministry is displayed in His sensitivity and response to the physical needs of those who would be His followers.

> "He said to the one who was paralyzed, 'I say to you, stand up and take your bed and go to your home.' Immediately, he stood up before them, took what he had been lying on, and went to his home glorifying God"
> —Luke 5:24–25

> "He took [Jairus's daughter] by the hand and called out: 'child get up!' Her spirit returned, and she got up at once"
> —Luke 8:54

An important message for us to glean from the scriptural stories of Jesus' healings is the fact that in so many instances Jesus directly interacted with and/or touched the sick to whom He ministered. Jesus did not just stand on a mountaintop and give a blessing or say to someone, "Be healed!" He "stood over" Simon's mother-in-law and "rebuked the fever." He "stretched out his hand and touched" the leper. He allowed the man who was paralyzed to be lowered down through a hole in the roof that he might be laid before Him for healing. He took Jairus's daughter "by the hand" and "called to her: 'child get up!'"; "He took the blind man by the hand and led him out of the village," then "putting saliva on his eyes," he laid his hands on him. Jesus repeatedly modeled for us the kind of loving interaction and caring touch that He would have His followers adopt toward those who are ill or disabled.

> "He took the blind man by the hand and led him out of the village; and when he had put saliva on his eyes and laid his hands on him . . . his sight was restored and he saw everything clearly"
> —Mark 8:23–25

> "He cried with a loud voice: 'Lazarus, come out!' The dead man came out, his hands and feet bound . . . Jesus said . . . 'Unbind him and let him go'"
> —John 11:43–44

There are also a number of scripture passages in which Jesus' disciples are directly mandated to care for the health of those to whom they will minister; these include such passages as: "The Commissioning of the Twelve": "Then Jesus summoned his twelve disciples and gave them authority over unclean spirits, to cast them out and to cure every disease and every sickness . . . [instructing them to] . . .

'cure the sick, raise the dead, cleanse the lepers, cast out demons'" (Matthew 10:1; 5; 8); and Paul's lesson to the Corinthians in which he used the analogy of one body with many parts to exemplify the responsibility of members of the Christian community to care for each other: "For just as the body is one and has many members . . . so it is with Christ. For in the one Spirit we were all baptized into one body . . . [and] the members of the body that seem to be weaker are indispensable. . . . If one member suffers, all suffer together with it" (1 Corinthians 12:12–13; 22; 26). It is suggested that scriptures, such as the latter, teach us that "the Church community, then, needs to embrace, protect and assist its poor, weak, sick and handicapped members" (Kern, 1984, p. 5).

> *"Then Jesus summoned his twelve disciples and gave them authority over unclean spirits, to cast them out and to cure every disease and every sickness . . . [instructing them to] . . . 'cure the sick, raise the dead, cleanse the lepers, cast out demons'"*
> —*Matthew 10:1; 5; 8*

> *"For just as the body is one and has many members . . . so it is with Christ. For in the one Spirit we were all baptized into one body . . . [and] the members of the body that seem to be weaker are indispensable. . . . If one member suffers, all suffer together with it"*
> —*1 Corinthians 12:12–13; 22; 26*

While not all of Jesus' ministry involved attention to the needs of the sick, the healing narratives were surely important in the gospel message of the evangelists. Theologian Thomas Droege poses a rhetorical question as to what, in fact, it means for us Christians that Jesus "healed people of physical diseases"? His response is, "At the very least it means that physical healing and health ought to receive as much attention from us as they did from Jesus" (Droege, 1991, p. 61). Droege goes on to explain that Christians need to be supportive of the contemporary interest in the relationship between health or well-being and faith, as this is the "second source of meaning in the healing stories of Jesus—whole person healing" (p. 61). One of my favorite examples is the woman with the 12-year hemorrhage who seemed afraid to bother Jesus with her troubles, yet had strong enough

> *"Daughter, your faith has made you well; go in peace, and be healed of your disease"*   —*Mark 5:34*

faith in His power and His caring that she believed that only "touching the hem of his garment" would cure her. When Jesus confronted her, and she confessed her need and her belief in His power to heal, He gifted her with the response: "Daughter, your faith has made you well; go in peace, and be healed of your disease" (Mark 5:34).

The Relationship of Faith and Health

Current scholarly and popular literature suggests a positive relationship between personal faith and wellness. Faith has been described as "an untapped health resource" (Kenniston, 1987, pp. 28–29), which "throughout the ages [has] played an awesome, albeit sometimes vague, role in facilitating health" (p. 28). Thus, "nurses," Kenniston adds, "need to be concerned about faith insofar as it relates to health" (p. 29). In support of Kenniston's point, a discussion of the relationship of religion to public health notes that while religion's role as a "modifier of health status" is "poorly defined and not universally accepted," population survey data "indicate a strong desire of people to have their spiritual needs addressed in concert with their health needs" (Becker, 2001, p. 351).

It is reported further that having a sense of spiritual comfort or peace may greatly enhance coping with illness or disability. Over the past few years, I have been exploring the relationship between spiritual well-being and quality of life among chronically ill persons. To date, 92 adults living with a chronic illness have been interviewed. Their ages ranged from 21 to 92 years; 44 percent of the group falling in the 51 to 70 years of age category. Twenty-nine individuals were over 70. As expected, older age groups were highly represented among the chronically ill. Thirty-three of the study participants were male, and 59, or 64 percent, were female. Just over half, 49 persons, were married; 29 were widowed, separated, or divorced; and 14 were single. Faith traditions represented among the group included 31 Protestants, 57 Roman Catholics, two Jewish persons, one Budddhist, and one individual who reported that he was "not sure" what his religion was.

The group's diagnoses included such conditions as diabetes, lung cancer, emphysema, rheumatoid arthritis, asthma, prostate cancer, malignant hypertension, breast cancer, colon cancer, Crohn's disease, congestive heart failure (CHF), chronic obstructive pulmonary disease, multiple sclerosis, muscular dystrophy, coronary artery disease, osteomyelitis, and cerebral palsy. Among the over-70 age group, individuals often presented a multiplicity of diagnoses; for example, a 92-year-old woman with hypertension, CHF, arthritis, depression, lung cancer, and fibromyalgia; and an 88-year-old woman suffering from diverticulitis, hypothyroidism, diabetes, uterine fibroids, and arthritis.

During the interviews, study participants were asked to respond to quantitative tools measuring spiritual well-being, hope, and life satisfaction. They were also requested to share their personal thoughts about the importance of spiritual well-being and/or personal faith in coping with their illness conditions. Overall, a significant relationship between spiritual well-being and quality of life (hope and life satisfaction) was evidenced in the quantitative interview data; the chronically ill persons' qualitative narratives also reflected the importance of this relationship in their lives.

A 66-year-old widow diagnosed with multiple sclerosis explained the meaning of spiritual well-being in light of her illness and disability: "To me, spiritual well-being means peace of mind and feeling good about myself and my condition. Thinking that, even though I am ill, God is always there protecting me and loving me. This gives me peace of mind." Two chronically ill women spoke about the importance of trust in God in dealing with their conditions: one, a 51-year-old woman with diabetes and severe degenerative arthritis, commented: "If you look at the half-empty glass, there would be a lifetime of depression and sadness. Each day I concentrate on the half-full glass, and things go better than I expect them to go. I look at what I can do, not at what I can no longer do. I trust that God has a reason for everything, a reason for me being alive, and I believe He has things for me to do, despite my pain; He knows I love a challenge." And a 52-year-old emphysema sufferer reported: "I could not get through my illness without God. I leave my illness and my prayers in God's hands. Spiritual well-being means being at peace with myself and with God. It means trusting in God and believing that all things are possible with Him."

A number of the individuals interviewed admitted that there were times when their illness conditions were very difficult to deal with; it was at those times, especially, that faith beliefs proved most crucial. A 56-year-old mother with severe arthritis and sarcoidiosis admitted: "My health is really declining. There are so many things wrong with my body and I'm always in pain." She added: "I just pray that God will see me through until my children are all finished with school and married. I thank God for giving me the strength He has given me up to now. God understands that I am trying to do for my children, so I do what I can and leave the rest to Him." A 49-year-old mother with chronic hepatitis reported: "With my current illness, I get depressed a lot. My mind gets cluttered with negative thoughts, like death, but when I direct my thoughts toward God, I feel better; I feel reassured that God is in control." And a 48-year-old social worker, diagnosed with breast cancer, asserted: "I find so much strength in my spiritual beliefs; they give me a focus when the cancer seems so irrational and destructive."

For chronically ill individuals whose conditions are life-threatening, thoughts of death are often close at hand; spiritual beliefs are frequently critical in helping them cope with their uncertain futures. A 79-year-old nurse, suffering from a multiplicity of illnesses including coronary artery disease and rheumatoid arthritis, spoke about death as being a "great adventure": "When I get depressed about my medical condition or when I'm in pain from my arthritis, I think about the new life that awaits me; my life with God." She added: "My dog will run to me, my parents will be waiting, I'll see my husband and hopefully I'll get my wings; could you think of anything better than flying?" A much younger woman, 29 years old and diagnosed with muscular dystrophy, asserted: "In your relationship with God, your spirituality, you understand that your mortality is not nescessarily the end of you but is, in fact, a new beginning; through spirituality you understand that dying may mean freedom instead of the end, and you feel at peace in your soul."

Finally, a theme repeated over and over in the narratives of chronically ill individuals related to the fact that it was indeed one's "faith" which enabled the person to cope with a particular illness or disability. A 78-year-old retired nurse with breast cancer commented: "My faith in God is what keeps me going. I believe that in the end I will be reunited with [those I love] but until then I live everyday, all day, and at the end thank God for it." And a 38-year-old woman living with fibromyalgia shared the fact that while in the past she had sometimes felt far away from God, now "faith in God gives me the courage to get up in the morning and start my day." She added: "I need Him in my life as my comforter and to guide me. My faith makes me count my blessings and remember the good in my trial and not the bad."

While the personal stories of many of those interviewed were inspiring and poignant, perhaps the account that best exemplifies the powerful impact of faith and spiritual well-being on the lived experience of life-threatening chronic illness is that of Mrs. Margaret Mullaney. Margaret, a 61-year-old grandmother, had been diagnosed for the past three years with stage IV ovarian cancer; she had one major surgery, a colostomy, and seven minor surgeries, as well as 10 different regimens of chemotherapy. She observed initially: "I believe in God who rejoices with me in times of health; He is there in His Holy Spirit to guide me." She added: "In times of sickness God is there to give me strength and the spiritual sustenance to get through this journey. And He makes me feel very loved, so I know that He is there in good times and in bad."

I'll let Margaret take up her story from here:

> When I was first diagnosed with cancer, I was filled with fear, and certainly a lot of crying and wondering what lay ahead. I was told it was incurable. There was no light at the end of the tunnel. It was almost claustrophobic; like things closing in on me. And I soon realized that I could not go on like this. And so I went into my bedroom and got down on my knees, and put my hands up to my God and said that I could only do it in His strength. If He was there for me; if He would be my strength, then I could do it. And I felt this peace that just washed over me; just like a balm.

> *It was a very physical feeling, this peace that God was giving me, and I knew then that it was the peace that the Bible speaks about, the peace that only God can give. And with it a calmness and a lack of fear. From then on, I had no fear of tests, of surgery, any situation that lay ahead with the cancer; and to this day I can say that God has relieved that fear and has left me with this beautiful peace of His.*

Margaret continued to speak of the importance of trust in God in the face of her illness:

> *God is in control. I have no control over the disease but I trust that God will give me the strength and the energy for the activities that each day holds. I trust Him to guide me in the daily discernment I must make concerning my treatments, so I feel that trust is probably one of the major feelings that I have toward God right now. Trust that He knows what he is doing, that He knows the results, and I need only put myself in His hands between now and the end of my journey. My belief in God makes me feel loved and humbled. I know that He cares for me and I know that He is with me in this. And He's using others, my husband and my family, to support and comfort me; that's the way I can feel His presence in the world; through others.*

Margaret also spoke about the importance of her church in the face of her devastating illness:

> *I am very at home in my parish where we have belonged for 41 years. Sometimes I miss church because of my illness but then my husband brings me Communion. My parish has really rallied to my support. The pastor has come to anoint me and bring me the Eucharist. The parishioners are very supportive. They bring everything from meals; they come to visit. They pray with me; they pray for me. They send cards. They are willing to drive me to the doctor's. I love going to church because when I do there are so many people there who are ready to give hugs and to support me with their love and their caring.*

Margaret described her personal religious practices such as prayer and spiritual reading:

> *I talk to God thoughout the day; thank Him for his goodness, for good health. My husband and I pray together and we pray with the children when they are here. We have always prayed together as a family. And, now especially, I read books on prayer that help me find out where God is in all this; or the lives of special people like Saint Therese. Doing spiritual reading at a time such as this, it gives me guidance to my prayer life. It also lifts my spirit. More and more I look for material that I can meditate on during this time.*

It brings me closer to God and helps me to look at my situation in a different light. With the fact that my mortality is right "smack-dab" in front of me, it helps me to prepare for the transition from this life to the next. I also have prayer cards that I love to say the prayers on. And we have lit candles in petition and others have lit candles in petition for my healing.

Margaret also asserted:

Religious music is a big thing for me. I love to listen to religious music. I love to sing along with it; just hum as I go along. I like to just keep music in my mind because it's both relaxing and uplifting and it's full of praise to God. And that is how I want to live my days—giving praise to God for his constantness in my life.

Finally, Margaret admitted:

My faith has so much to do with my illness that it is difficult to talk about where I am in this journey if I can't talk about my faith because it is so much a part of it. I have never felt angry at God. I don't like the circumstances I'm in. I don't like the cancer, but as long as I have it I'm going to try and use it to help other people. I don't think that God causes the cancer. I don't think that God gives people these kinds of things, but He does say, "I will be there for you in times of need," and that we can use adverse situations to bring about good. I feel that I have done this in going out to speak to cancer support groups and retreats and even speaking at our church. I've done a video to use my cancer to encourage and inspire others to keep going; to keep keeping on. That this isn't the worst thing that could happen to a person in life.

She concluded:

Sometimes, you know, when you're very, very ill, after surgery, or after certain kinds of chemo treatments, it's very difficult to pray for yourself so sometimes just knowing that others are praying for you, and holding you up before the Lord, and I know that if I do get that feeling of "where is God?" I know I have to keep telling myself that He isn't the one who is far away, but that I have moved away. And so I just talk to Him and tell Him how I'm feeling so that I can talk to and tell Him. My faith in God definitely affects the quality of my life; knowing that this life is not all there is certainly helps considerably. I know that; I have this saying, "I know that I'm in a 'win-win' situation"; if I get to stay here with my family and friends, then I win, and if I die, I'll be with my God. So this is a situation where I can say: my God walks with me, talks with me, journeys with me, in many forms and shapes and ways, and life is good despite the cancer.

Throughout Margaret's detailed account of the importance of faith in coping with her illness, the support of her church emerges as playing a key role. And yet, Margaret, by her own admission, also has significant social and emotional support provided by a caring network of family and friends. How much more critical, then, is the ministry of one's church for an ill parishioner who is elderly and/or alone, without loved ones to comfort and care for them in their times of need.

The Church as a Center for Health Ministry

In the early history of Christianity, the Church was viewed by its members as a community wherein all of one's needs might be addressed: physical, emotional, social, and spiritual. During this time, very few buildings were identified as churches; worship services were held at the homes of the early followers of Christ. There are a number of legends of the era describing church-related health care ministries carried out by the Christian disciples. One is that of the saintly twin brothers Cosmas and Damien; both were physicians who cared compassionately and unselfishly for the sick poor, never accepting recompense for their services. They believed that they had been called by God to their ministry of medical care. Because of the austerity of their personal lifestyles, they were labeled by the community as "the moneyless ones." Ultimately, Cosmas and Damien were martyred for openly practicing their Christian faith.

A contemporary understanding of *church* also includes both concepts of place and body of believers. Livingstone (1990) defines *church* as a "building and the Christian community, local or universal" (p. 108). The word *church* is derived from the Greek "*kuriakos*, meaning 'belonging to the Lord' or as a shorthand for *kuriakon doma* . . . meaning 'the Lord's house'" (Hill, 1990, p. 185). *Church* has, however, also been "used in versions of the scriptures to translate the word *ekklesia* . . . [meaning] an official assembly of people" (Hill, 1990, p. 186). In the scripture, Saint Paul envisions the church as describing the followers of Christ, possessed of "a common vision of community" (Doohan, 1993, p. 164). As well as imitating Christ and embracing virtues such as prayer and ethical behavior, Paul admonishes the disciples to "selflessly give themselves to the service of others and the spread of the gospel" (Doohan, 1993, p. 164).

The importance, as well as the validity, of the present-day relationship between religious faith, frequently associated with church membership and church support, and health was discussed earlier. Study findings from research with chronically ill persons reinforces the belief. Both nursing and pastoral care literature also identify the positive benefits of associating faith and health. In describing nursing as a "spiritual practice,"

Janet Macrae (2001) points out that "scientific research supports the thesis that religious beliefs can have a positive effect on health" (p. 26); and she cites study findings demonstrating the fact that religious "factors" have been associated with a number of health improvements such as reduced blood pressure and decreased drug and alcohol abuse (p. 26).

One other reason why the modern church might be considered a natural setting for health ministry was described early on in the parish nursing movement by Rev. Dr. Granger Westberg. Rev. Westberg (1990) cites the frequent laments of physicians regarding their inability to motivate patients to choose healthy lifestyles and health-promoting behaviors. "This," Westberg asserts, "is where the church comes in" (p. 9). He notes that motivation toward health behaviors is related to the way individuals "look at life"; and that such motivation "comes through spiritual commitment": "The church does such motivating of people on a weekly basis and continues to care about people throughout their entire lives" (p. 9). Thus, Rev. Westberg holds that a parish nurse working within the structure of a church or faith community might be able to offer "just the kind of needed inspiration" (p. 9) to assist an ill parishioner in embracing postive coping strategies and health behaviors.

Authors Margaret Clark and Joanne Olson (2000), who describe faith seeking and health seeking as "parallel processes," also believe that churches or faith communities "provide unique settings for health promotion" (p. 5). Because many "developmental and situational" life transitions occur within or are related to a church context, there is a significant opportunity to provide and promote health and health care in the setting. "Nursing within the context of a faith community," Clark and Olson perceive, is "an opportunity to respond to people in their times of departure, transition and integration" (p. 7). A number of developmental life transition–linked nursing opportunities come to mind immediately, such as those related to birth, childhood, adolescence, middle age, change of life, elderhood, and death. Some of these are formalized in individual churches with rituals such as baptism, confirmation, marriage, and anointing of ill elders. There are, however, many situational life transitions as well that may have church-related implications, such as the death of a parishioner's child, parent, or spouse; a marital separation or divorce; or age- or illness-related entrance into a nursing home or assisted care facility. At the point of and after such situational life transitions, parishioners often turn to a pastor or to church members for spiritual support and guidance; a parish nurse, working in the church context, has the mandate to assess and, if appropriate, intervene to assist the parishioner in such transitions in coping with both physically and spiritually related symptoms or stressors.

The Healthcare System–Affiliated Church Ministry Program

When considering parish nursing or health ministry programs, as described earlier, one generally thinks of a particular church or faith community within which the ministry is carried out. And because of the newness of the parish health nursing/health ministry field, most programs are begun by individual churches through the initiative of the pastor, nurse parishioner(s), and/or other members of the congregation, whose vision encourages and fosters the effort. In some urban areas, however, local healthcare systems are affiliating with neighboring churches to advise and support the initiation of parish nursing/health ministry within individual faith communities.

One such effort, located in the northeastern United States, is labeled "Parish Based Health Ministry" (PBHM); PBHM is described as a "pastoral outreach of the Caritas Christi Health System" (Caritas Christi Health System, 2002, p. 1). The description of the Parish Based Health Ministry program points out, "Churches have traditionally carried out health ministry through sponsorship of health care institutions and hospital chaplains" (p. 2). "Today, however," it is noted, "the face of health care is changing. Hospital stays are shorter, home care and community-based programs are more commonplace, and people are taking on greater roles in attending to their own health" (p. 2).

Thus, the PBHM description continues: "Churches now have the wonderful opportunity to reclaim the connection between health and religion and make it operative in the everyday lives of parishioners. . . . PBHM works with parish leadership to identify the health needs of the parish and, together with a health team of parishioners, cultivate programs that serve those needs" (p. 2).

The PBHM mission statement describes the organization's philosophy and theology of ministry: "Parish Based Health Ministry . . . is rooted in the compassionate witness of Jesus and in the conviction that all life is sacred. PBHM is: Gospel centered, modeled after the life of Jesus; Responds to the needs as identified by each parish; Self-sustaining, recruits, trains and supports parish volunteers to sustain the ministry; Collaborative, works with other groups . . .; Inclusive . . . [of] all generations (and) all peoples; Attentive, to both wellness and healing" (p. 5).

The central activities of the Parish Based Health Ministry program are to "establish health teams or parish nurse programs; recruit, screen and train volunteers; coordinate a parish needs assessment; design and implement a pastoral health plan; connect with external community resources; and remain available for consultation, evaluation and ongoing training" (Caritas Christi Health System, 2002, p. 3; selected portions of the *Parish Based Health Ministry* brochure were cited with permission; the Caritas Christi "Parish Health Assessment Profile," included in Appendix A, is also reprinted with permission).

Another healthcare system–affiliated parish nursing program is that sponsored by St. Vincent's Medical Center in Bridgeport, Connecticut; the parish nursing program is presently affiliated with a number of congregations of various faith traditions. The mission statement of St. Vincent's program states:

> *The Parish Nurse Program of St. Vincent's Medical Center extends the Mission of St. Vincent's into the community by assisting parishes and congregations to address the needs of their sick, poor and vulnerable and to steward the effective use of health care resources to benefit the community. As a member of St. Vincent's Parish Nurse Program, the volunteer professional nurse of each parish is guided by a respect for the dignity and sanctity of life and fosters the belief that quality, holistic care includes ministering to the body, mind and spirit of parishioners and their families. (The mission statement of St. Vincent's Parish Nurse Program is reprinted with permission.)*

The St. Vincent's Medical Center–affiliated Parish Nurse Program, associated with St. Vincent's College which offers a 36-contact-hour basic parish nursing education program, assists parish nurses by providing ongoing continuing education programs, monthly meetings, and a yearly retreat. The hospital-affiliated program also assists parishes in initiating parish nursing/health ministry programs by working with pastors and nurses interested in parish nursing (St. Vincent's Medical Center's "Parish Nurse [Activity] Report" and "Newsletter Submission Form" are reprinted in Appendix B, with permission).

A Theology of Parish Nursing

> I give you a new commandment, that you love one another.
> —*John 13:34*

Jesus' mandate, cited in the Gospel of John, provides the underlying posture for development of a theology of Christian parish nursing. For it is out of this love for each other, which Jesus taught must be a hallmark of His disciples, that parish nurses derive their God-given calling to minister to the ill and infirm of their congregations. If *theology* is the science or the study of God and of His teaching, then a theology of parish nursing must seek to understand how nurses, ministering within the context of faith communities, might carry out their mission in a God-proscribed manner. In *Visiting the Sick: A Guide for Parish Ministers*, Patti Normile (1992) asserts that the task of any pastoral caregiver visiting the sick is to "be present to patients as they attempt to find God in their life situation, to listen as they grow in awareness and understanding of themselves and their God, to encourage them to grow in faith" (p. 15).

Theologian William Rademacher (1991), in exploring God's call to lay ministry, cites four elements of the vocation described by H. Richard Niebuhr. These include the call "to hearing and doing the word of God"; "the secret call," or personal experience in which one feels "directly summoned by God" to engage in ministry; the "providential call," in which a particular ministry is specifically fitted to the "talents" of the individual; and the "ecclesiastical call," or the invitation by a specific church or faith community to ministry within that group or institution (p. 29). While the first and second items of Niebuhr's list of elements of call are surely appropriate for parish nurses, the latter two points are uniquely suited to the vocation of the parish nurse; that is, the "providential call," in which one is called to a ministry because of his or her specific talents, and the "ecclesiastical call," in which one is called to serve a particular church group in ministry. If a nurse considering the undertaking of parish nursing— even if only on a part-time basis—is uncertain about the call, seeking the guidance of the Holy Spirit in prayer, as well as talking with a trusted spiritual advisor or companion, is an important step to take. Regardless of the degree of commitment, parish nurses' activities are guided by both the role modeling and the gospel message of Jesus to care for each other, especially the ill and the disabled. As Jane Krafft (1988) reminds us: "Jesus heard the cries of his people, the afflicted, the poor and the outcast. He freely chose to live among them as a healer . . . we must take Jesus' command to minister seriously" (p. 15).

In describing a "theology of pastoral care," Robert Kinast (1990) observes that the purpose of the Church is "to care for the covenant which God has initiated with us" (p. 7). "The church cares best for God's covenant," he asserts, "when it liberates people to grow with God in all the dimensions of their lives" (p. 8). For the parish nurse, working in a church-related setting, the focus must then be on helping parishioners achieve the freedom to "grow with God" in the midst of their stressors and sufferings; this is the goal of the primary parish nurse role that we identify as "integrator of faith and health." This dimension of the theology of parish nursing is also in concert with the theology of healthcare ministry as described by pastoral minister Cornelius van der Poel (1999), who explains that healthcare ministry is "both a human and a Christian task" (p. 1). Van der Poel notes that while recognizing the physical and psychological needs and concerns of the person, we must also understand the spiritual dimension, beginning with "the premise that the human being is created in the image of God" (p. 2). This explanation of healthcare ministry fits well with the identified ministry of the parish nurse, whose roles include attending to parishioners' "human needs" as health advocate, health educator, and health counselor, yet whose pastoral goal, as representative of his or her faith community, is to care for the spiritual needs of the ill members of the congregation. While many practicing nurses are also attentive to patients' spiritual needs, as part of holistic nursing care, a particular focus on an ill person's spiritual concerns represents the uniqueness of the parish nursing role. In a similar vein, describing the goal of pastoral care provided in the context of a healthcare setting, hospital chaplain Lawrence Holst (1992) notes that such care "becomes uniquely pastoral when it helps to direct others to the source of life and power, to that which alone is infinite and eternal" (p. 46).

In beginning the discussion of a theology of parish nursing, I described the practice as a "God-given calling to minister" to parishioners, especially the ill and the infirm of one's faith community. Neville Kirkwood (1995), in discussing Christian hospital healthcare ministry, offers a related opinion: "Hospital ministry is as much a call of God to a specific area of Christian service as is a call into the ordained ministry, a religious order or a missionary challenge" (p. 117). "A person so called," Kirkwood adds, "must clearly possess a theology [that has] its roots in the person and work of Jesus Christ"(p. 117). Such a theological perspective is also critical for the Christian parish nurse, especially in ministering to ill parishioners who are experiencing suffering.

From my personal experience of hospital chaplaincy, I can attest to the fact that the "why" of suffering is probably the most difficult question for a healthcare minister to deal with. Patients and families desperately seek answers—some reason or rational explanation for what seems like an extreme and unfair burden levied upon themselves or their loved ones. One of the first things a novice chaplain or parish nurse must learn is that there are no answers to the why of suffering; no spiritual quick-fixes to relieve the pleading, pain-filled eyes of the sufferers. This is precisely why Rabbi Harold Kushner titled his best-selling book on suffering not *Why Bad Things Happen to Good People* but *When Bad Things Happen to Good People* (1981). Rabbi Kushner's message was not an explanation of the why of suffering, but rather a declaration of faith that "when" suffering occurs in our lives, the God of love, the God of care, the God of tenderness weeps with us and will not abandon us.

"If any want to become my followers, let them take up their cross daily"
                    —*Luke 9:23*

A similar message is that of the Christian gospel upon which, it is suggested, we must reflect "before we minister to the sick in the name of Jesus Christ" (Glenn, Kofler, & O'Connor, 1997, p. 7). While it is important to remember, that as described in the scripture passages cited earlier, Jesus did perform a number of healing miracles to cure illness and disability among his followers, he also preached a message of acceptance of sorrow, suffering, and even death: "If any want to become my followers, let them take up their cross daily" (Luke 9:23), and "Very truly, I tell you, unless a grain of wheat falls into the earth and dies, it remains just a single grain but if it dies, it bears much fruit. Those who love their life, lose it, and those who hate their life in this world will keep it for eternal life" (John 12:24–25). Jesus did not, however, value suffering in itself. That lesson is modeled in the account of His agony in the garden when He prayed to the Father: "Father, if you are willing, remove this cup from me; yet, not my will but yours be done" (Luke 22:42). And in the fragile humanity that He so lovingly embraced, Jesus Himself gave voice to the incredible suffering of His passion and crucifixion in a lament of frustration: "'*Eloi, eloi, lema sabachthani!*' which means, 'My God, my God, why have you forsaken me?'" (Mark 15:34). In the end, however, despite his agony, Luke recorded the fact that, just before He breathed His last, Jesus asserted His confidence in His God when He "cried out in a loud voice: 'Father, into your hands I commend my spirit'" (23:46).

> *"Very truly, I tell you, unless a grain of wheat falls into the earth and dies, it remains just a single grain but if it dies, it bears much fruit. Those who love their life, lose it, and those who hate their life in this world will keep it for eternal life"*
> —John 12:24–25

> *"Father, if you are willing, remove this cup from me; yet, not my will but yours be done"*   —Luke 22:42

> *"'Eloi, eloi, lema sabachthani!' which means, 'My God, my God, why have you forsaken me?'"*   —Mark 15:34

> *"Father, into your hands I commend my spirit"*   —Luke 23:46

Thus, a parish nurse ministering under the aegis of a Christian theology of health ministry must be prepared to assist and support his or her church members in accepting and perhaps even embracing their sufferings and disabilities. This is part of a theology of parish nursing that facilitates the efforts of ill parishioners in finding meaning in the experiences of illness and disability, and ultimately of achieving a state of spiritual well-being in illness, as described in the middle-range theory of spiritual well-being in illness presented in Chapter 5.

Beatitudes for Parish Nurses

Following Jesus' well-known "Sermon on the Mount" (Mark 5:3–12), in which He taught scriptural beatitudes to His disciples, the following paradigm of beatitudes for parish nurses is presented, identifying primary roles of the parish nurse such as health visitor, health educator, health advisor, health advocate, and spiritual companion in health and illness.

Blessed are parish nurses who care for the poor, for theirs is the kingdom of heaven.

Blessed are parish nurses who mourn for parishioners lost, for they will be comforted.

Blessed are parish nurses who visit the isolated and the elderly, for they will inherit the land.

Blessed are parish nurses who advocate for marginalized clients, for they will be satisfied.

Blessed are parish nurses who minister to those in pain and suffering, for they will be shown mercy.

Blessed are parish nurses who bring peace to patients who are anxious and afraid, for they will be called children of God.

Blessed are parish nurses who suffer misunderstanding for the sake of their ministry, for they will see God.

Blessed are parish nurses who comfort and care in the Lord's Name, for their reward will be great in heaven. (O'Brien, 2003, p. 292 , reprinted with permission).

This chapter is about Christian parish nurses' call to facilitate and support holistic health among members of their faith communities. There is spiritual support for the call to parish nursing in both the Old and the New Testament scriptures; thus, the Church is indeed an appropriate center of nursing ministry to the ill and infirm. The parish nurse responds to Jesus' great commandment that his followers "love one another," through a ministry of caring and compassionate service to brother and sister parishioners in need.

References

Becker, D. M. (2001). Public health and religion. In N. Schneiderman, M. Speers, J. Silva, H. Tomes, & J. Gentry (Eds.), *Integrating behavioral and social sciences with public health* (pp. 357–368). Washington, DC: American Psychological Association.

Caritas Christi Health System. (2002). *Parish based health ministry*. Norwood, MA: Author.

Clark, M. B., & Olson, J. K. (2000). Faith seeking and health seeking as parallel processes. In M. B. Clark & J. K. Olson (Eds.), *Nursing within a faith community: Promoting health in times of transition* (pp. 3–13). Thousand Oaks, CA: Sage.

Doohan, L. (1993). Church. In M. Downey (Ed.), *The new dictionary of Catholic spirituality* (pp. 163–173). Collegeville, MN: Liturgical Press.

Droege, T. A. (1991). *The faith factor in healing*. Philadelphia: Trinity Press International.

Glenn, G., Kofler, M., & O'Connor, K. (1997). *Handbook for ministers of care* (2nd ed.). Chicago: Liturgical Training Publications.

Hill, H. (1990). Church. In J. Komonchak, M. Collins, & D. Lane (Eds.), *The new dictionary of theology* (pp. 185–201). Collegeville, MN: Liturgical Press.

Holst, L. E. (1992). Hospital chaplain: One role, many functions. In L. E. Holst (Ed.), *Hospital ministry: The role of the chaplain today* (pp. 42–52). New York: Crossroad.

Kenniston, M. M. (1987). Faith: An untapped health resource. *Journal of Psychosocial Nursing, 25*(10), 28–30.

Kern, W. (1984). *Pastoral ministry with disabled persons.* Staten Island, NY: Alba House.

Kinast, R. L. (1990). Caring for God's covenant of freedom: A theology of pastoral care. In H. Hayes & C. J. van der Poel (Eds.), *Health care ministry: A handbook for chaplains* (pp. 7–21). Mahwah, NJ: Paulist Press.

Kirkwood, N. (1995). *Pastoral care in hospitals.* Harrisburg, PA: Morehouse.

Krafft, J. (1988). *The ministry to persons with disabilities.* Collegeville, MN: Liturgical Press.

Kushner, H. S. (1981). *When bad things happen to good people.* New York: Avon Books.

Livingstone, E. A. (1990). *The concise Oxford dictionary of the Christian Church.* New York: Oxford University Press.

Macrae, J. A. (2001). *Nursing as a spiritual practice: A contemporary application of Florence Nightingale's views.* New York: Springer.

Normile, P. (1992). *Visiting the sick: A guide for parish ministers.* Cincinnati, OH: St. Anthony Messenger Press.

O'Brien, M. E. (2003). *Spirituality in nursing: Standing on holy ground* (2nd ed.). Sudbury, MA: Jones and Bartlett.

Rademacher, W. J. (1991). *Lay ministry: A theological, spiritual, and pastoral handbook.* New York: Crossroad.

St. Vincent's Medical Center. (2002). *Parish nurse program mission statement.* Bridgeport, CT: Author.

Van der Poel, C. J. (1999). *Wholeness and holiness: A Christian response to human suffering; A theology of health care ministry.* Franklin, WI: Sheed & Ward.

Westberg, G. E. (1990). *The parish nurse: Providing a minister of health for your congregation.* Minneapolis, MN: Augsburg.

CHAPTER 2

THE SPIRITUAL HISTORY OF PARISH NURSING

Jesus went about all the cities and villages...curing every disease and sickness.
—Matthew 9:35

"All the Towns and the Villages"

Dear Lord Jesus,
You are the role model for parish nurses.
    You didn't minister only in the Synagogue;
You went out to the "cities and the
         villages" *(Matthew 9:35);*
You went to wherever the ill and the
    infirm were in need.

You went to Capernaum and cleansed the
    man with the unclean spirit *(Luke 4:35);*
You went to the home of Simon and visited
    his feverish mother-in-law *(Luke 4:39);*
You went to Lake Gennesaret,
      and touched a leper *(Luke 5:13);*
You went to Gallilee and healed a paralytic
                (Luke 5:24-25);
You went to meet a Centurian and
    cured his servant *(Luke 7:10);*
      and

You went to the house of Jairus and
restored his daughter *(Luke 8:34).*

Dearest Lord Jesus,
You taught:
"Daughter your faith has made you well."
(Luke 8:48);
You counseled:
"Those who are well have no need of
a physician," but the sick do.
(Luke 5:31);
You advocated:
"Her sins... have been forgiven,
[because] she has shown great
love" *(Luke 7:47);*
and,
You referred:
"I will ask the Father and he will
give you another Advocate to
be with you forever, the
Spirit of Truth" *(John 14:16).*

Teach me, Dear Lord, to learn from
Your Blessed example.

Parish nursing and parish health ministry, although not described in those terms, have been around from the beginning of the establishment of Christian faith communities. The most well documented of the efforts of early church members to care for their parishioners are those of deacons and deaconesses and Roman matrons of the young Christian Church. These men and women responded to the call to care for the sick, especially the sick poor, as heard in the gospel message of Jesus, their leader. His followers were especially moved to respond to the Master's words as recorded in the Gospel of Matthew, "For I was hungry and you gave me food, I was thirsty and you gave me something to drink, a stranger and you welcomed me . . . naked and you gave me clothing . . . sick and you took care of me . . . in prison and you visited me . . . just as you did it to one of the

"For I was hungry and you gave me food, I was thirsty and you gave me something to drink, a stranger and you welcomed me . . . naked and you gave me clothing . . . sick and you took care of me . . . in prison and you visited me . . . just as you did it to one of the least [of my brothers] you did it to me"   —*Matthew 25:35–36; 40*

least [of my brothers] you did it to me" (Matthew 25:35–36; 40). The power and attraction of that gospel message of 2000 years ago is evidenced even today; one of my nursing colleagues recently told me that her church has a "Matthew 25" group whose members minister to the ill and infirm of the parish.

The Christian Gospel as a Framework for Parish Nursing

Jesus as a Role Model for the Parish Nurse

I have several times identified Jesus as a nurse's role model in his activities as "healer" (O'Brien, 2001, pp. 34–41) and as "pastoral minister" to the ill and the infirm (O'Brien, 2003, p. 25). When I began to explore the gospel message of Jesus in regard to the roles of the parish nurse and the parish health minister (a nonnurse member of a parish health ministry team), I sought to determine how his teachings on caring for the sick had been understood by our nurse historians. One of the earliest nurses to chronicle the spiritual history of the profession was Minnie Goodnow, RN, who, in her 1916 history of nursing, explained the roles of the Christian deaconesses and Roman matrons as guided by the gospel of Jesus. A primary teaching of Jesus, to which the deaconesses responded, was that of ministering to the ill and the infirm of their church community. Since the deaconesses visited and cared for "the sick poor in their homes," Goodnow (1916) asserts, they might also be regarded as constituting "the first Visiting Nurse Association" (p. 22). Two of these early Christian Church nurses or "parish nurses," as we would label them today, identified by Ms. Goodnow were Paula, a Roman matron, who Goodnow believes was "one of the first persons who systematically trained nurses" (p. 21), and Phoebe, a deaconess, who might be considered "the first district nurse" (p. 22). Paula is described by a number of nurse historians as an early Christian nurse who cared for the sick both in their homes and in hospices (O'Brien, 2003, p. 27); as is Phoebe, whom Saint Paul described as a "deaconess of the church . . . (and) a helper of many" (Romans 16:1–2).

Also writing in 1920, historians Lavinia Dock and Isabel Stewart point out that "Christ's parables and miracles dealt much with disease and death"(p. 42) and that thus the "disciples' great love for their Teacher took the instant form of service to . . . the sick, the neglected and destitute" (p. 42). Dock and Stewart (1920) also note that, while women had been "degraded under paganism," the important nursing role of deaconess elevated women's place in the Christian community: "Visiting nursing arose then . . . as distinguished from mere visiting of the sick, for the care of the sick rapidly became the role of women" (p. 45). The deaconess of the early church, who might be single or married, also achieved significant status in the church community as she was formally consecrated in her role by the local bishop. Men were also ordained as deacons in the church; however, Dock and Stewart, as well as other historians, note that the work of nursing the sick fell primarily to the deaconesses.

Physician James Walsh, who published a history of nursing in 1929, proclaims, "Christianity made a great change in the matter of caring for the sick" (p. 1). Walsh's statement is grounded in is his belief that Christianity's emphasis on "the Fatherhood of God and the brotherhood of man (gave) a new dignity to humanity and (made) all men responsible for the care of the needy" (p. 1). Walsh also described the nursing activities of holy women and deaconesses in the young Christian Church. Similar to the parish nurses of today, early deaconesses were chosen or approved by the congregation. They were also, like many parish nurses, consecrated or commissioned in church ceremonies. Part of the consecration ceremony included a beautiful prayer to the Father that reads in part: "Do Thou now look on this thy handmaid, who is appointed unto the office of a deaconess, and grant unto her the Holy Spirit and cleanse her from all pollution of the flesh and of the spirit that she may worthily accomplish the work committed unto her, to Thy glory and the praise of Thy Christ" (Walsh, 1929, pp. 4–5).

In their classic four-volume nursing history, revised in 1935, M. Adelaide Nutting and Lavinia Dock describe the "marvelous activity of the early Church in works of love and mercy [which] swept into its current thousands of men and women [who] responded to the summons of one of the greatest Teachers [whose] love had changed the face of the earth for them" (p. 95). They add that "in this movement the large share taken by women was as conspicuous as it was significant" (p. 95). The Christian deaconess, they assert, "sang the Gospel": she "regarded it as a sacred duty to comfort the afflicted, it was the special duty of the deaconesses to attend the sick in their own homes" (p. 102). Nutting and Dock also describe the early deaconess as "the first parish worker, friendly visitor, and district nurse"; "and from her day," they add, "the work of visiting nursing has never been unknown" (p. 102).

Following the thoughts of the historians previously cited, Agnes Pavey (1938) supports the strongly positive impact of Christianity on the care of the ill and infirm: "All the teachings of Christ stressed the brotherhood of man, and the duty of every human being to render, ungrudgingly, all the service in his power to his suffering, or less fortunate neighbor, so that from being merely a virtue, the compassionate care of the sick became a sacred and obligatory duty" (p. 94). "By his own actions in the healing of the sick," Pavey points out, "and by his parables . . . [Christ] placed great emphasis . . . on the tending of the sick in their own households" (p. 94). "No longer," Pavey adds, was the care of the sick to be relegated to the work of the servant or slave but it was "the duty of every Christian, and [was] to be limited only by the needs of the sufferer" (p. 94). In public witness, Christians were observed to care selflessly for "the ailing poor" because of their adherence to teachings of Jesus' gospel (Robinson, 1946, p. 25).

Nurse historians, writing in the latter half of the twentieth century, also applauded the Christian gospel as a framework for compassionate care of the ill and the infirm. "Throughout his earthly life," Charles Marie Frank (1953) writes, "Christ gave by word and deed a living example" of the precept described by Saint James: "What will it profit, my brethren, if a man says he has faith, but does not have good works?" (p. 62). "One of the fruits" of this precept, Frank adds, "was nursing, not as a social service based on mere motives of utilitarianism but on the love for one's fellow man who is made to the image of his creator. This motive not only makes tasks less difficult, it makes them enjoyable and eminently worthwhile" (p. 62). "Such a motive," Frank concludes, "is the true foundation of the spirit of nursing" (p. 62).

Anne L. Austin, writing in 1957, as well as supporting the fact that the witness of Jesus' healing miracles had a "profound influence on the care of the sick," points out that "in three of the four gospels, the disciples of Christ are directed to heal the sick" and that "the ideal of service [was] also implicit in the institutions established by the early Church to carry out the Christian philosophy" (p. 38). Austin, as other historians, describes the importance the Church's establishment of ministerial roles related to caring for the sick, such as those of deacon and deaconess, derived from the Greek word *diakonein,* meaning "to serve or to minister" (p. 38). The "great value" that Christianity placed on "human life" is highlighted by nurse historians Lena Dietz and Aurelia Lehozky (1967): "It embodied a fraternal concept of equality and charity which forced the faithful to undergo sometimes severe sacrifices in order to alleviate the sufferings of others" (p. 22). The Christian gospel, they note, enhanced the dignity of women, widening their opportunities "to pursue useful and active" ministries: "The activities of these early women workers, deaconesses, matrons and saints," Dietz and Lehozky assert, "laid the foundations for trained nursing" as well as providing outreach from the early Church (p. 22).

"Christianity made charity one of the leading virtues," observe Vern and Bonnie Bullough (1978, p. 28): "Jesus had set an example of solicitude for the poor and the sick that could not be entirely ignored." Then, they add, "Christianity took an almost revolutionary step by making the poor and the humble the special representatives of Jesus" (p. 28). This dimension of the Christian gospel, Bullough and Bullough conclude, gave all who nursed the sick "a more exalted position than they had had before" (p. 29). Josephine Dolan (1978) asserts that "the teachings and example of Jesus Christ had a profound influence on the emergence of gifted nursing leadership as well as on the expansion of the role of the nurse" (p. 43). Christ's own healing activities and attitude toward the sick provided the best model of caring for the nurse, Dolan points out, for "instead of saying the word and healing the sick, Christ gave individual attention to the needs of all by touching, anointing and taking by the hand" (p. 43).

The concept of the Christian Church as a center for parish health ministry also has a significant history as pointed out by contemporary public health nurses Lundy and Bender (2001), who observe that "communicable diseases were rampant during the middle ages, primarily because of the walled cities that emerged in response to the paranoia and isolation of the populations. Infection was [thus] next to impossible to control [and] physicians had little to offer, deferring to the church for the management of disease" (p. 74). "Nursing roles," they add, "were carried out primarily by religious orders" (p. 74).

And, finally, in her classic illustrated history, *Nursing: The Finest Art*, M. Patricia Donahue (1996) makes the case that nursing history "first becomes continuous with the beginning of Christianity": "Pre-Christian records of nursing are fragmentary and scattered; however, records of nursing from the days of the early Christian workers to the present day are continuous" (p. 72). As do the historians before her, Donahue observes that the Christian gospel of "love and brotherhood" greatly influenced the "development of nursing": "Organized nursing was a direct response to these teachings and epitomized the concept of pure altruism initiated by the early Christians" (p. 72).

While the nursing historians highlight a number of different facets of the Christian gospel that profoundly influenced early nurses and the development of the profession, all basically agree on certain points of import for nursing, such as Jesus' teaching of the mandate for all Christians to care for the less fortunate, especially the ill and the infirm; the fact that in caring for the sick, a nurse was in fact caring for Christ himself (Matthew 25:36); Christianity's emphasis on the brotherhood of all persons, which thus elevated the dignity of all humankind and promoted the sacredness of life; the elevation of the role of women through their activities of nursing the sick; and the fact that caring for the ill and the infirm became, through Christianity, an altruistic labor of loving and caring rather than a menial task previously carried out by servants or slaves. Centrally integrated within their discussions of early Christianity, most nursing historians present some description of the roles of those men and women called to the vocation of deacon or deaconess in the young Church. This role of the early Church nurse closely approximates that of today's parish nurse.

Deacons and Deaconesses of the Early Christian Church

The title of a recent comprehensive history of the diaconal role in the Church seems analogous to a description of the contemporary "parish nurse." Author Jeannine Olson (1992) has titled her work *One Ministry, Many Roles: Deacons and Deaconesses through the Centuries*. It seems most fitting to identify the early Church deacon or deaconess, in his or her many roles, with the parish nurse of today. The Church diaconal role included responsibilities other than caring for the sick, such as assisting with liturgy, dispensing alms, and teaching. These activities, however, in a sense, also fall within the purview of the parish nurse, who, as well as visiting the sick and assessing their needs, serves as integrator of faith and health (in some churches, parish nurses are also Eucharistic ministers or ministers of Communion), patient advocate for those marginalized from health care services, coordinator of volunteers, and health counselor and educator. Thus, the modern-day parish nurse is, as the deacon or deaconess of old, a minister with "many roles."

Olson (1992) points out that, after the death of Jesus, his followers who were creating the first Christian communities came together to share not only worship but also their worldly possessions; thus, a need arose for "designated responsibilities," and it was out of this beginning church structure that the role of deacon/deaconess was instituted (p. 23). Olson defends the fact that very little is written in the New Testament about the roles and duties of deacons and deaconesses with the suggestion that "perhaps . . . then as now, there is a tendency to neglect to write about what is a familiar part of daily life" (p. 27). And we must remember that the activities of these early church workers were, in fact, centered on ordinary tasks related to the developing of a new community: organizing and leading worship services, counseling those who were anxious, educating new converts to the faith, distributing alms to the poorer members of the community, and providing for the care of the ill and the infirm.

In summarizing the creation and evolution of the diaconal ministry in the early Christian Church, theologian William Rademacher (1991) lists a number of "conclusions" that he believes "seem to flow from [the] event," such as: "a new ministry emerges in response to complaints from the community"; "need precedes the formation of ministry"; "the new ministers are indigenous to the community"; "this new ministry, even after the laying on of hands, remains very broad and flexible"; "the church . . . feels it can impose qualifications for the ministry"; and "it is the community that elects [those] who accept and confirm the community's selection" (p. 37). Virtually all of Rademacher's conclusions could be applied to the contemporary parish or congregational nurse, who is commissioned to respond to a need in his or her faith community; who is usually "indigenous to" (a member of) the church or congregation; who, after the church's commissioning or consecration, undertakes a number of roles in the course of her parish ministry; who must meet the Church's and the profession's proscribed qualifications for the role of parish nurse; and, finally, who must be approved and accepted by his or her pastor and congregation.

As noted earlier, one of the first women identified as a deaconess in scripture is Phoebe, who was so labeled by Saint Paul in the words: "I commend to you Phoebe our sister, who is also a minister [deaconess] of the Church . . . for she has been a benefactor to many" (Romans, 16:1–2). Phoebe, who is believed to have lived around A.D. 55, has been described as a wealthy woman who devoted her life as a Christian to nursing the ill and the infirm in their homes (Grippando, 1986, p. 4). It has been asserted that the ministry provided by the early deaconesses, such as Phoebe, probably included such activities as visiting the sick in their homes and "bringing physical and spiritual comfort to all, especially the dying" (Dolan, 1973, p. 50). Phoebe carried out her ministry to the sick as a representative of the Church, as does the parish nurse of today.

There were many other individuals in the early Christian Church who assumed deacon- and deaconess-like roles of ministering to the sick in their homes, although historians tend to categorize them with more specific labels; for example, the Roman matrons who had converted to Christianity in the third and fourth centuries and the Christian physicians. Some of the more famous of the matrons were Helena, the mother of Constantine the Great; Marcella, founder of a religious community; and Fabiola, who was described as one of the most popular of the matrons. Following her conversion to Christianity, Fabiola devoted her life to caring for the sick, even founding a hospital where she herself ministered to the ill and infirm. It is reported that after her death, Saint Jerome wrote of Fabiola: "She gathered together all the sick from the highways and the streets, and herself nursed the unhappy, emaciated victims of disease" (Dolan, 1973, p. 51).

The early Christian physicians, as well, carried out diaconal roles of ministering to the sick, such as the caring provided by the earlier-mentioned martyrs Cosmas and Damien, who are widely viewed as patrons of the medical profession. One of the first Christian converts and ministers associated with the healing arts was the Greek physician Lucanus, from Antioch, who became Saint Luke, the evangelist. Saint Paul, in his letter to the Christian community at Colossae, described Luke as the "*beloved physician*": "*Luke, the beloved physician*" sends greetings (Colossians 4:14). Historians suggest that Luke may indeed have formally studied medicine in Tarsus. In Luke's own gospel, the concepts of healing and medicine emerge centrally in Jesus' life. The gospel, written in Greek, stresses the Lord's love, understanding, and care for those in need, especially those who are ill or disabled.

Another deacon physician of the early Christian era was Saint Blaise, by legend a bishop who was martyred in the fourth century. His association with healing is reportedly due to an occasion of his saving the life of a child who was choking on a fish bone: "To this day his intercession is sought for the sick, especially those with throat trouble" (Livingstone, 1990, p. 67). And the physician Saint Pantaleon, as his brother Christian physicians Cosmas and Damien, was applauded for providing all medical care without fees. Pantaleon, who had been personal physican to two Roman emperors, was martyred when Diocletian purged the court of all Christians (Livingstone, 1990, p. 379).

Nurse historian Frank (1959) names several other distinguished early Christian physicians who carried out diaconal roles within the Church, including Aetius, Paul, and Alexander. She adds that some of the wrtings of these deacons had been published within the past century and studied by scholars of history; Frank concludes: "Christianity did not impede these great men in the practice of their professions" (p. 36).

The Kaiserswerth Deaconess Program

An early community of Protestant women, a great many of whom engaged in nursing the sick, were the Kaiserswerth Deaconesses, founded in Germany in the mid-nineteenth century by Lutheran minister Theodor Fliedner. The establishment of the Kaiserswerth Deacnoness community provides historical perspective for parish nursing, as Pastor Fliedner recognizes the important connection between the Church and health care. He states that the deaconess community was a "free religious association . . . [taking] its stand from the mother nature of the church founded by Christ" (Nutting and Dock, 1935, p. 33). Thus, the deaconess training included a significant emphasis on personal spirituality. The deaconesses, who wore religious garb and called each other "Sister," "attended morning and evening prayer in the chapel and also went there to meditate, read the Bible, or pray during a quiet half hour" (Olson, 1992, p. 203).

In their initial nursing ministry, the Kaiserswerth Deaconesses carried out activities very similar to those of the contemporary parish nurse in visiting the sick in their homes. This was a key church-related nursing ministry originally envisioned by Pastor

Fliedner's wife, and co-leader of the movement, Fredericka Munster. As the deaconess community grew and emigrated to other countries, such as the United States, the deaconesses also assumed duties in hospitals. The Kaiserswerth Deaconesses began their work in the United States in the mid-nineteenth century when they began to serve at Passavant Hospital in Pittsburg. To this day, Lutheran deaconesses minister in a variety of social service and nursing roles affiliated with parishes across the country; they also serve in hospitals and nursing homes. Several educational programs exist to prepare contemporary deaconesses for ministry (see O'Brien, 2003, pp. 42–44).

A Tradition of Service: Nursing Ministry within Faith Communities

The Holy Woman Veronica

One of the earliest role models for the parish nurse, as a volunteer caregiver within a faith community, is the holy woman Veronica, who is reported to have wiped the bleeding face of Jesus during his agonizing walk to Mount Calvary. According to legend, Veronica has been identified as the "woman with the 12-year hemorrhage" whom Jesus healed when she touched the hem of his garment (Matthew 9:20–22). And while at the time of Veronica the young Christian Church was not even formed as a community yet, tradition holds that there was a core group of Jesus' disciples who acknowledged him as Master and Lord; some of these followed along as he trod the painful procession to his Crucifixion. The account of Veronica's action is not found in the four gospels of the New Testament; it is, however, described in a fifth-century apocryphal work called "The Gospel of Nicodemus" (O'Brien, 2003, p. 102). Historians note that, although the narrative is legendary, the fact "that a compassionate woman wiped the face of our suffering Lord may well have happened, and Christians can do well to ponder her action and revere her traditional memory" (Thurston and Attwater, 1996, p. 83). A number of early nursing journals identify Veronica as a "role model" for the nurse (O'Brien, 2003, pp. 101–102); to consider Veronica a role model for the parish nurse seems even more appropriate, as she carried out her compassionate act of caring for the Lord as a member of the very first faith community of Christian disciples.

The Early Public Health Nurse and the Church

Although contemporary parish nursing is not associated with public health nursing, a search of the early public health literature reveals a historical relationship between church-related nursing and public health nursing. In a 1922 article, "History of Public

Health Nursing," Lavinia Dock cites as forebears of public health nursing women who carried out nursing in the community for religious motives, such as the Kaiserswerth deaconesses (p. 522). And, in a 1935 book titled *The Art of Public Health Nursing*, the introduction notes that "since the time of St. Paul when Phoebe went about nursing the sick in their homes, the successful district nurse, and her successor, the public health nurse, have practiced the art of public health nursing" (Thomson, 1935, p. 5).

In perusing public health nursing articles in the journals of the early twentieth century, one finds a wealth of material describing the spiritual as well as the physical nursing ministries of pioneer public health nurses, some of whom were forced to visit backwoods populations on horseback, as homes were inaccessible on the existing road-ways of the time. Public health nurses also taught disease prevention and health pro-motion in concert with local churches, especially in rural areas of the South. In a 1920 issue of *The Public Health Nurse*, a state supervising nurse documented her parish health education and health promtion experience in an article titled "Roaming through Virginia with the Public Health Nurse." The nurse author describes numerous instances of educating rural people about such public health issues as preventing the spread of contagious diseases, personal hygiene, and disease prevention. The nurse also notes that she had been requested to give a health education talk at a local church: "In came the congregation," she reports, "a few at first, later in crowds, and soon the church was filled. In such a gathering . . . it was easy to talk" (Webb, 1920, p. 842).

Around the same time, Rose Hawthorne Lathrop, founder of the Servants for Relief of Incurable Cancer, decided to study nursing so that she could care for the urban poor suffering from cancer in the New York City area. Although not formally a public health nurse, Rose visited and cared for many cancer sufferers in their residences: "She turned no one down. Going from tenement to tenement, she cared for the poor, the downtrodden and the dying in their own homes" (Farren, 1996, p. 202). She did this work as a ministry of the church, derived from the gospel message of Jesus to care for brothers and sisters in need. Currently, the religious community Rose Hawthorne founded continues to provide free care for cancer patients who are unable to afford other nursing services, in a number of homes located across the country (O'Brien, 2003, pp. 47–48).

"In the Parish"

It is appropriately noted in the literature on parish health ministry that the concept of parish nursing was introduced in the late 1970s and early 1980s by the Reverend Doctor Granger Westberg. There were, however, numerous instances of volunteer kinds of church-affiliated nursing occurring prior to that time even in the past century, although these activities were not described as parish nursing. One exception is reflected in the narrative published by nurse Anna Lee Cummings in 1960, titled "In the Parish." Cummings's description of her role as the "parish health counselor" is strikingly similar to that of the contemporary parish nurse.

Parish Health Counselor Cummings (1960) begins by noting that her pastor had responded to the challenge to provide health care for a large parish of "thirty-five hundred families" by developing a multidisciplinary program "combining social service, recreation and nursing with the spiritual" (p. 26). She notes that the pastor believed that such holistic services should be "administered from the parish center for the benefit of the parish" (p. 26).

One of the nursing/health care activities developed by the parish health counselor was "an educational program . . . to provide better nursing care for the home patients, to acquaint the parishioners with the health facilities of the community, and how to use existing agencies and community health programs" (p. 27). "To accomplish this," Cummings explains: "home nursing classes were started . . . [and in two years] sixty-nine women received certificates in home nursing" (p. 27). Nurse Cummings describes additional parish health ministries: "A polio clinic was set up to administer Salk Vaccine shots, and individual parishioners could come to the Parish Health Counselor for advice" (p. 28). Some parishioner needs included requests for advice about finding placements for loved ones "in nursing homes, homes for the aged, or mental hospitals" (p. 28). Other activities of the parish health counselor and volunteer team members involved "evaluation of [parishioners'] homes before patients are discharged from hospitals; [assessment of] the type of nursing care required or equipment needed; reassuring an anxious mother when she calls about her sick child; or investigating a neighbor's report that a lady is sick and living alone" (p. 28). "Whenever professional nursing care is required," however, Nurse Cummings asserts, "referral to existing agencies is made" (p. 28).

Parish Health Counselor/Nurse Cummings also coordinated a volunteer team, assisted by the pastor, and supervised a supply of equipment such as "wheel chairs, crutches and walkers" donated by patients; in contemporary parish health nursing terminology, this ministry might be described as a "loan closet." The author reports that the pastor received many letters of appreciation from parishioners who were recipients of the parish nursing. And Nurse Cummings concludes the account of her work "in the parish" with the comment: "As a nurse, I have worked in many fields, but as a parish health counselor, I have the opportunity to use all my experience with a new challenge and receive rewarding satisfaction every day" (Cummings, 1960, p. 29).

Another parish nursing effort identified in mid-twentieth century nursing literature is that described by the registered nurses Gabrielle Martin and Claire Lacoutre (1953). In their opening, the authors, members of a Christian nurses "guild," invite women who had the "real spirit of nursing" to embrace the "adventure upon which they had recently embarked" (p. 13). The nurses recount the story of how their guild developed a "Volunteer Nursing Program" to care for patients in their homes. Although some nurses, the authors admit, had family responsibilities, approximately 25 out of their 60 nurse guild members pledged at least one home visit a month. The guild nurses worked under the direction of a group of nursing sisters, associated with a local church, who designated which patients needed to be visited. One of the guild members was assigned as "chairman" of the group and gave the volunteer nurses their assignments. "Although the work may sound as though it is very arduous and painstaking," Martin and Lacoutre report, "it has proved to each one of us to be most gratifying" (p. 14). They conclude by noting that the patients are always pleased to see their nurses and that the volunteer "parish nurses" feel that they have now "entered into the true spirit of nursing and . . . are fulfilling [their] goal" of being good Christian nurses (p. 14).

And a third mid-twentieth century parish nursing project described in the literature was a church-affiliated volunteer nursing effort: the "Friendly Visiting" program for residents of nursing homes, boarding homes, or those living alone ("Council Projects," 1956, pp. 42–44). The individuals who would benefit from the visits were identified by the local community's "Division of Aid for the Aged"; the nurses, however, undertook the ministry of visiting as a "program of Catholic Action" associated with the local chapter of the Diocesan Council of Catholic Nurses ("Council Projects," 1956, p. 42). It was reported that the community agency's "supervisor of volunteers" was very receptive to a group of professional nurses doing this kind of Christian ministry, especially in the city's nursing homes, where many of the residents were very ill. It was also noted that "the time spent on the project varies from one hour every other week to several days per week, depending on how much time the individual [nurse] is able to contribute to the advantage of all concerned" (p. 43).

The Church Nurse in the African American Congregation

The image of a white-clad "nurse," present at worship services, has long represented an important and vibrant dimension of the culture of many African American churches. The presence of "church nurses," as they are usually labeled, at most services is both theological and practical. On the one hand, the nurse's availability and accessibility for the faith community are concretely witnessed by her visible presence during the church's worship experiences. The African American church nurse provides a symbol of caring and compassion that is part and parcel of the Christian theology of the brother-hood of all believers. On a pragmatic note, the church nurse actually assumes the duties of caring for and comforting members of the congregation who may become anxious or ill during the course of a worship service. These nurses are generally dressed in uni-forms so as to be readily identifiable in times of need.

Some African American churches, it has been reported, have "nursing boards" as well as "church nurses who serve a first-aid and/or social function. . . . The members of these boards are not required to be licensed nurses, and they serve in a lay capac-ity" (Chase-Ziolek and Holst, 1999, p. 203). While it is accurate to note that many of the early church nurses were not formally trained or licensed nurses, most of the women serving in the church-nursing capacity had been mentored or informally trained in the role by older and/or former church nurses; many church nurse units also required attendance at courses such as Red Cross first-aid instruction of their mem-bers. A tradition of wisdom regarding nursing service to the faith community has been handed down from generation to the generation in individual churches.

In a 2000 editorial in the *Journal of Christian Nursing*, editor Judith Allen Shelly raises the topic of the "African-American office of the church nurse" (p. 3). Dr. Shelly comments that when she asked about the role, she was often told that the church nurses were not "real nurses." Her response was that the church nurses may indeed "be closer to real nurses than those with a string of academic degrees" (p. 3). A problem is that it is difficult to find much in the nursing literature describing the role of the church nurse. A 1989 article in *The Washington Post,* titled "The Salve in Salvation: Church Nurses See to Medical Needs and More," explores church nurses' activities in several urban churches. The author observes that "the church nurse has been a beloved fig-ure for decades, primarily among Baptists and Methodists" (Waterman, 1989, p. B1); she adds that while in the past the church nurse was usually an "untrained volunteer," today "she is a licensed nurse who arranges health festivals, tests blood pressure on Sundays, and offers a shoulder to lean on" (p. B1).

In reviewing the nursing periodical literature for discussions of the church nurse, the only research report found was that identifying a study of five churches representing different African American religious denominations in which narrative accounts of church nurses' activities were presented (Newsome, 1994, pp. 134–137). The study data, which concludes that "church nursing was a Christian calling to serve others within the church" (p. 134), identifies key church nurse roles as assisting those "who display illness or the inability to help themselves"; taking "care of infants and children"; taking care of those who need "assistance in walking"; providing "emergency care"; calling family members in emergency situations; and carrying out the duties "with a prayerful, sincere, and Christian-like manner" (p. 136). The church nurses interviewed report their caregiving as involving such activities as assisting parishioners who faint or fall, calling an ambulance in emergency situations, and performing cardiopulmonary resuscitation (CPR) (p. 136).

With the approval of the senior minister, I was granted an interview with the head of the Nurses' Unit at a large East Coast metropolitan Baptist church. Mrs. Jackson is an LPN now retired from full-time nursing employment; she has been head of the church Nurses' Unit for the past 10 years. Mrs. Jackson explained that some of the nurses in her unit were not licensed: "We accept licensed nurses and unlicensed nurses because we have a class given at least once a year for CPR and first aid; it's a Red Cross First-Aid class. People in the church feel called to be nurses; as I said, some of my nurses are not professional nurses, some have been nurse's aides but some just want to join in our service." Mrs. Jackson added that the church's usher board members had recently decided that they wanted some of the ushers to take a CPR class also, as they may come in contact with an ill person before the nurse gets there.

The sanctuary of Mrs. Jackson's church holds several thousand worshippers. She currently has 12 nurses in her Nurses' Unit, but admitted that she would like to have more: "I have only two on Sunday but would like to have three or four because our congregation is getting so large. I told the church that we have to do something to get our young women to come into the nursing unit." Mrs. Jackson described the role of the church nurse in her congregation:

> These directions were given to us by the Red Cross and The Ladies First Aide Union of Churches (our church was one of the first churches to form a union of churches in the area; now about 50 to 70 churches belong and we all do the same service). The directions include about 10 points: (1) The nurse is on duty for all Sunday morning services; at least two nurses are also on duty for other services (such as funerals and wakes); (2) always be in proper uniform of the day (we wear white uniforms and caps; we wear caps because the deaconesses wear all white too and we also wear a red cross patch on the left sleeve of our uniform); (3) open the health room at least one hour before services; (4) check supplies for proper equipment (that means the blood pressure cuff, juice, and things like that); (5) have water always available; (6) never give medications of any kind; (7) keep good records of all nursing care given and equipment used; (8) notify the pastor of all sick and injured persons under

> *your care; (9) visit all sick or injured persons after release for update; (10)*
> *after the service, check all supplies and re-stock; close the health room (about*
> *20 minutes after the service).*

Mrs. Jackson explained that the church nurses serve according to the church covenant: "To remember each other in prayer; aid each other in sickness and distress; to cultivate Christian sympathy and feeling, and courtesy in speech, but always ready for reconciliation and mindful of the rules of Our Savior to secure it without delay. . . . That," she asserted, "is what we go by!"

Mrs. Jackson also shared some history of her congregation's Nurses' Unit:

> *The Nurses' Unit was organized, prior to 1937, by the usher board of the church.*
> *Mrs. N. was elected president of the Nurses' Unit and Mrs. S., vice president;*
> *these two ladies were also the founders of the Nurses' Unit. The original Nurses'*
> *Unit had 45 nurses, six of whom were male nurses; 28 were female nurses,*
> *three of whom were licensed. [During the early days] . . . a first-aid room was*
> *donated to the church and furnished by members and friends of the church.*
> *In 1937 the church decided that they needed a medical advisor, Dr. M., who*
> *served faithfully until God called him home in 1953. A nurse, Mrs. L., served*
> *the nursing unit from 1941 to 1991; and then I came in after her.*

Some other interesting bits of history of the church's Nurses' Unit are the fact that "during World War II the first-aid room was equipped for any emergency that may have occurred; and the church nurses were always ready for duty"; and, over the years, members of the Nurses' Unit, who "were always available to administer service to the congregation," and other church members had donated a number of health ministry items to the church, such as a wheelchair given in 1959 in memory of deceased members and a water pitcher presented on the 100th anniversary of the church.

Mrs. Jackson described a few of the contemporary church nurse's activities:

> *On a Sunday, if somebody faints we try to revive them. If we can't, we im-*
> *mediately call our church doctor and she will determine if we should call the*
> *EMS [emergency services]. We don't ever fan anyone because you fan away*
> *the oxygen. If anyone feels ill, we just go and sit with them; we can give them*
> *water or Kleenex or a mint but we just can't give medications. We can also*
> *take a temperature and a blood pressure until the doctor comes.*

I asked Mrs. Jackson whether the church nurses, as do many parish nurses, serve on a volunteer basis; she replied in the affirmative: "Yes, this is volunteer; we don't get paid. The church only gives us money to replenish our supplies." In conclusion, Mrs. Jackson observed: "I am looking forward to doing more in the future with the help of God; with the help of God our group will carry on. We will carry on especially in the part of our church covenant 'aiding each other in sickness and distress.'"

Following my conversation with Mrs. Jackson, I also spoke with Rev. Foster, a minister centrally involved with overall health ministries for a group of Baptist churches. Rev. Foster supports the fact that many church nurses in the past have been of the "lay nurse" tradition or "nurse's aides." Most churches, however, do require basic training in first-aid and CPR, as reported by Mrs. Jackson. "While each church is autonomous," Rev. Foster notes, "we require the nurses to have the basics to respond to an emergency." She also explained that the nursing credentials of the president of a church's nurses' unit may influence how "extensively" they view the nurses' role. Some church nurse groups are called "nurses' units"; others, "health ministries" or "nurses' guilds," depending upon the particular church.

Rev. Foster commented that as her denomination moves more into the area of health ministries, they are attempting to take a holistic approach to working with the sick in terms of attending to body, mind, and spirit. Rev. Foster's analogy was to consider a three-wheeled bicycle, or tricycle: "If," she pointed out, "one wheel is broken or not working well, the tricycle doesn't go."

Holistic Health Care and Spiritual Ministry

Holistic health care and holistic nursing are not new concepts; the terminology, however, began to be more universally acknowledged and accepted by the medical and nursing communities in the second half of the twentieth century. In that era, nurses began to write books with titles such as *Holistic Nursing: A Handbook for Practice* (Dossey et al., 1988) and articles describing topics reflecting "wholistic" issues, such as "Spirituality: Cornerstone of Holistic Nursing Practice" (Nagai-Jacobson and Burkhart, 1989). New nursing journals were initiated in the area also, including *Holistic Nursing Practice* and *The Journal of Holistic Nursing*. There has been some confusion and contention in certain quarters of the nursing community as to the understanding of what is meant when one uses the terms *holistic* and *wholistic* health care; concerns relate specifically to what kinds of "alternate" health therapies might be included under the label of holistic care. Overall, however, a basic understanding of holistic health care is that it includes attention by the caregiver to the body, mind, and spirit of the human person, whether in terms of health care, health promotion, or disease prevention.

The current importance of the concept of holistic health care to the nursing community is evidenced by the fact that a newly published *Fundamentals of Nursing* (2002) text contains an entire chapter titled "Health, Holism and the Individual"

(DeLaune and Ladner). The authors support the notion that the concept of holistic health care is not new but is rather "rooted in the origins of healing"; they give such examples as Hippocrates teaching that "doctors . . . observe the emotional states of patients" and Florence Nightingale's recognition of the fact that patients had both "physiological and spiritual" dimensions (DeLaune and Ladner, 2002, p. 267). DeLaune and Ladner explain that "the holistic viewpoint guides the total care of the individual as a complete being rather than fragmented care focused on parts of the person" (p. 267). The association between holistic health care and spiritual ministry is also evidenced in this contemporary fundamentals of nursing text in that the major discussion of a patient's "spiritual dimension" is included in the chapter on holism; other topics are also included, such as characteristics of spirituality, nursing process and spirituality, spiritual assessment (including a spiritual assessment tool), health implications for a number of world religions, nursing diagnoses related to spiritual needs, nursing interventions to meet clients' spiritual needs, and evaluation of outcomes related to spiritual needs of clients (DeLaune and Ladner, 2002, pp. 269–277).

Prior to the mid-twentieth century, a discussion of the relationship of holistic health care and spiritual ministry for nurses would probably not have occurred. Health care, in the physiological and psychological realms, was considered to be within the purview of the nurse; spiritual ministry was viewed as the responsibility of the minister, priest, rabbi, or other pastoral caregiver. While referrals might be made from one domain to the other, the idea of close collaboration between healthcare providers and pastoral caregivers was only infrequently considered. And the concept of a nurse providing spiritual care, as in the parish nurse role of spiritual companion or "clarifier of the relationship between faith and health" (Westberg, 1990, p. 49), was rarely addressed. Nurses were, of course, allowed to pray for their patients; they were also expected to assist at religious rituals such as the distribution of Communion or anointing in a hospital or nursing home setting. The nurse was not, however, to infringe on the "territory" of the pastoral care provider or on the patient's privacy; his or her responsibility in regard to patients' spiritual needs was primarily to respond to verbalized requests for spiritual care, which would then be referred to an appropriate pastoral caregiver.

By reminiscing about nursing history in terms of spiritual intervention, or the lack thereof, I do not mean to infer that contemporary nurses now have the mandate to invade patients' spiritual privacy or to assume the role of clergypersons. I do believe, however, that with our current understanding of the importance of spiritual ministry in relationship to holistic health care, nurses do have a responsibility to informally (and sometimes formally) assess patients' spiritual needs and respond, if appropriate, with spiritual intervention, either themselves or through referral to a pastoral caregiver. How this spiritual intervention is carried out, and by whom, varies significantly, depending on the patient's needs and desires and also on the availability of pastoral care personnel in a particular setting. In the case of the parish nurse, who officially assumes a role of pastoral minister for his or her church community, the boundaries are more clearly defined, according to the combined vision of the nurse's pastor, church administration, and congregation. This is an important point that is explored later in a discussion of initiating a parish health ministry program.

A parish nurse I spoke with related an incident that I believe demonstrates well the relationship between holistic health care and spiritual ministry within the realm of congregational health ministry. Jane had recently undertaken the parish nursing role for a large urban Episcopal church. She was well received by the pastor and by most of the parishioners who understood the concept of parish nursing. A few members of the congregation, however, informed the pastor, Father Martin, that when they were ill, they would prefer a visit from their priest, rather than from a nurse. One such parishioner was 82-year-old Mrs. Wolfe, who was frequently homebound due to a variety of ailments. Pastor Martin tried to accede to Mrs. Wolfe's wishes; one day, however, he asked if she would consider a visit from the parish nurse, who, he pointed out, would understand her health concerns even better than he or one of the other priests; reluctantly she agreed.

Jane described her first visit with Mrs. Wolfe: "She was feeling pretty down about a lot of things: her physical problems (which she really has a lot of); her husband's death; her children moving away; and especially the fact that she can't get out much anymore because of her arthritis. She really misses getting to church and feels that she's losing her connection to the congregation she's been a part of for most of her life." Jane reported that Mrs. Wolfe actually had a very supportive healthcare system in place to monitor her physical needs, but that she was nevertheless quite depressed about her overall condition.

After assessing her physical limitations, Jane offered a suggestion about how Mrs. Wolfe might still remain connected to the faith community she loved. At the church, Jane told her, there was a newly created prayer group for homebound seniors; the plan was to share individual parishioners' prayer needs with the seniors, who would then make a commitment to keep those needs and concerns in their prayers. Notes could be exchanged between the senior "pray-ers" and the parishioners who had requested to have their problems prayed about; this interaction, it was anticipated, would create a sense of church involvement for the homebound seniors and promote a spirit of community among the younger, more active members of the congregation. The idea of this spiritual participation with her faith community was very attractive to Mrs. Wolfe and seemed to alleviate her depression; she commented, "Well, maybe I am still good for something for the church after all!"

Jane's suggestion, flowing from her parish nurse role of clarifier of the relationship between faith and health for her congregation, is central to the practice of holistic nursing care. Jane realized that because of the multiplicity of physical problems with which Mrs. Wolfe was dealing, she probably would not be able to attend church worship services very often; she could, however, through the senior prayer group, continue to feel like, and to indeed be, a useful and participating member of her congregation.

The Beginnings of Contemporary Parish Nursing and Health Ministry

Granger Westberg and the Lutheran Experience

It is noted in the parish nursing literature that "in the 1980s, the Reverend Dr. Granger Westberg 'rediscovered' church based nursing and called it parish nursing" (Carson & Koenig, 2002, p. xvi). Westberg believed in the concept of holistic, or whole-person, health, understanding that the spiritual needs of ill persons may be as or even more important than their physical needs in times of suffering. He embraced a team approach to health care, including such personnel as physician, nurse, and pastoral care provider, admitting: "This triumverate of doctor, nurse and pastor symbolized for me a type of patient care I had always dreamed about" (Westberg, 1990, p. 15). Reverend Westberg, who had served as a hospital chaplain, identified the concept of parish nursing as a role dimension of his mid-1980s experimental holistic health centers jointly supported by the University of Illinois College of Medicine and the Kellogg Foundation (Westberg, 1990). It is reported that although a 10-year follow-up evaluation was positive, the centers were deemed not to be cost-effective; however, "Westberg had observed that the nurse's role in these centers seemed to provide the 'glue' connecting the faith community with the medical community" (Paul, 2000, p. 72).

The International Parish Nurse Resource Center

As an outcome of Westberg's experiment, a parish nursing program was undertaken at Lutheran General Hospital in Park Ridge, Illinois, which ultimately led to the creation of the International Parish Nurse Resource Center (IPNRC), under the leadership of Ann Solari-Twadell, in 1986 (sponsored by Advocate Lutheran General Hospital). One of the IPNRC's activities was to develop an initial curriculum plan for basic parish nursing education. The IPNRC also "served to educate interested congregations from across the United States about the idea of parish nursing" (McDermott, 2001, p. 598). In the fall of 2001, it was announced that the IPNRC would no longer be an agency of its original sponsor; IPNRC activities were to be transferred to Deaconess Parish Nurse Ministries in St. Louis, Missouri.

The history of Deaconess Parish Nurse Ministries is described as follows:

> *Deaconess was started by Evangelical clergy and laity in 1889. The Evangelical Church was one of four denominations who later merged to become the United Church of Christ (UCC). We continue our affiliation with the UCC, but our parish nurses are from, and serve, a variety of denominations. The UCC was one of two denominations to which Advocate Health Care was related, the other being the Evangelical Lutheran Church.... Currently DPNM has 28 parish nurses serving churches in the St. Louis metropolitan area. In addition [DPNM] has been offering educational programs, as well as overseeing research efforts, throughout the Midwest region (Deaconess Parish Nurse Ministries, 2002b, p. 2).*

As of December 31, 2002, sponsorship of the International Parish Nurse Resource Center was formalized under the aegis of Deaconess Parish Nurse Ministries, which is continuing to sponsor the annual Westberg Symposium, providing a forum for parish nurses from across the country to come together to share ideas and experiences, as well as a number of other initiatives begun by the IPNRC in Park Ridge. Some of these activities include "support of the [IPNRC-developed] curriculum and educational classes" (Deaconess Parish Nurse Ministries, 2002b, p. 1). The IPNRC, under Deaconess Parish Nurse Ministries' direction, "will continue to offer the Parish Nurse Basic Preparation class, and . . . the Parish Nurse Coordinator's and Faculty Preparation classes" (Deaconess Parish Nurse Ministries, 2002b, p. 1). Deaconess Parish Nurse Ministries has announced that the IPNRC in St. Louis will also "honor contracts with organizations offering the Basic Preparation Curriculum" and that the "curriculum developed by IPNRC is still available" (Deaconess Parish Nurse Ministries, 2002b, p. 2). Key staff of the IPNRC, under the sponsorship of Deaconess Parish Nurse Ministries, include Reverend Deborah L. Patterson, M.Div., MHA, executive director, an ordained clergyperson in the United Church of Christ; Alvyne Rethemeyer, RN, MSN, director of parish nursing; and Sheryl Cross, RN, MSN, M.Div., associate director of parish nursing (Deaconess Parish Nurse Ministries, 2002b, p. 3).

> *The parish nurse Basic Preparation Curriculum developed by the International Parish Nurse Resource Center, in consultation with the National League for Nursing (NLN) and the American Nurses Association (ANA), is being taught*

at over 60 colleges, universities, hospitals and other parish nurse programs around the U.S. and abroad. The curriculum is a comprehensive set of lesson plans written by two dozen experienced parish nurses and parish nurse educators. The primary objectives for this curriculum are five-fold: (1) understanding the integration of faith and health as central to the parish nursing role, (2) knowledge and skills to practice as a beginning parish nurse, (3) intercollegial peer support, (4) identification of networks for continuing development and support, and (5) commitment to continued spiritual formation to support the role of the parish nurse within a congregation (Deaconess Parish Nurse Ministries, 2002a, p. 2; all material from Parish Nurse Perspectives *is cited with permission of Deaconess Parish Nurse Ministries)*

Parish nursing, as selectively defined, is currently being carried out within a number of faith communities throughout the country, by nurses from a variety of faith traditions; these nurses possess myriad nursing/parish nursing educational backgrounds. Some churches or faith communities carefully define the educational and experiential background required for an individual to serve as a parish nurse within their congregations; others do not. A search for the concept of *parish nursing* in the literature reveals significant differences in these criteria, if they exist at all. The field of parish nursing is currently evolving as a subspecialty within the profession of nursing. A parish nursing membership organization, the Health Ministries Association, has now been created, as has an American Nurses Association (ANA)–accepted document delineating the scope and standards of parish nursing practice (these are discussed later in Chapter 4, which explores parish nursing education).

Parish nursing is a very new subfield of nursing, only recently recognized by the ANA, and yet it is also very old. Parish nursing, or nursing carried out under the aegis of the Christian Church, began with Jesus' mandate to care for each other. This nursing was undertaken as ministry by the first church deacons and deaconesses, the Roman matrons, the early and medieval monastic nurses, the military nursing orders, and the Protestant and Catholic religious nursing orders (O'Brien, 2003, pp. 26–51). Church-related nursing continued throughout the first two millennia through a variety of church-sponsored volunteer activities involving care of the ill and the infirm. Today parish nurses are blessed to carry on the tradition of a ministry of service, in the parish nursing role, within their various faith communities. What is old has become new again; parish health ministry has been reborn, and parish nurses are gifted to be called to this service of caring and compassion.

References

Austin, A. L. (1957). *History of nursing: Source book*. New York: G. P. Putnam's Sons.

Bullough, V., & Bullough, B. (1978). *The care of the sick: The emergence of modern nursing*. New York: Prodist.

Carson, V. B., & Koenig, H. G. (2002). *Parish nursing: Stories of service and care*. Philadelphia: Templeton Foundation Press.

Chase-Ziolek, M., & Holst, L. E. (1999). Parish nursing in diverse traditions. In P. A. Solari-Twadell & M. A. McDermott (Eds.), *Parish nursing: Promoting whole person health within faith communities* (pp. 195–204). Thousand Oaks, CA: Sage.

Council projects. (1956). *Catholic Nurse, 5*(1), 42–44.

Cummings, A. L. (1960). In the parish. *Catholic Nurse, 8*(3), 26–29.

Deaconess Parish Nurse Ministries. (2002a). Parish nurse curriculum. *Parish Nurse Perspectives, 1*(2). St. Louis: Author.

Deaconess Parish Nurse Ministries. (2002b). What is going on; INPRC transition. *Parish Nurse Perspectives, 1*(1). St. Louis: Author.

DeLaune, S. C., & Ladner, P. K. (2002). *Fundamentals of nursing: Standards and Practice* (2nd ed.). Clifton Park, NY: Delmar.

Dietz, L. D., & Lehozky, A. R. (1967). *History and modern nursing*. Philadelphia: F. A. Davis.

Dock, L. L. (1922). The history of public health nursing. *Public Health Nurse, 14*(10), 522–526.

Dock, L. L., & Stewart, I. M. (1920). *A short history of nursing: From the earliest times to the present day*. New York: G. P. Putnam's Sons.

Dolan, J. A. (1973). *Nursing in society: A historical perspective*. Philadelphia: W. B. Saunders.

Dolan, J. A. (1978). *Nursing in society: A historical perspective* (2nd ed.). Philadelphia: W. B. Saunders.

Donahue, M. P. (1996). *Nursing: The finest art* (2nd ed.). St. Louis: Mosby.

Dossey, B. M., Keegan, L., Guzzetta, C. E., & Kolkmeier, L. G. (Eds.). (1988). *Holistic nursing: A handbook for practice*. Rockville, MD: Aspen.

Farren, S. (1996). *A call to care*. St. Louis: Catholic Health Association of the United States.

Frank, C. M. (1959). *The historical development of nursing*. Philadelphia: W. B. Saunders.

Goodnow, M. (1916). *Outlines of nursing history*. Philadelphia: W. B. Saunders.

Grippando, G. (1986). *Nursing perspectives and issues* (3rd ed.). Albany, NY: Delmar.

Livingstone, E. A. (1990). *The concise Oxford dictionary of the Christian Church*. New York: Oxford University Press.

Lundy, K. S., & Bender, K. W. (2001). History of community and public health nursing. In K. S. Lundy & S. Janes (Eds.), *Community health nursing: Caring for the public's health* (pp. 70–99). Sudbury, MA: Jones and Bartlett.

Martin, G., & Lacoutre, C. (1953). Volunteer nursing. *Catholic Nurse, 2*(2), 13–14.

McDermott, M. A. (2001). Parish nursing: When the population served is a congregation. In N. L. Chaska (Ed.), *The nursing profession: Tomorrow and beyond* (pp. 597–607). Thousand Oaks, CA: Sage.

Nagai-Jacobson, M. G., & Burkhart, M. A. (1989). Spirituality: Cornerstone of holistic nursing practice. *Holistic Nursing Practice, 3*(3), 18–26.

Newsome, J. (1994). Nurses in the African-American church. *Association of Black Nursing Faculty Journal, 5*(5), 134–137.

Nutting, M. A., & Dock, L. L. (1935). *A history of nursing* (Vol. 1). New York: G. P. Putnam's Sons.

O'Brien, M. E. (2001). *The nurse's calling: A Christian spirituality of caring for the sick*. Mahwah, NJ: Paulist Press.

O'Brien, M. E. (2003). *Spirituality in nursing: Standing on holy ground* (2nd ed.). Sudbury, MA: Jones and Bartlett.

Olson, J. E. (1992). *One ministry, many roles: Deacons and deaconesses through the centuries*. St. Louis: Concordia.

Paul, P. (2000). The history of the relationship between nursing and faith traditions. In M. B. Clark & J. K. Olson (Eds.), *Nursing within a faith community: Promotion of health in times of transition* (pp. 59–75). Thousand Oaks, CA: Sage.

Pavey, A. E. (1938). *The story of the growth of nursing, as an art, a vocation and a profession*. London: Faber and Faber.

Rademacher, W. J. (1991). *Lay ministry: A theological, spiritual and pastoral handbook*. New York: Crossroad.

Robinson, V. (1946). *White caps: The story of nursing*. Philadelphia: Lippincott.

Shelly, J. (2000). Diversity: Enlarging our tents (editorial). *Journal of Christian Nursing, 17*(3), 3.

Thomson, E. E. (1935). Introduction. In E. S. Bryan, *The art of public health nursing* (p. 5). Philadelphia: W. B. Saunders.

Thurston, H. J., & Attwater, D. (1996). *Butler's lives of the saints* (Vol. 3). Allen, TX: Thomas More Publishing.

Walsh, J. J. (1929). *The history of nursing*. New York: P. J. Kennedy & Sons.

Waterman, K. A. (1989). The salve in salvation: Church nurses see to medical needs and more. *Washington Post*, August 15, Metro Section, p. B1.

Webb, B. (1920). Roaming through Virginia with the public health nurse. *Public Health Nurse, 12*(10), 839–870.

Westberg, G. E. (1990). *The parish nurse: Providing a minster of health for your congregation*. Minneapolis: Augsburg.

CHAPTER 3

THE PARISH NURSING ROLE: SPIRITUAL COMPANION IN HEALTH AND ILLNESS

And whoever gives even a cup of cold water . . . [in My Name, will not] lose their reward.

–*Matthew 10:42*

The "Cup of Cold Water" Ministry

Only a "cup of cold water," Lord;
    it seems like such a small thing?
Yet, to give it in "Your Name," that's
    the heart of the message,
        Isn't it?

But what does it really mean, Lord,
    to give the cup in Your Name?

And to give it to "little ones"; does
that mean to just anyone who
comes along?

I want to minister in "Your Name,"
Lord; that's the desire of my heart.
It's just that some days the fog is so
thick, I can barely see the road.

I need Your help, Dear Lord;
Please lead me to the place
where I may give:
a cup of cold water,
a bowl of soup,
a word of comfort,
a touch of caring,
in Your Blessed Name.

The roles of contemporary parish nurses may differ somewhat, by congregation, since the subfield of parish nursing is still evolving. Parish nurse role behaviors may be influenced by such factors as the needs and desires of a faith community, the background and experience of the parish nurse, and the number of hours that a parish nurse is able to commit to a congregation. The number of activities in which a parish nurse engages may also depend upon whether the nurse serves in a paid position (either full-or part-time) or purely as a volunteer. Currently, four basic models of parish nursing have been identified, including congregation-based volunteer parish nursing, congregation-based paid parish nursing, institution-based volunteer parish nursing, and institution-based paid parish nursing (Kuhn, 1997, p. 26). Regardless of the model to which a parish nurse adheres, or the number of hours committed to the activity, it is important to clarify some basic principles that explain parish nursing, to identify what parish nursing is and what it is not, and to describe the overarching role of the parish nurse as that of a *spiritual companion in health and illness*.

A Definition of Parish Nursing

And they brought to him all the sick, those who were afflicted with
various diseases and pains . . . and he cured them.

—Matthew 4:24

Who is the parish nurse serving in a faith community? He or she may be an older or a younger nurse, a veteran or a neophyte, educated in any of a variety of nursing specialties. According to the *Scope and Standards of Parish Nursing Practice* (discussed later in this chapter), the parish nurse must be a licensed registered nurse and may be prepared at any level: diploma, associate degree, BSN, MSN, or doctoral degree. Parish nurses' specialty educational preparation (examined in the following chapter) currently ranges from a day-long or weekend parish nursing workshop to a college credit program in parish nursing, which may include a significant amount of theological study. The most common type of parish nursing education, at present, is a three-to five-CEU (continuing education unit) course.

In contemporary congregations' educational and professional criteria for their parish nurse(s), variations abound. Some churches prefer that their parish nurse(s), as well as being licensed in the state, have several years of nursing experience; other congregations require that their parish nurse take a basic course in parish nursing (the parameters of the course content are rarely described); and a few churches identify no criteria, except the desire of the parish nurse to serve the congregation in health care ministry.

A definition of parish nursing presented in the literature states, in part, that "parish nursing is a health promotion, disease prevention role based on the care of the whole person . . . it is a professional model of health ministry using a registered nurse" (Solari-Twadell, 1999, p. 3). Solari-Twadell adds: "The focus for the practice is the faith community and its ministry" (p. 3). The growing practice of parish nursing is described by Ruth Stoll (1997), who explains that churches are "attempting to restore a ministry of health and healing": "The professional nurse functions as a member of the pastoral team to promote individuals' sense of wholeness and health . . . [and to] encourage the congregation to realize that they are whole persons—body, mind, and spirit, whom God desires . . . to be healthy . . . dwelling at peace in all [of their] relationships" (p. 18).

There begins to be a plethora of nursing journal articles, written by parish nurses, which describe the concept of contemporary parish nursing; some descriptions articulated by practicing parish nurses include the following:

> *"The health ministry role of the parish nurse . . . is two-fold: (1)assisting parishioners to experience ownership of their lives by encouraging active participation in health promotion and illness prevention behaviors, and (2) helping parishioners to understand the connection between spirituality and health" (Leetun & Saabye, 1996, p. 9).*

> *"Parish nurses seek to provide spiritual solace, community resources and health guidance to their fellow community members" (McGee, 1998, p. 4).*

> *"A parish nurse is a registered professional nurse who, as a member of the pastoral team, provides preventive care with a focus on health promotion and spiritual care. The parish nurse serves as health educator, personal health counselor, advocate, teacher . . . coordinator . . . and liaison . . . all within a framework that links spirituality and health"* (Adkins, 1998, p. 21).

> *"Parish nursing . . . operating within any faith community . . . combines the art and skills of nursing with attention to the spirituality of the client, providing truly holistic health care"* ("Parish Nursing in Saskatchewan," 1998, p. 14).

> *"Parish nursing is a unique, specialized practice of nursing that holds the spiritual dimension to be central to practice. A parish nurse focuses on the promotion of health within the context of the values, beliefs and practices of a faith community . . . the nursing practice includes the faith community's mission and ministry to its members"* (Matteson, 1999, p. 5).

> *"The parish nursing role may be different from congregation to congregation. The role is defined by the nurses' expertise and strengths, the support of the pastoral staff and the needs of the congregation"* ("A Parish Nurse Story," 1998, p. 12).

> *"Parish nursing takes a holistic perspective . . . you become a proactive professional empowering people to make wise decisions about their health instead of merely ministering to those who are already sick"* ("Parish Nursing: Taking a Holistic Approach Toward Patient Care," 1999, p. 19).

> *"[As a parish nurse] many times I respond to a request for information about a specific condition or make a referral to a local support group or community agency. Above all I try to bring a sense of God's healing presence as I minister to body, mind and spirit"* (Ambrose, 2000, p. 13).

> *"[Parish] nurses . . . assist individuals with personal health care decision-making, particularly by helping the client to identify his or her physical, emotional and spiritual needs, and by presenting the available options for care and for care settings"* (Linton, 1997, p. 3).

In summarizing the preceding comments defining and describing parish nursing, it appears that most nurse authors view parish nursing as a holistic health ministry, based within the context of a faith community and placing particular emphasis on caring for the spiritual needs of the parishioner, especially of the parishioner suffering from illness or disability.

The Language

As discussed in Chapter 2, the early history upon which parish nursing is based reveals that the concepts of *diaconia*, or service, and *church nursing* are labels that have been used for centuries to describe the ministry of nurses serving within faith communities. An early association of the terms *parish* and *nursing* was found in a 1960 article titled "In the Parish," in which the nurse author states that, in distinction to nurses who work in hospitals, or clinics, or the home, her job is "in the parish" ; that she is the "parish health counselor" (Cummings, 1960, p. 26). Pastor Granger Westberg, however, introduced the terminology *parish nursing* to describe nurses providing health ministry within faith communities in the mid-1980s (Westberg, 1990).

It has been suggested that the term *parish nursing* or *parish nurse* may be problematic for some communities, as not all faith communities, not even all Christian churches, use the label *parish* to describe their congregations. Thus, some other terminologies have been introduced to describe healthcare ministry within a faith community such as congregational nursing, church nursing, and faith community nursing. In their text on "Nursing Within a Faith Community," Canadian authors Clark and Olson (2000) admit that they "struggled with the question of what to call a nurse who functions as a member of a ministerial team . . . to facilitate the healing mission of a faith community" (p. 7). Clark and Olson conclude that because the term *parish* tends to be associated with the Christian faith, they wished to use a "more inclusive terminology . . . faith community, faith community nurse, and faith community nursing" (p. 8). The authors do admit that they will, in referring to specific faith traditions, use such terms as "parish, church, synagogue, mosque, temple and congregation" (Clark & Olson, 2000, p. 8).

I have chosen, in the present book, to embrace the terms *parish nursing* and *congregational nursing*. I desire the book, in its many examples of parish or congregational nursing, to reflect the interdenominational nature of parish nursing within the Christian community. I do not, however, personally have the experience or the expertise to place church-related nursing ministry in an interfaith context. My prayer and my hope is that nurses serving as health ministers of other religious traditions will be able to relate the philosophy and the theology of Christian parish nursing to the philosophies and ethics of their own respective faith communities.

The Role of the Parish Nurse in Health Ministry

Having said a bit about who the parish nurse is, it is important to point out that there are some behaviors accepted by their congregations that parish nurses are generally expected to assume. These activities might be identified broadly as serving as an advocate in terms of a parishioner seeking needed health care; advising parishioners about their health problems, questions, and concerns; making referrals to appropriate healthcare facilities and services; educating patients about issues relating to health promotion and disease prevention; coordinating a faith community's health ministry volunteers; and providing spiritual ministry or facilitating the ministry of a pastoral care provider, as desired and needed by the parishioner.

The parish nurse might best be described as a church-based consultant, teacher, and minister, rather than as a "hands-on" caregiver. In listening to the stories of parish nurses' experiences, one usually finds minor exceptions to the preceding description. For example, a parish nurse may engage in the taking of blood pressure (BP) in a home or at the church for a parishioner concerned about his or her BP levels (outside of a scheduled blood pressure screening open to all church members); the nurse may guide an elderly parishioner in learning to use a walker or a cane; or the nurse may assist a patient confined to a wheelchair (many examples of parish nurses' activities are presented in Chapter 8).

What the parish nurse is not is a "visiting nurse" or "community health nurse," mandated to provide physical care in the home. Parish nurses do not start IVs (intravenous injections), give intramuscular or subcutaneous injections, administer oral medications, carry out treatments such as dressing changes, give bed baths, or provide any other physical care that might be needed by the parishioner. The parish nurse does, however, assist a parishioner who might need these services in making contact with the appropriate agency and/or individual whose mission is to provide such care. Parish nurses may also offer advice to parishioners about compliance with therapeutic regimens, if they feel comfortable doing so; and the teaching and counsel of a parish nurse can also be invaluable in assisting parishioners and their families in negotiating the "minefield" of contemporary healthcare services.

Writing in 1990, Reverend Dr. Granger Westberg identified five key roles as falling within the purview of parish nursing; these include "health educator," "health counselor," "teacher of volunteers," "liaison with community health organizations," and "clarifier of the close relationship between faith and health" (pp. 46–49). Ann Solari-Twadell and Pastor Westberg, in a 1991 article in *Health Progress*, point out that parish nursing provides a "unique setting in which the patient is allowed to speak to the nurse about spirituality" (p. 26). They add: "The parishioner sees the parish nurse as a representative of the Christian community. Part of the counseling time [in a visit] is often devoted to prayer or meditation. Sometimes the nurse acts as Eucharistic minister and brings clients the Holy Eucharist" (p. 26). In a 1999 book on parish nursing, the nurse's activities were identified as encompassing seven roles, including "health educator," "personal health counselor," "referral agent," "trainer of volunteers," "developer of support groups," "integrator of faith and health," and "health advocate" (Holstrom, 1999, p. 69). In a contemporary nurse's Christian fellowship course on "parish nursing education," I was introduced to a similar list of parish nursing roles.

When one reviews church bulletins for individual parishes in a variety of denominations, however, identified parish nurse roles vary to some degree. The parish nursing roles that are consistently described by the majority of congregations are those of "health educator," "health counselor," "liaison with community health agengies," and "facilitator"; a number of churches include such activities as working with volunteers and developing support groups under the label "facilitator"; several churches note that the parish nurse also represents the healing "mission" of the church. Some churches consider the parish nurse role of counselor to include sharing the healing message of the Gospel with ill parishioners. This important role of supporting the faith of an ill or disabled parishioner is, perhaps, considered by some congregations to be so central to the role of the parish nurse who ministers within a faith community as to supercede all of his or her other activities. Thus, it is presented as the underlying framework or mission for the ministry of parish nursing, rather than being identified as one of a number of nursing roles. In this context, alternate terminology found to describe the parish nurse's spiritual ministry includes promoter of spiritual well-being; facilitator of the relationship between body, mind, and spirit; responder to the physical, emotional, and spiritual needs of the parishioners; and role model as a representative of the Christian community.

I conducted a nursing intervention study to determine which parish nursing activities were most important to the ill parishioners to whom the nurses ministered and to test whether parish nursing made a difference in the areas of spiritual well-being, hope, and life satisfaction for recipients of the ministry. The project employed four parish nurses and two nonnurse church health ministers to implement the key role behaviors identified in the parish nursing literature, such as educating, counseling, referring, and providing spiritual support, as needed and desired, for a group of 45 chronically ill homebound persons. Funding was requested and received to purchase devotional items, such as large-print bibles and religious music tapes, which might be used, if appropriate, to support an ill parishioner's practice of faith. The process of accessing study participants was supported by the pastors of six churches in a tristate area, as well as a part-time chaplain at a nonreligiously affiliated nursing home (the study design, implementation, and findings are presented in Chapter 9.)

The parish nurses and health ministers who carried out the parish ministry intervention engaged in such activities as education (one nurse spent a great deal of time during a parish nursing visit teaching a diabetic parishioner about his diet and medictions); counseling (an elderly patient expressed concerns about her potential future life in a nursing home or assisted care facility, which the nurse was able to discuss with her); referral (a parish nurse, on a second visit, assisted a parishioner's husband in getting hospital care for his spouse whose condition had rapidly deteriorated following a mild stroke); and advocacy (a parish nurse assisted a patient in seeking needed health care that he had been hesitant to ask for). The concept of working with volunteers or support group members was not included in the project intervention, which was directed specifically to the needs of homebound parishioners.

While I would in no way devalue the importance of the health counseling, education, referral, and advocacy parish nursing activities described, an overwhelming need and desire articulated by our more fragile project participants was for a *ministry of spiritual companionship in their illness*; they reveled in the visits from parish nurses and health ministers who understood their illness and the loneliness of their homebound conditions, and whose caring ameliorated their isolation from the churches to which they belonged. Frequently, when I asked project staff members if they needed a larger budget allocation to purchase devotional items for their parishioners, they responded in the negative, explaining that those they were visiting asked for very little in terms of material items; the most commonly verbalized request from a parishioner participating in the study was, "When are you coming back?" Over and over, the homebound project parishioners expressed their joy and gratitude for the parish health ministry visits; they reported great pleasure at having a representative of their faith community come to share with them a ministry of prayer and spiritual support.

 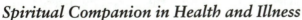

Spiritual Companion in Health and Illness

The overarching concept of the parish nurse as a *spiritual companion in health and illness* is derived from the parish nursing research the Gift of Faith in Chronic Illness, as described earlier and in Chapter 9, as well as from Granger Westberg's (1990) vision of the parish nurse as "clarifier of the close relationship between faith and health" (p.49). In his explanation of the activity, Pastor Westberg observes that parish nurses have the opportunity to discuss "deeper issues" that may impact a parishioner's health; he cautions, however, that "such counseling places a heavy load on the parish nurse" and notes that most nurses report that "it takes many years of experience and training to help counselees bring the two dimensions, faith and health, into productive dialogue" (p. 49). To describe the nurse as a "spiritual companion" in health and illness for the parishioner, however, places the relationship in a slightly different context. A parish nurse, as a spiritual companion, is one who journeys with parishioners in sickness and in health. While the parish nurse, as spiritual companion, may indeed help a parishioner "clarify" the relationship between faith and health, the primacy of the role is to be present, to listen and be listened to, and to touch and be touched by the parishioner with whom the nurse is journeying. When I embarked on a 10-week hospital chaplaincy internship, as part of a program of theology studies, the chaplain supervisor in our hospital's department of spiritual ministry asserted that the key role of a healthcare chaplain was to "journey" with patients in their illness experiences.

In his classic work *Introduction to a Devout Life*, Francis de Sales places great emphasis on what he describes as spiritual companionship or friendship among Christians who would support each other both in good times and in bad. He encourages Christians to find *spiritual companions* on their journey of life, asserting: "For those who live in the world and desire to embrace true virtue it is necessary to unite together in holy sacred friendship" (Ryan, 1966, pp. 175–176). Through such relationships, de Sales believed, friends could lead each other to a sense of spiritual peace and virtue (p. 176).

I have described a "nursing theology of caring" encompassing the previously noted roles of being present, listening, and touching (O'Brien, 2003, pp. 14–17). These, I believe, are the role behaviors of the spiritual companion, as described by Francis de Sales, as well as of the parish nurse as *spiritual companion in health and illness*.

Being Present

> You have upheld me because of my integrity, and set me in your presence forever.
>
> —*Psalm 41:13*

Psalm 41 is described as a psalm of "Thanksgiving After Sickness"; the psalmist gives thanks to the Lord for the gift of being allowed to "stand in His presence" in illness and in recovery. How important it is for us to have caring people "present" to us, and for us to be present to them, especially when we are in need either physically, emotionally, or spiritually. There are conditions and circumstances, for example, in the case of a parishioner who is terminally ill, when a parish nurse may not be able to really "do" anything in terms education, counseling, referral, or even advocacy. A parishioner might have excellent physical, emotional, and social support from family and friends, and yet the caring presence of a parish nurse can bring much additional comfort, for the nurse serving as a minister of faith represents the love and the care of the Lord, as well as of the parishioner's church community.

Some years ago, I wrote of the frustration I felt, standing at the bedside of 27-year-old Ricky, who was dying of AIDS. I lamented: "I felt so helpless. I stood there with the parents at Ricky's bedside and I wished that I had some deep well of spirituality out of which would emerge profound and comforting words, but nothing seemed to come—not for Ricky or for the family" (O'Brien, 1995, p. 133). I hugged Ricky and his parents as I left them but did not feel that I had done any ministry during my visit. When I returned to my office, I found a gift on my desk: a book written by Daniel Berrigan titled *Sorrow Built a Bridge: Friendship and AIDS*. As I leafed through the pages, I discovered a passage in which Berrigan also bemoaned not having words to say during a hospital visit to a young AIDS patient: "He would not offer false comfort or a quick fix . . . the priest's strength (or what passed muster for strength) was a simple act of the will. He wanted to be there. To be with this afflicted pair and their son. To go through it all with them" (Berrigan, 1989, p. 5; cited in O'Brien, 1995, p. 134).

Sometimes a parish nurse's act of simply "being there," of being fully present in mind and heart and soul to a parishioner's pain and the suffering, is the greatest gift he or she can give in the ministry of caring. The parish nurse can choose, as Berrigan, to "want to be there," to "go through it all" with parishioners and their families. This is a parish nursing ministry of presence, a ministry of caring, a ministry of love.

Listening

> Let everyone be quick to listen, slow to speak.
> —*James 1:19*

For a parishioner who is anxious or afraid, as well as being present, an important and blessed ministry for the parish nurse is that of listening—listening not only with a nurse's ears but also with a nurse's heart. I think all of us have had experiences of suffering during which we desperately needed to talk to someone about our pain. At those times we sought out a person in whom to confide whose caring we trusted unequivocally. And we can remember how blessed we felt to have a loving friend or family member to listen and to hear our pain, without judgment or condemnation.

There are many homebound or care facility–bound parishioners, who now in their senior years no longer have a supportive cadre of family and friends to be their "listeners." One of these was Mrs. McCracken, a study participant, who had for many years been active in her Episcopal church. Now 88 and suffering from myriad illness conditions including arthritis and congestive heart failure, Mrs. McCracken was mostly confined to her wheelchair in a long-term care facility; most of her family and friends had preceded her to their lives with the Lord. While her fragile body did not serve her well any more, Mrs. McCracken's mind was sharp, but "of course a little forgetful at times," she always admitted. But Mrs. McCracken loved to visit. She delighted in reminiscing about her days as a teacher in a rural, one-room school; and she worried about "getting old": "not the dying part" she asserted, "that comes to all of us and I'm ready to go whenever the Lord comes for me . . . it's just the 'getting there' that scares me."

Cathy, Mrs. McCracken's parish nurse, reported that her primary role with her parishioner during most visits was being a "listener." Cathy explained:

> *Sometimes I can tell Mrs. McCracken wants me to talk about God, to say a prayer with her; and we've talked about her death and her faith in heaven, when she'll get to be with all the people she loved. But a lot of times on my parish ministry visit, Mrs. McCraken does most of the talking and I just listen. I know she enjoys reminiscing because she seems to come alive when she talks about her teaching and her students; what it was like to teach in a small country school. But, you know, she likes to talk about the world too; you'd be surprised at how she keeps up with the news. She gives me information sometimes and I think she really likes that because then she has something important to share with me. We've really bonded because of these conversations. Mrs. McCracken is an inspiration to me and I tell her that; I know that makes her happy.*

For a parishioner like Mrs. McCracken, living in a long-term care facility, most needs for services relating to education, counseling, referral, or advocacy are taken care of by the professional staff. The gift that Cathy brings in her ministry of listening is the loving care and attention of Mrs. McCracken's faith community, the ministry of listening, as with the mind and the heart of God.

Touching

> And there was a leper who . . . knelt before him, saying "Lord, if you choose, you can make me clean." He stretched out his hand and touched him, saying "I do choose. Be made clean."
>
> —Matthew 8:2–3

> A woman . . . suffering from hemorrhages for twelve years (and unable to
> be cured) . . . came up behind [Jesus] and touched the fringe of his clothes
> and immediately her hemorrhage stopped. . . . Jesus said: "Someone
> touched me; for I noticed that power had gone out from me."
>
> —*Luke 8:46*

Jesus' ministries of touch, described in the two preceding gospel passages, provide important models for parish nursing. They are similar yet not the same, woven from the one seamless garment of Jesus' gospel message of caring, but colored with different threads of healing behavior. In the first narrative, Jesus takes the initiative, reaching out without fear and touching the leper; a risk to his person as the human Son of God. In the case of the woman with the hemorrhages, Jesus allowed himself to *be touched* by one considered "unclean," thus risking injury to his reputation as the Divine Son of God.

Several years ago, after writing a meditation to explain the meaning of the concept of "standing on holy ground" for nurses, I e-mailed the draft to a nurse friend for her comments. I had ended the piece with the sentence: "the nurse reverently touches the patient's heart, the dwelling place of the living God." My friend felt that the final sentence was missing a thought. She observed that we nurses are also "touched," in touching our patients, and that it is important to allow ourselves to be open to this happening. I thus revised the ending to read: "the nurse reverently touches, *and is touched by*, the patient's heart, the dwelling place of the living God" (O'Brien, 2003, p. vi).

How often when we reach out to touch or simply to open our hearts to the concerns of our patients we are deeply touched in return. One of my favorite stories involves the deep faith of a young man living with HIV infection. When I asked Peter whether his religious belief helped in coping with HIV, he replied that he "grabbed onto blessings" in many places; he gave an example of a prayer of his church that was very meaningful in his battle with life-threatening illness: "'We give Thee but Thine own; what'er the gifts may be. All that we have is Thine alone; a trust, O Lord from Thee.' What that says to me," Peter explained, "is I don't really own any of my things. They're on loan, and in a sense my life is on loan. It's a privilege to be here, and if that gets taken back, then it just means that the 'meter has run out,' you know; God is saying: 'OK, out of the pool,' time to move on. So really I'm not losing anything. I see it in the grander sense of what I'm gaining" (O'Brien, 1992, p. 47). My nurse's heart was truly "touched" by Peter's faith-filled response to living with the human immunodeficiency virus.

The Philosophy of Parish Nursing

The philosophy and theology of contemporary parish nursing is based in the Christian scripture, especially passages related to faith beliefs and caring for those in need such as Matthew 10:42: "And whoever gives only a cup of cold water in my name . . . he will surely not lose his reward," and Matthew 25:35–36: "For I was hungry and you gave me food, I was thirsty and you gave me drink, a stranger and you welcomed me, naked and you clothed me, ill and you cared for me, in prison and you visited me."

In describing the philosophy of parish nursing, Ann Solari-Twadell (1999), former director of the International Parish Nurse Resource Center, points out that a key statement in the philosophy is this: "Parish nursing holds the spiritual dimension to be central to the practice" (p. 3). The "spiritual dimension of the individual," Solari-Twadell notes, is the "focus" of the parish nursing role (p. 3). "The pastoral dimensions of nursing care are emphasized, with particular attention to the spiritual maturity of the nurse. This begins to distinguish the practice from the traditional community health nurse and to set the parameters for the role" (Solari-Twadell, 1999, pp. 3–4). The philososphy and theology of parish nursing are also derived from the basic philosophy and theology of the larger nursing profession. Contemporary professional nursing, as evolved from the era of Florence Nightingale, grew out of a "Christian worldview, in response to Jesus' teaching and example in caring for the sick" (Shelly & Miller, 1999, p. 39). In their exploration of the Christian theology of nursing, Shelly and Miller assert that "while other worldviews of the time focused on gaining control of the physical elements and spiritual powers, the early Christians looked instead to God as one who deserved love and obedience and who inspired loving service to others" (p. 39). They add: this "tradition of caring for others in the form of nursing has continued throughout church history" (p. 39).

Presently, the subfield of parish nursing is evolving, and as the practice develops so shall the philosophy. Nevertheless, some basic assumptions may be articulated.

"The parish nurse is considered by most parish nurse educators to be a registered nurse with well-developed clinical and interpersonal skills, a strong personal religious faith, and a desire or felt call to serve the needs of a parish or faith community. A parish nursing philosophy builds on the existing philosophy of caring and commitment already espoused by the nurse as a professional ethic" (O'Brien, 2003, p. 293).

Most parish nurses consider their practice to be a vocation or calling from the Lord to serve in a "ministry" of nursing, rather than in a profession. For many current parish nurses, although surely not all, the call to parish nursing came later in their careers; parish nursing became a ministry of service that could be undertaken on a volunteer basis following retirement from paid professional nursing. Because of the volunteer nature of much of contemporary parish nursing, the ministry naturally evokes a philosophy of caring for one's church members, unselfishly, as Jesus taught in a spirituality of Christian sharing and Christian community. This is, of course, consistent with the identified emphasis on caring for an individual's spiritual needs as identified by early leaders of the parish nursing movement, such as Reverend Dr. Granger Westberg (1990).

A Theology of Community

> They devoted themselves to the apostles' teaching and fellowship, to the breaking of bread and the prayers.
>
> —*Acts 2:42*

One cannot explain the Christian philosophy of nursing within a faith community, without also exploring the theology of Christian community. In the Acts of the Apostles, the evangelist Luke took pains to describe the communal life of the early Christians: in their sharing of goods and services; their coming together for meals in each other's homes, and their gathering together for prayer (Luke 3:43–47). Luke also reported that the Christians carried out these activities with "exultation and sincerity of heart" (3:46).

When one speaks of a "community," there is general understanding that a group of persons, bonded by some common interest or philosophy of life, is being described. Christian community offers "belief in a God who is the perfect community, who invites each of us into that community, and whose Spirit dwelling in our hearts enables us to cast out our fears and love one another" (Barry, 1992, p. 55). The Christian community is united by the members' common adherence to the gospel teachings of Jesus, the Christ, whom they worship as Lord and Savior. Christians are also taught that simple belief in Christ, a "personal relationship with God" is not enough; rather, salvation is achieved also "through an intensified life in community with other believers as members of Christ's body" . . . "the familiar Christian precept to love one's neighbor as oneself should then be understood as the mandate to remain in communication with others" (Bracken, 1990, p. 217).

The Christian community has been described sociologically as a "hybrid group": "It has some characteristics of a primary group, for members of a Christian community always minister to one another's needs. It has some characteristics of a secondary group as well for it is always in mission . . . [building] a new world with the transforming good news of Jesus Christ" (Lee, 1993, p. 188). In Christian community "there is a bonding that goes beyond human expectations . . . a bonding of prayer and spiritual caring that is not dependent on the externals of similar personalities, tastes or causes" (Dougherty, 1995, p. 13). Despite this bonding of prayer and caring, Henri Nouwen (1975) also points out that Christians need to constantly support each other in the understanding that the basis of Christian community is the "divine call": "we are together, but we cannot fulfill each other . . . we help each other, but we also have to remind each other that our destiny is beyond togetherness" (p. 153). God is "the source of our new life together," Nouwen observes, and "by our common call to the New Jerusalem, we recognize each other on the road as brothers and sisters" (p. 153).

Finally, Brother Roger Schutz, founder and prior of the Christian ecumenical religious community of Taize brothers, teaches that all Christians should live a "parable of communion, a simple reflection of that unique communion which is the Body of Christ, his Church, and through this, be also leaven in the human family" (Roger of Taize, 1990, pp. 88–89). Perhaps, Brother Roger (1991) also advises the Christian community, "you could place these Gospel words on the wall of your home; they come straight from the heart of Christ: 'Whatever you do to the least of my brothers, you are doing to me!'" (p. 13).

The *Scope and Standards of Parish Nursing Practice*

The publication of the *Scope and Standards of Parish Nursing Practice* is an important marker in the brief history of the subspecialty of parish nursing, for it represents the formal acknowledgment of the discipline by the larger nursing community. The 23-page document was prepared by the Practice and Education Committee of the Health Ministries Association (HMA). The document was first adopted by the HMA board of directors on September 23, 1996, and was revised in January of 1998 (American Nurses Publishing, 1998, p. iii). The American Nurses Association (ANA) Congress of Nursing Practice recognized parish nursing as a specialty in April 1997. The *Scope and Standards of Parish Nursing Practice* (SSPNP) was acknowledged by the ANA Congress of Nursing Practice in February 1998 (American Nurses Publishing, 1998, p. iii).

The introduction to the *SSPNP* states that the purpose of the document is to "describe the evolving specialty of parish nursing and to provide parish nurses, the nursing profession, and other health care providers, employers, insurers and their clients with the unique scope and competent standards of care and professional performance expected of a parish nurse" (1998, p. 3); it is added that "parish nursing promotes health and healing by empowering the client system (faith community, family or individual) to incorporate health and healing practices from its faith perspective to achieve desired outcomes" (p. 3). The standards of care and of professional performance included in the *SSPNP* are based on the ANA 1991 *Standards of Clinical Nursing Practice* (*SSPNP*, 1998, p. 4). The parish nurse is defined, according to the *SSPNP,* as being a "registered professional nurse who serves as a member of a ministry staff of a faith community to promote health and wholeness . . . [according to] the standards set forth" in the document (p. 7).

The *Scope and Standards of Parish Nursing Practice* includes proscriptions for such parish nursing standards of care as assessment, diagnosis, outcome identification, planning, implementation, and evaluation (pp. 9–14); and standards of professonal performance, including quality of care, performance appraisal, education, collegiality, ethics, collaboration, research, and resource utilization (pp. 15–21).

The Health Ministries Association (HMA), developer of the *SSPNP*, is a membership organization, originally conceived of by an advisory board of the INPRC, for individuals involved in any health ministry activities (the "faith–health movement"); its activities revolve around such foci as education, advocacy, and spiritual transformation. The HMA "serves as the professional specialty organization for parish nurses" and has been recommended by the ANA for "membership in the Nursing Organization Liaison Forum." HMA has also assumed a leadership role in exploring the possibility of "credentialing for parish nurses through a certification examination" (FAQ about HMA and Parish Nursing, 2001, p. 1).

The Credentialing Issue

It is generally understood that a significant number of nurses practicing in a specialty area is needed in order to develop and administer a credentialing exam through the ANA Credentialing Center; this is also a complicated and costly process. Most parish nursing educators, therefore, anticipate that it may be several years before formal ANA credentialing of parish nurses can be accomplished. This is an important point to clarify in explaining the specialty to potential employers, such as churches or hospitals, as well as to nurses interested in becoming parish nurses. On the opening day of the parish nursing education course in which I participated, one of our group members commented that she had been serving as a parish nurse, at her church, for several years and was "excited about finally getting *credentialed!*" One of the course faculty members immediately responded with the explanation that the students would be "commissioned," in a religious ceremony, at the end of the course but that we would not be credentialed, as credentialing does not yet exist for the parish nursing specialty.

Dr. Norma Small, Ph.D., CRNP, consultant, and educator for parish nursing and parish health ministries in Johnstown, Pennsylvania; former director of parish nursing at Georgetown University, Washington, D.C.; consultant for the *Scope and Standards of Parish Nursing Practice* (American Nurses Publishing, 1998); and archivist of the Health Ministries Association, observes that there has been "confusion and misunderstanding over terminology" related to credentialing among those involved with contemporary parish nursing. In order to bring some clarity to the discussion, Dr. Small (1999) wrote an article titled "Professional Credentialing for Parish Nurses." Dr. Small first notes the difference between the nursing license (to practice in one's state) and certification ("a professional recognition of excellence," p. 1); she then describes the current state of parish nursing as follows:

> *With the designation of parish nursing as a specialized practice of professional nursing by the ANA Congress for Nursing Practice in April 1977, parish nurses require the mandatory credential of a current license in the state in which practicing. Parish nurses must practice within the independent scope of practice and according to the minimum standards of practice of that state. In addition, states and courts recognize the ANA standards for clinical Nursing Practice (1991) regardless of specialty, and the scope and standards of specialized practice developed by specialty organizations as "usual and customary" practice.*
>
> *As a recognized specialty, parish nursing builds upon the generic scope and standards for clinical nursing. Through a membership organization of peers, parish nurses were responsible for further delineating and publishing the unique scope and competent standards of parish nursing practice. HMA (Health Ministries Association), as a professional organization representing parish nurses, accomplished this with the publication of ANA's* Scope and Standards of Parish Nursing Practice *(1998). The ANA Congress for Nursing Practice approved the* Scope *and "acknowledged" the* Standards of Practice for Parish Nursing *in February 1998. This recognition enabled HMA to contract with the American Nurses Foundation to publish, market and distribute the standards along with all other specialty standards (Small, 1999, p. 1).*

Dr. Small (1999) then explains that "the next step in credentialing parish nurses is the voluntary credential of *certification* which signifies professional excellence and achievement" (p. 1). The "cornerstone" of certification, Dr. Small notes, is the certification exam approved by the American Nurses Credentialing Center (ANCC). However, she adds, "it is estimated that the development, psychometric testing, testing reliability and validity, administering and maintaining test security for a specialty examination costs about $100,000" (p. 1). Thus, Dr. Small anticipates that it will probably be some time in the "distant future" before parish nursing certification becomes a reality (excerpts from Dr. Norma Small's [1999] article, "Professional Credentialing for Parish Nurses" are cited with permission).

The Health Ministries Association

Since the Health Ministries Association is still a relatively new organization, I interviewed Dr. Norma Small, as archivist and historian of HMA, in order to document the association's early history; Dr. Small explained:

> The "National Parish Nurse Resource Center" (NPRC) was started around 1985; it sponsored its first conference in 1986, which became the annual Westberg "Symposium." In the next few years people began talking about a parish nurse membership organization. But the NPRC stated that at that point they could be a resource center but not a membership organization because they were a part of the Lutheran hospital system. So, prior to the 1988 meeting, the NPRC put out a call for those interested in forming a parish nurse organization to come the day before the symposium started. And I think there were about 40 people there, as I recall (In 1998 we had the 10th anniversary of the founding of HMA). At that point in time, the resource center invited everyone who was interested in parish nursing, including clergy. There were some very vocal people there, including clergy, who stated that they felt the work of health promotion ministry in the church was broader than just parish nursing and they felt that the membership organization should include everyone who was interested in promoting health within a congregation. And that was one of the major decisions that was made at that time; that the group was not going to be just a parish nursing organization but a health ministries organization.
>
> They then formalized the Health Ministries Association (HMA) to begin meeting, and initially we had meetings each year following the Westberg Symposiums, so that really linked us to parish nursing; we probably did that for about the first three years, from about '89 to '91. Then we [Norma Small was a member of HMA from the formation the organization] decided that it was time that we broke off and had our own meetings. At first we received a grant to do this in Minneapolis; and from then on we've met in different places. We've stayed very much tied to the parish nurse resource center activities, but as a membership organization. We went through a lot of growing pains and typical organizational development during the next few years.
>
> Then in 1994 and 1995 we began to discuss development of a "scope and standards of parish nursing practice"; different people had a number of different ideas. And then state boards of nursing began increasingly calling

the health ministry association to ask about parish nursing, and if it was pro-
fessional nursing and something they should be regulating. And these ques-
tions kept coming up, so finally in 1996, it was decided that we had to go
forward with the establishment of the scope and standards of parish nursing.
At that point we formed a "Practice and Education Committee" (of HMA),
which I served on, and we just "went to town" and developed the scope and
standards of practice.

The first time we sent the scope and standards in to ANA, when they
arrived they were approved almost immediately with only a few comments
relating to terminology; ANA pointed out the fact that parish nursing was
the only specialty caring for three levels: patient, family and community; and
they commented on independence of practice. What the ANA was looking
for was to make sure that we were different from community health nursing;
they were satisfied that we were. They were pleased with the "scope and stan-
dards" as we submitted them.

The HMA will reevaluate the scope and standards in 2003, and resubmit
any changes to ANA, which will republish them with changes. We also learned,
in the process, that before the scope and standards could be formally ac-
knowledged, parish nursing had to be acknowledged as a specialty, which it
was after we submitted our application. We were told that this acknowledg-
ment had implications for the future of parish nursing because, as of 1998,
as a specialty, you must have a baccalaureate degree to go for certification
and so a curriculum at a higher level needed to be developed.

One of the things that we've struggled with over the years is our (religious)
identity and about five years ago we did declare that we were an interfaith
group. We discussed how to include others in worship; what we could do and
not do as an interfaith goup. We were advised by two theologians that we could
not have interfaith worship but that we could have a "celebration." But, even
though we have made this stand we still have not attracted many represen-
tatives from other (non-Christian) faiths.

Norma concluded her comments with the following note:

Currently HMA has a membership of approximately 1000; about two-thirds
are nurses and the others are in a variety of health ministry activities. Anyone
who wishes to support health ministry may join. We have an annual meet-
ing; periodic board meetings throughout the year and then local chapters, of
which there are about 23, meet more frequently. We also have a newsletter
Connections, *which is published quarterly, and a website, which gives infor-*
mation about the organization.

Ethical and Legal Issues in Parish Nursing

Marsha Fowler (1999) points out that the ethical issues that parish nurses face in ministering to members of their congregations are "much the same as those faced by other nurses" (p. 181). These include such concerns as "issues of respect for the parishioners' wishes, of capacity to give consent or understanding and informedness, of privacy and confidentiality, of end-of-life decisions including treatment cessation, of truthfulness and promise keeping, of advocacy and intercession, [and of] equitableness and discrimination" (p. 181). Fowler does admit, however, to potential differences in "meaning and emphasis to ethical practice" in congregational settings in which there is a "more intimate involvement" with parishioners' lives, "a commitment to pray for one another," and "a shared faith journey" (p. 181).

Ethics, derived from the Greek *ethos*, meaning "character," was originally related to the concept of behaving with good character; "later theories of ethics built other meanings onto the original concept" (Pense, 2000, p. 10). Ethics is currently understood as the study of "the principles of right and wrong conduct, of virtue and vice, and of good and evil as they relate to conduct" (Taylor, Lillis, & LeMone, 2001, p. 84). Nurse authors Taylor, Lillis, and LeMone add that "many people use the term *ethics* when describing the professional ethics incorporated into a code of professional conduct, such as the nursing code of ethics" (p. 84).

The American Nurses Association Code for Nurses includes 11 guidelines for ethical professional nursing behavior relating to such issues as "respect for the human dignity of the client"; "the client's right to privacy"; "safeguard[ing] the client [from] incompetent, unethical or illegal practice"; "accountability for individual nursing judgements and actions"; "competence in nursing"; "exercise [of] informed judgement"; contributing to the "ongoing development of the profession's body of knowledge"; participation in efforts to "improve standards of nursing"; participation in efforts to facilitate "high quality nursing care"; participation in efforts to "protect the public from misinformation . . . and to maintain the integrity of nursing"; and collaboration with others in "promoting community and national efforts to meet the health needs of the public" (cited in Broom, 2000, p. 87).

Two basic ethical theories that undergird behaviors, such as those identified in the ethical code for nurses, are utilitarianism and deontology. The utilitarian approach takes the position that "those acts that produce the greatest overall balance of good for the greatest number of people are right" (Taylor et al., 2001, p. 1354). In common parlance, the utilitarian might say that "the end justifies the means"; that is, it is the outcome of an action that determines its goodness. Deontological theory, however, holds that "actions are right or wrong independent of the consequences they produce" (Taylor et al., 2001, p. 1346). The deontologist would argue that a good "end" cannot justify a questionable "means" to achieve that end.

There are also some basic ethical principles that are universally accepted as appropriate and right to guide nursing behavior. These principles include "autonomy, respect for an individual's right to self-determination; respect for individual liberty"; "nonmaleficence, obligation to do or cause no harm to another"; "beneficence, duty to do good to others and to maintain a balance between benefits and harms"; "justice, equitable distribution of potential benefits and risks"; "veracity, obligation to tell the truth"; and "fidelity, duty to do what one has promised" (DeLaune & Ladner, 2002, p. 478).

Assuming that professional nurses value and behave according to accepted ethical standards, including the ANA ethical code of conduct for nurses, what unique ethical problems or concerns, then, might face the contemporary parish nurse? During the past few years I have interviewed, both formally and informally, approximately 30 practicing parish nurses; excerpts from some of their narratives appear in later chapters of this book. From the reports of their respective practices of parish nursing, I have no doubt that they practice, as the ANA code mandates, with respect for the dignity of their patient–parishioners, protecting privacy and safety, and practicing competently according to the standards of their profession and in concert with the *Scope and Standards of Parish Nursing*. I, nevertheless, agree with Marsha Fowler in the perception that there are some unique issues in parish nursing that may challenge the nurse to particular care in carrying out professional practice.

One issue I have heard discussed in parish nursing circles is the idea that it may be better for a parish nurse to serve in a faith community *not* of his or her own religious tradition, or at least not in the environment of his or her home church, in order to enhance privacy in terms of parishioners' faith or health problems. As a researcher, I understand the validity of such a suggestion; as a member of both a faith community and a religious community, I tend to disagree. I'm not suggesting that this cannot be done, nor that this kind of a parish nursing model would not be successful. In fact, I know of parish nurses serving congregations not of their own faith tradition very successfully and with many positive benefits for the parishioners. I simply feel that the trade-off between the anonymity parishioners may experience in confiding in a nurse not of their church may not always balance out the spiritual comfort of parishioners' trust that a parish nurse of their own religious tradition understands deeply their faith-related health and illness issues. The parish nurse who ministers in a church not of his or her own tradition must gain at least a modest knowledge of the theology of health and illness accepted by the church being served. Parish nursing is, however, still a very young subfield of the profession; this dimension of practice will be further clarified in the years to come.

Given the concern expressed by some analysts of parish nursing that a parishioner may be hesitant to divulge a particularly sensitive problem to a parish nurse of his or her own congregation, promulgating the ANA code of ethics in church bulletins, together with a description of the role of the parish nurse, might help alleviate parishioners' concerns around such areas as confidentiality (even in situations when a patient may be well known to the nurse as a fellow parishioner). I doubt that most church members are hesitant to choose a doctor or a lawyer from their own church congregation; a parish nurse of one's home church might be a similar choice.

Admittedly, counseling parishioners and families about certain ethical issues such as end-of-life decisions or treatment cessation (termination of life-saving hemodialysis treatments or the decision to terminate aggressive chemotherapy) may prove challenging for a parish nurse who has strong emotional ties to the patient and family as fellow church members. Such a situation, however, might be precisely the time for the parish nurse, following the ANA code, to seek consultation, both medically and spiritually, and, if necessary, excuse him- or herself from advising or participating in the decision-making process.

In discussing the topic of nursing ethics in chronic illness, McElmurry, Harris, Misner, and Olson (1998) assert that, aside form "everday ethics" such as the norms contained in the ANA code, there are two other key concepts in nursing ethics that "stand out as central factors": caring and relationships (p. 432). Caring is understood as critical to nursing's "efforts to delineate its own ethical base of practice" (p. 432); and nurse–patient relationships are "closely associated with caring" (p. 433). It would seem that these two nursing concepts are both deeply embedded in the earlier identified overarching parish nursing role of *spiritual companion in health and illness*; they are also incorporated in the individual parish nursing roles of educator, counselor, advocate, referral agent, and integrator of faith and health.

It is a given that many parishioners whom parish nurses serve will be members of the elder community. In exploring ethical considerations in gerontological nursing, Charlotte Eliopoulos (1997), who also cites the ANA code as a guide for nurses, admits that "although guidelines exist, no solid answers can solve all of the ethical dilemmas that nurses will face" (p. 432). She does, however, suggest some measures that may "minimize struggles in making ethical decisions," including the following: "encourage patients' expressions of desires"; "know thyself" (one's own personal values); "read" (medical and ethical literature); "discuss" (with colleagues, clergy, ethicists); "form an ethics committee"; "share" (seek guidance and support); and "evaluate decisions; even the worst decision holds some lessons" (p. 432).

Ultimately, I believe that a parish nurse practicing not only according to the ANA code and the *Scope and Standards of Parish Nursing Practice*, but also in concert with the moral and ethical philosophy of his or her faith community, and in prayer under the guidance of the Holy Spirit, will be able to cope successfully with the ethical challenges that this new dimension of practice may pose.

Legal Issues in Parish Nursing Practice

Legal issues in nursing are very often associated with ethical issues. Perhaps the most significant issue for a nurse, and thus for a parish nurse, is malpractice; this might occur as a result of failure to adhere to the ANA code, which mandates that the professional nurse "maintains competence in nursing." A related ethical and potentially legal issue is negligence, through which a nurse may fail in his or her professional responsibility. Issues involving breaches of privacy or confidentiality can also have legal as well as ethical implications. Basically, there are four sources of nursing practice rules: federal legislation (e.g., Medicare and Medicaid); state legislation (practice scope for different levels of nursing); boards of nursing (licensing); and healthcare institutions (nursing policies and procedures) (Taylor et al., 2001, p. 99). It is expected that all practicing nurses be familiar with the practice rules governing their area of specialization.

A director of a large, urban health ministries association told me that pastors usually ask three questions when the subject of parish nursing or parish health ministry comes up. The questions are "How much will it cost?" "How much of my time will it involve?" and "Will I be sued?" The latter issue, he commented, is usually the point of greatest concern.

To my knowledge, no parish nurse has, to date, been involved in litigation. I suspect that the reason for this is the fact that, aside from the ministry dimension and commitment involved in the role that is currently very much of a volunteer nature, the activities of the parish nurse do not lend themselves to the kinds of negligence or malpractice that might involve litigation. In their 2001 *Fundamentals of Nursing* text, Taylor et al. identify the most frequent allegations against nurses in terms of malpractice as being related to such issues as "failure to insure patient safety," "improper treatment," "failure to monitor and report," "medication errors," "failure to follow agency procedure," "documentation," "equipment use," and "adverse incident" (accidents) (p. 108). Basically, the only points of concern for parish nursing, as presently understood, might be related to issues of documentation or accidents;

nevertheless, many churches do suggest that their parish nurses carry malpractice insurance. In certain congregations, a parish nurse is able to be included under the church's staff liability insurance policy.

Some suggestions that nursing textbooks offer to minimize the potential for involvement in litigation, which might be applicable to parish nursing, include such behaviors as "communicate with clients," "acknowledge unfortunate incidents," "document," "report any concerns," "use appropriate standards of care," and "treat all clients and their families with kindness and respect" (Martin, 2002, p. 469). A final suggestion is that, as noted in terms of ethical behavior, nurses "be familiar with state regulations governing nursing and with standards of professional organizations" (Broom, 2000, p. 103). For parish nurses practicing at this time, the document setting out the *Scope and Standards of Parish Nursing Practice* provides guidelines that adequately address the primary ethical and legal issues the nurses and their congregations may encounter.

This chapter on the role of the parish nurse was a challenge to write because of the newness and the evolving nature of contemporary parish nursing. I have interviewed a variety of practicing parish nurses, of different faith communities; they described myriad activities within their congregations associated with the title. Most included such activities as education, counseling, advocacy, and referral as falling within their role behaviors; all, however, highlighted the importance of the pastoral ministry dimension of their parish nursing role. That is, the spiritual caring that the nurses provided, especially in ministering to those who were ill and infirm, was considered a treasured dimension of the parish nursing role. It was for this reason that I introduced the concept of the nurse as a *spiritual companion in health and illness* as an overarching role of the parish nurse.

The future for the subfield of parish nursing is wide open at this time, and hopefully the guidance of the Holy Spirit will lead us to acquire the knowledge and the skills to serve our faith communities with generosity and faithfulness. Our task is simply to be open and to "listen"!

References

Adkins, S. (1998). The human experience. *Tennessee Nurse, 61*(6), 21.

Ambrose, J. (2000). To be a nurse . . . one R.N.'s journey in faith. *New Mexico Nurse, 45*(93), 13.

American Nurses Publishing. (1998). *Scope and Standards of Parish Nursing Practice (SSPNP).* Washington, DC: Author.

Barry, W. A. (1992). *Spiritual direction and the encounter with God: A theological inquiry*. Mahwah, NJ: Paulist Press.

Berrigan, D. (1989). *Sorrow built a bridge: Friendship and AIDS*. Baltimore: Fortkamp.

Bracken, J. A. (1990). Community. In J. A. Komonchak, M. Collins, & D. Lane (Eds.), *The new dictionary of theology* (pp. 216–218). Collegeville, MN: Liturgical Press.

Broom, C. (2000). Ethical and legal concerns. In R. E. Craven & C. J. Hirnle (Eds.), *Fundamentals of nursing: Human health and function* (pp. 85–107). Philadelphia: Lippincott.

Clark, M. B., & Olson, J. K. (2000). Faith seeking and health seeking as parallel processes. In M. B. Clark & J. K. Olson (Eds.), *Nursing within a faith community: Promoting health in times of transition* (pp. 3–13). Thousand Oaks, CA: Sage.

Cummings, A. L. (1960). In the parish. *Catholic Nurse, 8*(3), 26–29.

DeLaune, S. C., & Ladner, P. K. (2002). *Fundamentals of nursing: Standards and practice* (2nd ed.). Clifton Park, NY: Delmar.

Dougherty, R. M. (1995). *Group spiritual direction: Community for discernment*. Mahwah, NJ: Paulist Press.

Eliopoulos, C. (1997). *Gerontological nursing* (4th ed.). Philadelphia: Lippincott.

FAQ about HMA and parish nursing. (2001). *Connections: The Health Ministries Association Information & Contacts, 1*(2), 1.

Fowler, M. (1999). Ethics as a context for the practice. In P. A. Solari-Twadell & M. A. McDermott (Eds.), *Parish nursing: Promoting whole person health within faith communities* (pp. 181–194). Thousand Oaks, CA: Sage.

Holstrom, S. (1999). Perspectives on a suburban parish nursing practice. In P. A. Solari-Twadell & M. A. McDermott (Eds.), *Parish nursing: Promoting whole person health within faith communities* (pp. 67–74). Thousand Oaks, CA: Sage.

Kuhn, J. (1997). A profile of parish nurses. *Journal of Christian Nursing, 14*(1), 26–28.

Lee, B. J. (1993). Community. In M. Downey (Ed.), *The new dictionary of Catholic spirituality* (pp. 183–192). Collegeville, MN: The Liturgical Press.

Leetun, M., & Saabye, J. (1996). Bismarck parish nurses respond to health reform. *Prairie Rose, 65*(2), 9.

Linton, M. A. (1997). The parish nurse as a congregational health minister. *Maryland Nurse, 16*(5), 3, 6.

Martin, J. (2002). Legal accountability and responsibilities. In S. C. DeLaune & P. K. Ladner (Eds.), *Fundamentals of nursing: Standards and practice* (2nd ed.). (pp. 459–474). Clifton Park, NY: Delmar.

Matteson, P. S. (1999). Parish nursing: A new, yet old model of care. *Massachusetts Nurse, 69*(3), 5.

McElmurry, B. J., Harris, B., Misner, S., & Olson, L. (1998). Nursing ethics in chronic illness. In I. M. Lubkin & P. D. Larsen (Eds.), *Chronic illness: Impact and interventions* (pp. 431–452). Sudbury, MA: Jones and Bartlett.

McGee, A. K. (1998). Parish nursing brings health care closer to home. *Texas Nursing, 72*(6), 4–5, 12.

Nouwen, H. J. M. (1975). *Reaching out: The three movements of the spiritual life*. New York: Image Books.

O'Brien, M. E. (1992). *Living with HIV: Experiment in courage*. Westport, CT: Auburn House.

O'Brien, M. E. (1995). *The AIDS challenge: Breaking through the boundaries.* Westport, CT: Auburn House.

O'Brien, M. E. (2003). *Spirituality in nursing: Standing on holy ground* (2nd ed.). Sudbury, MA: Jones and Bartlett.

A parish nurse story. (1998). *Connecticut Nursing News, 71*(3), 12.

Parish nursing in Saskatchewan. (1998). *Concern, 27*(2), 14.

Parish nursing: Taking a holistic approach toward patient care. (1999). *Nevada Reformation, 8*(3), 19.

Pence, G. E. (2000). *Classic cases in medical ethics.* Boston, MA: McGraw-Hill.

Roger of Taize. (1990). *His love is a fire.* Collegeville, MN: Liturgical Press.

Roger of Taize. (1991). *No greater love: Sources of Taize.* Collegeville, MN: Liturgical Press.

Ryan, J. K. (1966). *Introduction to a devout life, by Saint Francis de Sales.* New York: Image Books.

Shelly, J. A., & Miller, A. B. (1999). *Called to care: A Christian theology of nursing.* Downers Grove, IL: InterVarsity Press.

Small, N. (1999). Professional credentialing for parish nurses. *Connections 1*(2), 1.

Solari-Twadell, P. A. (1999). The emerging practice of parish nursing. In P. A. Solari-Twadell & M. A. McDermott (Eds.), *Parish nursing: Promoting whole person health within faith communities* (pp. 3–24). Thousand Oaks, CA: Sage.

Solari-Twadell, P. A., & Westberg, G. (1991). Body, mind and soul: The parish nurse offers physical, emotional and spiritual care. *Health Progress, 72*(7), 24–28.

Stoll, R. I. (1997). Parish nursing ministry growing. *Pennsylvania Nurse, 52*(8), 18.

Taylor, C., Lillis, C., & LeMone, P. (2001). *Fundamentals of nursing: The art and science of nursing care* (4th ed.). Philadelphia: Lippincott.

Westberg, G. E. (1990). *The parish nurse: Providing a minister of health for your congregation.* Minneapolis, MN: Augsburg.

CHAPTER 4

EDUCATION FOR PARISH NURSING PRACTICE

The Advocate, the Holy Spirit, whom the Father will send in my name,
will teach you everything and remind you of all that I have said to you.

—*John 14:26*

"He Will Teach You Everything"

Dear Father,
It's so easy to forget, in the
busyness of the day, all that your
Son has taught; thank you for
sending the Spirit, in His Name,
(John 14:26)
to "remind" us of the beauty
and the power of Jesus'
gospel message of
caring and compassion.

For it is only through the teaching
of the Spirit:
that our parish nurses' hearts
will be moved to love;
that our parish nurses' minds
will be inspired to counsel;
that our parish nurses' thoughts
will be directed to educate;

> that our parish nurses' souls
> will be guided to pray.
>
> Bless us, Lord God of our lives,
> with the teaching that will bring
> us to true understanding
> through the grace of Him,
> who alone, is the
> Spirit of Truth
> and
> wisdom.

The History and Current State of Parish Nursing Education

As with the specialty of parish nursing itself, education for parish nursing practice is still a relatively new field; and as the discipline of parish nursing practice has grown and developed in this country, so have the variety of educational offerings. In the very early years of parish nursing, a parish nursing education program might consist simply of a two-hour seminar or day-long or weekend workshop in parish nursing. In 1989, the International Parish Nurse Resource Center (then called the Parish Nurse Resource Center) in Park Ridge, Illinois, offered its first two-and-a-half-day continuing education program in parish nursing that "gave nurses basic information on the concept, how to get a program started, and a discussion of issues such as legal concerns and accountability" (McDermott, Solari-Twadell, & Matheus, 1999, p. 270). Over the next decade, the resource center continued to work on developing a "standardized" curriculum to prepare nurses for parish nursing practice. The work of the International Parish Nurse Resource Center (IPNRC) was carried out in collaboration with Marquette University in Milwaukee and Loyola University in Chicago. In 1998, a suggested curriculum for basic parish nurse preparation was developed by the IPNRC in consultation with the National League for Nursing (NLN) and the American Nurses Association (ANA) (McDermott et al., 1999, p. 273). As well as a number of other parish nursing issues, the basic curriculum recommended by the IPNRC included discussion of the parish nursing roles of "teacher," "counselor," "referral agent," "trainer of volunteers," and "integrator of faith and health" (McDermott et al., 1999, p. 274).

At the same time, both college- and university-affiliated schools of nursing and private nursing organizations were also developing basic programs in parish nursing. These programs varied in content to some degree but generally included key topics identified in the burgeoning body of parish nursing literature, such as working as a member of a ministerial team, working with the pastor, the theology of health, health promotion in a parish, initiating health ministry within a faith community, ministering to older or chronically ill parishioners, and working with volunteers. Many of the early courses in parish nursing did not include areas such as ethical and legal issues, multicultural diversity, or grant writing, as these did not seem relevant at the time; this was prior to the publication of the *Scope and Standards of Parish Nursing Practice* in 1998. Some of the programs offered continuing education units (CEUs); others offered college or university credits.

As noted in Chapter 2, on the spiritual history of parish nursing, sponsorship of the International Parish Nurse Resource Center and its basic parish nursing education preparation course was transferred from Lutheran Advocate Health System in Park Ridge, Illinois, to Deaconess Parish Nurse Ministries in St. Louis, Missouri, as of December 31, 2001. The curriculum developed by the IPNRC, as described in Chapter 2, is currently available from the Deaconess Parish Nurse Ministries IPNRC office.

In reviewing brochures on parish nursing education programs and in speaking with contemporary parish nurses, one continues to discover a significant variety of curriculum offerings in the field. The most frequently observed common denominator among the programs is the offering of CEUs rather than academic program credits. This is true even for university- or college-affiliated programs; CEU parish nurse programs are also sponsored by church-related organizations, such as healthcare facilities and seminaries. Some examples of existing programs include a 36-contact-hour, college-affiliated program that meets for four days and includes such topics as the theology of health and healing, history, ethics, accountability and documentation, legal issues, and roles of the parish nurse. Another college-affiliated program, with a similar curriculum, meets for six days and the student has the option of obtaining 3.8 CEUs or three college credits. A third university-affiliated program requires nine days of attendance, with the student being awarded 5.4 CEUs; this course also includes a clinical practicum in parish nursing. Most of these programs incorporate some worship experiences within the curriculum and generally conclude with a dedication or commissioning ceremony for the parish nurses completing the program. Parish nursing pins may also be distributed at the ceremony, which is usually held in a church or chapel.

In the early days of the movement, there were a variety of other workshops or courses that parish nurses attended to prepare them for ministry. A master's-prepared nurse, who has been the identified parish nurse at her Lutheran church for the past five years, told me that her formal parish nursing education had consisted of a day-and-a-half-long "weekend Christian workshop on parish nursing," with a dedication ceremony at the conclusion of the meeting. Another parish nurse, from a small rural town, explained that the nurses in her area could not afford to take an "expensive" course in parish nursing, so, she reported: "We all got together from the Methodist Church and the Baptist Church and the Catholic Church and we planned our own course and learned as we went along." This group had also begun its efforts prior to the publication of the *Scope and Standards of Parish Nursing Practice*, so it was primarily guided by the parish nursing literature and by the needs and desires of the respective pastors and parishioners. I also met a nurse practitioner, recently hired by a large urban Episcopal congregation as a paid, part-time parish nurse, who admitted that she had never taken a course in parish nursing; she had, however, participated in an elective university-based school of nursing course on spirituality and nursing.

Finally, regardless of what specific parish nursing education a nurse receives, it is suggested that the basic nursing education preferable for parish nurses is "a baccalaureate degree in nursing" (Olson, 2000, p. 159). A parish nursing course is, however, recommended by Joanne Olson, who points out that because "faith community nursing occurs in a unique setting, often without another nurse on the ministry team . . . [these factors] require additional educational preparation" (p. 160).

A Contemporary Parish Nursing Education Program: Parish Nursing: Connecting Faith and Health

In the process of trying to find a parish nursing education course for myself, and being ever the nurse researcher at heart, I not only reviewed many parish nursing program brochures and Internet sites, but also spoke with directors of 10 fairly well known programs in parish nursing. Four of these programs were college- or university-based, although they offered CEU credits; students of one of the programs also had the option of obtaining university credits upon completion of the course. The other six programs had university or college affiliations in order to validate the awarding of continuing education credits; not all of the programs awarded nursing CEUs. One parish nursing program offered the potential for continuing education credits, but recommended that students enroll in two sequential courses awarding college credits; this program contained a significant amount of theological exploration.

Among the 10 programs examined, some taught parish nursing content based on the curriculum developed by the International Parish Nurse Resource Center (IPNRC); others had created their own unique parish nursing curriculum plans. Ultimately, I decided to enroll in the Nurses Christian Fellowship (NCF) Parish Nursing Education Program described in the following pages.

A Christian group that has developed an excellent parish nursing curriculum is the Nurses Christian Fellowship (NCF). The Nurses Christian Fellowship is an organization of professional nurses and nursing students, founded in 1948, whose goal is "Bringing Good News to Nursing." The organization describes its purpose in these words: "NCF is both a professional organization and a ministry of and for nurses and nursing students. We are concerned for the nurse as a whole person and are advocates of quality nursing care. Our vision is to bring the good news of Jesus Christ to nursing education and practice" (Nurses Christian Fellowship [NCF], 2002, p. 2).

The NCF course, titled Parish Nursing: Connecting Faith and Health, offers content derived from the core curriculum recommended by the IPNRC; NCF has, however, added course materials supportive of Christian theology of parish nursing in accordance with the NCF Christian worldview. The NCF course is described as a "Christ-centered, biblically-based program."

The NCF Parish Nursing Education Program includes such topics as "congregational role in health, healing and illness, theology of health, history and philosophy of parish nursing, spiritual care, ethics, assessment, accountability and documentation, parish nursing roles, functioning within a ministry team, health promotion and maintenance, grief and loss, legal considerations, ministering to the underserved, and prayer and worship leadership" (NCF, 2001, p. 1). The Nurses Christian Fellowship parish nursing program offers 35 contact hours of continuing nursing education (CNE) credit; NCF is an approved provider of continuing nursing education by the Wisconsin Nursing Association Continuing Education Approval Program Committee. The NCF program concludes with a religious ceremony of commissioning for the program participants, in which the parish nursing pin is presented to those completing the course. A second, advanced NCF parish nursing course is offered for nurses who have participated in the basic curriculum. Recently, the Nurses Christian Fellowship has created its own parish nursing pin bearing the NCF logo.

A "Lived Experience" with the NCF Parish Nursing Education Program

Several years ago, I was blessed to be commissioned as a parish nurse after completing the Nurses Christian Fellowship program. The course in which I participated was conducted over a period of six days; the setting was a peaceful and prayerful rural

retreat center, Fellowship Deaconry, operated by a community of Christian deaconesses. There was a chapel available for quiet prayer and meditation, as well as a
large wooded area for walking, either alone or in groups. Our rooms were small and
simple; no television sets, phones, or computers, but they were impeccably clean and
quiet. The caringly prepared family-style meals, each of which began with the assembled
community giving thanks to the Lord, nourished our spirits as well as our bodies. At
the evening meal, we were inspired each day with a beautiful meditation and prayer
offered by the senior pastor, who was an administrator of the deaconry. Mealtime also
provided an opportunity for sharing and fellowship among the program participants.

Our course, coordinated and taught by a team of five seasoned parish nurse members of Nurses Christian Fellowship, consisted of 22 licensed RNs, including diploma
graduates, A.A degree, BSN, MSN, and doctorally prepared nurses. We were from a
variety of Christian denominations: Lutheran, Methodist, Baptist, Presbyterian,
Episcopalian, United Church of Christ, and Roman Catholic. Our ages ranged from
the mid-thirties to the mid-seventies; several nurses were retired from active nursing
and others maintained full-time professional nursing jobs. A number in our group had
already served as parish nurses in their respective congregations for several years; others had little or no prior experience in parish nursing. As it turned out, this variety of
age, nursing and parish nursing experience, and religious denomination was one of
the treasures of the program in terms of learning and growing in our knowledge of
the relationship of faith and health. Each course participant had her (we were an all-
female group) own wisdom to share, which greatly enriched the learning experience.

Our days began at 8 A.M., with breakfast in the deaconry dining room and lasted
well into the evening, with our closing worship concluding about 9 P.M.; the hours
were long and full but ample breaks were interspersed throughout the day to provide
times for rest and informal sharing among the group members. I especially enjoyed
taking outdoor walks with one or more of my classmates; I learned a great deal about
parish nursing in both my own and other Christian churches from listening to the stories and experiences of other group members. I remember taking a long walk during
one afternoon break with a nurse from a Southern Baptist church. We both delighted
in discovering that although our churches were quite different in some areas of worship and tradition, we had many similar needs and concerns related to the implementation of parish nursing in our respective congregations.

The students and faculty began each day of classes with a time of prayer and meditation to set the tone for our study, to remind us that the course in which we participated was about the relationship of faith and health, as understood in the Christian
tradition. The prayerful setting and prayerfulness of the NCF program was very im-

portant to me, as I believe that prayer is a critical dimension of parish nursing practice. I appreciated having early mornings and break times for personal prayer. Members of our group truly enjoyed sharing and learning from each other but most of us also chose to have some quiet times with the Lord during the program, and that was respected by fellow students. Our parish nursing class also received a special gift in the promise of prayers from the deaconess community during our week of study.

"The Spirit of the Lord is upon me. . . . He has sent me to proclaim liberty to the captives and recovery of sight to the blind"
—Luke 4:18-19

"For I was hungry . . . thirsty . . . a stranger . . . naked . . . sick and you took care of me"   —Matthew 25:35-36

"Jesus called [his disciples] . . . and said, 'You know that the rulers of the Gentiles lord it over them, and their great ones are tyrants over them. It will not be so among you, but whoever wishes to be great among you must be your servant and whoever wishes to be first among you must be your slave. Just as the Son of Man did not come to be served but to serve, and to give his life as a ransom for many"
—Matthew 20:25-28

As well as prayer, NCF faculty included both Old and New Testament scripture in their presentations, beginning, for example, with the biblical foundations of Jesus' healing ministry (Luke 4:18–19, "The Spirit of the Lord is upon me. . . . He has sent me to proclaim liberty to the captives and recovery of sight to the blind"; Matthew 25:35–36, "For I was hungry . . . thirsty . . . a stranger . . . naked . . . sick and you took care of me"), as well as Jesus' explanation of service or *diaconia* in ministry, as described in Matthew 20:25–28, "Jesus called [his disciples] . . . and said, 'You know that the rulers of the Gentiles lord it over them, and their great ones are tyrants over them. It will not be so among you, but whoever wishes to be great among you must be your servant and whoever wishes to be first among you must be your slave. Just as the Son of Man did not come to be served but to serve, and to give his life as a ransom for many." A particular goal of parish nursing ministry was associated with Jesus' admission reported by Luke in chapter 19, verse 10 ("For the Son of Man came to seek out and to save the lost").

"Your steadfast love, O Lord, extends to the heavens; your faithfulness, to the clouds. Your righteousness is like the mighty mountains"   —Psalm 36:5-6

Biblical caring was identified with Psalm 36, verses 5–6 ("Your steadfast love, O Lord, extends to the heavens; your faithfulness, to the clouds. Your righteousness is like the mighty mountains"). And parishioners' spiritual needs were associated with Paul's teaching to the Corinthians on the centrality of love as a Christian virtue (1 Corinthians 13:13, "Faith, hope, love abide, these three; and the greatest of these is love").

The history of health care in the Christian Church was described in terms of scripture passages, such as 1 Corinthians 4:2 ("It is required of stewards that they should be found trustworthy"). The theology of health and healing was grounded in both Old and New Testament scripture, as was the Christian nursing metaparadigm. Christian nursing was identified with the beginning of Jesus' Galilean ministry as described in Luke 4:17–19 ("And the scroll [of the prophet Isaiah] was given to him and [he] found the passage where it was written: 'The Spirit of the Lord is upon me, because he has anointed me to bring good news to the poor. He has sent me to proclaim release to the captives and recovery of sight to the blind, to let the oppressed go free, and to proclaim the year of the Lord's favor'").

"Faith, hope, love abide, these three; and the greatest of these is love"
—*1 Corinthians 13:13*

"It is required of stewards that they should be found trustworthy"
—*1 Corinthians 4:2*

"And the scroll [of the prophet Isaiah] was given to him and [he] found the passage where it was written: 'The Spirit of the Lord is upon me, because he has anointed me to bring good news to the poor. He has sent me to proclaim release to the captives and recovery of sight to the blind, to let the oppressed go free, and to proclaim the year of the Lord's favor"
—*Luke 4:17–19*

"Humble yourselves . . . under the mighty hand of God, so that he may exalt you in due time. Cast all your anxiety on him because he cares for you"
—*1 Peter 5:6–7*

"Righteousness and Justice are the foundation of your throne; steadfast love and faithfulness go before you"
—*Psalm 89:14*

While course content on all ministry topics was presented in light of both contemporary literature and practical examples relevant to parish nursing, biblical undergirding of the discussions was included wherever appropriate. A biblical maxim cited to support a parish nurse's initiation of a health ministry program in his or her congregation was taken from the First Letter of Peter, chapter 5, verses 6–7 ("Humble yourselves . . . under the mighty hand of God, so that he may exalt you in due time. Cast all your anxiety on him because he cares for you"). On the subject of ethics in parish nursing, faculty discussed ethical theories such as teleology and deontology, and principles of beneficience, nonmaleficence, veracity, fidelity, justice, and others and presented biblical models appropriate to medical ethics (e.g., Psalm 89:14, "Righteousness and Justice are the foundation of your throne; steadfast love and faithfulness go before you"). In discussions of the roles of the parish nurse as educator, counselor, integrator of faith and health, and advocate, while pragmatic examples of parish nursing activities were discussed, again the presentations were grounded in the biblical perspective.

An example from the discussion of the parish nursing role of coordinator or trainer of volunteers was that, as the parish nurse identifies the importance of the volunteer having a "compassionate heart," she consider the writings of Nehemiah who wept over the needs of the Jewish survivors of captivity who were "in great distress" when the "wall of Jerusalem [lay] breached" and its "gates . . . gutted with fire (Nehemiah wrote: "When I heard these words, I sat down and wept and mourned for days" [Nehemiah 1:4]). The class was reminded also that Nehemiah fasted and prayed about his ministry to the Israelites in 1:5–6, "I said, 'O Lord God of heaven . . . let your ear be attentive, and your eyes open to hear the prayer of your servant"; and 2:4–5, "The king said to me, 'What do you request? So I prayed to the God of heaven . . . [and] then said to the king: '. . . Send me to Judah . . . that I may rebuild it'"); but it was also pointed out that, even in attempting to initiate a project about which one has prayed, as did Nehemiah, things don't always go smoothly (2:10, "When Sanballat the Horonite, and Tobiah the Ammonite official heard [of] this [Nehemiah's visit], it displeased them greatly that someone had come to seek the welfare of the people of Israel").

> *"When I heard these words, I sat down and wept and mourned for days"*
> —*Nehemiah 1:4*
>
> *"I said, 'O Lord God of heaven . . . let your ear be attentive, and your eyes open to hear the prayer of your servant"*
> —*Nehemiah 1:5–6*
>
> *"The king said to me, 'What do you request? So I prayed to the God of heaven . . . [and] then said to the king: '. . . Send me to Judah . . . that I may rebuild it"*
> —*Nehemiah 2:4–5*
>
> *"When Sanballat the Horonite, and Tobiah the Ammonite official heard [of] this [Nehemiah's visit], it displeased them greatly that someone had come to seek the welfare of the people of Israel"*
> —*Nehemiah 2:10*

The heart of Christian nursing was described as a ministry of compassionate care to those in need (Luke 10:27, "You shall love the Lord, your God, with all your heart . . . and your neighbor as yourself"). And the importance of the parish nurse's spiritual self-care was identified as derived from the example of Jesus' own healing behavior (Luke 5:15, "The word about Jesus spread abroad; many crowds would gather to hear him and to be cured of their diseases").

The value of teamwork in carrying out parish health ministry was placed in biblical perspective (Exodus 17:11–12, The Battle with Amelek: "Whenever Moses held up his hand,

> *"You shall love the Lord, your God, with all your heart . . . and your neighbor as yourself"*
> —*Luke 10:27*
>
> *"The word about Jesus spread abroad; many crowds would gather to hear him and to be cured of their diseases"*
> —*Luke 5:15*

Israel prevailed . . . [but] Moses' hands grew weary . . . [so Aaron and Hur each] held up his hands, one on one side and the other on the other side, so that his hands were steady"), and a discussion of the importance of parishioners with a variety of talents functioning within a health ministry team was supported by Paul's teaching to the Corinthians (1 Corinthians 12:4–11, "There are varieties of gifts but the same Spirit and there are varieties of services but the same Lord").

The Battle with Amelek: "Whenever Moses held up his hand, Israel prevailed . . . [but] Moses' hands grew weary . . . [so Aaron and Hur each] held up his hands, one on one side and the other on the other side, so that his hands were steady"

—*Exodus 17:11–12*

"There are varieties of gifts but the same Spirit and there are varieties of services but the same Lord"

—*1 Corinthians 12:4–11*

The preceding biblical citations represent only a few examples of the many scripture passages that served as framework for the lectures and discussions in the Nurses Christian Fellowship Parish Nursing Education Program; this scriptural thrust reflected and substantiated the NCF goal of initiating and presenting a "Christ-centered, biblically-based" program in parish nursing. Time was also included for a question and answer period at the end of each class, allowing participants to question, clarify, or elaborate on specific topics, both biblical and nonbiblical, explored in the formal lecture; these sessions were lively and exhilarating, as students, especially those with previous parish nursing experience, shared their perceptions and anecdotes with the group. It also provided the faculty an opportunity to further explain any concepts about which individuals desired elaboration.

At this point in the narrative of my "lived experience" as a particpant in an NCF parish nursing education course, I need to insert a brief behavioral note; I do so lest it appear that our group interactions encompassed only the scholarly and the studious. While the newly emerging subfield of parish nursing does require study and attention to scholarly inquiry, as well as a lot of prayer, it is also important to recognize the human, and sometimes humorous, in situations, especially in those occurrences pertaining to ourselves. Thus, I must admit that during our week of learning and sharing we also laughed a lot! Sometimes students told funny stories about their past falls and foibles in attempting to live the gospel message of Jesus; other times the faculty delighted us with their own humorous admissions. I don't really know why, but for some reason an "aside" comment from the course coordinator, who had a wonderfully dry sense of humor, sticks in my mind. She was speaking, as I recall, about Jesus' mandate that we, as his disciples, should care for the "thirsty" and the "hungry" and the "ill" and, as preamble, began to read the passage from Matthew (25:31–40) that begins: "When the Son of Man comes in his glory . . . all the nations will be gathered before him. And he will separate people one from another, as a shepherd separates the sheep from the goats, and he will put the sheep at his right hand and the goats at the left. Then the king will say to those at his right hand, 'Come, you that are blessed by my Father, inherit the kingdom prepared for you from the foundation of the world.'"

At this point in the scripture passage, our faculty member abruptly stopped reading, and with a rather sheepish (pardon the pun) grin, exclaimed: "You know, I always feel so sorry for those goats! The sheep got to inherit the kingdom but we don't know what happened to the poor goats! I've decided that when I retire, I'm going to get some goats for my farm so they won't feel so left out; those poor old goats!" Of course, the student group disintegrated into gales of laughter, which was probably a very good thing, since it was late in the afternoon, and if any of us needed a wake-up jolt, our teacher's "goat story" was just the thing to do it. Having been a school of nursing faculty member for the past 25 years, I sincerely believe that humor, in an appropriate format, can be a wonderful asset in keeping a class alive and healthy.

> *"When the Son of Man comes in his glory . . . all the nations will be gathered before him. And he will separate people one from another, as a shepherd separates the sheep from the goats, and he will put the sheep at his right hand and the goats at the left. Then the king will say to those at his right hand, 'Come, you that are blessed by my Father, inherit the kingdom prepared for you from the foundation of the world.'"*
>
> *—Matthew 25:31–40*

As well as humorous bonding, our parish nursing group also did some wonderful spiritual bonding. This was supported in both formal and informal interactions, and especially though our interdenominational worship services. All of the class members were assigned to small groups, consisting of four or five students each, whose assignment was to organize and lead for one day of the week a communal evening worship service. I must confess, however, that there was, also, sometimes a little humor involved in our worship-planning sessions. Just imagine a group composed of a Baptist, a Methodist, a Presbyterian, a Lutheran, and a Roman Catholic, trying to put together a unified communal worship service! We chuckled over our differences as we attempted to get the services prepared; nevertheless, in the end, all of the groups created meaningful worship services in which all could participate. Were our services always "liturgically correct" in ecclesiastical terminology? Well, perhaps not, but in Christian charity and caring, we students all congratulated each other warmly after the services for planning such prayerful experiences. And, more importantly, in the eyes of the Lord, I'm sure that "liturgical correctness" becomes a relative term.

Sister Minnie

I cannot leave the concept of community, and the communal bonding that took place within our NCF parish nursing group, without telling the story of Sister Minnie. Our parish nursing course did not include a congregationally based clinical practicum. For the six days during which the class lived and studied and prayed at Fellowship Deaconry, however, the German Lutheran sister deaconesses and pastors became, in a sense, our temporary church community. And, as the following anecdote reflects, this communal setting provided the parish nursing class the opportunity to come together in a small act of pastoral ministry to one of our church members.

Being a sister myself, I was very interested in learning about the Lutheran deaconess community, which operated Fellowship Deaconry at which our course was held. Sister Minnie was an elder deaconess who used to sit in the hallway outside of the dining room and greet all of us as we arrived at and departed from meals. One afternoon, I introduced myself and had a lovely conversation with Sister Minnie (Sister Whilhelmina was her real name, she admitted, but she preferred Sister Minnie!). Sister Minnie told me that she had been a deaconess for 65 years: "Well, tomorrow," she said, would be the "65th anniversary of her commitment as a deaconess." When I asked whether there was to be a great celebration, Sister Minnie replied modestly, "Oh, no, 65 isn't a special anniversary. The next big one will be 70, but by then, I think," she said laughingly, "I'll be up there with the Lord" (Sister Minnie poined upward).

That evening, I was telling some of our group about Sister Minnie, and I admitted to feeling that although 65 years as a deaconess might not be a special anniversary in the community, it surely seemed like enough years to celebrate. I asked those around me if we could make a card to give to Sister Minnie and then perhaps everyone would write a little note of congratulations on it; they all agreed. We quickly realized, however, that we didn't have appropriate card-making materials with us, so one of the nurses who had a car offered to drive me to the nearest town to pick up an anniversary card and a box of candy to give to Sister Minnie with our good wishes. Because of the incredibly supportive response from a small group of classmates, I asked the entire class if they would be willing to sing a hymn for Sister Minnie the next day when we presented the gifts. There was lots of enthusiasm for our community project; many in the group had lovely voices, and a nurse who was a skilled pianist volunteered that as soon as I could discover Sister Minnie's favorite hymn, she would learn to play it to accompany the singing. Also, before the evening was over, most of the nurses had tucked dollar bills into my pocket so that we could also have a small "purse" to include in Sister Minnie's card. The next morning, we got one of the other deaconesses involved in our surprise. She told us that Sister Minnie's favorite hymn was "Blessed

Assurance" and that the parish nursing group could come into the deaconesses' dining room and sing to Sister Minnie at the close of the noon meal; she promised not to let Sister leave before we got there.

Sister Minnie looked very shy as we began to sing, but then, with tears in her eyes, she gently joined us in completing her favorite hymn. The Sisters and their pastor told us that the day had been an occasion Sister Minnie would not soon forget. Our remembrance of Sister Minnie's anniversary, I think, represents the beauty of pastoral ministry when a communal effort takes place and the gifts of all are given freely for the joy of others. Our small celebration seems even more special now, as I recently learned that Sister Minnie has, in fact, gone to live with her Lord, whom she loved and served so faithfully; I trust that her 70th will indeed be a grand anniversary in His heavenly mansion.

Finally, I believe that our most meaningful worship service during the NCF parish nursing course took place on the last morning, when we were commissioned as parish nurses and received our certificates and pins. A Fellowship Deaconry pastor, who had at one time himself served as a nurse, shared beautiful and powerful thoughts on the meaning of nursing as ministry; he spoke of our parish nursing service as a living expression of the gospel message of Jesus. Many in our group had, as I mentioned earlier, served their congregations for some time as parish nurses. Having the opportunity to participate in a parish nursing course and being formally commissioned by the Nurses Christian Fellowship as parish nurses, however, meant as much to them as to those of us who had only recently begun to work in parish health ministry. The NCF parish nursing course was a gift and a blessing for all of us and forged a bond that will remain for many years.

Because of this felt bonding among us, one of our group members with well-honed computer skills offered to create an e-mail Listserv so that we could continue our communicating and learning, as well as praying for each others' ministries, after we left the formal parish nursing program. I recently asked, via e-mail, whether any of the group would care to share her thoughts about the NCF parish nursing course and/or the impact of the course on her current parish nursing ministries. The following are some of the replies I received:

From an NCF faculty member:

> *My comment about the Parish Nurse preparation course, as one of the faculty, is that the class is like a weeklong Bible study, where I have the privilege of learning how to better praise God and attempt to be obedient to Him—and to learn and share with the other nurses with similar purposes in life. Probably the preparation for each topic is especially refreshing to me, because*

*it is like finding gems in the scripture to improve our lives and our ability to
serve as nurses. The greatest gift is that God can love each of us, small and
insignificant as we are!!*

*In one class, a nurse asked me to reread one scripture. After I did, she re-
marked, "That's what it's all about!!" She looked like a light had been turned
on for her; and she keeps in touch with me, and her "light" was turned on,
but by the power of the scripture! That is my greatest reason for wanting to
continue teaching this course, and others, where nurses come to know God,
accept Jesus, and enjoy the strength of the Holy Spirit.*

From one of my parish nurse classmates:

*Looking back on the course, one of the most helpful and meaningful things
would be the honesty with which we spoke and shared. The worship services
every night gave depth to my faith and in turn have helped me with my Parish
Nursing ministry. The humor, also, definitely was a memorable high point and,
again, I utilize that quite often. Lastly, the "game" we played with the pieces
[of paper] and how the group dynamics unfolded was not only fun but a great
tool.*

(Note: For the game mentioned in the preceding response, our class was divided up
into about five groups with four or five students per group. Each student received an
envelope with a number of pieces of cardboard of different sizes and shapes. We were
told that each of us had to create a perfect square, as if putting together a puzzle; the
problem was that we did not each have the appropriate pieces to make a square, but
there were enough appropriate pieces within the overall group for four or five squares
(depending on the number of us assigned to the group). The catch was that for each
of us to achieve success and make our completed square, each person would have to
give up some of her pieces in order to help the others, *trusting that others would in
turn help her.* It was a great exercise.

I remember having my square almost completed but needing one more geometric
cardboard piece to finish it. I looked down the table and spotted the appropriate size
piece already fitted into one of my classmate's squares, which still needed several more
pieces. She noticed the dilemma at the same time. Oh, and I forgot to mention that
we could not speak during the exercise; that is, we had to become aware of each other's
needs, but no one could ask for help. Anyway, after a brief hesitation, my classmate
removed the piece from her own puzzle and handed it to me. Now I had achieved success; I had finished my puzzle but my classmate still needed several more cardboard
pieces. Ultimately, they all came her way and she completed her square also!

After the exercise was over, my classmate, who became my friend, told me that it was really hard for her to give away that little cardboard piece, which she seemed to need; it was already fitted into her puzzle and by giving it away, she was giving up the security of being at least partly successful. She admitted: "I really didn't want to give it up but then I saw that you couldn't finish without it, so I gave it to you; it was a great learning experience in letting go. I had to trust that other people would help me." When I returned home, I found a small refrigerator magnet, bearing a scripture quotation, which was the exact size of our shared puzzle piece and sent it to my friend as a memento. Games can be great experiences in the exercise of Christian virtue!)

Two other classmates commented on worship and the program's communal sharing: "I found being exposed to the different worship styles was really enlightening for me. I have heard of 'Healing Services' but never experienced one and thought it was beautiful. Our commissioning was so good too; experiencing the differences yet oneness in Christ was beautiful."

And, "I think of two things right off the top of my head: the name tags we designed for ourselves. It was a great way of introducing our favorite things [and thus our focuses]; and the meditative walks" (that we took during the course).

Finally, one of the class members described not only her experience at the parish nursing course but also her call to attend the program:

> When I applied for admission [to the NCF Parish Nursing Education Program], the greatest challenge of all turned out to be completing the application form. "Along with this registration, please submit a one-page essay describing why being a parish nurse is important to you at this time of your life." This seemed to me to be "a statement of purpose." Now, I like to talk, but putting my ideas on paper is difficult and subject to much procrastination. However, the commitment I'd made to the program and the roommate served to be strong motivators. Actually, I began to realize my response to this assignment would become the cornerstone of my experience. I was asked an important question, and if I could not answer it honestly and with some degree of substance, perhaps I shouldn't attend. Even more importantly, perhaps I shouldn't be a parish health minister.
>
> Looking back and thinking about the word "purpose," I'm prompted to ask, "Whose purpose?" Certainly mine, but what was the nucleus of the cell that grew into this intention? That's where the word "call" comes to mind. Who or What was the prompt, the stimulus which was exerting its power upon me to become something new and very much different from what my life had been? I truly believe it was a call from the Holy Spirit. And, I now realize it

was a two-fold summons, first to decide to become a parish health minister, second to follow the path to Liberty Corner.

My statement began with a short description of who I am, and at what stage of life. Following was a description of the resources I am fortunate to have which would, I hoped, make it possible for me to serve in this new role. More importantly, and closely related to my sense of the presence of the Spirit, was a strong desire at last to include my religious faith as part of the work that I would do.

Then, I described two significant phrases that have been an integral part of my nursing practice since my first day in nursing school. The first, the motto of my school of nursing, was "Corpus Sanare, Animam Salvare," "To heal the body and save the soul." The other, etched in the stone of the entrance to the infirmary which was for many years so much a part of my life as a college health nurse, is "Non Ministrari, Sed Ministrare," "Not to be ministered unto, but to minister." I concluded by saying, "Parish health ministry provides an opportunity to blend the professional skills and experiences of a successful nursing career and a lifelong, faith-centered system of values and behaviors with a generous amount of flexible time.

The main reason I decided to attend the [NCF] program was that I was seeking validation. I was new to parish health ministry and uncertain about how the system worked in theory and in practice. Intellectually, I accepted that each parish probably had its own, unique way of doing things. However, completing a formal orientation program that included "commissioning" would give me two important gifts. One was a tried-and-true system to follow while I was developing my own, and the other was permission, if that's the word, to be trusted with entering into a special relationship with people in need for the purpose of easing their lives. Therefore, along with my presence comes the unspoken but ever-present promise to "do no harm." I would leave with a lovely lapel pin, an official piece of paper, and the prayers of those I had gotten to know. I hoped also to acquire a greater feeling of confidence and stronger identity as a parish health minister.

Of course, the inspiration to begin having faith in myself and my prayerful intent began at Liberty Corner with the people around me, the faculty, the other students, and the staff. We were generously provided with a comfortable, nourishing environment which made possible separation from worldly concerns and focus on the new life that possibly lay ahead.

Information about parish health ministry was provided in abundance by a richly qualified and dedicated faculty. Formal lectures were made lively, touching, funny, challenging by the real-life stories that rose spontaneously from the students throughout each day. Integration of the formal and informal naturally took place as the words on the paper of our notebooks came to life through these shared experiences. It was also present as the words of scripture and the prayers of those present were continuously woven into the fabric of familiar nursing process.

Each day ended quietly and peacefully in congregation set aside for reflection and unified prayer as a group. Then, back in my dormitory room, my roommate fell asleep as soon as her head hit the pillow, leaving me time and spiritual space for my system to turn itself off gradually as I engaged in meditation, the attentive search for the Spirit.

This request for recollection has presented me with the opportunity for thoughtful evaluation. Did I achieve what I hoped I would achieve? Was I validated? Actually, at the end of the program it became clear to me these qualities could not be acquired in a workshop setting alone. There would be much more testing and proving to be done back home. Did I learn new information? Absolutely. Was I freshly inspired? Without a doubt. Did I become fully integrated into a different system of behaviors? That's a question which will be answered as my life in parish health ministry unfolds. I know now that part of the process will be one which always is evolving and, I hope, responsive to the dynamic nature of my church community and its particular needs for service.

Since that week I can attest to the fact that the Spirit which took me to [the NCF Parish Nursing Education Program] has remained. I have experienced moments of great satisfaction as I become ever more free to provide care not just for the body and mind of those I visit, but also the spirit in a fully synthesized manner. In contrast, at times of great discouragement, I have been strengthened and sustained by my memories of caring people who predicted these occasions and told me I would not falter.

What I am finding most rewarding about my new nursing role, however, is that the technology, which has increasingly come between nurses and their patients, is no longer a part of the picture. I am not laying hands on tubes, bottles, and monitors. I am sitting with my patient at the bedside, or the kitchen table, or the lounging chair, listening, offering suggestions, often completing the simplest of tasks. For this I regularly receive the greatest of rewards, a rich feeling of accomplishment and spiritual satisfaction. When things don't always work out just the way we might prefer, we always can turn the challenge completely over to our Heavenly Father through prayer. We are never completely helpless. Neither of us is alone. We are together in the loving company of the Holy Spirit.

Nurses Christian Fellowship Parish Nursing Advanced Seminar

For parish nurses who have completed the NCF basic preparation course in parish nursing, Nurses Christian Fellowship offers an advanced seminar. This offering is a two-and-one-half-day Christ-centered program that addresses, in depth, the topics of suffering and grief, ministerial team dynamics, ethical dilemmas, accountability in parish nursing, and documentation systems in parish nursing (NCF, 2002, p. 2). The course objectives for the advanced seminar proposed that at the conclusion of the seminar, participants should be prepared to:

> *participate in a ministry support group; utilize principles of group facilitation; articulate a biblical perspective on suffering; develop a plan for supportive working relationships with the ministerial team; problem-solve ethical dilemmas common to parish nursing; plan a system of accountability within the work environment; establish a system for documentation of nursing care; [and] begin writing a grant proposal. (NCF, 2002, p. 2).*

At the completion of the course students are awarded 14 contact hours of CNE credit.

As with the NCF basic preparatory course in parish nursing, the advanced seminar is a biblically based program. For example, the topic of suffering and grief is discussed in light of such scripture passages as Romans 5:3–5: "We also boast in our suffering, knowing that suffering produces endurance . . . and character and . . . hope, and hope does not disappoint us because God's love has been poured into our hearts through the Holy Spirit that has been given to us." And a discussion of ministerial team dynamics is grounded in such biblical passages as Acts 6:2–4: "And the Twelve called together the whole community of disciples and said . . . 'Friends, select from among yourselves seven men of good standing, full of the Spirit and of wisdom, whom we may appoint to this task, while we . . . will devote ourselves to prayer and to serving the word.'"

Although I was not personally able to participate in the NCF advanced seminar because of my teaching schedule, I did interview one of my classmates from the basic course who attended; she described the experience as very positive:

"We also boast in our suffering, knowing that suffering produces endurance . . . and character and . . . hope, and hope does not disappoint us because God's love has been poured into our hearts through the Holy Spirit that has been given to us"
—*Romans 5:3–5*

"And the Twelve called together the whole community of disciples and said . . . 'Friends, select from among yourselves seven men of good standing, full of the Spirit and of wisdom, whom we may appoint to this task, while we . . . will devote ourselves to prayer and to serving the word.'"
—*Acts 6:2–4*

This NCF program, both the basic and the advanced course, is actually based in scripture, which is very different than a program that just tacks on spirituality as a part of the course. This course is definitely bible-based and directed by parish nurses who are serious Christians.

In the advanced course, there were 12 students and two faculty members. We all introduced ourselves first to tell what we were doing in parish nursing; although we were only there for two and a half days, we divided into groups to prepare worship services for the two evenings we were there. We were supposed to prepare a group service. And while being in the first group we only had about 15 minutes to prepare something but the Holy Spirit was at work; it was very Holy Spirit–driven. It worked for the group [considering the interdenominational nature of the groups]. I was amazed that we were able to put something together so quickly that was so profound, so that's why I knew that the Holy Spirit was working.

The advanced course was led by two NCF faculty members. We met in a lovely room which was conducive to listening and reflecting. It was less formal than the first course. The topics on which we had teaching included: grief and loss, ethics, ministry teams, and accountability and documentation; but there was a lot of discussion. An important part of the sharing was that we were supposed to all come with an ethical dilemma and this ended up also in ministry for those involved. Because the dilemma was part of their ongoing parish ministry. When someone presented a situation, we got into why did that happen; what is the scriptural basis for a response. What can we learn from the Word of God, and we prayed for each other and we ministered to each other. It was a beautiful experience because of the chemistry that was going and the ministry.

The setting, instead of being like a classroom format, we were either sitting at tables in a circle or in chairs around the circle and it was more collegial. In other words, parish nursing is now in its beginnings and so there were opportunities for other students to tell us what they were doing. And everybody was really listening; not just trying to tell their own story but [they] really wanted to hear what other people had to say and to learn from them. People were truly interested in what everyone else was doing and what their experiences were so there was more Christian behavior or opportunities for Christian behavior. We did learn from each other.

The parish nurse gave an example of her own ethical dilemma, which occurred within the context of counseling in which she was invited to visit the home of a young woman who had had a serious psychotic break. The parents did not want their daughter to be hospitalized but requested that the parish nurse pray for healing. This posed a serious dilemma, as the nurse felt that the parents were exhausted and the young woman actually needed the safety and protection of hospital care and therapy.

> *She was having an acute psychotic break and I went to the home of the parents, and she was suicidal and they wanted us to pray for healing and for deliverance, which I am not against, but the nurse part of me said that this person needs to be in a protected environment; she needed a safe place. The parents wanted to keep her at home and protect her but they had been doing this for some time and were exhausted. She had not been to sleep in three days, so the dilemma was that the nurse in me said that this person needs to be hospitalized where she can be safe and be medicated so that her body can get some rest, but the counselor in me wanted to say that "all things are possible with God" and "let's pray for her." In the end, I prayed for her, and I asked her some questions about whether she would like to be free of the torment she was suffering, and so we led her to pray for deliverance herself and she calmed down a lot. So when I left I instructed the parents that they could not leave her alone and if [they got] too tired to continue, to call an ambulance to come and bring her to the hospital. This is what they ended up doing.*

The nurse added:

> *I think that this is the thing about parish nursing that when you walk into a home you have to meet the person where they are and try to work with that and encourage them to work with their medications or treatment. So that's what came out of this particular scenario for me that yes, you pray and yes, you use scriptures, and yes, you encourage the person to exercise their faith, and yes, you involve the family members but you don't throw nursing out. You still have to protect the patient; you still have to use your common sense and refer patients that we have these services and you can use them.*

She concluded:

> *I think that in sharing our ethical dilemmas we were building relationships and it turned out in a very positive way. And the facilitator was strong enough in her faith, and strong enough in her nursing, and strong enough in interpersonal relationships to allow the Holy Spirit to minister to people. And she let things happen that needed to happen. One of the group said that her sharing had been a life-changing experience for her and for that reason she was so glad that she had come to the group.*
>
> *Another important topic that we discussed the next day was accountability and documentation. The most important thing I remember is that we said: "document, document, document!" People did this in very different ways, but*

how is not as important as that we do document. We also talked about issues of confidentiality and care in protecting records of patients you have seen as a parish nurse. A final topic of the program was on grant writing for nurses.

Distance Learning in Parish Nursing Education: A Biblically-Based Program

Distance-learning parish nursing courses are now beginning to be offered online; one newly developed course, the Virginia Parish Nurse Education Program, endorsed by the Women's Missionary Union of Virginia in conjunction with the College of Health Sciences of Roanoke, Virginia, offers core content in an online format. The course does, however, additionally include two directed retreat weekends to support the parish nurse's spiritual formation and the course's faith community component. The theology of the Virginia Parish Nurse Education Program (VPNEP) is centered in the New Testament account of Jesus' life, which the coordinators of the course point out describes more of Jesus' healings than of any other dimensions of his ministry.

The VPNEP Christian education parish nursing program is open to licensed registered nurses of all denominations: "it offers registered nurses with a strong spiritual faith the knowledge to implement and facilitate a parish nurse ministry" (College of Health Sciences, 2002, p. 2). As well as the two retreats, the program described as "Education That Makes Housecalls" offers "instruction and support on software and computer use," "distance learning through 'Blackboard' that is currently the standard for most educational institutions," "more interactive discussion than conventional classrooms," "continual access to expert Parish Nurse Consultants," and "networking . . . during and after completion of the program" (College of Health Sciences, 2002, p. 2).

The Virginia Parish Nursing Education Program (distance-learning portion) includes such courses as history and models, philosophy of parish nursing, theology of health, multicultural issues, use of humor in ministry, children's and older adults' educational considerations, entering sacred space, legal considerations, getting started, accountability and documentation, volunteer issues, ethics, and wise counsel (College of Health Sciences, 2002, p. 3)

The VPNEP retreat courses include such topics as mission statement, devotion, journaling, introduction to "Blackboard," role of the church in health, spiritual care, spiritual assessment, what parish nursing is, discerning the call, importance of rituals, sacraments, symbols, spiritual care prayer walk, working with churches, functioning within a ministerial team, educator role, spiritual gift assessment, music therapy, referral agent role, grant proposal writing, sharing the journey, grief and loss, and mental health issues (College of Health Sciences, 2002, p. 3).

It is suggested that an advantage of this distance-learning format, which the parish nurse coordinators estimate takes approximately five months to complete, is the flexible study schedule for nurses who must be able to access parish nursing education as work or family responsibilities permit. The Virginia Parish Nursing Education Program in a quarterly weekend retreat format has, over the last five years, graduated 110 parish nurses from seven Christian denominations and five states. From that experience, the need for the newly created distance-learning format was identified and has been developed without compromising competency of the program (material from the College of Health Sciences brochure is cited with permission).

University-Based Programs in Parish Nursing

In their book *Parish Nursing: Stories of Service and Care*, Verna Carson and Harold Koenig (2002) speculate about the future of parish nursing education. Carson and Koenig report that many parish nurses with whom they spoke had participated in a parish nursing course employing the curriculum recommended by the International Parish Nurse Resource Center (INPRC) (p. 143). The authors observe that "the INPRC's emphasis on standardization has served parish nursing well in launching and expanding the specialty"; they also see signs that the future education of parish nurses will develop and change as the subspecialty grows (p. 143).

A number of university-based parish nursing education programs currently exist. Some programs offer both academic credit and continuing education credit (CEU) as options for potential students. Many of the courses also teach the basic IPNRC curriculum. The introduction of parish nursing education has been suggested, though not yet implemented, at my own university-affiliated school of nursing. I have taught a three-credit elective course on spirituality and nursing at the university for the past seven years; during the past three years, I have included several classes on the subfield of parish nursing within the course to introduce students to the specialty. Some nursing faculty at my institution have suggested that we add both a CEU and an academic credit course in parish nursing to the curriculum. Material for this new elective could be derived from my course on spirituality and nursing; from the current literature in parish nursing, especially the *Scope and Standards of Parish Nursing Practice* (1998); from the findings of our parish nursing intervention study, the Gift of Faith in Chronic Illness, described in Chapter 9; and/or from the basic parish nursing curriculum of the IPNRC.

Major topics in the course might include: spirituality and the healing arts (a theology of health and healing); the spiritual ministry of parish nursing: standing on holy ground (ethical issues); the spiritual history of parish nursing; definition and philosophy of parish nursing; the role and functions of the parish nurse (the nurse–patient relationship: a sacred covenant); grand and middle-range theories of parish nursing; prayer in parish nursing; working with a congregation (initiating a healthcare ministry within a faith community); assessment of health needs of a faith community; assessment of parishioners' spiritual needs; spiritual care of chronically ill parishioners; spiritual care of acutely ill parishioners; spiritual care of ill child parishioners (and their families); spiritual needs in parishioners' deaths and bereavement; spiritual needs in mass casualty trauma; accountability and documentation; legal and ethical issues; and parish nursing research.

As with the spirituality and nursing course, a parish nursing offering for academic credit would carry both undergraduate and graduate course numbers, with assignments and clinical experiences varying according to the students' levels of experience. Both graduate and undergraduate students participating in the class for university credit could be mentored in a parish nursing research experience in order to assist in further developing and validating the specialty area.

The formal education of the parish nurses with whom I have spoken over the past decade has been found to be as brief as a weekend workshop on parish nursing and as broad as a 54-contact-hours CEU course including both practical as well as theoretical experience. Some nurses have taken a parish nursing course based on the initial curriculum developed by the International Parish Nurse Resource Center (IPNRC); others have not. Because of the evolving nature of current parish nursing education, I described both an overview and "lived experiences" with one IPNRC parish nursing course, as well as descriptions of two other models of parish nursing education. This gives some sense of the present state of the parish nursing educational milieu. The future of parish nursing education currently rests, appropriately, in the hands of the Lord and of those nurses who follow His call to serve within their faith communities.

References

American Nurses Publishing. (1999). *Scope and standards of parish nursing practice*. Washington, DC: Author.

Carson, V. B., & Koenig, H. G. (2002). *Parish nursing: Stories of service and care*. Philadelphia: Templeton Foundation Press.

College of Health Sciences. (2002). *Virginia parish nurse education program*. [Brochure]. Roanoke, VA: Author.

McDermott, M. A., Solari-Twadell, P. A., & Matheus, R. (1999). Educational preparation. In P. A. Solari-Twadell & M. A. McDermott (Eds.), *Parish nursing: Promoting whole person health within faith communities* (pp. 269–276). Thousand Oaks, CA: Sage.

Nurses Christian Fellowship. (2000). *Bringing good news to nursing*. Madison, WI: Author.

Nurses Christian Fellowship. (2001). *Parish nursing: Connecting faith and health*. Madison, WI: Author.

Nurses Christian Fellowship. (2002). *Parish nursing: Advance seminar*. Madison, WI: Author.

Olson, J. K. (2000). Components of optimal nursing practice within a faith community. In M. B. Clark and J. K. Olson (Eds.), *Nursing within a faith community: Promoting health in times of transition* (pp. 157–168). Thousand Oaks, CA: Sage.

CHAPTER 5

CONCEPTUAL MODELS OF PARISH NURSING PRACTICE:
A MIDDLE-RANGE THEORY OF SPIRITUAL WELL-BEING IN ILLNESS

Jesus Called the twelve…and he sent them out to proclaim the kingdom of God and to heal.

—*Luke 9:1*

"To Proclaim the Kingdom"

Dear Lord Jesus,
    You call me, and you "send"
  me *(Luke 9:1)* to "proclaim the
kingdom . . . and to heal" the sick.
        (Luke 9:2)

You ask me to "take nothing" for
the "journey"; neither walking
stick . . . nor food, nor money."
(Luke 9:3)

This is not a very comforting
message, Dear Lord: no food,
not even a little money
in case I get hungry?

You know I'll be taken care of,
My Lord and my God, for
your faith is infinite; but my
hope is so fragile.

What if I don't have the strength,
or the courage, or the talent to
heal the sick and proclaim
the kingdom? These are heavy
mandates, Lord Jesus. You
yourself, appointed disciples
to carry them out

But, then, that's the heart of this
call, isn't it, Dear Lord?

Its not my mission to proclaim
the gospel and heal the sick,
but Yours!

It's not my task to worry about
the talent and the courage,
and the strength,
but Yours!

It's not my grace that makes me
a minister of the gospel,
but Yours!

Teach me to trust.

Actually, I was just in the process of considering whether I should include
an entire chapter on conceptual models of parish nursing practice in this
book when my advanced copy of the summer 2002 *Journal of Christian*

Nursing arrived in the mail. I couldn't believe my eyes when I saw that the theme of the issue, displayed prominently on the cover, was "Thinking Christianly About Nursing." Two of the lead articles were titled "Who Needs Theories, Anyhow?: Critical Thinking About Faith, Reason and Nursing Theory" (Miller, 2002, pp. 6–10), and "Faith and Nursing: Adjusting Nursing Theories to Christian Beliefs" (Stegmeier, 2002, pp.11–15). These are both excellent articles that explore the Christian perspective on current and future nursing theories.

In her issue editorial "Why Nurses Need to Think," Judy Shelly (2002) responds to the posture of some nurses who might say of nursing theory: "I'll leave that kind of thinking to the academics; I don't have time for such heady stuff" (p. 3). Shelly asserts: "God doesn't let us off the hook. He created human beings with the unique ability to consider the reasons for our existence and the consequences of our actions. It is not good enough for nurses to know what to do; we must also know *why* we are doing it. Otherwise, we may end up doing more harm than good" (p. 3). Citing a scriptural basis for contemporary Christian nursing theory efforts, Shelly observes: "Paul challenged the Philippian church to think when he wrote to them: 'Finally, beloved, whatever is true, whatever is honorable, whatever is just, whatever is pure, whatever is pleasing, whatever is commendable, if there is any excellence and if there is anything worthy of praise, think about these things' (Phil. 4:8). His exhortation," Shelly concludes, "stands worthy of our attention today" (p. 3; portions of J. Shelly's editorial cited with permission).

Basing it on the articles in the contemporary issue of the *Journal of Christian Nursing*, and especially moved by editor Judy Shelly's advice, I decided that a chapter on conceptual models of parish nursing practice, including both grand theories of practice and a middle-range theory of spriritual well-being in illness, was not only appropriate but also timely and necessary for the new specialty of parish nursing.

During the decades of the 1970s and 1980s, especially, both academicians and practicing nurses began to incorporate theories of nursing into their research and practice. The majority of these early nursing models fell into the category of "grand theories" of nursing, or those conceptual frameworks that attempted to present a way of describing and understanding the overall discipline of professional nursing practice. Each model contained some exploration of the concepts: person, health, nursing, and environment. There were a number of nursing theory conferences organized to analyze and discuss the logical adequacy and practicality of these theories for use in research and practice. The meetings often included presentations by key nursing theorists of the day, such as Dorothea Orem, Callista Roy, Martha Rogers, and Betty Neuman. Some of the most frequently cited conceptual frameworks were Orem's self-care model for nursing, the Roy adaptation model, the Neuman systems model, and Rogers' model of unitary person. Despite focus on the work of the theorists of the late twentieth century, as contemporaries of that era, most nurse metatheorists, however, acknowledged and still acknowledge Florence Nightingale as the first nursing theorist; this accolade is based on Nightingale's exploration and understanding of the need for a framework for nursing practice as described in her 1859 book *Notes on Nursing*.

While some nurse researchers have attempted to use grand theories of nursing to undergird their studies, the breadth of these models makes such efforts difficult. Usually, the grand theory is dissected by an investigator, a portion of the model being employed to provide the framework for research. While the grand theories of nursing provide valuable parameters to delineate and explain the practice of professional nursing, metatheorists have called for and continue to advocate the development of middle-range nursing theories, or those theories that strive to explain more discrete phenomena of interest to practicing nurses.

In distinction to the grand theories of nursing, which attempt to incorporate myriad concepts representing a broad range of phenomena within the discipline, a number of middle-range theories have begun to emerge in the professional literature. Some of these include frameworks dealing with such issues as pain control, chronic sorrow, end of life, uncertainty of the illness experience, and skill acquisition. The concept of "middle-range theory" was introduced in the sociological literature by Robert Merton in 1957 (p. 9); midrange theories were viewed as bodies of knowledge that would encompass a more limited number of variables than grand theories and could be empirically tested. Middle-range nursing theories cluster "around a concept of interest" (Chinn & Kramer, 1995, p. 40), such as those identified previously. They are also described as "theories that focus on specific nursing phenomena that reflect clinical practice" (Meleis, 1997, p. 18); "not covering the full range of phenomena that are of concern within the discipline" (Chinn & Jacobs, 1987, p. 205); sharing "some of the conceptual economy of grand theories but also [providing] the specificity needed for usefulness in research and practice" (Walker & Avant, 1995, p. 11); and "made up of a limited number of concepts and propositions that are written at a relatively concrete . . . level" (Fawcett, 1992, p. 5). As middle-range theories address a specific phenomenon, their goal is thus to "describe, explain or predict phenomena" (Fawcett, 1992, p. 5). In sum, middle-range theories fall somewhere between the more abstract or grand theories/conceptual models and circumscribed practice theories.

Grand Theories of Parish Nursing

In a literature review on the emerging subfield of parish nursing, a number of broad conceptual models for parish nursing are found, each framework reflecting the existing structure of the grand theories of nursing in focusing on four components of practice: person, health, nursing, and environment. Four of these conceptual models for parish nursing practice include the Berquist and King conceptual model of parish nursing, the Miller model of parish nursing, the parish nursing continuity of care model, and the circle of Christian caring model of parish nursing.

A parish nursing conceptual framework incorporating the concepts of client, health, nurse, nursing process, and environment was developed by nurses Sandra Berquist and Jean King (1994). The Berquist and King model assumes that the client is a "physiological, emotional and spiritual person" (p. 156). The parish nursing environment is identified as the faith community (p. 156). Parish nursing practice incorporates one or more roles, including "health educator," "health counselor," "leader of individuals and groups," and "community liaison" (p. 158). The goal of parish nursing is "to enhance the holistic health and well-being of individuals, families and groups within the faith commuity" (p. 161). Physical, emotional, and spiritual health and wellness are identified as the immediate goals of parish nursing practice. Nurse theorists Berquist and King suggest that their framework "can provide the basis for implementation of a parish nurse program" (p. 167); they also note that the model may be further developed and validated in "future nursing research" (p. 167).

The Miller model of parish nursing, developed by Lynda Whitney Miller (1997), is based on the theological perspective of evangelical Christianity and contains four basic components: person/parishioner, health, nurse/parish nurse, and community/parish (p. 18). The model's "core integrating concept" is that of "the Triune God: God (Father)/Christ (Son)/Holy Spirit" (p. 18). Miller explains that while many nursing frameworks incorporate spiritual care for patients as a dimension of practice, the uniqueness of her parish nursing model lies in the fact that "the spiritual is central and personhood is defined as a spiritual relationship with the Triune God" (p. 19). The concepts of health, nurse/parish nurse, and community/parish are also undergirded by Old and New Testament biblical theology in the Miller model of parish nursing. In viewing the church as an appropriate setting for parish nursing, Miller points out that "health and healing are integral to the Christian Church's mission and ministry" (p. 21); and that faith communities can promote health philosophically by "nurturing spiritual values" and practically by "sponsoring health related programs" (p. 21).

Ultimately, Miller observes that her model, like parish nursing itself, is a "work in progress" (p. 21).

The parish nursing continuity of care model, created by parish nurse Rita Wilson (1997), is a holistic framework that emphasizes "harmony in mind, body and spirit" (p. 14). Key elements in the Wilson model include the person (body, mind, and spirit), health (physical, emotional, and spiritual), the parish nurse (health care services, pastoral care services, and community services), and the congregation (birth to death) (pp. 14–15). The parish nursing continuity of care model is based on "caring which is enveloped in the healing spirit of the Lord" (p. 14). "The Church becomes the nurse's community," Wilson points out, "in which wellness is promoted by holistically addressing members' physical, emotional and spiritual needs" (p. 13). The parish nurse practicing within a congregational setting "becomes God's representative of love and caring" (p. 13) to the members of the faith community. As do theorists Berquist and King, nurse theorist Wilson advises that "further conceptual development and validation" of the model's components may be provided in future research (p. 16).

A fourth model for parish nursing practice described in the literature is the circle of Christian caring, created by Margie Maddox (2001). Dr. Maddox developed the circle of Christian caring model of parish nursing while serving as the parish nurse for a large Presbyterian church in the Southeast. As a basis for the model, parish nursing is envisioned as "an opportunity to combine the spiritual and physical dimensions of caregiving and to affirm the church as a place for disease prevention and health promotion" (p. 12). The parish nurse roles are identified as "health educator," one who teaches parishioners in such areas as blood pressure screening and control, cardiopulmonary resuscitation (CPR), age-related illness conditions, and preschool handwashing techniques (p. 12); "health counselor," involving such activities as hospital and nursing home visiting and working with church groups; "referral resource/client advocate," employing the parish nursing role to serve as community liaison primarily in terms of finding a variety of health care–related services for the parishioner; and "facilitator," or leader of the health ministry group within a faith community (pp. 12–13). An important component of the circle of Christian caring model of parish nursing is the concept of "visitation." The author suggests that visitation of homebound parishioners and assessment of their needs provides the opportunity to determine what resources the church may provide and/or what external community referrals may be needed (p. 13). Dr. Maddox concludes the discussion of her parish nursing model with the "hope that someday every church will have a parish nurse" (p. 13).

Each of the models described provides a broad organizing framework that parish nurses or faith communities may use to assist in the development of a parish health ministry program. The essential areas of discussion for initiating a faith community's parish health ministry include the church's philosophy of person (as a physical, emotional, and spiritual being); the religious tradition's attitudes toward health and healing; the role of nursing/parish nursing within the congregation; and the environment of the faith community as a potential setting for selected parish nursing/health ministry activities. These broad parish nursing models provide information to assist in development of the overall structure and processes of a parish nursing/health ministry program.

As noted earlier, however, nursing metatheorists also call the profession to develop middle-range theories, which will guide specific areas of practice and research with particular patient populations. To respond to that call, I have developed a middle-range nursing theory, spiritual well-being in illness, which can be used to direct parish nursing practice with seriously ill or disabled parishioners.

A Middle-Range Theory for Parish Nursing Practice: Spiritual Well-Being in Illness

While a middle-range theory of spiritual well-being in illness can be useful in orienting the practice of any nurse carrying out holistic health care, which includes attention to the needs of body, mind, and spirit, it is especially important for the parish nurse whose primary role is that of "spiritual companion," as integrator of faith and health. As discussed in earlier chapters, the parish nurse is not a glorified community health nurse or visiting nurse; those roles already exist within the overall practice of contemporary nursing. The uniqueness of parish nurses is that, while they do present themselves as professional nurses, they are also representatives of faith communities with the dual mission of providing holistic nursing care (within the scope and standards of parish nursing practice) and the pastoral care usually associated with ministry representatives of a parish or congregation. Thus, while the parish nurse may, in her or his multiple roles as advocate, educator, and referral agent, give significant attention to a parishioner's physical, emotional, and social health and well-being, a primary dimension of the ministry is to assess and support ill or disabled church members' spiritual well-being. The latter activity is at the heart of the vocational call of the parish nurse.

In Chapter 1, under the heading "The Relationship of Faith and Health," qualitative data reflecting the importance of spiritual well-being in coping with illness were presented; both quantitative and qualitative data supporting the relationship between faith and health are also presented in Chapter 9. Recent studies in the area of parish nursing combined with past research on the spiritual needs of such populations as end-stage renal disease (hemodialysis) patients, elderly long-term care residents, and persons living with HIV (human immunodeficiency virus) and AIDS (acquired immune deficiency syndrome) have continued to support my work on developing a midrange nursing theory of spiritual well-being in illness, the seeds of which are evident in the earlier publication of a Spiritual Assessment Scale (O'Brien, 2003, pp. 65–66).

Development of the Theory of Spiritual Well-Being in Illness

The nursing literature suggests that "middle-range theories generally emerge from combining research and practice, and building on the work of others" (McEwen, 2002, p. 207). The latter point is validated by nurse theorists who assert that middle-range theories may be derived or deduced from grand theories or conceptual frameworks (Ruland & Moore, 1998, p. 170) or from established clinical guidelines (Good, 1998, p. 120). The midrange nursing theory of spiritual well-being in illness was derived from earlier conceptualizatons in the area of spiritual well-being and also from the nursing model conceived by Joyce Travelbee, in which a central focus of the framework is the concept of finding meaning in an illness experience.

The core component of the nursing theory of spiritual well-being in illness is the concept of finding *spiritual* meaning in the experience of illness. While Travelbee (1971) indeed introduced the importance of spiritual concerns: "the spiritual values a person holds will determine to a great extent his [sic] perception of illness" (p. 16), she never explicitly described the concept of "spiritual well-being" in her model. Rather, Travelbee developed an interactional framework based upon "human-to-human," nurse–patient relationships, viewing the nurse's role as assisting "the ill patient to experience hope as a means of coping with illness and suffering" (Chinn & Kramer, 1995, p. 176); illness was envisioned as a "spiritual, emotional and physical" experience that might be defined both "subjectively and objectively" (Chinn & Jacobs, 1987, p. 188).

For Travelbee, one's definitions of illness and suffering depended very much on "the symbolic meaning attached to these concepts by the individual" (Thibodeau, 1983, p. 90); she further postulated that "a person's attitude toward suffering ultimately determines how effectively he [sic] copes with illness" (Meleis, 1997, p. 361). Finally, Joyce Travelbee (1971) taught that "the professional nurse practitioner must be prepared to assist individuals and families not just to cope with illness and suffering but to find meaning in these experiences" (p. 13). "This is the difficult task of professional nursing," she admitted, (but) "it must not be evaded" (p. 13).

Joyce Travelbee, a psychiatric nurse practitioner and educator, died at age 47 just as she was beginning doctoral study; thus, we do not know how she might have expanded her beginning conceptual model for nursing practice. Travelbee has been described as a deeply spiritual woman, whose human-to-human vision of nursing practice was importantly influenced by her early educational experience at Charity Hospital in New Orleans, by the work of the great psychotherapist Viktor Frankl, and by the writings of nurse theorist Ida Orlando. Although Joyce Travelbee did not live to further explain and validate her interaction model, her groundbreaking work on the concept of a sick person finding meaning in the experiences of illness and suffering provides a solid and scholarly basis for the development of a midrange-level theory exploring and describing the spiritual meaning of illness and suffering: a nursing theory of spiritual well-being in illness.

As noted, the middle-range theory of spriritual well-being in illness was also inductively derived and concretized through several nursing studies exploring the importance of spiritual well-being in coping with chronic illness and disability. Overwhelmingly positive associations, both quantitatively and qualitatively, were found between spiritual well-being and quality of life. That is, those persons who reported a higher degree of personal faith, spiritual contentment, and religious practice were much more positive about and satisfied with other aspects of their lives and had greater hope for the future, despite sometimes painful and debilitating illnesses. Several case examples are those of Mr. Jones, a 62-year-old Methodist parishioner who was suffering from leukemia; Mrs. Manley, an 82-year-old Lutheran parishioner with a multiplicity of disease conditions, including osteoporosis, congestive heart failure, and diabetes; and 75-year-old Mrs. McDermott, a Roman Catholic parishioner who was disabled with rheumatoid arthritis, among other diagnoses. In completing the *Spiritual Assessment Scale* (O'Brien, 2003, pp. 65–66), which measures spiritual well-being, all three scored very positively on the items measuring faith, religious practice, and spiritual contentment or lack of spiritual distress. Similarly, all three were also most positive in their responses related to quality of life: hope for the future, for example, being positive about life, being able to get through difficulties, and feeling loved; and life satisfaction, for example, agreeing that they are "just as happy as when younger" (O'Brien, 2001). In looking back, they agreed they were "fairly well satisfied" with their lives (more detailed research findings reflecting the importance of spiritual well-being in coping with chronic illness are presented in Chapters 1 and 9).

Philosophy and Key Concepts

Every theory must have a philosophical basis undergirding the concepts and relationships articulated in the framework. The middle-range theory of spiritual well-being in illness is grounded in the belief that the human person, as well as being possessed of a physical and psychosocial nature, is also a spiritual being capable of transcending and/or accepting such experiences as pain and suffering in the light of his or her higher nature. Over and over, clinical nurses have witnessed ill or disabled patients rise above constraining physical or psychosocial deficits to live extraordinarily positive and productive lives. This ability to accept, and in some cases even embrace, illness and suffering is primarily a function of the patients' personal spiritual resources. It is for the purpose of identifying, supporting, and strengthening the influence of these spiritual resources, in relation to sickness or disability, that the nursing theory of spiritual well-being in illness has been developed.

The key concept of the middle-range theory of spiritual well-being in illness is, of course, that of spiritual well-being itself. In the conceptual model (Figure 5.1), an ill individual is presented as having the ability to find spiritual meaning in the experience of illness, which can ultimately lead to an outcome of spiritual well-being for the sick person. The capacity to find spiritual meaning in an occasion of illness or suffering is influenced by a number of factors. First and foremost, an individual's perception of the spiritual meaning of an illness experience is influenced by personal spiritual and religious attitudes and behaviors. These attitudes and behaviors include variables related to *personal faith*: belief in God, peace in spiritual and religious beliefs, confidence in God's power, strength received from personal faith beliefs, and trust in God's providence; *spiritual contentment*: satisfaction with faith, feeling of closeness to God, lack of fear, reconciliation, security in God's love, and faithfulness; and *religious practice*: support of a faith community, affirmation in worship, encouragement of spiritual companions, consolation from prayer, and communication with God through religious practices.

The impact of these spiritual and religious attitudes and behaviors on one's finding spiritual meaning in illness may also be mediated by such potentially intervening variables as *severity of illness*: degree of functional impairment; *social support*: support of family, friends, and/or caregivers; and current *stressful life events*: emotional, sociocultural, and/or financial.

The first step in developing a middle-range theory is to conduct an analysis of the core concepts in the model. Nurse metatheorists Walker and Avant (1995) identify a series of "steps" to be included in a "concept analysis," which include (among others) determining the "aims of the analysis," identifying "uses of the concept," and "defin[ing]

Figure 5.1 Parish Nursing Practice: A Conceptual Model of Spiritual Well-Being in Illness

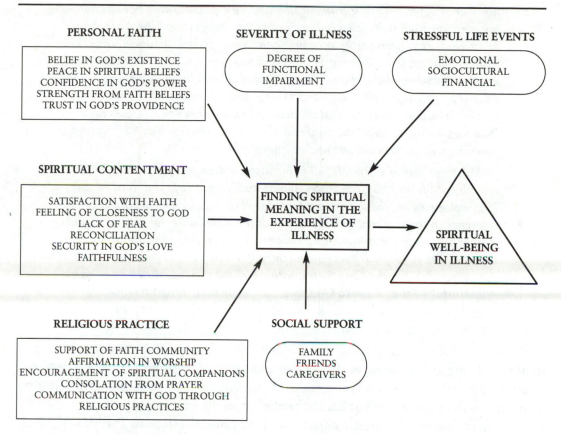

empirical referents" (p. 39). The aim of exploring the concept of spiritual well-being is to identify and describe its meaning in terms of contemporary usage, especially in relation to experiences of illness and suffering. The usage and empirical referents of the concept have been examined from the extant literature as well as nursing practice and nursing research. As I was developing the earlier referenced instrument to measure spiritual well-being, the Spiritual Assessment Scale (O'Brien, 2003), I explored the concept in both the nursing and the sociological literature:

> *The term* spiritual well-being *is described historically as having emerged following a 1971 White House Conference on Aging. Sociologist of religion David Moberg (1979) identified spiritual well-being as relating to the "wellness or health of the totality of the inner resources of people, the ultimate concerns around which all other values are focused, the central philosophy of life that*

guides conduct, and the meaning giving center of human life which influences all individual and social behavior" (p. 2). The concept of hope is central to a number of definitions of spiritual well-being. In a discussion of holistic nursing care, spiritual well-being is described as "an integrating aspect of human wholeness, characterized by meaning and hope" (Clark, Cross, Deane, & Lowry, 1991, p. 68). Lindberg, Hunter, and Kruszewski (1994) included "the need to feel hopeful about one's destiny" (p. 110) in a litany of patient needs related to spiritual well-being; and Droege (1991), in discussing the "faith factor" in healing, suggested that when an individual does not experience spiritual well-being, serious "spiritual maladies" may occur such as "depression, loneliness, existential anxiety and meaninglessness"(p. 13).

Most notions of spiritual well-being also contain some reference to philosophy of life and transcendence. Blaikie and Kelson (1979) described spiritual well-being as "that type of existential well-being which incorporates some reference to the supernatural, the sacred or the transcendental" (p. 137); and Barker observed that spiritual well-being is "to be in communication, in communion with that which goes beyond oneself in order to be whole in oneself" (1979, p. 154). For the Christian, spiritual well-being is identified as a "right relationship of the person to God, and, following that, a right relationship to neighbor and self" (Christy & Lyon, 1979, p. 98) (O'Brien, 2003, pp. 60–61, reprinted with permission).

Based on prior nursing practice and nursing research, I envision the concept of spiritual well-being as consisting of two dimensions: that of spirituality or one's personal relationship with God or the Transcendent; and religiosity or religiousness, reflecting an individual's practice of his or her faith beliefs (this dimension of spiritual well-being may or may not involve participation in an organized religious tradition). Thus, empirical referents of spiritual well-being are conceptualized in terms of *personal faith* and *spiritual contentment* (spirituality) and *religious practice* (religiosity or religiousness).

The three empirical referents of spiritual well-being are defined as follows:

Personal Faith. *Personal faith, as a component concept of the spiritual well-being construct, has been described as "a personal relationship with God on whose strength and sureness one can literally stake one's life" (Fatula, 1993, p. 379). Personal faith is a reflection of an individual's transcendent values and philosophy of life.*

Religious Practice. *Religious practice is primarily operationalized in terms of religious rituals such as attendance at formal group worship services, private prayer and meditation, reading of spiritual books and articles, and/or the carrying out of such activities as volunteer work or almsgiving.*

Spiritual Contentment. *Spiritual contentment, the opposite of spiritual distress, is likened to spiritual peace (Johnson, 1992), a concept whose correlates include: "living in the now of God's love," "accepting the ultimate strength of God," knowledge that all are "children of God," knowing that "God is in control," and "finding peace in God's love and forgiveness" (pp. 12–13). When an individual reports minimal to no notable spiritual distress, he or she may be considered to be in a state of spiritual contentment"* (O'Brien, 2003, pp. 61–62, reprinted with permission).

Theory Synthesis

Theory synthesis is defined as "a strategy aimed at constructing theory, an interrelated system of ideas, from empirical evidence" (Walker & Avant, 1995, p. 155). In theory synthesis "a theorist pulls together available information about a phenomenon. Concepts and statements are organized into a network or whole, a synthesized theory" (Walker & Avant, 1995, p. 155). In the preceding discussion, a diagrammatic model of the theory of spiritual well-being in illness is presented (Figure 5.1) to identify the relationships between key concepts and potentially mediating variables relevant to the framework. A sick or disabled individual's ability to find spiritual meaning in an experience of illness or suffering is perceived as being influenced by his or her spiritual and religious attitudes, beliefs, and practices, including those reflecting the concepts of *personal faith*, *spiritual contentment*, and *religious practice*.

An ill person's personal faith—not only whether or not he or she believes in the existence of God, but also his or her trust in the power and the goodness of God's care, sense of peacefulness about these beliefs, and courage and strength derived from them—is critical to whether the individual will be able to identify and/or accept an illness experience as having a spiritual dimension. If one believes in God, yet does not truly trust in or feel at peace in accepting His loving providence, an illness experience may be considered an unwarranted and unfair burden at best, or a punishment for some perceived past indiscretion at worst. In terms of the concept of *spiritual contentment*, an ill person may indeed *believe* in God's existence, His power, His care for all of humankind, and yet not personally feel close to the Lord; his or her faith may be based on a relationship that incorporates fear of God's judgment rather than security in His love. In such a situation, again, it may be very difficult for the individual to perceive an experience of illness or suffering as anything more than a possible retaliation or punishment for past sins.

While *religious practice*, in the formal sense of attending church services, may not be necessary for one to find a spiritual meaning in illness or disability, coping with illness can be greatly facilitated if a sick person has the support of such devotions as prayer or spiritual reading. The encouragement of a faith community with whom one may occasionally share worship or whose members pray for sick parishioners during communal worship services and/or the guidance of a pastor or spiritual companion can also be very comforting spiritual supports in times of illness and suffering.

A parish nurse, serving in his or her primary role as spiritual companion or "integrator of faith and health," can provide important nursing intervention in helping an ill parishioner who may be struggling with a number of spiritual issues. First, as parish nurses are representative of the ill person's faith community, they provide a dimension of spiritual support simply by their caring interaction with a sick parishioner. Parish nurses also may encourage ill parishioners' prayer lives as they frequently pray with patients during home or hospital visits; or they may choose to share a passage from scripture if a patient wishes. Very often, as will be seen in the many empirical examples presented in Chapter 8, parish nurses facilitate either the enhancement of, or in some cases the return to, religious practices that may have waned or even been abandoned by a parishioner during the onset of an illness experience.

Also, as demonstrated in the diagrammatic model presented in Figure 5.1, there are a number of potentially confounding variables that may interfere with a sick person's ability to achieve a sense of spiritual well-being in his or her illness. A parish nurse may have the opportunity to intervene in relation to a number of these factors hindering the ability to find meaning in the illness experience. For example, a parish nurse may be able to serve as a referral agent assisting sick parishioners in finding some relief for a functional impairment. For instance, if an ill parishioner is hard of hearing, the parish nurse may recommend audiology testing if this has not been done and/or may assist the individual in obtaining a hearing aid if necessary.

A parish nurse may also serve as a "bridge" between the congregation and the ill parishioner, thus providing social support from the faith community. The nurse may also facilitate communication with family and friends if these relationships have become strained due to illness or disability. Finally, through the various roles of integrator of faith and health, educator, referral agent, counselor, and patient advocate, the parish nurse may have the opportunity to guide, advise, teach, or support an ill parishioner in regard to a variety of emotional, sociocultural, and even financial concerns that may interfere with the individual achieving a sense of spiritual well-being in the illness experience.

Hypotheses Derived from the Theory

Based on the middle-range theory of spiritual well-being in illness, as described, several hypotheses might be derived related to the association between spiritual well-being and quality of life for those dealing with illness and/or disability. First, it can be proposed that there will be a significant relationship between the degree of a sick person's personal faith and his or her perceived quality of life in an illness experience. Second, there will be a significant relationship between the activity of a sick person's religious practice and his or her perceieved quality of life in an illness experience. Third, there will be a significant relationship between the degree of a sick person's feeling of spiritual contentment and his or her perceived quality of life in an illness experience. An overall hypothesis might be stated as follows: there will be a significant relationship between spiritual well-being (personal faith, spiritual contentment, and religious practice) and quality of life among sick persons experiencing illness or disability, controlling for the variables of severity of illness, social support, and stressful life events.

Empirical Testing

As presented in Chapters 1 and 9, testing of the preceding relationships has already begun. Empirical findings support both the subhypotheses and the overall hypothesis, correlating spiritual well-being (as a total concept and in its subcomponents: personal faith, spiritual contentment, and religious practice) with quality of life, measured in terms of hope and life satisfaction. The research was conducted among chronically ill adults experiencing myriad illness conditions; study participants belonged to a variety of religious traditions and faith communities. It is anticipated that similar parish nursing studies might be carried out with other patient populations experiencing both similar and different illness conditions and disabilities. Such research would greatly assist in validating the importance of the parish nursing role of integrator of faith and health; positive findings would strengthen and potentially expand the pastoral care role of the parish nurse while also supporting the health care dimension of parish health ministry.

It is suggested that, as in the studies presented in this book, parish nursing research to test the middle-range theory of spiritual well-being in illness employ methodological triangulation; that is, the collecting of both quantitative and qualitative data to explore the relationship of spiritual well-being to coping with illness and disability. While the quantitative data would provide a strong statistical basis for the relationship, the qualitative data elicited in focused conversational interviews with ill parishioners could provide the detailed narrative examples from which guidelines for the parish nurse role of integrator of faith and health could be further expanded and clarified. In essence, this was the goal of the project the Gift of Faith in Chronic Illness described in Chapter 9.

References

Barker, E. (1979). Whose service is perfect freedom. In D. O. Moberg (Ed.), *Spiritual well-being: Sociological perspectives* (pp. 153–171). Washington, DC: University Press of America.

Bergquist, S., & King, J. (1994). Parish nursing: A conceptual framework. *Journal of Holistic Nursing, 12*(2), 155–170.

Blaikie, N. W., & Kelson, G. P. (1979). Locating self and giving meaning to existence. In D. O. Moberg (Ed.), *Spiritual well-being: Sociological perspectives* (pp. 133–151). Washington, DC: University Press of America.

Chinn, P. L., & Jacobs, M. K. (1987). *Theory and nursing: A systematic approach* (2nd ed.). St. Louis: C. V. Mosby.

Chinn, P. L., & Kramer, M. K. (1995). *Theory and nursing: A systematic approach* (4th ed.). St. Louis: C. V. Mosby.

Christy, R. D., & Lyon, D. (1979). Sociological perspectives on personhood. In D. O. Moberg (Ed.), *Spiritual well-being: Sociological perspectives* (pp. 91–98). Washington, DC: University Press of America.

Clark, C. C., Cross, J. R., Deane, D. M., & Lowry, L. W. (1991). Spirituality: Integral to quality care. *Holistic Nursing Practice, 3*(1), 67–76.

Droege, T. (1991). *The faith factor in healing*. Philadelphia: Trinity Press International.

Fatula, M. A. (1993). Faith. In M. Downey (Ed.), *The new dictionary of Catholic spirituality* (pp. 379–390). Collegeville, MN: Liturgical Press.

Fawcett, J. (1992). *The relationship of theory and research* (3rd ed.). Philadelphia: F. A. Davis.

Good, M. (1998). A middle-range theory of acute pain management: Use in research. *Nursing Outlook, 46*(3), 120–124.

Johnson, R. P. (1992). *Body, mind, spirit: Tapping the healing power within you*. Liguori, MO: Liguori.

Lindberg, J. B., Hunter, M. L., & Kruszewski, A. Z. (1994). *Introduction to nursing: Concepts, issues and opportunities*. Philadelphia: Lippincott.

Maddox, M. (2001). Circle of Christian caring: A model for parish nursing practice. *Journal of Christian Nursing, 18*(3), 11–13.

McEwen, M. (2002). Middle-range nursing theories. In M. McEwen & E. M. Wills (Eds.), *Theoretical basis for nursing* (pp. 202–225). Philadelphia: Lippincott, Williams & Wilkens.

Meleis, A. I. (1997). *Theoretical nursing: Development and progress* (3rd ed.). Philadelphia: Lippincott.

Merton, R. F. (1957). *Social theory and social structure*. New York: Free Press.

Miller, B. J. (2002). Who needs theories, anyhow?: Critical thinking about faith, reason, and nursing theory. *Journal of Christian Nursing, 19*(3), 6–10.

Miller, L. W. (1997). Nursing through the lens of faith: A conceptual model. *Journal of Christian Nursing, 14*(1), 17–21.

Moberg, D. O. (1979). The development of social indicators of spiritual well-being and quality of life. In D. O. Moberg (Ed.), *Spiritual well-being: Sociological perspectives* (pp. 1–13). Washington, DC: University Press of America.

Nightingale, F. N. (1859). *Notes on nursing: What it is and what it is not.* London: Harrison.

O'Brien, M. E. (2001). *Spiritual well-being in chronic illness.* Unpublished study report, Catholic University of America, Washington, DC.

O'Brien, M. E. (2003). *Spirituality in nursing: Standing on holy ground.* (2nd ed.). Sudbury, MA: Jones and Bartlett.

Ruland, C. M., & Moore, S. M. (1998). Theory construction based on standards of care: A proposed theory of the peaceful end of life. *Nursing Outlook, 46*(4), 169–175.

Shelly, J. A. (2002). Why nurses need to think. *Journal of Christian Nursing, 19*(3), 3.

Stegmeier, D. (2002). Faith and nursing: Adjusting nursing theories to Christian beliefs. *Journal of Christian Nursing, 19*(3), 11–15.

Thibodeau, J. A. (1983). *Nursing models: Analysis and evaluation.* Monterey, CA: Wadsworth Health Sciences Division.

Travelbee, J. (1971). *Interpersonal aspects of nursing.* Philadelphia: F. A. Davis.

Walker, L. O., & Avant, K. C. (1995). *Strategies for theory construction in nursing* (3rd ed.). Norwalk, CT: Appleton & Lange.

Wilson, R. P. (1997). What does a parish nurse do? *Journal of Christian Nursing, 14*(1), 13–16.

CHAPTER 6

INITIATING A PARISH NURSING/HEALTH MINISTRY PROGRAM

Bear one another's burdens, and in this way you will fulfill the law of Christ.
—*Galatians 6:2*

"Bear One Another's Burdens"

Dear Lord Jesus,
   the apostle Paul taught that
Your followers should "bear one
   another's burdens" *(Galatians 6:2).*
Those who do so, he promised,
   would fulfill Your law.

But how can I take on "another's
   burdens" when I already have
so many of my own, Dear Lord?

What if I help another, and no
   one helps me?

That's the frightening part of
   this teaching, Lord Jesus;
Will I have more burdens
   than I can bear?

But . . . You have taught that
   in giving, I will receive;
   in grieving for others,
      I will be comforted;
   in being merciful, I will
      be shown mercy;
         and
   in becoming poor in spirit,
   I will inherit the kingdom
      of heaven *(Matthew 5:3–10).*

Grant me the courage, and the
   strength, and the love to
      bear another's burdens
         and so fulfill the law
            of the Lord.

One of the most challenging tasks of a parish nurse is that of initiating a parish nursing/health ministry program within a congregation. As with the beginning of any effort, especially when the concept underlying a program is new to potential participants, there are many issues to be considered and may pitfalls to avoid. This chapter discusses the process. In the relatively new era of contemporary parish nursing and health ministry, it is important, first, to recognize that even the terminologies used by churches for their health ministry programs can differ; thus, parish nurses need to be sensitive to adopting the most appropriate and acceptable language for their respective faith traditions. And, of course, there may also be differences within the various churches of a religious denomination.

In examining brochures and parish bulletins distributed by churches with parish nursing/health ministry programs, one finds this diversity. The following are just a few examples of denominational differences and similarities in health ministry terminology both within and among churches: Presbyterian congregations (Parish Health Ministry, Health Ministry Committee, Healing Ministry, Parish Nurse Ministry); Lutheran congregations (Congregational Health Ministry, Parish Health Ministry, Parish Health Committee); Episcopalian congregations (Parish Nursing Health Ministry, Parish Health Committee); United Methodist congregations (Congregational Health

Ministry, Parish Nursing Ministry); Baptist congregations (Congregational Health Ministry, Congregational Nursing Ministry); Roman Catholic congregations (Parish Health Care Ministry, Parish Health Ministry, Parish Wellness Committee); and Church of the Nazarene (Health Care Fellowship). Some labels suggested in the literature for health ministry teams are faith and health cabinets, wholeness in health teams, parish nurse advisory committees, and congregational health councils (Chandler & Berry, 2001, p. 987). A few churches highlight the role of the parish nurse, as in "parish nursing health ministry" or "parish nurse advisory committee." The more usual label, however, for a congregation's overall health ministry is that of either parish or congregational health ministry. In this chapter, I employ the terms, sometimes interchangeably, *parish health ministry* and *congregational health ministry*. I do so to emphasize the nature of the ministry being inclusive of parishioners, other than parish nurses, called to serve a congregation in healthcare ministry.

Initiating a Parish Health Ministry Program

Prayer as a Spiritual Support

In the book *Prayer in Nursing: The Spirituality of Compassionate Caregiving*, I wrote, paraphrasing Benedictine Mary Clare Vincent (1982) who asserted that "life without prayer doesn't work" (p.1), "nursing without prayer doesn't work" (O'Brien, 2003, p. 4). I would now expand the thought to add that parish nursing without prayer doesn't work! As the work of nursing represents the response to a call from God, a vocation to serve His "least ones" at their most fragile and most vulnerable, so the undertaking of parish nursing is a vocation, with unique emphasis on the dimension of pastoral ministry—the ministry of being a *spiritual companion* to one's patients as described in Chapter 3. The spiritual ministry of the parish nurse's role may be the most important for many parishioners, especially those for whom good health has long been a thing of the past, and yet who strive to live as fully as possible, despite limiting illnesses and infirmities.

For the parish nurse to carry out this ministry of spiritual companionship as well as the the tasks of education, counseling, advocacy, and referral that provide support and comfort during an illness trajectory, the nurse must be a man or woman of prayer. One parish nurse told me that she never knew "what kind of situation" she might find on making a home visit; thus, she needed all the spiritual support she could get to guide her nursing ministry for the "unexpected."

I am reminded of the importance of prayer in my hospital chaplaincy training, during which we also dealt with the unexpected. I, as did the rest of our chaplain intern group, arrived on the first day of the program very anxious about whether we would be capable of providing spiritual support to the seriously ill patients at the research medical center where our training was situated. We spoke among ourselves about our need for prayer and guidance from the Lord. At the conclusion of the first week of our 10-week internship, we decided, as a group, to begin meeting in the medical center chapel for 15 minutes each morning before class, to share prayer for the coming day's ministry. All of us found this to be not only an extremely comforting and bonding experience, but also a graced time for prayerful reflection; a time when we could give over the coming eight hours of study and ministry to the Lord and seek His blessing and His guidance on our day. We also encouraged each other to pray silently prior to entering a patient's room.

There are myriad kinds of prayer and times for prayer that may be adopted by parish nurses; the important thing is that we try, as Paul admonished the early Christians, to "pray without ceasing" (1 Thessalonians 5:17). We may pray individually before meeting with a parishioner, seeking the guidance of the Holy Spirit to direct our nurse–patient interaction. We may pray with other members of a parish nursing/health ministry team, asking that our activities be blessed and fruitful as we serve in the Name of the Lord. And we may pray quietly, during our leisure time, giving thanks for the blessing and the joy that is our call to serve in the ministry of parish nursing.

Parish nurses must be men and women of prayer! We are servants of the Lord; called to follow Him and minister to Him as He taught in Matthew 25:36: "and you cared for me." This is the heart of the parish nurse's vocation; this is the grace of the parish nurse's vocation; this is the gift of the parish nurse's ministry.

The Call to Christian Parish Health Ministry

In his book *Healthcare Ministry*, Gerald Arbuckle (2000) asserts that today's Christians are called to the "refounding" of healthcare ministries within faith communities (p. xxii). "For the process to begin and continue," he notes, "we need people with the qualities of the founders of Christian healthcare, people with similar imagination and creativity, who first hear and live the healing message of Jesus Christ, and then devise ways to reinterpret it in the turbulent world of contemporary healthcare" (p. xxi). These Christians, Arbuckle adds, will be able to "go to the heart of the story of the healing Jesus" (p. xxi). Many individual parishioners within faith communities, associated with a variety of Christian religious denominations, are presently attempting to do exactly what Arbuckle advises: They look to the gospel healing message of

Jesus and carry out His teachings through the creation of parish health ministry programs within their faith communities.

The majority of Christian health ministry programs identify a statement of scripturally based philosophy or mission underlying the ministry. Included in these mission statements are the goals of the ministry, for example, promotion of healthy bodies, minds, and spirits among members of the faith community. The philosophy and/or theology of the church may also be included in a comment related to the ministers' vocation to serve that is derived from Jesus' gospel message to care for those who are ill. Some mission statements add that the church's parish nurses and health ministers are witnesses of Christ's love and healing ministry in serving their brothers and sisters in the faith community to which they belong. The ministry's mission statement may also address the church's perception of the important linkage between faith and health/illness, which is the undergirding framework for the development of health ministry within the context of a faith community. The importance of prayer, as a dimension of parish health ministry, is included in the description of some congregational health ministries, as well.

Before exploring parish health ministry further, it is important to say a few words about Christian ministry in general. *Christian ministry* has been defined theologically as "the public activity of a baptized follower of Jesus Christ, flowing from the Spirit's charisma and an indvidual personality, on behalf of a Christian community to proclaim, serve and realize the kingdom of God" (O'Meara, 1999, p. 150). In describing the spirituality of ministry, O'Meara adds: "Ministry lives out of the theology of a ministering community, out of a church's tradition of Christian life and faith, and out of the minister's silent conversation with grace" (p. 225). Ministry is "intended action," Michael Lawler (1990) asserts, and "to be Christian ministry . . . action must flow from Christian being, from the belief in and the commitment to represent Jesus, the Christ" (pp. 28–29). "The one decisive element that distinguishes ministry from ordinary acts of kindness is motivation," Gerding and DeSiano (1999) point out, "and the motivation singularly necessary for ministry is discipleship. . . . Christian ministry . . . flow[s] out of the relationship that one has with Jesus Christ" (p. 22). "A minister," they note, "lives the life of Christ. A minister follows his teachings. A minister follows his way. A minister follows his example. A minister continues his deeds" (p. 22).

"Jesus came among us to heat up the chemistry of human encounter": "Christ . . . increases your ability to love beyond what human logic says you should have," assert DiGiacomo and Walsh (1993, p. 74). This point is supported by the principle that "the first rule of ministry is to shift attention away from ourselves and onto those we are called to serve" (Paprocki, 2000, p. 119). Because in this ministry of unselfish service we are called to witness the gospel message of Jesus, it is also advised that "knowledge of the scriptures is . . . crucial as a source of prayer and piety and a source and resource of [the] ministry" (Cooper, 1993, p. 15).

And, in discussing the subject of "confidence" or lack thereof in ministry, the authors of *Called to Parish Ministry*, Greg Dues and Barbara Walkley (1997), remind us that "we are in good company if we feel inadequate sometimes" (p. 86); and they cite the example of Moses' attempt to "slip away from the Lord's call with the plea that he was inadequate: 'O Lord, I have never been eloquent . . . even now that you have spoken to your servant'" (Exodus 4:10) (p. 87).

From the many accounts I have heard of nurses being called to Christian parish health ministry, there does not seem to be any unique vehicle, other than the whispering of the Holy Spirit, that accounts for hearing and responding to the parish nursing vocation. In some cases individual nurses, perceiving healthcare needs within their faith communities, initiated a health ministry by approaching a pastor or parish council. In other cases, nurses were approached by their pastors and asked to develop a parish health nursing and health ministry program. This latter occurrence, while probably less frequent, is beginning to occur more often as parish nursing becomes better known and understood by clergy and parishioners. The following case examples of how parish nurses in different denominations heard their "calls" demonstrates the variety of ways nurses become involved in health ministry.

A parish nurse, serving in a part-time paid position for an Episcopal congregation, reported that one of the church members, herself a retired nurse academician with a graduate degree, was the moving force behind the initiation of the church's health ministry. This nurse–parishioner was aware of the concept of parish nursing, as well as the needs of the older members of her congregation; she thus suggested that a parish nurse be hired to facilitate the beginning of the ministry. While the parish nurse was not actually a member of this particular Episcopal church, the pastor and parishioners felt that she had the nursing skills and the spirituality for which they were looking. The nurse herself had not participated in a parish nursing course, although she did have a strong interest in the relationship of faith and health.

A parish nurse serving in a Roman Catholic church explained that when the pastor learned she had just retired from a full-time nursing career, he approached her husband, first, with the idea that his wife might initiate volunteer parish nursing at the church. "My husband said I'd do it!" she laughingly added. The nurse had not taken a parish nursing course at the time, but was currently enrolled in a program. She added that there were more than 20 other nurses from her congregation who were also interested in participating in parish nursing.

When asked why she felt called to parish health ministry, a younger parish nurse ministering in a Lutheran congregation responded this way: "I was trying to remember that. As a new graduate in my church, I remember that one of the active nurses in our congregation brought it [parish nursing] up and we had a meeting with [a local hospital parish nursing program], and that's how we got started." The nurse added: "I am very thankful that I am involved in this church ministry. It has brought so much meaning into my life; I find that the parish nursing program, because I am trained as a nurse, this is a way I can give back to my church community."

As can be seen from the three preceding examples, a parish nurse may be "called" to health ministry in a variety of ways. As parish nursing and health ministry become more well known and well accepted among pastors and congregations, many new parish nurses will be joining already-established programs within their faith communities. At the present stage in the development of the parish nursing specialty, however, most nurses called to this ministry become either the "founders" or at least one of the founding members of their churches' health ministry programs. Thus, it is important to describe some basic steps in establishing a health ministry, such as identifying the administrative and religious cultures of the church, working with the pastor and/or other clergy or parishioners, establishing a health cabinet, conducting a parish health needs assessment, and creating a health ministry team.

The Pastoral Leadership Culture of the Faith Community

It is essential for a potential parish nurse to possess a clear understanding of the church culture, both pastoral and religious, in which he or she will be working. The pastoral leadership culture relates to the pastoral administrative style of the church in terms of power and decision making. For example, in some churches, the pastor has final decision-making authority about new programs to initiate in the church. In other congregations, decision making about or recommending of programs such as health ministry is delegated to fall within the purview of a body such as a church vestry or parish council. Thus, the key individual(s) whom a nurse, wishing to initiate a health ministry program, should approach initially may vary from congregation to congregation.

The Pastor

Regardless of the pastoral administrative structure, however, a first basic step in initiating parish health ministry is to approach the church pastor (if the impetus for the program was not initially suggested by him or her). The relationship between a parish nurse and his or her pastor is critical to the success of a health ministry program; this must be even more carefully established if the nurse and pastor are not of the same religious denomination. Trust between a pastor and parish nurse is a key element in promoting a seamless initiation of the ministry. As parish nursing and parish health ministry programs grow and develop, it is anticipated that seminaries will begin to orient their clergy students to the existence of such ministries. At present, however, some seasoned pastors may be only vaguely aware of the concepts of parish nursing and parish health ministry, and serious work might need to be done by a parish nurse to educate a congregation's pastor.

Once a pastor has accepted the concepts of parish nursing and health ministry, he or she may well refer the nurse to a designated church committee, such as the social ministry committee, to seek further support and approval. Nevertheless, it remains essential that a pastor be fully informed and supportive of all the activities involving a potential parish nursing initiative within his or her church for the effort to flourish. It is the task of the pastor to announce the program from the pulpit in order to generate parishioners' interest and participation; the pastor also must approve, in most cases, advertising a parish nursing/health ministry initiative in a church bulletin or newsletter. And, finally, any expenses incurred by the initiation of a health ministry program, even if minor, will, in most churches, need the final blessing of the pastor. Two additional contributions of the pastor supportive of a health ministry effort suggested by Granger Westberg (1990) are the pastor's contacts with other parishes in the community that may wish to initiate a parish health ministry, and the provision of a strong biblical context within which to situate the ministry activities (p. 24).

To work collegially with a church pastor, it is important for a parish nurse to learn and understand his or her pastor's earlier noted administrative "style." If a pastor assumes a "hands-on" approach for church activities, he or she may wish to attend meetings related to a newly forming health ministry team; if the pastor believes in delegating selected church activities to associates or church committees, a written or verbal report of ongoing health ministry activities may be adequate.

In discussing important "elements of collaboration in ministry partnerships," Margaret Clark (2000) highlights three concepts: "learning," shared reflection related to the meaning and parameters of a topic; "boundaries," "lines of separation" distinguishing ministry roles; and "dialogue," discussion of ministry activities characterized by "openness," "meekness" (peacefulness), and "trust" (pp. 314–316). These "elements of collaboration" provide an excellent basis for establishing a pastor–nurse relationship for the parish nurse seeking to establish a health ministry program within a faith community. While some of the elements may need to be worked at by both pastor and nurse, an underlying presentation of self by the nurse as having a willingness to learn from the pastor's ministerial experience, an understanding of the boundaries between pastor and church staff, and a readiness to talk about parish nursing and health ministry openly, peacefully, and trustingly, greatly facilitates the nurse–pastor relationship.

As mentioned previously, now that parish nursing/health ministry is becoming better known among clergy, in some instances a pastor may suggest the initiation of a program. The pastor, however, may still need more detailed information about the parish nursing role; and he or she should be a participant in the planning of the church's health ministry program, if only from the posture of final approval. It is also important to meet with other clergy associated with the church, such as associate pastors or deacons, to keep them informed of a health ministry initiative, obtain their feedback, and hopefully gain their full support of the program.

If, after speaking with a church's pastor and associate clergy, a parish nurse(s) is directed to meet with a parishioner group within the church, such as the vestry, the parish council, or a social concerns committee, it is important to determine which member(s) of the body to approach first. For example, most parish councils or social concerns committees are led by chairpersons who coordinate the meeting times and activities of the groups. It can greatly facilitate the approval of a potential program if the relevant committee chair has been given a "heads up," a preliminary explanation of the initiative, prior to bringing the issue to committee. As with the pastor and clergy, it is anticipated that if a committee chairperson is supportive of a program, the presentation to the group will be received in a more positive light.

The Religious Culture of the Faith Community

The religious culture of a church relates predominantly to the way in which a faith community's spirituality is lived out in terms of personal prayer, worship services, community service, religious gatherings such as bible study, and the administration of the sacraments. For some congregations, the religious orientation tends to be more "activist" in living out the gospel message of service to those in need; that is, the parishioners who are able engage in volunteer service activities, such as feeding the homeless, visiting prisoners, or working with youth groups in underserved areas. Such churches may already have active social concerns committees or similar bodies, which may be willing to either assimilate a parish nursing/health ministry initiative as a new dimension of the social gospel ministry or might provide support and guidance as the program begins.

If a faith community tends to focus more on ministering to the spiritual needs of the congregation, the initiating of a parish nursing/health ministry program may need more discussion among the church community. The concept of a parish health program may be viewed, initially, as an activity that falls outside the usual spiritual ministries of the church. In the very early days of parish nursing, a question frequently raised was this: "What is the difference between parish nursing and community health nursing?" That difference has now been clarified and acknowledged by the American Nurses Association, as well as by many parishes with existing parish nursing programs. For a congregation unfamiliar with the concept, however, a parish nursing initiative may have to move more slowly and with more explanation and discussion. Informing and gaining support of pastors, associate clergy, and parishioners is essential to the success of any parish health ministry program initiative.

The Health Cabinet

Pastor Granger Westberg (1990) asserts that "every church with a parish nurse should have a health cabinet or committee that can become a true support for the nurse" (p. 26). A faith community may already have an existing health cabinet or a similar group with a different label, such as a "health and wellness cabinet," a "wellness committee," or a "health and welfare committee," or no such group may exist within the church. Most health cabinets or wellness committees are composed of approximately seven to 10 parishioners who have an interest is advising and supporting a church's ministry to the ill and infirm but who may not themselves be able to carry out health ministry activities, for physical, logistical, or other reasons. In smaller congregations, members of a health cabinet might also be health ministers. Having a separate body to oversee and advise a health ministry team, however, can be a distinct advantage if the congregation is large enough for this kind of administrative structure. Health cabinet members are generally volunteers, serving with the approval of the pastor, and are usually men and women representing a variety of ages and professional backgrounds. The parish nurse is generally not a member of the health cabinet, although, again, this may occur, especially within very small faith communities.

The parish nurse initiating a health ministry program will find the work greatly facilitated if he or she is supported by a health cabinet. Because the parish nurse is, in most cases, introducing a new concept and a new program to his or her church community, things may not always go as smoothly as desired, even with the support of a pastor and majority of parishioners. Some individual members of the church may express a preference for spiritual ministry to be carried out only by ordained clergy of the denomination; others may feel that health issues are not within the purview of the church ministry. Most parish nurses will admit to some "rocky places" along the path to integrating a health ministry program within their congregations. The health cabinet provides an oversight group to support, counsel, and even mediate if any problems or concerns occur relative to the conduct of the ministry.

Health cabinet members may also take over the responsibility for such activities as fund-raising; suggesting health and wellness programs for the parish; educating the congregation about the importance of the parish nurse/health ministry activities; setting health ministry policy; soliciting and approving potential health ministry volunteers; developing promotional materials for the church bulletin, newsletter, and/or bulletin board(s); and evaluating the ongoing success or needs of the health ministry program.

Perhaps the most important point to remember in initiating a parish nursing/health ministry program is that, despite early difficulties and potential roadblocks, in the end the programs are generally appreciated and deeply valued by both pastors and parishioners who have benefited from the ministry. Parish nurses beginning a new health ministry program must, however, be willing to take risks. When I began hospital chaplaincy training, the medical center's Catholic chaplain commissioned me as a Eucharistic minister that I might be able to offer the sacrament of Communion when I made rounds; he felt this could be an added dimension of ministry for the Catholic patients I visited. The chaplain warned me, nonetheless, not to feel hurt if a patient refused to receive Communion from my hands because I was not a member of the "ordained" clergy in the Catholic Church. He reminded me that even though I had been commissioned as a Eucharistic minister, with his blessing, some Catholics feel that only clergy should administer the sacraments, and he advised: "We have to respect their attitude in this." It was, thus, with some trepidation that I began to offer Communion to patients when visiting; to my delight, the response was joy and gratitude. No one refused to accept Communion from me! The point I needed to remember, however, was that if a patient did refuse, his or her response must be respected.

After gaining the support of a congregation's pastor, administrative staff, and, hopefully, a significant number of parishioners, the next important step in initiating a parish health ministry program is to carry out a parish health needs assessment. This not only provides important health/illness data to assist the ministry team in setting priorities in healthcare activities, but also serves as a vehicle to introduce the ministry.

Conducting a Parish Health Needs Assessment

The goal of a parish health assessment is to determine the overall health/illness needs and concerns of the congregation. It is also an important way of letting the parishioners know about the health ministry initiative within their church and of giving them the opportunity for input into the offerings and activities of the ministry. In discussing the concept of parish health assessment, Olson and Clark (2000) point out that the process itself is a way to introduce the congregation to parish nursing and parish health ministry: "As the nurse is conducting a complete assessment of congregational needs, she or he will also be finding ways to educate the congregation about the types of needs or issues that could be brought to the faith community nurse" (p. 237). They add: "It often takes up to two years from the time a nurse is hired by a faith community before most of the members of that community are aware of the services offered by the new staff member" (p. 237).

A parish health needs assessment may be conducted in a variety of ways, depending on such factors as a congregation's size, number of parishioners needing assistance in completing the questionnaire (e.g., elderly with vision difficulties), and available methods of distributing the survey tool. These issues can be discussed with the faith community's health cabinet or health ministry advisory committee. In one church community assessment effort, carried out by the University of Massachusetts Amherst School of Nursing, focus groups were added to the process to discuss such issues as individual or family health concerns, whether the church has "a role to play in meeting the health needs" of members, and "type of services" that the parish nurse should offer (Swinney, Anson-Wonkka, Maki, & Corneau, 2001, p. 42). Interestingly, although the school of nursing project was well developed and implemented (it had been requested by a "large urban parish"), of the 800 questionnaires made available during a weekend period (the assessment had also been advertised from the pulpit and in the church bulletin), only 53 percent, or 421 questionnaires, were returned (Swinney et al., 2001, p. 42). It would be important to know why almost 50 percent of the parishioners did not complete the tools.

In carrying out a parish health needs assessment, some procedures should be built in to distribute and assist those who are homebound and unable to pick up and/or fill out the tool because of disabilities. If a newly created parish nursing/health ministry team does not find it feasible to make home visits for the health assessment data collection, phone interviews with homebound parishioners might be conducted.

Based on the findings of the parish nursing/health ministry study the Gift of Faith in Chronic Illness, presented in Chapter 9, an individual parishioner health assessment form was developed (see Fig. 6.1).

Initiating the Program: The Parish Nurse as Health Ministry Team Leader

In terms of the initial organizing of any parish social ministry, several basic concepts should be considered, some of which include the following: the ministry is "linked to faith development" . . . with a focus on bringing about "a more just and loving world"; "the effort touches a system of values"; "thought and planning [go] into organizing and developing leadership"; the "efforts are . . . supported by the entire parish community"; "the ministry team involves the people experiencing the problems" that the program is attempting to alleviate; and volunteers are recruited in a "systematic way" (Ulrich, 2001, pp. 25–26). Ulrich's latter suggestion regarding the systematic recruiting of ministry team members is supported by Baard and Aridas (2001), who emphasize the importance of carefully describing ministry positions within the church; they advise preparing descriptions of "the ministry [title]"; "position"; "purpose of the position"; "responsibilities"; "qualifications"; "amount of time required"; "where ministry is performed"; "length of commitment"; who the "on-site training [is] provided by"; who the position is "responsible to"; who "support [is] provided by"; and "benefits" (e.g., spiritual/emotional) (pp. 123–124).

There are a number of suggestions in the literature as to how to approach the actual task of beginning a parish health ministry program. Carol Zarek (1990) offers five steps that she believes "any parish can apply," including "locate the sick, the frail elderly and the homebound," "assess their needs and those of their families," "execute an appropriate pastoral response," "evaluate the effectiveness of the first three steps," and "revise the process" (p. 105). These steps might well be carried out following the earlier suggested activities of praying, experiencing a call to parish health ministry, learning about the administrative and religious culture of the faith community, speaking with the pastor and church leaders, establishing or working with a health cabinet or wellness committee, and conducting a parish health needs assessment.

Some other important issues that must be addressed early on in the ministry-planning process include: identifying the theology and philosophy undergirding the health ministry, such as the gospel message contained in Matthew 25:36; stating the goals of the ministry, both short-term and long-term aims and desired outcomes;

Parish Health Needs Assessment

Come, you that are blessed by my Father, inherit the kingdom prepared for you from the foundation of the world . . . for I was . . . sick and you took care of me.

—Matthew 25:34–35

Introduction: The purpose of this parish health needs assessment questionnaire is to help [church name]'s parish nursing/health ministry team identify priorities in planning activities for the ministry. All information will be kept confidential; placing your name and address on the questionnaire is purely OPTIONAL.

A. *Personal Data (Optional)*

1. Name _____

   Address _____

   Phone Number _____ E-mail _____

B. *Demographic Data and Personal Health History*

2. Age _____ 3. Gender _____

4. Marital Status   Single ◯   Married ◯   Widowed ◯   Divorced ◯   Separated ◯

5. Household Members (who you live with)

   Alone _____

   Spouse _____

   Spouse and Children _____

   Adult Children _____

   Minor Children _____

   Other Relatives/Friends _____

6. Frequency of Church Attendance   Daily ◯   More than once a week ◯   Once a week ◯

   Once a month ◯   Less than once a month ◯   2 to 3 times a year ◯   Never ◯

7. Occupation (current/former) _____

8. Employment Status   Full-time ◯   Part-time ◯   Retired ◯

   Volunteer (Please specify number of hours per week) ◯ _____

9. Primary Illness Diagnosis (if any) _____

Parish Health Needs Assessment, page 2

10. Disability (if any) _____

11. Current Medications or Treatments (if any) _____

12. Other Diagnoses (please specify if any) _____

  Respiratory Conditions (e.g., COPD) _____

  Neurological Conditions (e.g., stroke) _____

  Psychiatric Conditions (e.g., depression) _____

  Circulatory Conditions (e.g., heart disease) _____

  Musculoskeletal Conditions (e.g., arthritis) _____

  Endocrine Conditions (e.g., diabetes) _____

  Gastrointestinal Conditions (e.g., reflux) _____

  Integumentary (skin) Conditions (e.g., dermatitis) _____

  Other Diagnosis(es) _____

13. Please specify any other medical or illness history that you would like the church health ministry team to know about:

  _____

  _____

C. *Specific Health/Illness-Related Needs*

1. Physical needs in the home (e.g., shopping; preparing meals) _____

  _____

2. Psychosocial needs at home (e.g., companionship; assistance with letter writing)

  _____

  _____

3. Spiritual needs at home (e.g., visit from a spiritual minister; prayer; the sacraments)

  _____

  _____

4. Health education/counseling at home (e.g., diabetic teaching)

  _____

  _____

Parish Health Needs Assessment, page 3

5. Legal advice at home (e.g., preparing a will; advance directives) _____

6. Transportation (e.g., to physician's office; church; grocery store) _____

    _____

7. Family respite assistance _____

    _____

D. *Suggested health promotion workshops that you would like to see the church's health ministry sponsor*:

1. Women's Health Issues _____

2. Men's Health Issues _____

3. Teen Addictions/Eating Disorders _____

4. Aging with Grace _____

5. Healthy Nutrition and Exercise _____

6. Stress Reduction Techniques _____

7. Diabetes Education _____

8. Alzheimer's Disease _____

9. Medicare and Medicaid Insurance _____

10. Advance Directives (Living Wills) _____

11. Coping with Grief and Bereavement _____

12. The Relationship between Faith and Health _____

E. *Suggestions for/response to the church's support of the parish nursing/health ministry initiative*:

    _____

    _____

Thank you for completing this questionnaire. Please feel free to add additional comments in the space below as desired.

    _____

    _____

    God bless you,
        the Parish Nursing/Health Ministry Team of [church name]'s Church

identifying the role of the parish nurse, whether the position is to be a paid or a volunteer activity and the approximate number of hours per week the nurse(s) might be expected to be available; describing what activities the health ministers will carry out and what activities fall outside of their roles; specifying who may become a health minister and what kind of personal experience or training he or she should have; identifying a space in which the parish nurse/health ministry may be located; describing resources within the church and the local community (and identifying any potential links with existing church programs, such as a Stephen Ministry); determining how the program will be funded and approximately what funding will be needed for start-up costs; planning how health ministry activities will be recorded or documented; describing lines of accountability within the program and the congregation; exploring whether issues of possible liability need to be discussed with the congregation's legal advisor(s), for example, discussing whether the parish health ministry program can be covered under a parish's general liability insurance; and finally, deciding how, when, and by whom the program will be evaluated.

While faith communities may vary greatly in ways of approaching these suggested phases in implementing a parish health ministry program, some more detailed explanations of the activities may prove helpful. These descriptions are derived from conversations with parish nurses from a variety of religious denominations who have already been through the process of initiating a health ministry program within their congregations (at the conclusion of the chapter, a case study of the initiation of parish nursing and a health ministry program in a West Coast church is presented as a lived experience, recorded by one of the nurses who facilitated the process).

Identifying the Theology of the Health Ministry.   This topic has been discussed broadly earlier. Suffice it to say here that regardless of how the theology of the health ministry is to be articulated, it is important to have key individuals involved in the conduct and oversight of the parish health ministry program involved, to some degree, in drafting and/or approving the ministry's mission statement. This provides an important sense of ownership of the ministry among parishioners who will be centrally involved in the work of the ministry. Involving the ministry team members, health or wellness cabinet (if one exists), and the pastor and/or church administrative staff in the process of developing the health ministry's mission statement also serves to facilitate the acceptance of the ministry within the congregation at large.

Stating the Long- and Short-Term Goals of the Health Ministry.   These goals, both short and long, might differ greatly depending upon multiple factors such as the congregation size, whether there is to be one or several parish nurses (the time to be committed to the ministry), and/or the availability of funding to support the ministry.

Nevertheless, it is essential that some goals be identified for the program to get off the ground. Some parish nurses report that they began very simply by planning monthly Sunday morning blood pressure screenings for the parishioners following worship services. A next step, in some cases, was to add a monthly or bimonthly column in the parish bulletin or newsletter on a health-related topic, such as nutrition and exercise or smoking-cessation modalities. A ministry may, thus, begin with one or two volunteer nurses identifying short-term goals such as the initiation of health education and blood pressure screening, with the hope that the effort will eventually develop into a functioning parish health ministry program. If a church has significant resources, both in terms of personnel and funding, at the initiation of a parish health ministry program, a plan identifying carefully delineated short- and long-term goals should be drafted to provide a blueprint for the future of the ministry.

Identifying and Describing the Parish Nurse Role.   The usual role behaviors of the parish nurse, educator, counselor, advocate, and referral agent, falling under the overarching role of spiritual companion in health and illness, are discussed in Chapter 3. Because parish nurses are currently functioning in a variety of logistical and functional parameters, the nurse's role must be clarified for each individual congregation. If the nurse is employed under a "congregation-based paid model," he or she will probably be expected to identify "office hours" in the church setting, as well as the possibility of home visits or phone consultations. Parish nurses working as "congregation-based volunteers" generally identify those activities and times that can be fitted around other work and/or family obligations. Some parish nurses begin to serve in a volunteer capacity with the hope that in the future the parish nursing position will become a paid position under the church staff budget.

Exploring Resources in the Church and the Community.   Depending, again, upon the size of a congregation and the kind of parish nursing/health ministry personnel who are available to initiate a ministry, this kind of exploration may vary significantly. It is important, however, even with a very small team or an individual parish nurse attempting to begin a program, to identify the helpful resources that may be available both in the community and in the church. Within the parishioner community itself there may be a number of retired persons who, if approached with an explanation of the concept, would be more than willing to give of their time and their resources to assist in the work of a health ministry; such volunteer work could provide meaningful personal satisfaction and pleasure for the parishioner, as well as greatly aid the parish nursing team. Another important resource for the ministry can be a cadre of homebound parishioners who, while they may not be able to support the work physically or financially, could add a magnificent *contemplative* dimension to the program through a ministry of prayer.

A parishioner group resource in some churches is a "Stephen Ministry." This ministry of service provides counseling and spiritual support for parishioners who are currently experiencing crises or great difficulties in their lives. Stephen ministers receive approximately 50 hours of training in such areas as listening, confidentiality, crisis intervention, prayer, and the Bible. Stephen ministers, who generally make a two-year commitment to the service, are excellent resources for referrals from a parish nurse or health minister who has identified a person needing this particular ministry.

In terms of community resources, many churches with social action committees already have compiled listings of local resources such as the VNA (Visiting Nurses Association), hospice care, meals-on-wheels, legal aid, and other groups that could be helpful both to homebound and active parishioners in need of such services. If such information is not available within a church directory, it can usually be obtained from local social service agencies.

Activities of Parish Health Ministers.   It is very important to identify early on a number of anticipated activities of parish health ministers, as this may stimulate the interest of potential parishioner volunteers who might otherwise have thought that they did not have the talents or skills to participate in such an effort. While activities such as home visiting, hospital visiting, or long-term care facility visiting of ill or disabled parishioners might be very appealing to some volunteers, these ministries might be intimidating to those who have no background in or affinity for working directly with the sick. Volunteer opportunities, however, such as running errands for the homebound—grocery shopping, picking up medications from a drugstore, or taking clothes to a dry cleaner—might capture the interest of those more reluctant to have direct involvement with the ill. Other viable options besides one-on-one patient contact should be offered to volunteers, such as assisting with paperwork (drafting of parish bulletin materials), organizing and setting up educational programs or blood pressure screening events, and assisting with communicating information about the health ministry program throughout the congregation.

A final issue is to plan educational offerings for those health ministry volunteers who wish it. Hospice training is excellent for volunteers willing to visit with terminally ill parishioners or to provide respite hours for the parishioners' families. And there are a variety of videos that teach the importance of nonmedical persons providing care and support during illness; a fine example is the video titled *Almost Home,* in which Franciscan Thea Bowman describes the value of her family and friends' caring companionship during the experience of terminal cancer.

Specifying Who May Become a Health Minister.   As noted earlier, presenting a congregation with examples of expected activities of nonnursing or medical health ministry volunteers opens the door to the program to many parishioners who may not have thought they had the skills to fulfill a health ministry role. Generally, churches welcome all adults who feel called to participate in a health ministry program. If the team thinks creatively, there should be no exceptions; even parishioners who are physically or cognitively impaired may be able to contribute to the ministry with small tasks such as stuffing envelopes for mailing a health assessment questionnaire, collating materials, or serving as a "prayer partner" for one of the more actively involved parish nurses or health ministers.

Identifying a Space for the Health Ministry.   In most churches, large and small, "space" is a very treasured, and often limited, commodity. Thus, a parish's allocation of space for a parish nursing/health ministry program, even a very small space, represents an important public witness of the value placed on the ministry by the pastor and the overall congregation. Most nurses are accustomed to working out of relatively cramped quarters and would not initially expect that an entire infirmary be set up. It is important, however, that a room affording some degree of privacy for parishioner consultations is assigned to the health ministry. Equipment may be limited, but simple assessment tools such as stethoscopes, sphygmomanometers, thermometers, and a scale can hopefully be purchased, or may even be donated from local physicians or clinics. A few basic items such as band-aids, cotton balls, ace bandages, hydrogen-peroxide and alcohol should also be available.

Locating Funding for Start-Up Costs.   The need for some basic equipment and supplies can be covered by a relatively low budget, which may be donated by one or several parishioners, or may be derived from a church social concerns committee allocation. As most parish nurses beginning health ministry programs hope that in the future, their jobs as well as the equipment and supplies needed for the ministry will be included in their church's overall budget, it is important to keep a record of equipment and supplies used, even if these have been donated or funded privately. Thus, the parish nurse leading the effort will be able to submit an adequate and appropriate budget to church administration for a coming fiscal year.

Defining Lines of Accountability within the Ministry and the Church.   It is important to determine at the initiation of a health ministry program who is the ministry leader and to whom that leader reports in the church administration. Generally, a parish nurse is the leader or coordinator of a parish health ministry program; initially, he or she may *be* the program, as some churches begin simply by announcing that they now have a "parish nurse." Nevertheless, in planning for the future, these roles should be clearly identified; this is essential for large churches that begin with several parish nurses, nonnurse volunteers, and a complex administrative clergy structure. As ministry coordinator, a parish nurse may designate other nurses to assume such roles as soliciting and training volunteers, recommending community resources, or planning health/illness educational offerings for parishioners. Ultimately, the parish nurse coordinator will be responsible for communicating with the pastor or his or her designated representative, submitting reports of ministry activities, and managing the ministry budget.

Identifying Legal Liability Issues.   A discussion of legal and ethical issues related to parish nursing is discussed in Chapter 3. The important task of the parish nurse initiating a health ministry program is to understand his or her church administration's wishes in terms of liability insurance related to the newly created ministry. Some churches ask that their parish nurses, even though not practicing nursing involving invasive procedures, do carry individual malpractice insurance. Other churches have been able to include parish nurses on their overall church staff liability insurance plans. It would be helpful for a parish nurse coordinator to speak not only to the pastor and/or his or her representative, but also to the church's legal counsel, about this issue.

Conducting a Program Evaluation.   A final yet very important dimension of initiating a parish health ministry program is to include a plan for ministry evaluation. Depending upon how many nurses and volunteers are involved, and how quickly it is anticipated that the program will be "up and running," a cursory evaluation as early as three or six months into the ministry can be very helpful in straightening out beginning "wrinkles" or rough spots in the conduct of the ministry. The evaluation may also result in the provision of some excellent suggestions for additional ministry activities to be included in the coming months. If the ministry team is smaller and it is expected that the beginning effort will move more slowly, the coordinator may wish to wait until the end of the first year for an evaluation, when some more substantive results and/or problems may be identified (Table 6.1 presents a list of important guidelines for developing a parish health ministry program).

TABLE 6.1 GUIDELINES FOR DEVELOPING A PARISH HEALTH MINISTRY PROGRAM

1. Describe the role of the parish health minister.
2. Explain the biblical spirituality of the parish health minister's vocation.
3. State who may become a parish health minister.
4. Specify the kind of training/orientation required to become a parish health minister.
5. Give examples of potential parish health ministry activities.
6. Share a statement of support for the ministry from the church pastor (and other clergy or church leaders, if appropriate).
7. Broadly describe who the potential recipients of parish health ministry might be.
8. Identify a parish contact person (usually a parish nurse) with whom parishioners interested in parish health ministry might consult.
9. Present a brief description of the commissioning ceremony for parish health ministers (if appropriate) as a formal validation of a parishioner's response to God's call to serve.

Working with Volunteers

> There are varieties of gifts but the same Spirit; and there are varieties of services, but the same Lord; and there are varieties of activities, but it is the same God who activates all of them in everyone. To each is given the manifestation of the Spirit for the common good.
>
> —*1 Corinthians 12:4–6*

While all of the activities listed previously need not be carried out by a parish nurse personally, he or she will most probably be the congregational minister identified to coordinate the planning and execution of all phases of the health ministry. Again, this is greatly determined by the size of the congregation and the overall administrative structure. If a health cabinet exists separate from the designated parish nurse(s) and health ministers, a number of supportive ministry activities can be assigned to volunteers from that committee; if not, more of the ground work may fall on a parish nurse (or nurses) and nonnurse health ministry volunteers.

Once the basic parish health needs assessment is completed, the data must be analyzed to get an overall sense of the needs of the church's individual parishioners. The nurse may choose to work with the data personally, or may solicit volunteers from the congregation to assume the responsibility. If the faith community is not too large, summary of the data might be done by a homebound person capable of working with questionnaires; if the database is quite large, perhaps a parishioner trained in research and possessed of good computer skills may be willing to process and analyze the data. After the parish nurse or a fledgling parish nursing committee has the findings of the parish health needs assessment, the members can begin to identify the number and types of volunteers who might be needed to assist in initiating the ministry.

William Bausch (2000), in his book *The Parish of the Next Millennium*, observes that in the past church volunteers used to just "help out." Today's volunteers, he asserts, "are apt to have a sense of ownership whose larger objective is the overall need and benefit to the parish as a whole" (p. 104). This "sense of ownership" can be a very positive asset to a parish health ministry team, provided the volunteer's initial sense of calling and enthusiasm can be sustained over time. In a parish handbook, *Attracting and Managing Volunteers*, Donna Pinsoneault (2001) offers a number of suggestions to "generate retention" of parish volunteers; some of these include offering "meaningful work," planning "orientations to set the tone," scheduling "training as needed," "respecting everyone" as members of the faith community, "sharing faith" (e.g., prayer, scripture reading, song), building in "continuing learning opportunities," expecting individual "needs" and "charisms," "creat[ing] space" for volunteers to work and meet, and "say[ing] thank you frequently" (pp. 83–88). Admittedly, some of these activities may be implemented later on as the volunteer team grows and develops; they can, however, be useful thoughts to integrate into an initial plan for working with volunteers.

A last point about working with church volunteers is the importance of letting parishioners know that their potential services are of value; that, as Saint Paul pointed out: "There are different kinds of gifts . . . and to each individual the manifestation of the Spirit is given for some benefit." Sometimes very talented parishioners, especially those who are older, may feel that they no longer have anything to give to their faith communities; yet, because of their life experience these may be some of the very individuals a parish nurse would most like to recruit as volunteer parish health ministers. In exploring the situation of "ministering when you think you can't," Joe Paprocki (1998) discusses the "reluctant minister" who may have a variety of seemingly legitimate excuses for avoiding the ministry, such as not having time, inadequate theological background, or lack of church finances for a project (pp. 15–16). While it is certainly true that physical or logistical exigencies might truly prevent some parishioners from participating in volunteer ministries, Paprocki argues, "Jesus . . . challenges us to see beyond logical limitations . . . to explore the possibilities and potential that exist despite the logical limitations" (p. 16). "When you get down to it," he argues, "the very notion of living as a Christian is not logical" (p. 16).

I think that perhaps one of the most "logically" valid excuses in a potential volunteer's mind for not participating in a ministry is a feeling of inadequacy, not just of theological background, but of the gifts or talents needed for a particular project. Such an excuse may indeed be appropriate and valid. For example, if a parishioner becomes very distressed or anxious being around sick people and/or admits to fainting upon seeing blood, the health ministry task of visiting the ill in the hospital or in a long-term care facility is not a good idea. If, however, this same parishioner feels called to support the church's health ministry, he or she might help with preparing promotional materials about the program, assisting with planning health education workshops for the congregation, or even doing parishioner interactional ministry by volunteering for grocery shopping or picking up of prescriptions for homebound congregants. And one never knows where these activities may ultimately lead.

One of my favorite "volunteer conversion" stories was told to me by a dear friend, Sister Anna, a "retired"—and I use the word *retired* very loosely—sister who had been a schoolteacher all of her professional life. Although her mother was a nurse, Sister Anna never felt called to work with the sick; she did not even particularly like to visit the hospital. Then one summer, Sister Anna needed a place to stay while finishing a graduate degree in education. And, as it happened, the most convenient and available location was the convent wing of a local Catholic hospital. Although she was a boarder, Sister Anna asked the superior of the community for a small "charge," or housework assignment, to assist with the upkeep of the convent that was providing her hospitality. She commented: "I expected her to ask me to tidy up the community room several times a week or something like that." After some thought, the superior sought out Sister Anna and explained that she had decided upon a task that would be very helpful to the "hospital sisters." Sister Anna's summer charge was to visit all of the Catholic patients each evening in order to prepare a Communion list for those who wished to receive the sacrament the next morning. Sister Anna related, laughing, "When I volunteered I thought I'd be dusting the community room; I almost fainted when Sister said I had to go and visit patients!"

Although she undertook her task with no little anxiety and trepidation, in a very short time Sister Anna's loving heart and generous spirit had been completely captivated by the experience of hospital ministry. She loved the patients and they loved her. At the end of the summer, the superior announced that there was to be an evening picnic for all of the visiting sisters in the house and asked them to indicate their plans to attend by signing a list on the bulletin board. When Sister Anna did not add her name, the sister superior asked why she did not plan to attend the celebration. Sister

Anna replied: "Well, it's in the evening and that's my time to visit the patients; I can't miss that!"

In concluding this narrative, it is important to explain that at the time Sister Anna told me the story of her "volunteer conversion," she had been, for the past seven years (and still is) director of pastoral care at the same hospital where her love of working with the ill had been born and nurtured. In describing her role in hospital pastoral ministry, Sister Anna observed: "God has been so good to me; I wouldn't want to [be] doing anything else!"

The Health Ministry Team Members

Health Ministry Activities

It has been pointed out that there are "as many examples of health ministry activities a congregation can initiate as there are creative ideas within the congregation" (Chandler & Berry, 2001, p. 986). As well as providing a vehicle for sharing the "personal and professional gifts" of a church's parishioners, "starting a health ministry can have a galvanizing effect on a community; few people are politically opposed to health," observe Chandler and Berry, "and the resultant shared goals have the serendipitous effect of forging bonds in disparate groups within the community" (p. 986). And, as mentioned earlier, health ministry volunteering may also call forth, refine, and develop skills and gifts of which an individual was previously unaware.

Some of the most well received activities carried out by the two health ministers who participated in the study described in Chapter 9, the Gift of Faith in Chronic Illness, involved "presence" and the bringing of the sacrament of Communion to homebound or long-term-care-facility-bound parishioners. While these two members of our research team were not parish nurses, they did have significant experience both in pastoral ministry and in working with people. The health ministers were very positively received when making "home" visits to assess and intervene in regard to the spiritual needs of study participants; study members also greatly appreciated the ministry of Holy Communion being carried out on their visits.

Aside from visiting as spiritual companions to those who are ill and infirm, health ministers can carry out a multitude of important and helpful tasks, a number of which have already been identified, such as grocery shopping, picking up prescriptions, and providing several hours of respite for family caregivers in the home. Some other health ministry–related activities appropriate for nonnurse volunteers might include assisting an elderly parishioner with reading or letter writing; reading scripture and praying with homebound parishioners; bringing a parishioner up to date on the local and national news if he or she has difficulty watching/hearing television; assisting a frail parishioner with eating, if necessary; straightening up a bedroom or nursing home room to make the environment more comforting to the infirm parishioner; organizing a card-writing project among Sunday school children to send notes to those who are home-bound; planning phone follow-up for the homebound; and, most important, simply becoming a loving friend who represents the care and support of the parishioner's faith community.

Another activity that might well fall within the purview of a parish health minis-ter is the creation of a "loan closet" or a "care equipment closet," in which usable but no longer needed healthcare articles donated by church members are collected. The closet may include such items as crutches, walkers, bedside commodes, overbed tray tables, air mattresses, wheelchairs, blood pressure cuffs, and stethoscopes. These items are often given to the loan closet for other parishioners to use, after a congre-gant's loved one who used them has passed away. New or clean and slightly used cloth-ing that an infirm parishioner may appreciate can also be collected, for example, bed jackets, warm slippersocks, house slippers, robes, nightshirts or nightgowns, and pa-jamas. The donation of both equipment and clothing that may be of use to others can often be a turning point in the grieving process for a parishioner who has lost a loved one. The act of charity may also be of great assistance to the recipient and his or her family who may not have to purchase the items, some of which are very expensive.

A well-received activity that, as mentioned earlier, may fall within the role of the health minister is the planning and organization of parish education workshops that would be of interest to a large number of parishioners. Some of the topics identified in the Gift of Faith in Chronic Illness study are included as potential topics in the Parish Health Needs Assessment; these include men's and women's health issues, teen ad-dictions, aging issues, nutrition and exercise, stress reduction, disease conditions such as diabetes and Alzheimer's disease, Medicare and Medicaid issues, advance directives (living wills and durable power of attorney), coping with grief and bereavement, and the relationship between faith and health. Some additional parish education topics that might be planned and coordinated by a health minister are parenting, first aid in the home, coping with pregnancy: prayer and meditation, child bike safety, and re-tirement planning.

And a final activity that may be coordinated by the parish nurse with the assistance of a number of health ministers is the planning of a church "health fair"; the fair may be open to the local community, as well as to the faith community parishioners. "Encouraging positive choices is basic to health fairs," asserts nurse Pattie Boyes

(2001, p. 17). Boyes adds: "Health fairs encourage well-being in a festive atmosphere," and that well-being may include both spiritual as well as physical health (Boyes, 2001, p. 17). A health fair is usually, though not always, open to a church's local community, thus providing both outreach to and connection with the church's neighbors. Health fairs generally include a number of booths presenting both services and education related to health and illness. There is no charge for admittance to the fair; donations may be accepted.

Each year my school of nursing conducts a very successful health fair, on campus, for the university community and for our neighbors in the local urban community. The planning and carrying out of the health fair is done by junior and senior nursing students under the guidance of a faculty advisor. Some of the educational and service activities presented in the 20 to 30 booths at the fair include blood pressure screening; cholesterol screening; hand-washing education (for children); spiritual counseling; blood sugar testing and diabetes education; educational materials on cardiovascular disease, osteoporosis, Alzheimer's disease, mental health, and alcoholism; and nutrition and exercise demonstrations.

A similar health fair could quite easily be organized by a church health ministry committee, employing resources from local hospitals and social service agencies to man some of the booths, as well as eliciting volunteers from the church community. This is an excellent team activity to acquaint church community members with each other, as well as with representatives from local community agencies and visitors from the immediate neighborhood who have come to participate in the event (Table 6.2 presents a list of suggested activities that might be carried out by parish health ministers).

Accountability and Documentation

It is important for both nurses and health ministers to document their activities; this is for the protection of the ministry, as well as to provide an ongoing witness of the value and usefulness of the program and its impact on improving the quality of parishioners' lives. Because of the newness of the disciplines of parish nursing and parish health ministry, those involved in carrying out the ministry roles are currently employing a great variety of methods of documentation. In practice, it often seems to be a case of "whatever works" for a particular faith community. A parish nurse who recently attended a parish nursing education course reported that it was suggested to the participants that different methods might be used but the important thing to remember was to carry out the activity in some way. "The bottom line, we were taught," she reported, was "document, document, document!"

Table 6.2 SUGGESTED ACTIVITIES FOR PARISH HEALTH MINISTERS

1. Home, hospital, and nursing home/assisted care facility visitation

    Praying with parishioners

    Bringing holy Communion (if appropriate)

    Reading scripture or other spiritual books

    Listening and visiting with parishioners; sharing news of the church or other areas of interest

    Counseling/advising on spiritual/health-related issues (as appropriate)

2. Running errands such as grocery shopping or picking up prescriptions (for homebound elders)

3. Phone ministry to homebound parishioners

4. Providing periods of respite for family caregivers

5. Writing notes/holiday cards to parishioners who are hospitalized, homebound, or living in nursing homes/assisted care facilities

6. Writing parish health ministry articles for the church bulletin

7. Assisting with the planning and coordinating of health education programs for the congregation

8. Assisting with organizing and coordinating health promotion programs such as blood pressure screening

9. Organizing a prayer partner program for the church

10. Organizing and maintaining a loan closet of healthcare supplies for ill or disabled parishioners

11. Planning and coordinating a church health fair

12. Communicating with other interested parishioners about the health ministry and its needs

The Commissioning Ceremony

A "commissioning ceremony" for both parish nurses and parish health ministers may in some congregations consist of one celebration. Most parish nursing education programs, such as that described in Chapter 3, include a religious ceremony of "commissioning" or "blessing and sending forth" at the conclusion of the course. At that time the newly commissioned parish nurse is presented with a pin, similar to a nursing graduation pin, identifying the university, school, or organization sponsoring the parish nursing education. A health minister may have attended a seminary or college health ministry program.

Regardless of whether a parish nurse or health minister has been commissioned by an educational organization, it is important to have a religious ceremony of commissioning take place either during or immediately following one of his or her home church's worship services. At that time, the pastor may say a few words related to the ministry. Then the parish nurse(s) and health ministers can then be called forth and blessed by the pastor and deacons and, in some churches, the entire congregation. A health ministry lapel pin, designed by the church, may be distributed along with flowers to the newly commissioned team members.

This commissioning of parish nurses and health ministers within the church setting validates the ministerial role of the health ministry participants, acquaints the parishioners with the underlying concept of the program, and allows for the blessing of the pastor and parishioners on their newly commissioned parish nurses and health ministers. The commissioning represents a joyous event of celebrating the parish health ministers' response to the gospel message of Jesus: "I was ill and you cared for me."

The Lived Experience of Initiating a Parish Nursing/Health Ministry Program

One of the best ways for a parish nurse to get some practical suggestions about initiating a health ministry program in his or her church is to explore methods used by those who have already gone through the process. To provide one detailed example, I asked a new bachelor of science in nursing graduate who had recently helped her pastor and two other nurses initiate a parish nursing and health ministry program within their faith community whether she would describe the history and process. This is her response:

> The parish, located [on the West Coast of the United States] was founded in 1906 in a predominantly Italian community. Today, the parish serves 2500 families and has a large elderly population. As the population aged, the need for parish nurses became painstakingly clear as fewer and fewer long-time, devout parishioners were seen attending services or other parish functions. The one priest, accompanied by one deacon, assigned to the parish were beginning to find it extremely difficult to meet the needs of the growing congregation. [The parish currently serves roughly 10,000 people.] Having long depended on the volunteer hours of the senior citizens of the parish, who are now slowly aging and dying off, the pastor had to find alternate means to reach all of his parishioners. In addition to revitalized youth programs, the pastor turned to parish nursing for a portion of the answer.

[Several years ago] one woman, a retired RN, tried to implement a parish nursing program. She met a lot of resistance from the clergy that were in-house at that time. After two years of trying to work with the clergy, and finding minimal interest from the congregation, she gave up on the program and eventually even left the parish. In 1998, the present pastor of the parish recognized the need for parish nursing. Not being able to convince the council in charge of budgeting for the parish, he was not able to find the funding necessary to make this a paid position. In the winter of the year 2000, the pastor learned of my involvement with a research study involving parish nursing, and was greatly interested in what we were doing. He and I communicated throughout the spring of 2001 about the study and how home visits were conducted.

In August of 2001, my pastor approached [me] and two other long-time parishioners, who were RNs, about beginning a small parish nursing ministry within the parish. One of the RNs had just completed her parish nursing certificate and was very enthusiastic about the prospect of beginning a program; [she], however, felt overwhelmed with what it might mean. The other [nurse] was very enthusiastic as well, but claimed to not know a thing about parish nursing, what her role would be, or if she would be able to find the time. She has since received her certificate in parish nursing as well and does all she can to aid the program.

In the beginning, my contribution to the group was nominal since I was not a parish nurse; I merely had experience with home visiting. I functioned as a consultant, really, as the program was launching. After meeting with the two nurses and my pastor several times [last year], we formed a group [parish nursing committee], whose initial function was going to simply make parishioners aware of our existence, write small informative entries once a month into the church bulletin related to prominent medical issues (hypertension, diabetes, breast cancer, etc.), and to run a monthly blood pressure screening. Our pastor has been supportive from the first day and does what he can to make our ideas realities; however, all funds must be raised by us. Initially, our reception within the parish, although not cold, was less than we desired. Attendance at our blood pressure screenings was minimal, and people simply seemed not to grasp what we were trying to do. Our pastor suggested combining the blood pressure screening with the monthly "coffee and doughnuts" Sunday, hoping that would at least bring people through the area. Although this was clearly not a "healthy" solution to our attendance problem, we thought it could be a great temporary solution.

Our next screening [a few months later] had over 100 people come to it. People began to depend on the service and appreciated what it did for them.

We were able to talk to them about hypertension or other health problems, and the parishioners really came to know us and trust us. [Several months later, the parish nursing group] began conducting two BP screenings each month, neither of which are on "coffee and doughnut" Sunday. Attendance [at the screening] was up on both Sundays; we now have about 350 parishioners having their BPs taken monthly. The RNs have suggested that some hypertensive patients seek medical advice. We document these referrals and follow up on them over the phone.

[The parish nursing committee] had a meeting a few months ago and we made it open to all parishioners who felt they had a "gift to serve God's people through parish nursing [and health ministry]." Fifteen people attended the meeting: five current RNs, one physical therapist, one physician's assistant, and eight retired RNs, MAs, and MDs. Our main goal was to discuss and establish some sort of home visiting program to help alleviate the strain on our clergy, and this was accomplished. The five current RNs will be doing the visits, and each of us is going to pursue our parish nursing certificates [for those who have not had a parish nursing course]. The other members of [the health ministry group] are going to contact parishioners who have requested Communion visits to determine if they were open to visits by parish nurses and to schedule times for us to visit if they in fact are.

This program has kicked off and is going beautifully. The five RNs had a small in-service/retreat day with the pastor to discuss duties and responsibilities. We have met and discussed this ministry since it began, and we all agree that it is doing the parishioners a lot of good. However, we all also concur that we feel very richly blessed by God to be a part of such a ministry and that the graces we have received as a result of the ministry are immeasurable.

[The parish nursing and health ministry group] also decided to publish a parish health survey in order to determine the concerns and needs of the parish related to health care. This was distributed and the response was incredible. During our meeting [the following month], it was decided that an informative and interactive booth would be created for "coffee and doughnut" Sunday each month. The booth would be related to one of the topics suggested in the survey. This idea was strongly supported by all 15 members of [the group] and our pastor was elated with our progress as a group. The topic for this month was diabetes; a retired RN, as well as a volunteer parishioner who is an endocrinologist, received patients after each mass and gave out advice and information. The endocrinologist donated a glucometer that was raffled off. Hypertension will be the focus of the booth the coming month.

One of the retired RNs commented that she had just been to a senior expo in Sacramento, and she found that extremely informative and proposed the idea of a health fair. I was the only one with any experience with health fairs, so I was placed in charge of this. We have planned it for a Sunday [several months from now] and the response from the community has been amazing. Each of the now 20 members of [the parish nursing and health ministry group] has agreed to create and staff a booth; and many parishioners involved in the medical profession have stepped forward to create booths related to their specialties. There will be over 40 booths in all, ranging from hypertension to stress relief to smoking cessation. The booths will be staffed with parishioners ranging from LVNs to psychiatrists, orthodontists, optometrists, surgeons, and podiatrists. One of the local hospitals will be providing cholesterol screenings, and [the local blood bank] is sending a representative to talk about blood donation, but more importantly their bone marrow program. We would like to coordinate a bone marrow drive; however, the [blood bank] program is still working on obtaining the funding for such a large-scale drive. The idea of the health fair spread so well and became so large that it has even been advertised throughout other local parishes.

[The parish nursing and health ministry group] has met an incredible amount of success, and by the grace of God, we hope to continue to do so. The first few months were difficult, but with three determined RNs and one pastor, who all long to serve God's people, we hope to continue to have the parish support and create programs that will make us a healthier parish! A seed was planted, and although it took an extremely long time for that seed to bear fruit, it now has; the parishioners even requested that [the parish nursing and health ministry group] be represented at the parish festival in August, and [the group] looks forward to using this opportunity to make the parish more aware of all of our ministries; and to perhaps begin to reach out to the youth and young adults of the parish.

In interviewing my pastor individually about [the parish nursing and health ministry group], he had many things to say. He stated that the ministry was a "Godsend" and he is still amazed at how much we have done in the past weeks. He knows that nothing is impossible with God, but he never dreamed that [the ministry] would receive the reception that it did. He stated that [the ministry] "helps me to be a better priest and pastor. I am able to depend on others to assist with non-emergency visits, and I can focus my energy on a greater variety of things. I am able to reach more people more effectively with this program and spend many fewer hours worrying that I am not doing enough to serve God and His people here."

The pastor stated that he would never get rid of this program and hopes that it is around for years to come. He also feels confident that with the reception [the ministry] has received in the past few months and with the useful programming planned entirely by volunteers and funded through donations, that he will have no problem having the council allocate funds from the budget toward the parish nursing [and health ministry] program in the coming year[s]. He also stated that he has received extremely positive feedback from the parishioners involved in the home visiting program. Many of the parishioners involved have reported that it helps them remain positive, that they have something to look forward to, and that they feel very comfortable with the parish nurses and parish health ministers that visit them.

The two parish nurses that are currently "certified" [sic] took four-day courses (Friday through Monday) offered in a city [on the West Coast]. They both had very positive experiences and were so very pleased to be combining their spirituality with their nursing in the way that they are. Our pastor has been outstanding and checking in with each of us frequently to be a spiritual support and in many instances a spiritual director to each of us. [The parish nursing and health ministry committee] convenes every three weeks as a group with our pastor to discuss our ministry. We praise positive happenings and pick apart negative occurrences so that we might become better servants. The meetings generally last 90 minutes to two hours and are always prayerful, positive experiences. We are doing all we can to live up to our motto of "humbly and compassionately serving God's people, one sniffle at a time!"

There are myriad tasks involved in initiating a parish nursing/health ministry program within a faith community. The effort must, of course, be grounded in prayer and supported by the blessing of the congregation's pastor and parishioners. The parish nurse initiating the ministry, whether a member of the faith community or not, must have or gain a clear working knowledge of the administrative and religious culture of the church he or she seeks to serve. And, after a beginning parish nursing/health ministry team is assembled, a parish health needs assessment should be conducted; this will guide the parish nurse in setting ministry priorities for the coming months. Finally, a religious ceremony of commissioning for the parish health ministry team is important, not only to introduce the program to the church at large, but also to witness the importance and the validity of the ministry in the perception of the church's pastor and other clergy.

References

Arbuckle, G. A. (2000). *Healthcare ministry: Refounding the mission in tumultuous times.* Collegeville, MN: Liturgical Press.

Baard, P. P., & Aridas, C. (2001). *Motivating your church.* New York: Crossroad.

Bausch, W. J. (2000). *The parish of the next millennium.* Mystic, CT: Twenty-Third Publications.

Boyes, P. (2001). Church health fairs: Partying with a purpose. *Journal of Christian Nursing 18*(3), 17–19.

Chandler, E., & Berry, R. D. (2001). Health ministries: Health and faith communities. In K. S. Lundy & S. Janes (Eds.), *Community health nursing: Caring for the public's health* (pp. 985–997). Sudbury, MA: Jones and Bartlett.

Clark, M. B. (2000). Nurses and faith community leaders growing in partnership. In M. B. Clark & J. K. Olson (Eds.), *Nursing within a faith community: Promoting health in times of transition* (pp. 297–316). Thousand Oaks, CA: Sage.

Cooper, N. P. (1993). *Collaborative ministry: Communion, contention, commitment.* Mahwah, NJ: Paulist Press.

DiGiacomo, J. J., & Walsh, J. J. (1993). *So you want to do ministry* (2nd ed.). Maryknoll, NY: Orbis Books.

Dues, G., & Walkley, B. (1997). *Called to parish ministry.* Mystic, CT: Twenty-Third Publications.

Gerding, S. B., & DeSiano, F. (1999). *Lay ministers, lay disciples, evangelizing power in the parish.* Mahwah, NJ: Paulist Press.

Lawler, M. G. (1990). *A theology of ministry.* Kansas City, MO: Sheed & Ward.

O'Brien, M. E. (2003). *Prayer in nursing: The spirituality of compassionate caregiving.* Sudbury, MA: Jones and Bartlett.

Olson, J. K., & Clark, M. B. (2000). Promoting inquiry: Assessment processes. In M. B. Clark & J. K. Olson (Eds.), *Nursing within a faith community: Promoting health in times of transition* (pp. 235–252). Thousand Oaks, CA: Sage.

O'Meara, T. F. (1999). *Theology of ministry* (Rev. ed.). Mahwah, NJ: Paulist Press.

Paprocki, J. (1998). *You give them something to eat; Ministering when you think you can't.* Notre Dame, IN: Ave Maria Press.

Paprocki, J. (2000). *Renewing your ministry: Walking with Jesus in all that you do.* Notre Dame, IN: Ave Maria Press.

Pinsoneault, D. (2001). *Attracting and managing volunteers: A parish handbook.* Liguori, MO: Liguori Publications.

Swinney, J., Anson-Wonkka, C., Maki, E., & Corneau, J. (2001). Community assessment: A church community and the parish nurse. *Public Health Nursing, 18*(1), 40–44.

Ulrich, T. (2001). *Parish social ministry: Strategies for success.* Notre Dame, IN: Ave Maria Press.

Vincent, M. C. (1982). *The life of prayer and the way to God.* Petersham, MA: Saint Bede's Publications.

Westberg, G. E. (1990). *The parish nurse: Providing a minister of health for your congregation.* Minneapolis: Augsburg.

Zarek, C. (1990). Parish health care: Unique needs, special responses. In H. Hayes & C. J. van der Poel (Eds.), *Health care ministry: A handbook for chaplains* (pp. 105–113). Mahwah, NJ: Paulist Press.

CHAPTER 7

THE SPIRITUALITY OF PARISH NURSING

Remove the sandals from your feet, for the place on which you are standing is holy ground.

—*Exodus 3:5*

"Remove the Sandals from Your Feet"

Lord God of Israel,
   You taught us, through Moses,
that when we stand before You,
   the ground is holy and we
      must "remove the sandals
         from our feet" *(Exodus 3:5).*

But . . .
   removing the sandals from
our feet may leave us:
         anxious,
            vulnerable,
               fragile,
                  insecure,
                     penitent,
      and yet receptive; and humbly
      open to Your compassion
         and Your care.

> Teach us to "remove the sandals
> from our feet" permanently, that
> we may stand forever on the
> "holy ground" of Your
> Blessed Presence.

Parish nurse Linda Miles (1997) observes that parish nurses must be attentive to their own spirituality: "We cannot be comfortable in dealing with clients' spiritual concerns, until we address our own values and belief systems and what gives our life meaning and purpose" (p. 23). I agree with Linda Miles and, thus, although the parish nurse's spirituality is interwoven throughout both the conceptual and practical issues discussed in this book, I feel that a separate chapter dealing with the spirituality of parish nursing is warranted.

The Spirituality of Parish Nursing: Standing on Holy Ground

In an earlier book, I describe all nurses as "standing on holy ground" (O'Brien, 2003b, pp. 1–2). The analogy is to the Old Testament scripture in which Moses is described as meeting the Lord in a burning bush; as Moses approaches the bush, God asks him to take off his shoes, for the place on which he is standing is holy ground (Exodus 3: 4–5). I believe that when we, as parish nurses, stand before our parishioners we stand on "holy ground" as truly as Moses did, for these meetings also represent encounters with God; they are opportunities to meet Him in the "burning bushes" of our parishioners' pain and loneliness and fear. And, thus, we must also humbly "take off our shoes" in recognition that the place where we are standing is holy.

But what does taking off one's shoes, spiritually, mean for the parish nurse? I envision the metaphor as the undergirding framework of a parish nurse's spirituality. For the taking off of our shoes places parish nurses in the best position for ministry, humbly standing before the presence of the Lord and seeking His guidance, or as the old hymn both poetically and graphically puts it, "Leaning on the Everlasting Arms." If we should ever find ourselves literally "shoeless," it can be very difficult to negotiate the path before us, depending on such conditions as the heat of the pavement, the chill of the earth, or the rockiness of the land. I can still vividly remember a childhood incident when, as summer campers, a young friend and I were forced by a frightening thunderstorm to beach our canoe about a mile from the place where we were staying. We had begun our paddling trip several hours earlier, under then-sunny skies, dressed in shorts and tee shirts, but without shoes! To our dismay, we discovered that the only route back to our cabin was by walking a narrow dirt road covered with a multitude of small, sharp pebbles. That painful trip home, and our very sore feet, still live in my memory.

When we choose to remove our psychological, emotional, or even our spiritual shoes—those dearly held thoughts, perceptions, or feelings that might serve to cushion a belief in our own abilities—and stand shoeless before the Lord, the path before us may also appear to be covered with small, sharp pebbles and may become both frightening and seemingly impossible to negotiate.

One of my favorite spiritual guides for traveling the sometimes difficult path set out for us by the Lord is the poignant and poetic allegory *Hinds' Feet on High Places*

> *"God, the Lord, is my strength; he makes my feet like the feet of a deer and makes me tread upon the heights"*
> —*Habakkuk 3:19*

written by Christian missionary Hannah Hurnard (1975). Hurnard's work is a scripturally based narrative, whose theme is derived from the final chapter of one of the smaller books of the Old Testament, the Book of the Prophet Habakkuk: "God, the Lord, is my strength; he makes my feet like the feet of a deer and makes me tread upon the heights" (3:19). In the allegory, the author allows the reader to journey with the protagonist Much Afraid on the Chief Shepherd's invitation to the High Places, through tortuous mountain climbs, frightening forest treks, and barren desert detours accompanied by fierce battles with such enemies as fear, pride, anxiety, loneliness, loss, and, finally, even despair of ever reaching the High Places. In essence, Much Afraid, who has crippled, crooked feet, is frequently made "shoeless" by her overwhelming terror and feelings of inadequacy. It is precisely during those times, however, that, in desperation, she is able to cry out for the assistance of the Chief Shepherd, who promised from the beginning of the journey: "I assure you . . . that never for a moment shall I be beyond your reach or call for help, even when you cannot see me. It is just as though I shall be present with you all the time, even though invisible" (p. 63). This is, I believe, the message of "standing on holy ground" as described in the book of Exodus; the message that once we recognize the holiness and the presence of the Lord in all aspects of our life journey, we must, indeed, "take off our shoes" that the "bare feet" of our spirits, as the crooked feet of Much Afraid did, may ultimately be made as "swift as those of hinds," that we may "go upon the heights" as we minister in His name.

To say to the Lord: "I've taken off my shoes, and now I'm not sure I'm equipped to travel this road, but I place my trust in You," is the spirituality needed to become a true instrument of the Lord. To become an *earthen vessel*. We cannot do this parish nursing ministry of ourselves, for earthen vessels are very fragile; and yet we hold a "treasure" that "the surpassing power may be of God and not of us" (2 Corinthians

> *"The surpassing power may be of God and not of us"*   —2 Corinthians 4:7

4:7). Saint Paul, it is suggested, chose the image of the "poor earthenware vessel" because "it helps Christians realize that the grace they bear in their souls is such a wonderful treasure, God Himself" (Gavigan, McCarthy, & McGovern, 1999, p. 187). This spirituality of *earthen vesselness*, as of standing on holy ground, is the spirituality of the nurse as minister (O'Brien, 2001, pp. 19–31); this is the privilege of the parish nurse as minister.

In considering the spirituality of the parish nurse as minister, it is important also to understand that God may call parish nurses to a variety of kinds of service within this new subfield of nursing. Some parish nurses may serve as leaders in the field, assisting with the professionalization of the discipline, such as those involved in articulating the *Scope and Standards of Parish Nursing Practice*. Other parish nurses may be committed to the specialty's growth though developing and conducting parish nursing education programs. Still others may initiate parish nursing research in order to validate the impact of the nurses' interventions through scholarly inquiry and dissemination of findings. And, finally, the largest number of parish nurses may place their energies into the direct practice of parish nursing through carrying out health-care ministry within their faith communities.

A parish nursing ministry choice will come about through each nurse's personal prayer and reflection. Barbara Fiand (1987) observes that "men and women ministers for the most part know that they have been touched by love and surrender creatively in whatever manner seems most fitting to them" (p. 1). It is important to remember that when one seeks to follow the Lord's call in ministry, God may "reveal that call . . . through the very talents, experience and gifts" an individual already possesses (Rademacher, 1991, p. 212). "Every believer has been given unique gifts for ministry . . . [and] even if a gift seems the same as someone's else's, it is not the same because each person is a unique individual; thus, the ways the gift is experienced and expressed will differ" (Williams & Sturzl, 2001, p. 9.) Because God has "gifted each person to serve others in some specific area," Don Hill (1994) notes, one should embrace the virtue of "meekness" in submitting to "individual roles as service members of His church" (p. 32). Rademacher (1991), in exploring the topic of "finding" one's "work and place in the vineyard," explains additionally: "You need to be aware that God, as a jealous lover, is constantly calling the beloved, often through new needs and new situations. While the call comes from inside through faith and personal gifts, it also comes from outside through changing needs and community discernment" (p. 212). These "outside factors," Rademacher asserts, are all part of the sometimes "more difficult obedience to which you are called" (p. 212).

Rademacher's latter point is particularly relevant for the contemporary field of parish health ministry in that some parish nurses are beginning to be solicited by pastors and/or parishioners to serve a congregation. This is a recent occurrence related to the growing understanding and appreciation of the specialty by clergy and laity alike. Recently, the archdiocesan director of parish health ministry in a large New England urban area told me that several years ago pastors in his city were "suspicious" of parish nursing; they did not understand the concept or the validity of their parishes having a parish nurse. "That has changed significantly," he observed. "Within the last few months I've had four or five pastors call me and say: 'I need a parish nurse!'" This anecdote is validated by several of the parish nursing/health ministry examples described in Chapter 5.

Whether a parish nurse is called to the ministry through his or her own felt call or through the invitation of a pastor or congregation, the spirituality of the mission is the same. The parish nurse is called to minister to the hungry, to the thirsty, to the naked, to the stranger, to the ill, and to the imprisoned in His Name. This is the treasure; this is the gift; this is the blessing of the parish nurse's spirituality.

Prayer and Parish Nursing: Praying with Parishioners

In the preceding chapter, I address a parish nurse's personal prayer as a spiritual support for parish health ministry; I have also written an entire book on the history and the importance of prayer for all practicing nurses (O'Brien, 2003a). Personal prayer provides a critical spiritual support to strengthen and guide the day-to-day conduct of parish nursing practice. Prayer encourages the parish nurse's vocation, nourishes the spirit, and consoles in suffering. Prayer is truly the heart of this ministry in which the nurse, as well as being a skilled educator, counselor, advocate, referral agent, and leader of volunteers, also has the mandate to become a spiritual companion to his or her clients; to assist them in integrating or, as Pastor Westberg puts it, "clarifying" the relationship between faith and health.

Praying with the parishioners we serve as parish nurses can be a vitally important dimension of the health ministry role, deeply appreciated by those who are ill and infirm; it can also be one of the most challenging elements of the practice for some nurses.

How a parish nurse prays with parishioners may vary significantly, sometimes related to personal experience and religious denomination, sometimes related simply to personality characteristics such as shyness or reserve. I mention religious tradition because in some denominations the concept of verbal, personal prayer shared with others or for others in a faith community is a more usual occurrence; that is, some parish nurses may have grown up with the experience of listening either to spontaneous verbal prayers of a pastor or other church members. In my earlier experience of Roman Catholic worship, the participation of the congregation tended to be quite structured, including only the recitation of specifically designated prayers such as the Our Father, Hail Mary, and so forth. In others words, spontaneous prayer was not included in most religious services. That has changed somewhat, especially in smaller contemporary Catholic churches, which may allow parishioners to participate in the Prayers of the Faithful during a Mass.

When I was about to begin my hospital chaplaincy internship, and knew that I would be ministering to persons of faiths other than my own, I called a friend whose father is a Methodist minister and said: "How do I pray with my patients?" She advised me to pray simply, as if I were talking to God. "Call the persons' names," she noted, "and pray about whatever is happening in their lives, their illness, their therapy, impending surgery, or whatever it is that they want you to pray about." Another bit of advice that my friend gave was to ask the patient whether he or she wished to join in the prayer. And, if family or friends were present, to invite them to join in. "Sometimes joining hands with a patient and family member during the time of prayer," she concluded, "can be very comforting to the person who is ill and to their loved ones."

I found my friend's advice incredibly helpful as I made my pastoral visits at the medical center of my chaplaincy internship. While most parish nurses will be praying with members of their own congregations and will be familiar with the prayer style parishioners are most used to, there may well be differences in prayer style preference among individual congregants. I have found that most sick people are accepting of and grateful for any kinds of prayer offered during their illness. Some individuals, however, may be more comfortable with a silent time of prayer with the nurse, affording them the opportunity to pray communally and yet to express their concerns and anxieties privately to the Lord. Other persons find comfort in verbalizing their needs, both in their own words and in those of the one ministering to them. And still others, sometimes because of their illness-related disabilities, prefer the nurse minister to pray aloud for their needs while they listen or join in a petition silently.

I have written previously about nurses needing to take risks in praying with patients (O'Brien, 2003a, pp. 62–63). There are times when we need to overcome our own insecurities or fear of saying the wrong words and must just plunge in, leaving the spiritual intervention to the True Minister, for whom we are simply humble servants. On patient rounds during my very first week of chaplaincy training, I stopped in to see Mark, a 17-year-old suffering from lymphoma: he had been extremely ill for some time and the prognosis was not good. We students had been warned by one of our chaplain supervisors that sometimes on an initial visit a patient would not be willing to open up about his or her spiritual needs or concerns, that it might take several meetings before the degree of trust and rapport was established for more in-depth spiritual ministry. As one supervisor put it: "On the first two or three visits a patient may spend the time talking to you about football scores and then on your fourth meeting, the person will begin to tell you about spiritual needs."

I am not terribly familiar with the interests of teenage boys but attempted to engage Mark in conversation about his love of sports (his room was filled with sports magazines, videos, and other sports paraphernalia). The discussion kept us occupied during most of my visit. Although I had introduced myself as a chaplain, Mark had not brought up the topic of spirituality and, quite frankly, I was too shy to do so, fearing I might "turn him off" to a future visit. As I was about to leave, however, with my hand on the doorknob, the Holy Spirit intervened and somehow out of my mouth came the question: "Mark, would you like me to pray with you before I leave?" To my astonishment, this charming young man replied with a very bright smile: "Yes, I sure would like that; I've been thinking that I needed to do some praying and this would really be a good time. Thank you." And I had been about to leave the room. We need to take risks!

Scripture and Parish Nursing: Sharing the Word

Because "all who respond to the call of ministry are invited to a vocation of service that proclaims gospel values," it is advised that "knowledge of the scriptures is . . . crucial as a . . . source and resource of ministry" (Cooper, 1993, p. 15). To share a comforting or encouraging passage from scripture, the holy word of God, with a parishioner who is struggling with physical or emotional suffering can be a very important dimension of the parish nurse's ministry. New Testament passages reflecting the healing miracles of Jesus demonstrate the love and the caring of the Lord for those who were ill and infirm. Old Testament scriptures display the power of God in supporting and caring for his people in times of great trouble and stress. The Psalms, the beautiful prayers that Jesus prayed in the synagogue, can become an ill person's own prayers in an experience of suffering and sorrow.

The following are some of the Old and New Testament scripture passages that I have used in hospital chaplaincy and that might be comforting to parishioners who are in need.

Old Testament Passages

Ecclesiastes 3:1; 4

"For everything there is a season,
            and a time for every matter under
                        heaven:
a time to be born, and a time to die;
        a time to plant, and a time to
                    pluck up what is planted.
A time to weep, and a time to
        laugh; a time to mourn
                    and a time to dance."

The book of Ecclesiastes is considered in the biblical genre of "wisdom literatuture"; it observes life "as man lives it" and points out that "God can inject joy into every aspect of living" (Alexander & Alexander, 1992, p. 362). The preceding beautiful passage can be very comforting for one who is suffering illness or infirmity related to the aging process, especially in terms of the verses that observe that there is "an appointed time for everything . . . a time to be born and a time to die . . . a time to seek and a time to lose." What the passage affirms is that God is in control and he has determined the times for things to happen in our lives, and from this knowledge we can derive peace related to the happenings both to us and around us.

Isaiah 40:28; 31

"Have you not known? Have
        you not heard?
The Lord is the everlasting God, the
            Creator of the ends of the earth. . . .
Those who wait for the Lord shall renew
        their strength,
they shall mount up with wings like eagles,
they shall run and not be weary,
            they shall walk and not faint."

The first of the prophetic books, the Book of Isaiah, is described as appropriately leading the writings of the other prophets, for "there is nothing to equal [Isaiah's] tremendous vision of God and the glory in store for God's people" until the book of Revelation (Alexander & Alexander, 1992, p. 376). The preceding passage from Isaiah is well known to many of us; poignant poems and hymns have been written about our hope in the Lord allowing us to "soar as with eagles' wings." The final verses can provide great support and encouragement for a person who is suffering from a disabling illness or infirmity. Recently, I experienced a very nasty and, to a degree, disabling bout of middle-ear-related infection. I could sit at my computer but had great difficulty maintaining my balance when attempting to walk, especially in the early mornings. When I went to my physician, a distinguished otolaryngologist, who I was certain was familiar with the Book of Isaiah, I announced that I was asking him to help fulfill, for me, the promise of the great prophet Isaiah in chapter 40, verse 31. I said: "I'm 'hoping in the Lord' and also hoping in you, as his instrument. I'm not asking to 'soar as with eagles' wings,' and I don't even need to 'run and not be weary,' but I really would love to be able to *walk and not faint!*"

Isaiah 43:1–3

"But now, thus says the Lord,
  he who created you . . . and
    formed you . . .
Do not fear, for I have redeemed you;
  I have called you by name:
    you are mine.
When you pass through the waters,
  I will be with you;
and through the rivers,
  they shall not overwhelm you;
When you walk through fire, you
    shall not be burned and the flame
      shall not consume you."

This second passage from the Book of Isaiah is also well known to many of us for its message of God's loving protection in times of trouble. A commentary on the verses notes that even though God had been distressed by the behavior of his people, he nevertheless redeemed the community and "promised to protect it from any ordeal, be it fire or water" (Collins, 1986, p. 94). For me, the most comforting aspect of the passage are the words: "I have called you by name: you are mine." This gift of being chosen and blessed by the Father is a reminder that no matter what happens in our lives, we still belong to Him and have been redeemed.

Jeremiah 18:1–6

"The word that came to Jeremiah from the Lord: 'Come, go down to the potter's house and there I will let you hear my words.' So, I went down to the potter's house, and there he was, working at his wheel. The vessel he was making of clay was spoiled in the potter's hand, and he reworked it into another vessel, as seemed good to him. Then the word of the Lord came to me: Can I not do with you . . . just as this potter has done? says the Lord. Just like the clay in the potter's hand, so are you in my hand."

It is always difficult to say which scripture passage is a favorite, but I believe this to be one of the most important for me personally. It's the passage I always keep marked with a ribbon in my several bibles. Peter Ellis (1986) comments that the image of the potter at his wheel, "one wheel at the top holding the clay and the other at the bottom rotated by the feet," represents the potter as "master of what he will create" (p. 45). My prayer whenever I meditate on this image is that if somehow I am molding my life in way that the Divine Potter can see will "turn out badly," he will make of my clay "another object of whatever sort he pleases." I also believe that Jeremiah's narrative of his visit to the potter's house provides a spirituality guide for all nurses, that we may become "beautiful earthen vessels . . . God's vessels, for him to fill and use as he chooses in the service of the ill and the infirm" (O'Brien, 2001, p. 125).

Jeremiah 29:11–14

"For surely I know the plans I have for you, says the Lord, plans for your welfare, not for harm, to give you a future with hope. Then when you call upon me, and come and pray to me, I will hear you. When you search for me, you will find me; if you seek me with all your heart, I will let you find me with you, says the Lord, and I will restore your fortunes."

The scripture passage, included in chapter 29 of the Book of Jeremiah, describes the prophet's advice to a group of embattled peoples, that they should pray and trust in the Lord, for ultimately, "God will reverse their fortunes and bring them back to their own land" (Ellis, 1986, pp. 64–65). This prophecy also models how the Lord acts with those who suffer and are exiled from places or things or people they love by illness or disability, and how he reminds us to have faith: "to call on" the Lord, to "seek" him with "all [our] hearts"; in the end, he will bring us back to the place from which we were exiled.

The Song of Songs 2:10–11; 13

"My beloved speaks and says to me, 'Arise,
 my love, my fair one and
  come away;
for now the winter is past,
 rain is over and gone . . .
Arise, my love, my fair one,
 and come away.'"

The Song of Songs or Song of Solomon is one of the most beautifully moving love poems of the Old Testament literature. Chapter 2 includes the image of the bridegroom calling to his bride "in the idyllic beauty of springtime" (Alexander & Alexander, 1992, pp. 367–368). Sometimes the bride is interpreted as being a metaphor for the Church; sometimes for the individual within the Church. For those who may be recovering from a serious illness or surgery, the imagery presented in verses 10 through 12 can be very meaningful and uplifting, as it invokes the image of the voice of the Lord saying: "Arise . . . my love and come away, for now the winter is past, the rain is over and gone. The flowers appear on the earth . . . and the voice of the turtle-dove is heard in our land."

Micah 6:6; 8

"With what shall I come before the Lord . . . ?
He has told you, O mortal, what is good,
 and what does the Lord require of you,
but to do justice and to love kindness
 and to walk humbly with your God."

The teaching of the eighth-century prophet Micah can be very consoling for parishioners who, because of illness or disability, may have lost their jobs or been unable to continue in a former profession that they believed allowed them to provide an important contribution to the community or the world. Micah reminds us that God does not want great or expensive gifts or sacrifices from us; he desires only that we "do the right," "love goodness," and "walk humbly" before him. This final verse, it is suggested, "gives us the essence of true worship. God accepts no substitute" (Alexander & Alexander, 1992, p. 450). It doesn't matter to the Lord whether one is physician, prophet, priest, or bricklayer; all that he asks of us is to be just, loving, and humble.

Psalm 27:1; 4; 5

"The Lord is my light and my salvation;
    whom shall I fear?
The Lord is the stronghold of my life;
    of whom shall I be afraid?
One thing I asked of the Lord,
    that will I seek after:
To live in the house of the Lord
    all the days of my life . . .
For he will hide me in his shelter
    in the day of trouble;
he will conceal me under the cover
    of his tent, he will set me
       high on a rock."

Psalm 27, verses 1 to 5, has been described as a "song of trust" in which "the psalmist's conviction of the Lord's protecting presence is intense" (Clifford, 1986a, p. 30). This is a wonderful prayer for parishioners struggling with any kind of threat or challenge in their lives, be it from their own or a loved one's illness or some other physical or emotional challenge. The psalm reminds one that since the Lord is his or her "life's refuge" there is no one and nothing to be afraid of. And, in fact, that is the reality. Any of us may, of course, be psychologically "afraid" of serious illness or accident, yet in the larger scheme of the Christian worldview, if we trust in God's providence, "all," as the mystic Julian of Norwich liked to say simply, "will be well!"

Psalm 121:1–4; 7–8

"I lift up my eyes to the hills,
    from where will come my help?
My help comes from the Lord,
    who made heaven and earth.

He will not let your foot be moved;
    he who keeps you will not slumber.
He who keeps Israel will never
    slumber nor sleep. . . .

The Lord will keep you from all evil;
    he will keep your life.
The Lord will keep your going out
    and your coming in,
from this time on and forevermore."

Psalm 121 is one of my very favorite psalms because it always reminds me of my childhood faith—which I would sometimes love to recapture—in having my own personal guardian angel. I hope that I still have a special angel to watch over me. But I am certain that we each do have a guardian in the Lord, who, as the psalmist notes, "never slumbers nor sleeps" and who "will not let our foot slip." This latter assurance of the psalmist provides a very practical aspect of comfort in physical disturbances. And, it is noted, "this blessing assures those embarking on [any] dangerous journey of the Lord's protection" (Clifford, 1986b, p. 64).

Psalm 139:1–5

"O Lord, you have searched me and
    known me.
You know when I sit down and when I rise up;
you discern my thoughts from far away.
You search out my path and my lying down, and
    are acquainted with all my ways.
Even before a word is on my tongue,
    O Lord, you know it completely.
You hem me in, behind and before,
    and lay your hand upon me."

Psalm 139, the beautiful prayer describing God's infinite knowledge of each of his children, as well as his interest in our lives, can be very supportive for parishioners faced with a challenging decision related to health and illness or related to other dimensions of their lives or the lives of their loved ones. Because the Lord knows us so well and knows what is best for us, we can place great trust that, in prayer, he will guide our decisions and lead us on the right path. How blessed we are to have a Divine Companion who knows us even better than we know ourselves.

New Testament Passages

Luke 8:43–44; 46–48

"There was a woman who had been suffering from hemorrhages for twelve years . . . [and] no one could cure her. She came up behind [Jesus] and touched the fringe of his clothes, and immediately her hemorrhage stopped. . . . Jesus said, 'Someone touched me; for I noticed that power had gone out from me.' . . . she declared in the presence of all the people why she had touched him and how she had been immediately healed. He said to her, 'Daughter, your faith has made you well; go in peace.'"

I have always loved the New Testament story of the "woman with the hemorrhage," partly, I think, because of the woman's great humility. She did not feel worthy, because of her condition which was considered unclean by some, to ask Jesus to lay hands on her and cure her affliction. Yet she had such incredible trust and faith in his caring and his healing power that she believed by simply touching the tassel of his cloak she would be cured. And, of course, her faith was rewarded. This is a very consoling message for those who may be too ill or disabled to attend church or participate in a healing service. Such a parishioner can be confident that if he or she touches the "hem of his garment" in prayer, Jesus will respond. The healing may not be physical, as the gospel woman's was, but whatever healing of the spirit is needed will take place.

Luke 11:9–13

"So I say to you, Ask, and it will be given to you; search and you will find; knock and the door will be opened for you. For everyone who asks receives, and everyone who searches finds, and for everyone who knocks, the door will be opened. . . . If your child asks for a fish, will [you] give a snake . . . or a scorpion? If you then . . . know how to give good gifts to your children, how much more will the heavenly Father give the Holy Spirit to those who ask him?"

In commenting on this passage of Saint Luke's gospel, Jerome Kodell (1989) points out that the extreme examples, such as a father giving his child a snake or a scorpion, serves to "drive home the absurdity of thinking of the heavenly father as harsh or cruel" (p. 63). "God wants the best for us," he asserts, "which ultimately is the Holy Spirit, the gift of the age to come" (p. 63). This can be an important scripture for one who may be hesitant to petition the Lord in prayer. In discussing this scripture passage with a parishioner, an important thought to remember, however, is that a loving father does not always, perhaps cannot always, accede to a child's wishes, dearly as he may desire to do so. In the same way, our Heavenly Father may not respond to our seeking with the answer we would like; he will, however, respond with the answer we need.

Luke 12:22–23

"He said to his disciples, 'Therefore I tell you, do not worry about your life, what you will eat, or about your body, what you will wear. For life is more than food, and the body more than clothing. Consider the ravens: they neither sow nor reap . . . yet God feeds them. Of how much more value are you than the birds!'"

In this passage of Luke, describing the Father's care for his children, we are reminded that despite all of our many worries about obtaining the material necessities of life, we can trust that God is on top of things. Kodell (1989) comments that this gospel message is not meant to condemn "foresight and industry, but an anxious approach to life that subconsciously denies that God is a loving Father who has everything carefully under his control" (p. 69). This is a very consoling thought for those facing the uncertainty of a serious illness outcome.

John 12:24–26

"Very truly, I tell you, unless a grain of wheat falls into the earth and dies, it remains just a single grain; but if it dies, it bears much fruit. Those who love their life lose it and those who hate their life in this world will keep it for eternal life. Whoever serves me must follow me, and where I am, there will my servant be also. Whoever serves me, the Father will honor."

This scripture passage may be particularly meaningful to a parishioner with a terminal illness. Jesus reminds us that the grain of wheat must fall to the ground and die to produce fruit, and he uses his own life as an example. What Jesus is teaching in this metaphor is that "life will be offered to the world through his death. If he is buried like the seed . . . then much fruit will come; then he will draw all to himself" (Flanagan, 1989, p. 56).

Matthew 10:26–28

"So have no fear. . . .Nothing is covered up that will not be uncovered, and nothing secret will not become known. What I say to you in the dark, tell in the light; and what you hear whispered, proclaim from the housetops. Do not fear those who kill the body but cannot kill the soul."

This brief passage from Saint Matthew's gospel provides support and comfort for a parishioner who may feel besieged by the enemies of illness and infirmity. The Lord is reminding his disciples not be afraid, for the Father knows even all the "hairs" of their heads. The message was meant to "encourage the disciples . . . in the face of opposition" (Harrington, 1991, p. 48).

John 14:1–3

"Do not let your hearts be troubled. Believe in God; believe also in me. In my Father's house there are many dwelling places. If it were not so, would I have told you that I go to prepare a place for you? And if I go and prepare a place for you, I will come again and will take you to myself, so that where I am there you may be also."

This scripture passage from the gospel of John may be helpful to a parishioner who entertains doubts or questions about whether his or her life has been worthy to merit an eternal reward. Jesus, in these comments, is assuring us that there are places for many different people in the eternal kingdom and that he himself will prepare a place for his followers.

Romans 8:31; 35; 37

"If God is for us, who is against us? He who did not withhold his own Son, but gave him up for all of us, will he not with him also give us everything else? . . . Who will separate us from the love of Christ? Will hardship, or distress, or persecution, or famine, or nakedness, or peril, or the sword? . . . No, in all these things we are more than conquerors through him who loved us."

This portion of Paul's letter may serve to comfort a parishioner facing intense suffering related to illness, infirmity, loss, or bereavement. For one is reminded that no anguish or distress, no matter how great, can separate us from the "love of God in Christ Jesus." The final verses are described as possessing a "hymn-like celebration of the reality of the victory, the reality of being in the Spirit" (Pilch, 1991, p. 50). Pilch adds: "The chief message" of the scripture "is that God is for us, and the verses describe what 'God-for-us' looks like" (pp. 50–51).

Philippians 4:4–7

"Rejoice in the Lord always, again I say: Rejoice! Let your gentleness be known to everyone. The Lord is near. Do not worry about anything, but in everything, by prayer and supplication, with thanksgiving, let your requests be made known to God. And the peace of God, which surpasses all understanding, will guard your hearts and your minds in Christ Jesus."

In these two short verses, contained in a letter to the Philippians, Paul was assuring the young Christian community that, in truth, they had nothing to fear; that they should simply turn all of their anxieties over to the Lord. Then, he promised, they would be filled with a peace that was beyond all imagining. Very often, parishioners, even very devout Christians, are plagued with anxiety related to an illness, their own or that of a loved one. The sharing of a brief scripture passage, such as Paul's message to the Philippians, can have an enormous impact, for it is recognized as the word of God, rather than human counsel.

The preceding passages represent only a few examples of scripture citations that a parish nurse may share in counseling parishioners who are ill or in need. Each parish nurse will have his or her own favorites scriptures to use in ministry. The sharing of scripture with a parishioner, especially the choice of passage(s) and the time of sharing, will primarily be directed by the Holy Spirit who is present in all such interactions. I think virtually all of us who have done ministry involving the sharing of scripture can relate instances of when a person being counseled has said something to the effect of "that was exactly the scripture I needed to hear today; how did you know?" And the minister's answer, of course, is "I didn't, but the Lord did!"

Religious Ritual and Parish Nursing: The Rites of the Church

> For where two or three are gathered in my name, I am there among them.
> —*Matthew 18:20*

It is important to briefly address the topic of religious ritual, for involvement with the rites of the church may become an important dimension of the parish nurse's ministry. The discussion can only be presented in general terms, however, as some churches among the Christian denominations differ significantly in the carrying out of their religious rituals. Of course, prayer is a religious ritual, especially communal prayer. And it may become a role of the parish nurse to assist in the planning of some opportunities for communal prayer among parishioners. One example that comes to mind is a service organized yearly by a local church for those who are disabled and who cannot ordinarily attend communal worship. Families with homebound members, as well as staff members of nearby nursing homes, make every effort to get the physically challenged individuals they care for into cars or vans so that they may be able to attend a service with others in similar circumstances. The service is an eagerly anticipated aspect of worship for the disabled attendees and their families. Obviously, a project like this takes a great deal of planning and organization; however, an ecumenical worship service might be an excellent project for a local group of parish nurses to coordinate for their disabled parishioners.

Another role of the parish nurse related tangentially to the religious ritual of his or her church is the organization or coordination of transportation to and from regularly scheduled worship services for those who can no longer drive or take public transportation. This can be one of the most important parish nursing roles falling within the domain of leader or coordinator of volunteers.

A third role of the parish nurse, treasured by many homebound parishioners, is the role of Eucharistic minister, or one who brings the sacrament of Holy Communion to the home. In a number of Christian denominations, a parish nurse is allowed to carry out this pastoral ministry for parishioners; if the role is not within the tradition of a church, the nurse may be able to coordinate a visit from the pastor or assistant clergyperson ordained by the denomination to fulfill such a ministry.

Finally, a small home or nursing home prayer service for homebound or nursing home–bound parishioners and their families and friends might be organized by a parish nurse to include the sacrament of Communion. Any religious ritual involving the spiritual coming together of a group of family and friends makes all more fully aware of the grace of the Lord, who promised his disciples that wherever two or three are gathered in his name, there he is in the midst of them.

Spiritual Companionship and Parish Nursing

Among the generally identified roles of the parish nurse, including such activities as educator, counselor, advocate, referral agent, coordinator of volunteers, and integrator or clarifier of the relationship between faith and health, the latter concept is clearly the most important and, as I have observed earlier, the overarching role of the parish nurse. For it is in his or her role as integrator of faith and health, as spiritual companion in health and illness, that the "parish" dimension of parish nursing truly resides. There are many fine home health and community health nurses who carry out the activities of educating, counseling, advocating, referring, and even sometimes soliciting volunteers to help with care for their patients. And, of course, some of these nurses may also provide spiritual care for their clients as a dimension of the holistic health care to which they are committed. For the parish nurse, however, the conduct of spiritual caring, of spiritual companionship, must be central to the conduct of professional practice as defined in the *Scope and Standards of Parish Nursing Practice*; that is, the parish nurse "serves as a member of the ministry staff of a faith community" (American Nurses Publishing, 1998, p. 7). The role of *ministry* defines the uniqueness of parish nursing practice.

The Ministry of Spiritual Companionship

The author of a classic work on pastoral care and counseling, Howard Clinebell (1991), has observed that "in recent decades there has been a dramatic rediscovery of a striking fact, *all Christians have a ministry because they are Christians*, whether or not they are ordained" (p. 394). "This awareness," Clinebell asserts, "gives laypersons a new self-image. They are no longer second-class Christians who leave spiritual work to the pastor" (p. 394). The current "lay renaissance," Clinebell notes, "is based on the rediscovery of the New Testament understanding of the church; the people of God, the Body of Christ, and the community of the Holy Spirit in which each member has her or his ministry" (p. 394).

Howard Clinebell's observations are strongly supportive of the parish nurse's ministry role of spiritual companion within the Christian tradition. Spiritual companionship, sometimes described as spiritual direction, involves an individual, ordained or non-ordained, ministering through spiritual counseling and spiritual listening as a vehicle for the Holy Spirit in guiding or supporting the faith development of another. In discussing the ministry of spiritual direction or spiritual companionship, William Barry (1992) points out that "the real guide in the spiritual life is the Holy Spirit" (p. 89). The tradition of the church, he adds, "has consistently believed that everyone who wants to develop his or her relationship with God needs to seek the help of someone else, even granted that the ultimate spiritual director is the Holy Spirit" (p. 89). "Spiritual direction," Barry asserts, "helps people to pay attention to and to share with another member of the community experiences of God and in the process to learn how to discern what is authentically of God from what is not. In this way they also learn how to talk about their experiences of God with other members of the community" (pp. 91–92).

The role of serving as a spiritual companion, spiritual director, or "spiritual friend," as some describe the ministry, may be more or less formalized according to the needs and desires of the parishioner seeking spiritual counseling. Several years ago, I participated in an excellent course on spiritual direction, which included both a didactic dimension and a clinical practicum in providing spiritual companionship. In support of William Barry's observation, one of the first things we learned was that there really is no such thing as spiritual direction! That may seem a strange lesson in a course titled "The Ministry of Spiritual Direction," which was taught by two seasoned "spiritual directors": a Lutheran pastor and a Catholic deacon. The point of the faculty members' assertion, however, was to remind the student group that we, as future ministers of spiritual companionship, would not ourselves be "directing" or "guiding" a counselee's spiritual life. The "real guide," in Barry's words, "is the Holy Spirit." We who serve in this ministry are simply his instruments in helping to facilitate an individual's openness to hearing his whisperings. This is also validated by spiritual director Rose Mary Dougherty (1995), who affirms that "success" in spiritual direction is not dependent upon the skills of the minister or the spirituality of the person seeking counseling. "Rather," she points out, "the critical element in spiritual direction, which those involved share, is the intention to rely on God, to seek God actively and wait for God's leading. Where this can happen, between two individuals . . . hearts are opened, private agendas are put on hold and God's Spirit is given free rein" (p. 2).

The understanding of experienced spiritual directors regarding the role of the minister vis-à-vis the role of the Holy Spirit in spiritual companionship should be comforting to parish nurses seeking to minister as integrators of faith and health, especially if they feel inadequate to the task. Prior to my taking the spiritual direction course, Margie, a young baccalaureate student living on my university campus, approached me at a Holy Week liturgy and asked out of the blue whether I would be a spiritual companion or director for her; we had never met, but her explanation for the request was that the rather distinctive silver medal I wear reminded her of the sisters who had taught in her high school. I told her that I would pray about it, and we set a time to meet and discuss her request further.

Because, at the time, I had never formally done any spiritual direction, I called my school's director of campus ministry, a priest, and asked his advice; I specifically asked whether he thought I should send the student to campus ministry to meet with an ordained pastoral caregiver. Interestingly and surprisingly to me, at the time, he immediately responded: "If the student asked you to be her director, then I think you should do it; your job will be helping her to listen to the voice of the Holy Spirit." I have to confess that I planned our first meeting with some trepidation, as the ministry of helping someone, especially a young person seeking to follow God's call for her life, seemed a graced yet also a heavy responsibility. Because of my insecurity, I realized that I needed the Lord's help, so when the student arrived at my office for our first meeting, I suggested lighting a candle and beginning with a prayer to the Holy Spirit for guidance. Margie was very responsive to the time of prayer, and it became part of the routine for all of our following meetings.

What exactly does the minister do in a spiritual-counseling meeting? Well, actually, that also depends upon the Holy Spirit! If both minister and counselee are open to His inspiration, a meeting may sometimes go in a different direction than initially expected. Spiritual director Maureen Conroy (1995) describes spiritual direction as helping "people grow in a personal relationship with God" and in assisting them "to discover God's presence in their lives" (p. xvii). This was the goal of my meetings with Margie. Thus, many of our initial interactions, after the time of prayer, involved Margie relating experiences in her spiritual life so that we could discuss these in light of scripture and the call of God for her future. One day, however, it seemed that I was doing all, or at least a great deal, of the talking. Something Margie had asked or commented on stimulated my response, which became much longer than I expected. At any rate, near the end of our time together (we usually planned to meet for approximately an hour), I realized how much I had been talking and apologized for seeming to dominate our discussion. Margie started to laugh and said: "Oh, Sister, you said all the things I needed to hear. I'm really tired and on my way over here I thought: 'I'm not up to talking a lot this morning,' and you did it for me. It was great!" The Holy Spirit is, indeed, in the words of some of my younger students, "totally awesome"!

Although sometimes, as in the preceding example, a spiritual minister may need to talk, to facilitate the progress of the counseling, the more usual role of the minister is to listen. That message is beautifully articulated by hospice physician and spiritual writer Sheila Cassidy (1999) in her book *Sharing the Darkness*: "Those of us who are carers must listen in particular to the 'little ones' who have been given to us to cherish. Children, the handicapped, the sick and the dying often have a directness and simplicity which gives them an access to the truth which is denied to the more complex of us" (p. 156).

Many of the ethical guidelines for spiritual counseling, such as confidentiality, respect for an individual's self-determination, counselee autonomy, and the obligation to do good and not harm (beneficence and nonmaleficence) are virtually identical to the ethical concerns identified for parish nurses in the *Scope and Standards of Parish Nursing Practice*. An important point related to the concepts of beneficence and nonmaleficence, which was highlighted in my spiritual direction course, and which is important for parish nurses, is the notion that the spiritual counselor must take care to sort out a counselee's psychological problems and needs from his or her spiritual ones. In other words, an individual needing psychological or psychiatric counseling or care should not be allowed to use spiritual counseling to meet those ends. It is not within the expertise or the role description of most ministers to provide in-depth psychological counseling; counseling offered by an untrained minister could result in harm to the counselee, and the counselee may feel that he or she is getting help and thus avoid the initiation of appropriate and needed psychotherapy.

A note about this concern of keeping spiritual counseling "spiritual" must be added, however. It would be naïve to think that many parishioners' spiritual problems are not in fact closely related to psychological or emotional issues, as well as to physical concerns. The point for the minister of spiritual counseling to remember is that the focus of the counseling sessions should be spiritual. If a counselee is interested in discussing only issues that fall within the psychological/emotional realm and does not seem to respond to or be willing to discuss the spiritual context of his or her concerns, the effort can turn into psychological counseling rather than spiritual counseling. The bottom line, my spiritual direction faculty emphasized, was that all of a counselee's joys and sorrows, anxieties and worries, problems and concerns should be discussed in light of spirituality, if it is to truly be called spiritual direction or spiritual companionship.

A final bit of advice given in my spiritual direction course, which I believe is very important for parish nurses also, is to *pray*; to pray not only with and for those to whom we minister, but to pray for the guidance of the Holy Spirit in all of our ministry activities. One of our student assignments—I had never experienced a class assignment such as this before—was to engage in a half hour of contemplative prayer each day. This could be done how, when, or in whatever setting we chose, but it was, we were advised, a necessary support for spiritual counselors. (For a description of some suggested methods of contemplative prayer, see *The Nurse as a Contemplative Caregiver*, O'Brien, 2003a.)

Although the "spirituality" of parish health ministry represents a unifying thread running throughout this text, the importance of the concept for practicing parish nurses warrants a focused discussion. The theme of a parish nurse's posture in ministering to parishioners in both health and illness is that of "standing on holy ground," as described in Exodus 3:5. And, in this place of holy ground, parish nurses, as spiritual companions, as integrators of faith and health, must often call upon personal spiritual resources such as prayer, scripture, and religious ritual both for themselves and for those to whom they minister. The parish nurse's personal spirituality supports both the calling to and the carrying out of this blessed ministry to church members in need.

References:

Alexander, D., & Alexander, P. (1992). *Eerdmans handbook to the bible.* Grand Rapids, MI: William B. Eerdmans.

American Nurses Publishing. (1998). *Scope and standards of parish nursing practice.* Washington, DC: Author.

Barry, W. A. (1992). *Spiritual direction and the encounter with God: A theological inquiry.* Mahwah, NJ: Paulist Press.

Cassidy, S. (1999). *Sharing the darkness: The spirituality of caring.* Maryknoll, NY: Orbis Books.

Clifford, R. J. (1986a). *Psalms 1–72: Collegeville bible commentary.* Collegeville, MN: Liturgical Press.

Clifford, R. J. (1986b). *Psalms 73–150: Collegeville bible commentary.* Collegeville, MN: Liturgical Press.

Clinebell, H. (1991). *Basic types of pastoral care and counseling: Resources for the ministry of healing and growth.* Nashville, TN: Abingdon Press.

Collins, J. J. (1986). *Isaiah: Collegeville bible commentary*. Collegeville, MN: Liturgical Press.

Conroy, M. (1995). *Looking into the well: Supervision for spiritual directors*. Chicago: Loyola Press.

Cooper, N. P. (1993). *Collaborative ministry: Communion, contention, commitment*. Mahwah, NJ: Paulist Press.

Dougherty, R. M. (1995). *Group spiritual direction: Community for discernment*. Mahwah, NJ: Paulist Press.

Ellis, P. F. (1986). *Jeremiah, Baruch: Collegeville bible commentary*. Collegeville, MN: Liturgical Press.

Fiand, B. (1987). *Releasement: Spirituality for ministry*. New York: Crossroad.

Flanagan, N. M. (1989). *The gospel according to John and the Johannine Epistles: Collegeville bible commentary*. Collegeville, MN: Liturgical Press.

Gavigan, J., McCarthy, B., & McGovern, T. (Eds.). (1999). *The Navarre bible: St. Paul's Epistles to the Corinthians*. Dublin: Four Courts Press.

Havener, I. (1991). *First Thessalonians, Phillipians, Philemon, Second Thessalonians, Colossians, Ephesians: Collegeville bible commentary*. Collegeville, MN: Liturgical Press.

Harrington, D. J. (1991). *The gospel according to Matthew: Collegeville bible commentary*. Collegeville, MN: Liturgical Press.

Hill, D. (1994). *Life by design: A guide to personal devotions and daily bible study*. (Book 3). Danville, KY: Lay Leadership International.

Hurnard, H. (1975). *Hinds' Feet on High Places*. Wheaton, IL: Tyndale House.

Kodell, J. (1989). *The gospel according to Luke: Collegeville bible commentary*. Collegeville, MN: Liturgical Press.

Miles, L. (1997). Getting started: Parish nursing in a rural community. *Journal of Christian Nursing, 14*(1), 22–24.

Nassal, J. (1997). *The conspiracy of compasson: Breathing together for a wounded world*. Leavenworth, KS: Forest of Peace Publishing.

O'Brien, M. E. (2001). *The nurse's calling: A Christian spirituality of caring for the sick*. Mahwah, NJ: Paulist Press.

O'Brien, M. E. (2003a). *Prayer in nursing: The spirituality of compassionate caregiving*. Sudbury, MA: Jones and Bartlett.

O'Brien, M. E. (2003b). *Spirituality in nursing: Standing on holy ground* (2nd ed.). Sudbury, MA: Jones and Bartlett.

Pilch, J. J. (1991). *Galatians and Romans: Collegeville bible commentary*. Collegeville, MN: Liturgical Press.

Rademacher, W. J. (1991). *Lay ministry: A theological, spiritual and pastoral handbook*. New York: Crossroad.

Williams, D. R., & Sturzl, J. (2001). *Grief ministry: Helping others mourn*. San Jose, CA: Resource Publications.

CHAPTER 8

PARISH NURSING MINISTRY WITH DIVERSE POPULATIONS

For everything there is a season, and a time for every matter under heaven: a time to be born, and a time to die; a time to plant and a time to pluck up what is planted.

—Ecclesiastes 3:1-2

There Is a Time

Dear Father in heaven,
   You have taught us that, for
     everything, there is a time:

"A time to be born
   and a time to die" *(Ecclesiastes 3:2).*
Teach us to embrace both the
   beginning and the end of life,
     as Your gifts.

"A time to mourn and a time to
    dance" *(Ecclesiastes 3:4).*
Grant us the understanding to honor
   You in our gifts; and the wisdom to
    bless You in their loss.

"A time to seek and a time to lose"
(Ecclesiastes 3:6).
Help us to know when to rejoice in
our good health; and when to
glory in our infirmity.

"A time to keep silence and a time to
speak" *(Ecclesiastes 3:7).*
Grace us with the ability to accept
the things we cannot change; and the
courage to advocate for the things
we can influence.

"A time for war and a time for
peace" *(Ecclesiastes 3:8).*
Counsel us to fight valiantly against
illness and disability; but endow us
with acceptance when the
battle is lost.

Help us, Dearest Lord, to remember
that, in all things, there is a time;
a time that is not ours, a time
that, blessedly, is Yours.

As I was preparing to begin the parish nursing intervention study described in the following chapter, I spoke with the pastor of a large multicultural and multiethnic parish about the needs of his parishioners in terms of parish nursing and health ministry. The pastor, who was the only clergyperson in church administration at the time, did not have a parish nurse but was very supportive of the concept; he suggested that we probably could find many of the homebound project participants we were seeking for our study right in his parish. He explained that he could identify a number of ill and infirm parishioners who were visited by the church's Eucharistic ministers. The pastor feared, however, that there were also a number of other infirm parishioners or former parishioners who had "slipped through the cracks," as they had stopped attending church; their names were no longer listed on the congregational membership rolls.

In support of the need for parish nursing, the pastor described a phone call he had received the previous day from Mrs. McDonald, a long-time church member. Mrs. McDonald reported that her "heart condition" was now getting worse and the doctor had told her that she would need to begin using oxygen at home. She was calling, she told the pastor, to say that she would no longer be attending worship services with the parish community but was hoping to stay connected to the church. While the pastor told me that he did have a group of Eucharistic ministers who would bring weekly Communion to parishioners like Mrs. McDonald, some of the ministers were becoming older themselves and could not assume a heavy visiting schedule. He also admitted that some of the parishioners complained that the Eucharistic ministers came and brought Communion but did not stay for a visit, something for which the homebound church members longed. The pastor assured me that he felt the presence of a parish nurse and a health ministry program could be a real blessing for his church and his parishioners.

The Parish Nurse as Health Minister
Identifying the Parish Ill and Infirm

> Jesus said to them: "Which one of you, having a hundred sheep and losing one of them, does not leave the ninety-nine in the wilderness, and go after the one that is lost until he finds it?"
>
> —*Luke 15:4*

One of the central concerns of the pastor described previously is the ability of the church to find parishioners, or former parishioners, who might, as he put it, have "fallen through the cracks" in terms of the church membership roll. An ill or infirm parishioner being dropped from a church's membership, even inadvertently, can be very traumatic for both the parishioner and his or her family. A colleague recently told me how hurt and angry she was that her elderly father never received a visit or in fact heard from the church he had supported for many years after he became homebound by infirmity. One would hope that this is the exception rather than the rule; however, as parishes of all denominations grow larger, pastors and assistant clergy are often stretched to the limit in ministering to actively involved members of their churches. Thus, the introduction of the concept of parish nursing is truly a blessing for many large urban and rural congregations.

One of the first tasks of a newly commissioned parish nurse, in concert with initiating a cadre of health ministry volunteers and planning a parish health assessment, is to identify the parish ill and infirm who may become recipients of the ministry. In some parishes, the information may be well documented; in other faith communities, parish nurses might have to use creative strategies to locate the sick of the congregation. Some of these parishioners will be living in their own homes; some in long-term care facilities such as nursing homes or assisted living communities; and some, perhaps, in hospices. A few parishioners may be hospitalized, and, while critically ill parishioners are usually known to a church, a patient may get lost over the course of a very long-term hospitalization.

In addressing parish health care, Cyrilla Zarek (1990) explores the topic of "locating the sick." First, she advises that for the search process to begin, it is important that the person (parish nurse) coordinating the effort "know and be known by the parishioners" (p. 106). "Next," Zarek suggests, "contacts are made with neighbors and family members," as well as the coordinator "speaking at weekly liturgies, writing bulletin articles, talking to a senior citizens club and other organizations" (p. 106). The pastor and clergy can also support the search effort through announcements made during sermons. Zarek observes that "although some health care facilities notify the parishes when a parishioner is admitted, those confined to their own homes seldom contact the parish" (p. 107). "Therefore," she concludes, "it is essential to enlist the help of the entire parish in locating the sick, the frail elderly and the homebound" (p. 107).

I would strongly support Cyrilla Zarek's proposal that a combination of approaches be used in order to locate the ill and infirm who may be lost to a parish. For the parish nursing project described in Chapter 9, one local parish, hoping to find some of its lost members, put a notice in the church bulletin, asking if anyone in the parish knew of a homebound or nursing home–bound or hospitalized parishioner who was not currently receiving pastoral ministry. The notice requested that the names of those to be visited be submitted to the church office. The pastor allowed his private telephone number to be used and added his personal words of support to the effort to carry out this health ministry in the parish. Although the request ran in the church bulletin for three or four weeks, no calls were received. Ultimately, some ill parishioners desirous of parish health ministry were found through referrals from the Eucharistic ministers.

In another church, although the pastor was also very interested in finding parishioners who might benefit from health ministry visits, he admitted that he did not know whether some of his former parishioners might be in local nursing homes or life care communities; he suggested that these might be places to seek out ill and infirm elders. Again, through the processes of referral and of approaching both the nursing home and the assisted care facility in the neighborhood, a number of ill parishioners who were delighted to have a parish nurse or health minister visit were located.

A last suggestion, which also supports Zarek's multifaceted approach to locating the ill and infirm in a parish, is to work closely with active parishioners in terms of referral. A parish nurse recently told me that she has been getting some excellent referrals from a woman who has been very involved in parish activities and is supportive of parish nursing for parishioners who needed health ministry. It began with the parishioner suggesting one person who might appreciate a visit from the parish nurse. When the nurse immediately followed through with a visit and expressed her appreciation for the referral, the parishioner began to enlist the assistance of others who might make similar referrals. The parish nurse described this as a wonderful "case-finding" effort on the part of one committed parishioner.

The Ministry Visit

> I give you a new commandment, that you love one another. Just as I have loved you, you also should love one another. By this everyone will know that you are my disciples, if you have love for one another.
>
> —*John 13:34–35*

The previous chapter addresses the ministry of spiritual companionship; that ministry, I reaffirm, is central to the role of the parish nurse. As a spiritual companion, the parish nurse may, however, engage in a number of practical health/illness-related activities during a home, nursing home, hospital, or office visit. These might fit into the category of what my hospital chaplaincy program director labeled the "cup of cold water ministry" (O'Brien, 2001, pp. 7–10). Chaplain Cornelius van der Poel (1999) points out that healthcare ministry may have a variety of meanings such as "spiritual care of patients in hospitals," "administering sacraments . . . to the sick," or initiating "any form of involvement with health care delivery" (p. vii). Essentially, van der Poel asserts, healthcare ministry has as "its immediate concern": "the restoration of the individual's personal balance and integrity at [a] time of disharmony. It is a direct contribution to the patient's peace of mind, physical comfort, and friendship with God" (p. viii).

It is the carrying out of whatever activity is needed during a meeting with a parishioner, in the context of the gospel message, that categorizes the visit of the parish nurse as ministry. A few reminders about ministry might be helpful. "The first rule for ministry," Paprocki (2000) asserts, " is to shift attention away from ourselves and onto those we are called to serve. The Emmaus story reveals to us that Jesus sought out the two disciples on the road to Emmaus. He was in search of those who needed healing" (p. 119). This thought is supported by Corita Clark (1991) in her book *A Spirituality for Active Ministry*. Clark comments that she was moved by the words of a speaker who pointed out that the purpose of ministry "is not to deliver services, but to empower people" (p. 43). "This," Clark adds, "resonated with my own experience of how I had been ministered to in my life by persons who loved and cared and thus sparked me, empowered me. Ministers empower people by helping [them] to believe in God's love and care, to value themselves and their gifts, to discover their own role in promoting God's reign in their family, their work situation, community and world" (p. 43).

Hospital chaplain Florence Smithe (1990), in discussing healthcare ministry, explains that the minister "approaches each new encounter, not as one sent to find solutions to . . . problems but rather as a vessel, open to receive, to listen and to share the pain" (p. 115). The minister, she notes, is "open to be with others in their sacred space. The vessel has windows as well, to allow the reflection of God's love and grace to emerge from within" for those to whom one is ministering (p. 115).

And finally, pastoral counselor Howard Clinebell (1991) shares thoughts on ministry in four areas that might be considered analogous to key roles identified for the parish nurse: counselor, educator, advocate, and referral agent. Ministers are natural counselors, Clinebell asserts, because of such attributes of their role in "ongoing relationships with their people; their entre to many family systems; the trust that many people have in ministers; their accessibility; and their presence during many of the developmental and accidental [unexpected] crises in peoples' lives, including illness, death and bereavement" (p. 183). Ministers also participate in "educative counseling," or "a helping process that integrates the insights and methods of two pastoral functions with the single objective of fostering the wholeness of persons" (p. 323). Client advocacy is incorporated in ministry through "supportive care and counseling," during which the minister "uses methods that stabilize, undergird, nurture, motivate or guide troubled persons, enabling them to handle their problems and relationships more constructively within whatever limits are imposed by their personality, resources and circumstances" (p. 170). And parishioner referral may be handled through "referral counseling," which Clinebell views as an art "indispensable in a minister's caring and counseling" (p. 310). "Because," he notes, "many people trust a [minister's] judgment and turn to him or her spontaneously when trouble strikes, a minister is in a strategic position to assist them in finding competent, specialized help" (p. 310.) Ministers, Clinebell concludes, "bridge the gap between informal social support systems and more specialized formal helping professionals" (p. 310).

Each ministry visit, as is the overall process of spiritual companionship, should be committed to the guidance of the Holy Spirit. The parish nurse's activities, if placed in prayer and undergirded by the gospel teachings of caring and compassion, will indeed bear "good fruit" in the service of the Master.

Home Ministry

Ministering to the Chronically Ill Parishioner

Within the current U.S. healthcare system, more and more clients who might in the past have been hospitalized are now receiving long-term care in their own homes. The chronically ill, receiving care in their homes, include such populations as "psychiatric clients, infants, children, perinatal clients, the disabled, and acutely and chronically ill adults" (LeMone & Burke, 1996, p. 52). LeMone and Burke assert that "today, almost any medical-surgical issue dealt with in a formal clinical setting can be addressed in the home" (p. 52). They also report that "about half of the all home care clients are over the age of 65" (p. 52).

There are surely advantages to home care, especially for an older adult, such as being able to remain in a familiar setting close to family and friends and not being subjected to the rigid schedule of an institution carrying out simple activities of daily living such as nutrition and hygiene. A disadvantage of home care may be a heavy caregiving responsibility imposed on the family. And it has been pointed out that several factors such as "the aging of the American population, the decreased reproduction rate among 'baby boomers,' plus the growing number of younger individuals needing care at home, has led to a predicted shortage of family caregivers, especially caretakers of the frail elderly" (Lubkin & Payne, 1998, p. 262). All of these factors support the need for the ministry of parish nurses to parishioners receiving home care in the local community.

In a former work describing the spiritual needs of the chronically ill person, I began with the assertion, " For the chronically ill individual, personal spirituality and/or religious beliefs and practices often constitute an important, even critical, dimension of coping with the life changes necessitated by the illness experience" (O'Brien, 2003, p. 176). The relationship between personal spirituality and coping with illness has been supported repeatedly in nursing research (Georgesen & Dungan, 1996; Post-White et al., 1996; Toth, 1992). Recognizing the role of a chronically ill person's spirituality or spiritual/ religious support system will help the nurse facilitate the individual's "drive to growth, to wholeness, to fullness" (Muldoon & King, 1991, p. 99) as a human person, despite his or her illness or infirmity.

One of the most important things to remember in preparing for a ministry visit to a chronically ill parishioner is that, although of course there are always exceptions, most chronically ill persons, especially elders, need to spend some time telling you about their conditions. An infirm parishioner may want to give you a history, if this is a first-time visit; or he or she may simply wish to update you on the progress of a disease and, hopefully, the remission of symptoms. A few years ago, one of my students was studying the spiritual needs of homebound elders; her plan was to visit disabled individuals in their homes and interview them about their needs. One of her initial concerns was whether older persons would be willing and able to speak with her to participate in the interview sessions. After the student's first few days of meeting with homebound elders, she called, laughingly, to report that she need not have worried about getting her study participants to talk—the problem was getting them to stop! The student had to come up with some creative strategies to delicately move the elders away from talking about their illnesses and onto talking about their spiritual needs.

While it's true that some chronically ill parishioners may find it cathartic to talk about their illnesses or disabilities, a parish nurse may also meet homebound persons, especially men, who prefer not to discuss their health. General information might be obtained from family members prior to a visit; this can help the nurse in knowing how to approach a potentially sensitive topic, such as a terminal cancer diagnosis. I have also learned, in my years of conducting research interviews with the chronically ill, that many times a significant degree of rapport needs to be established between client and nurse prior to the patient "opening up" about painful issues. As mentioned, in relation to the spiritual companion role and the ministry visit in general, beginning a parish health ministry meeting with a prayer can set the tone for openness for both client and nurse, and also for openness to the guidance of the Holy Spirit.

Depending of course upon myriad variables, such as a parishioner's age, severity of illness or disability, and personality, a health ministry visit may include such activities as listening, advising, teaching, praying, reading scripture, playing music, or simply sitting by the bedside of the person. One of the elder participants in our parish nursing intervention study, described in the following chapter, told her parish nurse, on a first visit, that she enjoyed listening to the "old hymns" and to "gospel music." On subsequent health ministry visits, the nurse brought taped religious music that they could listen to together, and the hymns became part of the opening prayer of their health ministry meetings.

All of us have spiritual needs; it is often only at a time of illness, however, especially an experience of serious or chronic illness, that "spiritual needs previously unnoticed or neglected become apparent" (O'Brien, 2003, pp. 178–179). Some important spiritual needs of chronically ill persons that have been identified in the literature and in research include faith (in religious beliefs), peace (inner strength), hope, trust (Boutell & Bozeht, 1988, p. 174), courage, and love (O'Brien, 1992; 1995). In the previous chapter, some magnificently consoling and encouraging scripture passages that a parish nurse may find appropriate to share with a parishioner struggling with such needs are identified. Some other brief Bible passages related to the needs of faith, peace, hope, trust, courage, and love are these:

> Faith: *"If God is for us, who is against us? He who did not withhold his own Son, but gave him up for all of us, will he not with him also give us everything else?" (Romans 8:31–32).*

> Peace: *"May the Lord give strength to his people: may the Lord bless his people with peace" (Psalm 29:11).*

> Hope: *"And now, O Lord, what do I wait for? My hope is in you" (Psalm 39:8).*

> Trust: *"But I trust in you, O Lord; I say, 'You are my God'" (Psalm 31: 15).*

> Courage: *"I took courage, for the hand of the Lord, my God, was upon me (Ezra 7:28).*

> Love: *"Even though I walk through the darkest valley I fear no evil; for you are with me. . . . You anoint my head with oil; my cup overflows. Surely goodness and mercy shall follow me all the days of my life, and I shall dwell in the house of the Lord my whole life long" (Psalm 23:4–6).*

Ministering in Pain and Suffering

> This poor soul cried and was heard by the Lord, and was saved from every trouble.
>
> —Psalm 34:7

Many of the patients a parish nurse visits may be experiencing some degree of pain and suffering; this can set the stage for serious spiritual questions or discussion on the part of a parishioner and/or a family. Of course, the "why" question of illness or suffering is sometimes raised, especially in cases of young persons who are sick. Some people seek to find a spiritual message in an experience of suffering; for example, "Is God attempting to teach me something through this pain?" or "Am I being punished for not living as holy a life as I should have?" There is no answer to the "why" of human suffering. However, spiritual writers Emeth and Greenhut (1991) respond that "to those who feel that God is somehow responsible for human suffering, we would call to mind the example of Jesus, whose ministry is characterized by a commitment to healing. Everywhere Jesus went, he touched, healed, forgave, set free, exorcised demons, and restored sight, hearing, mobility, even life itself. He was clearly opposed to anything that limited people's experience of the fullness of life and personal relationship with God" (p. 64). And the authors conclude: "God's will for us is revealed in Jesus' ministry: healing and abundant life. If we are to follow his example, we are not to settle for less for ourselves or for those who seek our help" (p. 64).

The parish nurse, visiting as a spiritual minister in health and illness, can support the response to suffering through his or her caring response and attempt to alleviate a parishioner to the degree possible. In describing some elements of ministering to those at home, Marcy Heidish (1997) suggests three concepts that she describes as "a focus on feelings," "a language of listening," and "a ministry of presence" (p. 40). The "focus on feelings" means that a caregiver must carefully examine his or her own feelings as well as those of the patient; the nurse's feelings may need to be put aside if they interfere with the caring ministry. The "language of listening" includes "active listening," "reflective listening," and "listening of a feeling level"; and the "ministry of presence" includes such aspects as being "fully present" with the ill person, "calling forth stories" (allowing patients to tell joys and sorrows), "following up" (continuity), "widening the support system," and letting the "visiting take many forms" (writing notes, listening to music, sewing) (pp. 41–58).

Visiting a suffering parishioner can, of course, make such spiritual ministry difficult on a practical level, depending upon the severity of a parishioner's symptoms. Despite the fact that a parish nurse may feel that an individual seems too ill for a visit, having a minister spend some time of quiet prayer at the bedside can be incredibly comforting for both the patient and the family. A cancer patient speaking at a meeting of pastoral care providers at which I was present addressed this issue. He recalled a period in his disease trajectory when he was very ill; he described being besieged by symptoms of pain and nausea and attempting to sleep a great deal in order to escape the suffering. He also, however, spoke of the importance of support from his pastor and church members. He admitted, nonetheless, that when he was recovering, some church members told him that they had "thought about" visiting but felt that he was too ill and "didn't want to bother him." The patient's response to us as ministers was: "Bother me! If I am feeling very ill, if I fall asleep during your visit, just sit with me. I will know that you came; that you are there, and that means a lot to me. Don't you make the decision that I don't want to see anyone, especially a minister or a church member."

This patient's experience provided an important lesson for me. I tend to be shy and might have behaved precisely as some of his church members did because of my fear of disturbing him. Having said this, it is also important to remember, however, that there may be times when a parishioner–patient really does not want visitors; the patient may appreciate a brief prayer, but may not feel up to carrying on a conversation at that time, spritiual or otherwise. Most nurses have witnessed suffering patients, both at home and in healthcare facilities, fighting to remain alert and responsive to visitors, while hoping desperately they would soon leave! A somewhat humorous example of a well-meaning and caring, yet intrusive, visitor immediately comes to mind.

Many years ago when I was evening house supervisor at a large medical center, I always made early rounds to the Labor and Delivery Unit to check up on whether the staffing was adequate to the number of moms who were getting ready to give birth. As I arrived, the L and D charge nurse was coming out of one of the labor rooms where a mom-to-be was resting; she was laughing and shaking her head. She told me she had just had to send one of the young student nurses "packing." During pregnancy visits to the hospital clinic, each mother-to-be was assigned an individual "student coach" who would be present to provide "support" during the labor and delivery. The mother-to-be, whose room the charge nurse had just left, had been receiving the student coach's "support" for several hours. When the student left the room briefly, the laboring woman immediately summoned the charge nurse and asked if there was any way she could kindly but firmly send her student home. The mother-to-be, in her seventh pregnancy, knew the drill: she reported that although the student was very caring, her "support" was exhausting! The mother-to-be wanted to rest between pains, and the student wanted to talk. "I appreciate the student's coming to be with me," the mom-to-be told the charge nurse, "but I'm so tired; I need to get some sleep."

The preceding somewhat extreme and opposite examples of patients' desire or lack of desire for visitors when suffering or in pain demonstrate that the parish nurse may at times be in a quandary as to when, where, and/or for how long to visit a patient. Certainly, advice from friends and family can be helpful in providing guidelines. Once when I was doing some pastoral visiting at a nursing home, a mildly cognitively impaired resident's daughter called and suggested that closing the door to her mother's room facilitated visiting, as the resident could become distracted by the hall "traffic"; this proved a very helpful suggestion.

In the end, however, as with the art and science of all nursing activities, the art (and the spirituality) of the parish nurse will be especially called into play in the planning and carrying out of health ministry visits to the ill and infirm. On some occasions, and in some situations, nurse–parishioner interactions may seem very fruitful; at other times, the nurse may feel that the suffering patient was either not aware or only mildly aware of his or her visit. Nevertheless, any visit from a parish nurse brings the caring and compassion of the parishioner's faith community, and as such represents also the living out of the gospel message to care for the "little ones" in His name.

Ministering to the Older Adult

> The righteous flourish like the palm tree, and grow like a cedar in Lebanon. They are planted in the house of the Lord; they flourish in the courts of our God. In old age they still produce fruit.
>
> —*Psalm 92:13–14*

Contemporary language describing older adults has changed from a generation ago. Currently, gerontologists tend to describe the "young old" as individuals from 65 to 75 years of age; the "older old" as persons from 75 to 90; and elders over 90 are labeled the "oldest old." It has been suggested, however, that the young old group "may soon include people as old as 84" (Roen, 1997, p. 348). The elderly population in our country is growing daily; this has both positive and negative implications for health care in general and parish nursing in particular. It is true that "Americans are living longer and healthier lives, but extended life spans also bring increased need for both medical care and support in day-to-day activities. . . . [Additionally], the rapidly increasing proportion of aging persons, particularly the frail elderly, threatens to overwhelm the present system of healthcare and support" (Catholic Health Association of the United States, 1999, p. 7). Parish-based programs for the elderly living at home may include such services as "personal support," for example, food delivery and transportation; "emotional support," including family and grief counseling; "enrichment," spiritual development and education; "caregiver support," counseling and respite care; and "advocacy," or representing the interest of the parishioner and his or her family" (Catholic Health Association of the United States, 1999, pp. 13–14).

Elders face significant losses related to such factors as retirement and the illness and death of loved ones; supporting their personal spirituality "may provide a means to help individuals through these difficult adjustments and late-life developmental tasks" (McCulloch, 1997, p. 137). In later life, the elder must transition in self-image; a shift in identity occurs as one becomes an "older adult." The elder may feel that he or she is no longer contributing to society as in younger days. One role of the parish nurse may be to help older parishioners find some meaningful volunteer activities. This is especially important for the Christian elder "who is called to be a forerunner until the end of life. . . . If one has identified with [the concept] of 'forerunner', the conviction remains, even after retirement, that one has a purpose to fulfill. One must still contribute to the kingdom of God" (Swift & Rench, 1991, p. 70).

As with the chronically ill, nursing research has also demonstrated the importance of spirituality in the lives of ill and infirm older adults (O'Brien, 2003; 1989). One reason suggested for the importance placed on personal spirituality among older adults is the fact that elders "must find answers to why they are losing their roles, identities, and capacities" (Berggren-Thomas & Griggs, 1995, p. 6). Berggren-Thomas and Griggs add: "Spirituality can help [elders] find meaning in these late-in-life struggles" (p. 6). Another rationale for an increased interest in spirituality and spiritual practices among older adults is the fact that now, as retired or at least semi-retired persons, they have more time to focus on these dimensions of their lives. In an ethnographic study of 12 older, chronically ill adults, geriatric nurse practitioner Cathy Young (1993) also found that "spiritual practices provided something to do for people who could not be as active as before their chronic illness" (p. 3000).

A list of "nursing roles relevant to spirituality of elders" identified in a text on gerontological nursing might well be likened to the primary roles described for the discipline of parish nursing. They include "friend," which might be likened to the role of spiritual companion or integrator of faith and health; "advocate," or mediator, as the parish nurse advocate role; "caregiver," assessor of spiritual needs and advisor, similar to the counselor role of the parish nurse; and "case manager," coordinating care as the parish nurse who serves as referral agent (Halstead, 1995, pp. 418–419). Halstead adds one additional role that she labels "researcher," in which the nurse seeks to better understand the spiritual needs and concerns of the patient (p. 419).

It has been pointed out that the minister to the older adult must be sensitive to the "coping techniques that people use to manage the stresses overwhelming them . . . anger, protest, hostility, withdrawal, apathy, display of helplessness, and dependence" (Hynes, 1989, p. 43). Hynes observes that these behaviors can "make people difficult to reach," but the minister must continue to be a "source of support and encouragement" for the parishioner. "Sometimes," she adds "it is a long, slow process, but our goal is to share the love of God, not to have all the answers" (p. 43).

As with chronically ill parishioners, a ministry visit to an ill or infirm older adult may include such activities as listening, advising, teaching, and sharing prayer, religious music, or scripture reading. Of these parish nursing roles, sometimes the ministries of presence and listening prove most supportive. The act of reminiscence can provide much pleasure for an older adult if carried out in the presence of a caring and interested listener. Religious rituals and symbols are also important to ill and homebound or facility-bound elders, as was observed repeatedly in the study the Gift of Faith in Chronic Illness (Chapter 8). Treasured religious symbols "can facilitate the tasks of aging persons by providing a link with the past as well as being a concrete reminder of hope in the future" (Maltby, 1990, pp. 102–103). Maltby notes that it is important for a pastoral minister to keep in mind that beloved religious symbols may have less to do with an elder's "theology" than with the "unique meaning they have given to their lives" (p. 103). "Ritual activites," Maltby adds, "are powerful expressions in ministry with the elderly. Even those with a language impairment can frequently sing familiar hymns and become involved in a community ritual" (p. 103). Other rituals suggested for ill elders are "anointing of the sick" and "spontaneous prayer" (Maltby, 1990, p. 103).

It is anticipated that a parish nurse ministering to ill elders at home will probably meet some parishioners who may be categorized as the "oldest old." Ministry to these elders will, of course, be modified according to physical and/or cognitive limitations. In describing ministry to the oldest old, however, four important issues must be considered by the pastoral caregiver: "preparation for dying," including consideration of the afterlife; "coping with chronic illness" and the associated pain and suffering; "coping with dependency," both physical and emotional; and "expressing the potential for spiritual development" or the understanding that "continued spiritual growth" is to be supported and desired for the oldest-old elders (Ellor, Thibault, Netting, & Carey, 1990, pp. 105–107).

Finally, some practical information that a parish nurse may be able to share with both chronically ill elders and younger parishioners who are homebound by illness and infirmity is a listing of community resources such as local pharmacies that deliver physician-prescribed medications; grocery delivery services; home healthcare services; home companion services; house-cleaning services; meals-on-wheels; respite care services (for families); "senior connections" (local hospitals); and transportation services. An ill parishioner, newly homebound, and/or a family may not have had the time or the energy to identify the availability and accessibility of some of these very important services; providing a list of community service agencies and phone numbers can be an important dimension of health ministry (Table 8.1 presents key issues in carrying out parish health ministry visits to homebound parishioners).

Hospital Ministry

Parish nurses are in uniquely positive positions to provide spiritual ministry to the hospitalized patient because of their in-depth understanding of the operation and management of the contemporary hospital. When I undertook an intense 10-week hospital chaplaincy training program, although I was well received by the medical center's department of spiritual ministry, my chaplain supervisor told me that, as I was in the program to become a chaplain, I must "leave my 'nurse's cap' in the trunk" of my car. I understood the advice in terms of placing my immediate focus on learning the

Table 8.1 **PARISH HEALTH MINISTRY VISITS TO HOMEBOUND PARISHIONERS**

1. Check with the parishioner or family about a convenient time to visit.
2. Prior to the visit, ask whether the ill parishioner has any visual, hearing, or speech impairments.
3. Seek to determine areas of the parishioner's interest for a pastoral visit, such as Holy Communion, prayer, scripture reading, spiritual counseling, or health counseling.
4. Listen actively; allow the parishioner to talk about things that are important to him or her.
5. Bring Holy Communion (if appropriate), a Bible, and a list of local community healthcare resources (if appropriate).
6. Draw the visit to a conclusion if parishioner begins to appear fatigued.
7. Begin and end the health ministry visit with prayer.

hospital chaplaincy role. The nursing staff on the pediatric oncology unit to which I was assigned rejoiced when they learned that they had a "nurse" as "chaplain" for the summer. When I related my supervisor's comment about my nurse's cap, however, the charge nurse replied: "No, don't leave your cap in the trunk of your car; keep it in your back pocket!" Since I was a nurse, I was allowed to be with patients during some therapeutic procedures, such as bone marrow aspirations and chemotherapy treatments, to which other student chaplains might not have been invited.

The charge nurse's advice seems appropriate also for the parish nurse, who, while functioning in the role of chaplain or spiritual minister, can still keep her (and figuratively, his) nurse's cap in a back pocket. Having lived through the anxieties of some of my nonmedical theology classmates who anticipated their hospital chaplaincy training experiences, I realized how blessed we are, as nurses, to be able to carry out spiritual ministry in a setting in which we are at home. Parish nurses visiting hospitalized patients can also be supportive of families and friends unfamiliar with the setting; they may able to explain hospital norms and rules related to such issues as visiting in intensive care settings, the need for lengthy recovery room periods after surgery, and strategies for obtaining information about a loved one's medical or surgical condition.

Ministering to the Acutely Ill Parishioner

As mentioned previously, whether, as well as when and for how long, a parish nurse should visit a hospitalized parishioner fall within the dimensions of both the art and the science of parish nursing. In a book titled *Pastoral Care in Hospitals*, Dr. Neville Kirkwood (1998) offers the advice that "the wisdom of your visit at a particular time has to be considered in light of the best interests of the patient" (p. 7). As Chaplain Kirkwood notes, one patient may be too ill for a visit, another already receiving pastoral care, and yet another may need privacy (p. 7). Most of us involved in pastoral ministry altruistically want to rush to the hospital when we learn that a parishioner or someone to whom we have ministered is seriously ill. However, as a wise friend has reminded me on occasion, it is important to stop and pray first about whether we are making the visit to meet the patient's needs or our own.

Having made a determination that a visit is appropriate, even if brief and perhaps for the benefit of the family as much as for the acutely ill parishioner, the parish nurse must pray about the ministry. Arnold (1982) comments that pastoral visits are "primarily symbolic during an acute stage of treatment" (p. 180). "Seldom," he adds, "are persons able or willing to engage in deep reflection during the acute phase [of illness] because of pain, discomfort, fear, or distractions" (p. 180). Because the onset of an acute illness may be sudden and unexpected, families are often left in the background (or waiting rooms), while all of the medical attention is lavished appropriately on the patient. Family members, however, can be critically important recipients of ministry during this acute period. Arnold asserts: "Often we will have knowledge about some procedures and can serve as a guide though some of the technicalities" (p. 181). The minister may also be a "contact person" with other hospital professionals and may serve as an "interpreter of language" that may be difficult for family members to understand (p. 181).

One of the most stressful experiences for the family of an acutely ill hospitalized patient is not knowing, waiting to learn the condition and prognosis of their loved one. The minister may be able to obtain some information or may possess some personal information about the professional staff treating the parishioner that can provide comfort to the relatives that their family member is in "good hands." And often simply the ministerial act of sitting with, being present to, the family of a seriously ill patient in a waiting room is something that provides great comfort to all.

A few years ago, a colleague at my university told me that she was scheduled to have surgery. While it was not emergency surgery, there was an initial diagnosis of cancer and it would not be known until the surgery was carried out just how serious were the situation and the prognosis. My friend was very anxious and asked for prayers. She was a member of a very large family, and she told me that a number of her relatives were planning to be at the hospital during her surgery. I asked whether she would like me to be there also, and she responded very enthusiastically; she immediately wrote down the date and time of the surgery and directions to the hospital. On the day of surgery, I arrived to learn that although I had allowed plenty of time to say a prayer with my friend before her departure for the operating room, the schedule had been moved up and she had been taken off on a guerney just minutes before I got there. I was, however, able to find seven family members in a nearby waiting room, and I sat with them during the surgery.

After about four hours, the primary surgeon came out of the OR to tell us the good news that my friend's cancer appeared localized with no sign of metastasis. He was very positive and said the surgery had gone as well as he could possibly have hoped; he did tell us, however, that our patient was not yet even out of the OR and following that she would be in the recovery room for several hours. As it was evening, he advised most of us to go home. One sibling planned to stay until his sister awoke; he promised to tell her that we had all been there and that we were rejoicing at the positive outcome.

The conclusion to my story is that although during my time at the hospital I never got to see the person I had come to pray with, my friend was deeply appreciative of my effort. For some time after the surgery, whenever I stopped by her office, she would say to friends and coworkers: "You know, Sister Mary Elizabeth was with me during my surgery!" The value of a parish nurse's presence during acute illness or crisis cannot be underestimated!

Ministering to the Parishioner in the Intensive Care Unit

Depending upon the size and sophistication of a hospital or medical center, there may be myriad intensive care units (ICUs) in which a parishioner may be placed for treatment: medical ICU, surgical ICU, transplant ICU, coronary care unit, pediatric ICU, neonatal ICU, and others. Regardless of the particular specialty designation, admission to an intensive care setting indicates the presence of a very serious medical or surgical problem and the need for intensive monitoring and care. The anxiety of being admitted to an ICU can be very traumatic for both patients and their loved ones. Many former ICU patients and their families admit that they felt something akin to panic on initially seeing such ICU technology as ventilators, nasogastric tubes, cardiac monitors, arterial lines, multiple intravenous setups, and other specialized equipment used intermittently such as a hemodialysis machines or chest tube drainage vacuum bottles.

Related to the frightening abundance of technology employed in the ICU environment, as well as the powerlessness of one's situation, it is suggested that patients' spiritual needs at the time often include "searching for meaning in the face of crisis, identifying and accessing one's inner resources for strength, reformulating one's spiritual identity in the face of disruption, developing effective coping strategies, and finding healing in the midst of brokenness" (Gillman, Gable-Rodriguez, Sutherland, & Whitacre, 1996, p. 10). Obviously, such immense needs, especially that of "finding healing in the midst of brokenness," pose an incredible challenge to the parish nurse as minister to parishioners in the ICU and to their families.

A parish nurse ministering to the ICU patient and family, however, represents not only his or her own caring and concern but also that of the Lord and of the faith community to which the parishioner belongs. Sometimes the most important dimension of the nurse's visit is not the words he or she says but the simple act of being there; of being present to the patient and family in their hours of greatest need. This is the healing brought by the parish nurse. For it has been pointed out that "healing" may or may not involve a "physical cure," but rather the minister "offers to the patient or family member the fullness of his or her personal presence and, in that receptive presence, the possibility of 'meeting' . . . [which provides] the opportunity to experience the healing that needs to take place" (Gillman et al., 1996, p. 13). Taylor (2000) describes a nurse's being present spiritually to those who are suffering as "presencing" which she explains as a "practice that relies heavily on the nurse's instinct or intution. To know if, when and how to touch or to speak should reflect the uniqueness of the situation and the nurse–client relationship" (p. 95).

One of the very specialized intensive care settings in which a parish nurse's ministry can be most comforting to a family is the neonatal intensive care unit (NICU). Infants may be admitted to the NICU for a variety of reasons: gestational age in the range of threshold viability (approximately 22 to 28 weeks), respiratory distress, apnea, stridor, seizures, and a multitude of other physical anomalies requiring such procedures as ventilation, tube feeding, intravenous therapy, and cardiac monitoring. Admission of an infant to the NICU can be terrifying to parents who realize that their baby might not survive the experience. Within the tradition of some denominations, a parish nurse may be asked to baptize a NICU infant in danger of death, or the nurse may request a visit from the pastor or other clergyperson to administer the sacrament. In the case of death of a NICU infant, the parish nurse can provide a caring presence to support grieving parents; the parish nurse can also advise and assist parents making plans for a wake and funeral. The nurse is an appropriate minister in bereavement, especially if he or she has been through the illness and death experience with parents and family of the NICU infant.

Ministering to the Child and Family in the Pediatric Unit

Chaplain Jim Arnold (1992) points out that "the crisis of a sick child usually begins days before the entrance to the pediatric unit" (p. 95). While Arnold acknowledges that some illnesses, and of course accidents, are of sudden onset, in many cases parents have been "struggling to prevent and stop pain and suffering from overcoming their child" for some time prior to hospitalization (p. 95). "It is during these hours," he notes, "that spiritual needs first begin to be felt in the family" (p. 95). Based on my personal experience of pediatric hospital chaplaincy, I am in complete agreement with Chaplain Arnold's point.

My chaplaincy internship, which, as I mentioned earlier, took place on a pediatric oncology unit, allowed me the opportunity for interaction with parents as well as with the "peds" patients I ministered to. Very often, by the time a child was admitted to the unit, the family members were already anxious and exhausted from care and from worrying about the progress of the child's cancer. I learned, as Arnold observed, that parents had indeed been feeling spiritual needs for some time. Initially, I was concerned with not being intrusive when I approached a parent whose child was undergoing treatment; I wasn't sure whether their anxiety for their child might override the need to talk about their own needs and worries. Of course, the parents' care was centered on their sick child, but I quickly discovered that as soon as I entered a room and said the words: "I'm a chaplain," a parent would quickly pull up a chair and invite me to sit down. A similar reception, I'm sure, would be afforded a parish nurse visiting a pediatric unit.

Obviously, the age and severity of illness of the child will guide the ministry that a parish nurse may carry out in a peds hospital setting. For the toddler or very young child, the parents are the primary recipients of listening ministry and the ministry of presence; a parent will generally, however, request that a prayer be offered for his or her child and some parents will join in the prayer themselves. For an older school-age child or a teen or preteen, parents will occasionally take a coffee break after spending some time with a visiting minister, allowing the child privacy to talk and to pray with the visitor; this may depend on the tradition of ministry that the parents and child or young person have experienced in the past.

When I first began my internship on the peds-oncology unit, I felt very insecure, as I am not a pediatric nurse; when I confessed my shyness about ministering to children to one of our pediatric residents she replied simply: "Let the children lead you." That was excellent advice; it worked. I think perhaps my greatest surprise was that the children, especially the very ill teens, were willing and even anxious to talk about their spirituality; they were also forthcoming in talking about their possible deaths, a topic which I had surely been hesitant to raise. My experience is supported by Verna Benner Carson (1998), who notes that "sometimes children display spiritual maturity beyond their years" (p. 1079). "Nurses," she adds, "who work with dying children frequently comment on the level of spiritual development present in the very young" (p. 1079).

I have written previously about the spiritual needs of children and families, both in terms of assessment and intervention (O'Brien, 2003, pp. 211–237). It can be helpful for a parish nurse to have some knowledge of children's "stages of faith development," such as those identified by James Fowler (1981), and of assessment strategies, such as those described by Judith Van Heukelem-Still (1982). In the moment of ministry, however, it is the nurse's personal spirituality and trust in the Lord that are his or her greatest assets in providing meaningful pastoral care. I have learned from hospital chaplaincy experiences, both during my internship and later as a volunteer in a local hospital, that there is no lecture or book or video, however helpful these tools may be, that will totally prepare ministers or parish nurses for what they may encounter when they enter a hospital room. Prayer and an absolute sense of dependence upon the Holy Spirit for guidance are the best approaches in ministering to all hospitalized patients, especially children, and to their families.

Ministering to the Parishioner in the Psychiatric Unit

The parish nurse ministering in a psychiatric unit also must depend heavily upon the previously suggested tools of prayer and dependence on the Holy Spirit. As nurses and ministers in psychiatry know, it is sometimes quite difficult to sort out spiritual problems and needs from imagined or delusional concerns for the neurotic or psychotic patient. A classic spiritually related symptom manifested by some psychiatric patients is the state of being beset by "scruples," or "unfounded fears that there is sin where there is none" (Livingstone, 1990, p. 465). Although this may be related to a parishioner's psychiatric diagnosis, the caring support and encouragement of a pastoral care provider, such as a parish nurse, may be very helpful in alleviating the patient's concerns; the parish nurse's support comes cloaked in a spiritual mantle and thus may, in spiritual matters, have greater meaning for a parishioner than the comfort of the psychiatrist or psychiatric nurse.

In discussing ministry visits to psychiatric units, Fernando Poyatos (1999) advises that the pastoral care provider be very careful about giving patients certain spiritual books, which might cause "more harm than good" (p. 79). He does suggest that the minister can share "prayers of trust" with a parishioner, such as those found in scripture, for example, Psalm 31: "Incline Your ear to me, make haste to rescue me! Be my rock of refuge, a stronghold to save me. You are my rock and my fortress, for your name's sake lead and guide me" (Poyatos, 1999, p. 79). And Lucien Sawyer (1990) asserts that ministers for psychiatric patients should have some familiarity with the "structure and categories of the *DSM*," the *Diagnostic and Statistical Manual* of mental disorders, "in order to have some handle on the patient's problem, and to understand the insight of the other therapists" (p. 95).

Conversation with a psychiatric patient–parishioner may help a parish nurse sort out some of the individual's spiritual needs, which may appear confounded by his or her illness. Some areas of exploration suggested by chaplain and psychiatric mental health nurse Saundra John (1983) include questions related to such areas as whether a patient's "religious behavior . . . seems to create emotional disturbance," whether "the religious aspect of the person's behavior [is] an indirect precipitating factor in the emotional disorder," whether "the religious concern [is] a symptom of a deeper conflict," whether "the religious concern [is] a defense that is not healthy long term," whether "the religious behavior and thinking [are] realistic, comforting and supportive," "what part religion plays in the choice of symptoms," and whether "the religion merely provides the content ideation for the illness or delusion" (pp. 81–83).

Ultimately, "attempting to analyze and understand the spiritual needs of a mentally ill patient, especially a depressed individual, is extremely challenging to the nurse. Much time may be spent in simply encouraging the patient to verbalize his or her concerns. During the interaction, however, the nurse can communicate a sense of care and empathy, sometimes opening the door to the possibility of therapeutic intervention in the area of spiritual need (O'Brien, 2003, p. 193; see also pp. 190–193). Table 8.2 identifies some specific issues to remember in preparing for a parish health ministry visit to a hospitalized patient; while, admittedly, these areas of concern are familiar to parish nurses, they may not be as easily remembered by nonnursing/medical parish health ministers.

Table 8.2 PARISH HEALTH MINISTRY VISITS TO HOSPITALIZED PARISHIONERS

1. Call the parishioner or family to find out whether a parish health ministry visit is desired or acceptable.

2. Check with hospital staff to identify appropriate visiting hours (and visitor restrictions/time limitations), especially for areas such as intensive care.

3. Be aware of possible ministry visit interruptions related to medical/nursing interventions.

4. Be alert to parishioner–patient's level of energy/fatigue (don't overstay a visit).

5. Pray with the patient (and family, if present) at the beginning and the end of the visit.

Nursing Home and Assisted Care Facility Ministry

Ministering to the Long-Term Care Parishioner

The Lord of the Nursing Home

Nursing homes are not places we look
    forward to visiting;
even the best of them, gifted with a
    spirit of caring and compassion.
Nursing homes remind us of things we
    know, but would rather forget:
We are grateful, Lord, for our years
    of youth and strength; but we beg
      You mightily to delay our years
      of age and fragility.

And yet we need not fear the nursing
    home, Lord God of life, and death,
    and glorious resurrection.
For You are there, Dear Lord,
    as surely as You are in the cloistered
      monastery;
        as surely as You are in the
        silent chapel;
          as surely as You are in the
          majestic Cathedral.
You are there, O Lord of the Nursing Home:
    in the gentle caring of a frail elder, who
      bravely maneuvers her walker to visit
      a bedridden comrade.

You are there, O Lord of the Nursing Home:
    in the tender commitment of a faithful
    daughter, who lovingly undertakes
      a frantic commute to sit beside
      her senile mother.

You are there, O Lord of the Nursing Home:
    in the kindness and compassion of a geriatric
    nurse who caringly keeps watch at
      the bedside of a dying patient.

> You gift the nursing home with Your
> presence, O Lord; and all who
> meet You there are blessed
> by Your love.

Ministering to parishioners residing in nursing homes or assisted care/life care communities and their families involves the parish nurse adopting many of the same attitudes, behaviors, and periods of prayerful preparation as home visiting or hospital visiting. There are, however, unique characteristics to the nursing home that need to be considered (for simplicity, I will from now on use the term *nursing home* to also include assisted care and life care communities in which the parishioners of a faith community may reside). In a study of long-term adaptation to nursing home life titled *Anatomy of a Nursing Home* (O'Brien, 1989), we became acutely aware of the importance of these resident and facility characteristics in terms of scheduling visits with the project participants.

Initially, the project team visited 71 cognitively alert nursing home residents; 62 women and nine men; our visits lasted anywhere from 15 minutes to one and a half hours according to the resident's abilities and desire to converse (O'Brien, 1989). One of the most important findings in regard to the scheduling of resident visits, which has implications for the planning of nursing home ministry visits by a parish nurse, is that one needs to be aware of a resident's activity schedule in the home and must plan meetings accordingly. This was somewhat of a surprise; we had naïvely thought that for planning meetings, we had a "captive audience" in terms of physical location, provided, of course, that the resident was agreeable to a visit. We quickly learned that, for the more active residents, visits needed to be planned around such activities as chapel services, physical therapy appointments, hair-styling appointments, outside trips, occupational therapy, physician's rounds, resident committee meetings, and a variety of seasonal celebrations planned by the nursing home administration.

A resident's personal schedule of activities of daily living must be considered also. While hygiene activities usually are carried out in the early morning, some elderly nursing home residents need a substantive afternoon nap in order to carry them through the day. Another important consideration is the presence of family members, who, if visiting the resident, may or may not wish to be present during ministry meetings. Evenings are generally unavailable for the more frail residents, as early bedtimes become the norm in many facilities. Often, the best times to visit with nursing home residents is between 10 A.M. and the noon lunch hour, or between about 3 P.M. and the evening meal at 5 or 5:30 P.M. Saturdays, Sundays, and holidays can also be very good times to visit with residents, depending, again, upon the planning of family visits in the facility; in some cases, especially on holidays or birthdays, family members will also take the resident home for a day or two.

A final note about the visiting of family members, or more specifically the absence of family visits, is important. The pastoral ministry visit of a parish nurse on a holiday, such as Thanksgiving, Christmas, or Easter, can be a treasured gift to an elderly nursing home resident who no longer has family or friends who come. During the project Anatomy of a Nursing Home, I made it a point to visit the nursing home where our study was being conducted on each of the major holidays. For some residents, the holidays were happy days, filled with the love and support of family and friends; for others, the lack of a familial support system served to increase their sense of loneliness and isolation. Another dimension of the latter suffering was manifested in Mrs. James, a long-time nursing home resident who, although physically active, was beginning to be quite confused and forgetful; she lived in a domiciliary unit (for self-care residents).

I stopped by to see Mrs. James around 11 A.M. on my Christmas Day visit. She was sitting up in a chair, dressed in a lovely Christmas dress, her hair combed attractively, and holding her coat and purse on her lap. When I asked whether she was going out for the day, she smiled brightly and replied: "Oh, yes, my family is coming for me!" She then added: "I'm all ready to go; could you see if they've arrived yet?" I relayed Mrs. James's question to the unit charge nurse, who shook her head sadly and replied: "I'm afraid there is no family coming for Mrs. James. Her only relatives are a niece and a nephew who live 500 miles away and we haven't received any notice that they will be coming to see her, or take her anywhere today. We've tried to explain that to Mrs. James, but she just doesn't want to hear it; in her mind, she's convinced that they're coming."

I remained at the nursing home to attend a specially prepared Christmas dinner and tried to get Mrs. James to come with me. She refused, however, insisting that she needed to remain in her room to wait for the family. My silent prayer was that, by the end of the day, the Lord would bless Mrs. James, in her dementia, with forgetfulness of the anticipated visit; at the moment, her futile hope and anticipation were breaking the hearts of the staff working on the unit.

In their book *Pastoral Visiting in the Nursing Home*, Simmons and Peters (1996) address issues of when and for how long to visit, as well as advise ministers to get focused prior to visits. They point out that while pastoral visiting of the institutionalized elderly can be very rewarding, it can also be challenging, and they suggest that before "beginning a visit . . . it [is] helpful to spend a few minutes in prayer, focusing on the compassion of Christ" (p. 37). "If," they add, "the facility you are visiting has a chapel, you might spend a few quiet moments there. If . . . not . . . find a quiet space . . . be attentive to God's presence; ask for strength and guidance" (p. 37). Actually, the facility in which the study Anatomy of a Nursing Home was carried out did have a chapel, which was adjacent to the front entrance, and I found that spending a few minutes with the Lord prior to making my way to the nursing units provided much spiritual support for my meetings with residents and staff.

Simmons and Peters (1996) also offer a "basic pattern" for the pastoral visit to a nursing home, which they identify as consisting of four dimensions: the greeting, speaking the word, sharing communion, and sending them home (ending the visit) (pp. 44–45). Greeting a resident is described by Simmons and Peters as "creating a hospitable space in which you and the other person come together in the name of Jesus Christ" (p. 44). "Speaking the word" as a central part of the visit may be done in one of several ways: sharing the word "explicitly, as that is appropriate," sharing ourselves "in service to the people we visit," or sharing the word "in silence because human words fail" (p. 45). Sharing communion means "coming to a moment of intensity and depth in God's presence" through prayer, shared silence, or touch (p. 45). And, finally, end the visit with "some form of closure . . . some form of looking forward," perhaps with a prayer or blessing, depending upon one's faith tradition (p. 45).

Ministering to the Cognitively Impaired Parishioner

In the study Anatomy of a Nursing Home we included 24 mild to moderately cognitively impaired nursing home residents as a subsample of the study population; the goal was to carry out simple conversational interviews to determine the needs and concerns of this resident group. I had been advised by a seasoned gerontological nurse to orient our meetings with some simple direct questions such as "How are you?" "What did you do today?" and "Is there anything you need?" It was also suggested that the nurse meeting with the cognitively impaired residents make an initial visit to say hello, introduce herself, and tell the resident that she would be coming back in the next day or two for a longer visit. Our gerontology consultant advised that while a cognitively impaired resident might not remember the nurse's name, he or she may remember her face or have a sense of familiarity at the next meeting. I realize that parish nurses may well not have the time for this kind of an introductory visit to a cognitively impaired nursing home resident; however, the idea has implications for the same nurse consistently making visits to a particular parishioner, if a faith community has the luxury of several parish nurses and/or health ministers.

In a ministry visit to any cognitively impaired person, Pastor Kent Miller (1995) advises: "Begin each conversation by calling the person by name, touching gently and identifying yourself" (p. 149). He also suggests that the pastoral visitor use "short sentences"; short words"; "sensory language: see, look, imagine"; and "ask questions that may be answered with yes or no or with a gesture" (p. 149). Miller's suggestions are supported by Simmons and Peters (1996), who also advise that the minister begin with a simple personal introduction using a few words or a "touch on the hand" and perhaps a simple reassurance to the person: "God loves you and you matter to God" (p. 60). The authors observe that even in the later stages of dementia, the minister may perceive "glimmers of a reaction that signal a response, however uncommunicable in words" (p. 60). This latter point is validated by Sister Anne, the director of pastoral care at a large nursing home where I did some volunteer parish nursing. Sister Anne told me that when she blessed the cognitively impaired residents and made the sign of the cross on their foreheads, she always sensed a response, even in those with advanced dementias; she commented that it was not a response in words but rather the look in the residents' eyes that told her they understood.

A last study finding from Anatomy of a Nursing Home, which might be helpful to parish nurses ministering to cognitively impaired nursing home residents, is the description of the categories of ideation that residents manifested in conversational interviews. These were labeled conformity, privacy, activity, externality, and reminiscence (O'Brien, 1989, pp. 37–39). *Conformity* relates to the residents' desire to please, especially the physician and nursing home staff. Most residents told us that they "tried to go along" with everything in the nursing home (p. 37). One elder commented, "This is the only place I have; what would I do if they put me out?" *Privacy*, closely related to the issue of conformity, meant minding one's business and not causing any trouble for the staff or other residents (p. 37). *Activity* was a label used to categorize the daily "work" of the resident, which was an important dimension of their conversations. *Externality* represented a theme found in a number of the residents' activity descriptions, in which they perceived their identities as related to family or a former life, for example: "They brought my baby to see me; the baby is named after me so it's 'my' baby, so to speak. It's special when a child is named after you" (p. 38). And *reminiscence* describes how residents retell the important occurrences in their lives (p. 39). Having some sense of the themes that may run through a cognitively impaired resident's thoughts may be helpful in directing a ministry visit or in responding to seemingly illusory thoughts or questions.

Ministering to Families

In the Anatomy of a Nursing Home project we also interviewed a subgroup of 32 significant others; as suggested earlier, not all of the residents we met had close family or friends who visited. The family/significant other group consisted of 12 daughters of residents, five sons, seven nieces, one nephew, three sisters, one brother, two wives, and one friend, a Catholic Sister who had become a legal guardian (O'Brien, 1989, p. 52). What surprised me most on attending my first "family" meeting, held periodically at the nursing home, was the number of attending family members with gray hair; many looked as if they themselves could become nursing home residents in the not-too-distant future.

One of the nursing home social workers commented on the "adult children" of the home's residents, noting that in recent years, and continuing until the present, residents admitted to the home were older and sicker than in earlier decades; many, she reported, "are in their 80s or 90s , so the children are in their 60s and they are dealing with their own impending aging process" (p. 54). The social worker's point was validated by the comments of several adult children themselves: "The 65-year-old daughter of Mrs. Elsie Decker [pseudonym], an 89-year-old third-floor resident [cognitively impaired unit] suffering from senility and depression, reported 'When she was with me it was like a senior citizen taking care of a senior citizen'"; and the son of 94-year-old Mrs. Englejohn admitted: "I feel guilty about putting Mother in a nursing home because I should be taking care of her myself, but we're in our sixties and it would be like the old taking care of the old" (p. 54).

I share the preceding examples with parish nurses because I believe that an important spiritual issue in nursing home visiting is ministering to the family members, as well as to the residents. A significant spiritual concern and need, which a parish nurse may help alleviate, is that expressed by Mrs. Englejohn's son: guilt over admitting a family member to a home. In fact, guilt was found to be a central concern of most of the family members we interviewed for the study, especially in the cases of nuclear family, including sons and daughters, siblings and spouses. As a social worked commented: "The family, it's almost like they are going through the same processes that they would if somebody died. . . . They're dealing with a tremendous amount of guilt . . . even though they know it's best for everybody concerned. They were brought up that your parents raised you and then you turn around and help them, and it's really difficult for them" (O'Brien, 1989, p. 62).

A parish nurse ministering to a family dealing with guilt feelings about admitting their loved one to a nursing home may not be able to take away the pain of the family's loss; he or she might, however, be able to help the family members face the reality of their situations that in fact necessitated such a step, for example, the family caregiver's own age and physical limitations. A parish nurse can also pray with the family members and support them spiritually as they struggle to cope with the realization that they can no longer provide the personal care for their loved ones as they might wish.

Table 8.3 presents some points to keep in mind for visiting parishioners residing in nursing homes or assisted care facilities.

Ministry in Death and Bereavement

Perhaps the most challenging pastoral ministry that a parish nurse will be called upon to perform is to provide support for dying parishioners and their families. Many factors impact this particular spiritual ministry such as the age of the dying parishioner; the severity of the illness; the length of time of physical disability; and whether the dying process follows a sudden onset physical assault, such as an accident or a stroke, or comes as the termination of a long period of suffering, as with certain malignancies. All of these variables impact a family's stress and coping at the time of a loved one's dying. Generally, the most traumatic of all deaths are those involving younger parishioners: infants, children, and young to middle-age adults. In such cases, families often feel that their dying loved ones did not have a chance to accomplish certain life goals, and they decry the brevity of their lives. As with all of parish nursing, ministry to each dying parishioner and his or her family will be unique and cannot be planned or prepared for according to any specific procedural directives. Having accepted that fact, however, there are some suggestions of general need and ministry

---

Table 8.3 **PARISH HEALTH MINISTRY TO PARISHIONERS RESIDING IN LONG-TERM CARE FACILITIES**

1. Check with the resident or facility staff for appropriate visiting times.
2. Arrive when expected by the resident (elders, especially, look forward to visitors with much anticipation).
3. Plan to spend enough time, during which the resident can share problems and concerns, if needed; loneliness is a prevailing issue in long-term care facilities.
4. Visit facility-bound residents on major holidays if possible (these are particularly lonely times for elders with little or no family to take them home for a visit).
5. Begin and end the visit with prayer.

guidelines that a parish nurse can then modify to fit the specific situation in which ministry is provided.

Ministry to Terminally Ill Parishioners

A terminally ill parishioner may have come to terms with concerns related to his or her life and death; or there may be some unresolved issues with which the parish nurse, as spiritual minister, can assist. In the past, I have done a number of psychosocial and spiritual nursing studies with persons facing life-threatening illnesses, especially those suffering from chronic renal failure, HIV (human immunodeficiency virus), and AIDS (acquired immune deficiency syndrome) (O'Brien, 1983; 1992; 1995). One of the most significant concerns that emerged from our interviews with patients close to death was not the fear of death, but the fear of dying. In other words, the patients had for some time prepared for their deaths, especially the AIDS patients; most even had specific details documented for their funerals or memorial services. Their greatest anxieties, however, revolved around the manner of dying, the possible pain, suffering, and humiliation of losing control of their bodily functions. Many also expressed the fear of being alone at the time of their deaths.

These fears were also documented in a study of 37 home hospice patients; among some of the identified death-related anxieties were "worry about dying; worry about dying before finishing everything; worry about being sick a long time; worry about others seeing him or her suffering; worry that dying may be painful; worry about being alone when dying"; and others related to concern for "loved ones left behind" (Reese & Brown, 1997, p. 34). Nancy Conrad (1985), a nursing consultant in death education, in describing the "inward journey" of the dying person, identifies three key overlapping needs of the dying: a "sense of forgiveness," the "need for love," and the "need for hope" (pp. 417–418). Forgiveness relates to the dying person's need for God's forgiveness for perceived "acts of omission or commission toward themselves or others" (p. 417). The need for unconditional love may, Conrad notes, be met by a caregiver "when family and friends are non-existent" (p. 418); and the need for hope "can be equated with transcendent hope . . . [which incorporates] theological meanings" (p. 418).

Hospice chaplain Barbara Derrickson (1996) describes the spiritual needs of dying patients as "the spiritual work of the dying," which she envisions as including four central tasks: "remembering," "reassessing," "reconciliation," and "reunion" (p. 11). The task of remembering is essentially a dying person's life review, the process that allows him or her to "affirm an essential goodness in life and to bless . . . [his or her] participation in that goodness" (p. 14). Reassessing allows terminally ill patients to redefine their contributions and "worth in the world" (p. 17). Reconciliation means attempting to resolve or at least come to terms with relationships that may have been broken during the person's lifetime (pp. 20–21). And Derrickson describes reunion as the dying person envisioning "the spiritual world as a reality"; it is "a definable spiritual process that allows [one] to disconnect with this world and reconnect with the spiritual world which is our true home" (p. 23).

For parish nurses ministering to dying parishioners, having an awareness of their potential needs and "spiritual work" can very helpful in understanding some parishioners' fears and frustrations. It can also sensitize the health minister to certain topics that might be approached in spiritual counseling. Nevertheless, as noted earlier, each dying patient is unique, and thus it is imperative that a parish nurse's spiritual ministry be carried out in prayer and humility and under the guidance of the Holy Spirit.

Hospice staff member David Praill (1995) supports my belief regarding the uniqueness of any ministry to a dying person: "More than any other aspect of care," he asserts, the "spiritual dimension [of ministry to the dying] defies rational explanation or the development of 'how-to' techniques" (p. 55). Praill observes that most of the dying have "shed [their] masks" and developed a great openness to spiritual ministry. He remembers one patient saying: "No, no reading. I only want what is in your mind and in your heart" (p. 56). Thus, Praill concludes: "When in the presence of a dying person, it is not simply what we say or do that counts, but how we are, our whole way of being" (p. 56). David Praill's thoughts are validated by hospice chaplain Richard Grey (1996), who asserts, "Those who work with the terminally ill quickly come to learn the importance of 'being with' . . . patients" (p. 21). Grey quotes the comment of a terminally ill oncologist who, playing on a well-known cliché, wrote: "Don't just do something, stand there"—caregivers are encouraged to "stand there with their suffering patients" (p. 21).

In discussing the topic of "being there" with dying patients, hospice chaplain Sharon Burns (1991) asserts, "One of the greatest spiritual gifts a pastoral care provider or any compassionate person can give a suffering human being is listening" (p. 51). "Listening," she notes, "involves paying attention not only to the words but also to the feelings contained in or hidden behind the other person's statements" (p. 51). Chaplain Burns points out that the spiritual role of one ministering to the dying is primarily that of "companion, of the friend who walks alongside, helping, sharing and sometimes just sitting empty-handed" when the minister "would rather run away" (p. 51).

Finally, and most importantly for some dying parishioners, prayer both with and for the patient can provide immense consolation in times of fear, depression, or loneliness. "For some patients," observes hospice nurse Rosemary Elsdon (1995), "prayer can counteract the loneliness of dying, by offering intimacy with God" (p. 643). Prayer, she continues, "can also provide a framework for reflections on regrets, hopes and meanings" (p. 643). In my own hospital chaplaincy experience, much of which was carried out with those who were terminally ill, I found praying with and for patients to be one of the most comforting aspects of ministry for those I visited. Some patients join in and pray with the visiting minister; more often, patients ask the minister to pray aloud for them. On a number of occasions, I have been amazed when a patient responded that the prayer I had prayed was just exactly what they needed to hear, especially when I realized that I really had no idea which words might come out of my mouth when I began to pray. I always trust the Holy Spirit when praying with another; these kinds of experiences, however, always humble me and reassure me about who is actually doing the "ministering" when I meet with a patient.

I cannot leave the subject of ministering to dying parishioners without some comment on the needs of the parishioners' families. Interestingly, though, often during the final stages of a loved one's life, family caregivers are energized with amazing strength and fortitude to carry on, focusing totally on the needs of their dying loved one, rather than on themselves; it is only after the death that caregivers' physical and emotional collapse may come. However, if a loved one's dying process constitutes a lengthy experience, some family members, especially the primary caregiver, may need a few days or even a few hours respite in order to be able to continue their caring presence at the deathbed. A parish nurse is in the ideal position to organize respite care, mobilizing volunteer support within the faith community. Some volunteers may be willing to sit with dying parishioners; others may prepare meals or do errands for the family; and still others will undertake a ministry of prayer support for the ill parishioner. Whatever the task, these activities carried out by members of the faith community provide encouragement, support, and comfort for both patient and loved ones.

Ministering to Bereaved Parish Families

Howard Clinebell (1991) asserts that "bereavement is the universal human crisis, striking everyone sooner or later" (p. 218). "Clergy," he suggests, "are the key professionals in helping people with this crisis" (p. 218). I believe that now we should add parish nurses to Clinebell's category of key professionals who can help those experiencing bereavement; this is particularly true for parish nurses who have ministered to a family and their dying loved one prior to the bereavement. Although I was not a parish nurse at the time, a number of family members of persons with AIDS, to whom I had ministered in life, sought me out for counseling after their loved one's death. In fact, family members of the AIDS patients participating in the project Coping Response in HIV Infection who had died suggested that I add a second phase to the project, titled Bereavement and Coping Response in HIV Infection, to give the bereaved families an opportunity to share their experiences and especially their pain.

The bereavement experience is multifaceted and influenced by a multitude of variables, just a few of which are relationship of the bereaved person to the individual who died, age of the deceased, whether the death was expected or unexpected, whether the death involved a great deal of suffering or occurred peacefully, religious beliefs of the bereaved about the existence or nonexistence of an afterlife, and personal theology of pain and suffering (see O'Brien, 2003, pp. 278–285).

An important point for parish nurses ministering to bereaved family members to keep in mind is the vast symptomotolgy, both physical and emotional, that often accompanies a bereavement experience. Elkin and Miller (1996) point out that "it is important to be aware that normal grief includes many feelings that tend to make people think they are ill or 'crazy'" (p. 692). Some of the physical symptoms they identify are "fainting, diaphoresis, anorexia, nausea, diarrhea, rapid heart rate, restlessness, insomnia, fatigue, sensations of tightness in the throat, choking, shortness of breath, weakness, anxiety attacks, and pain without any physical cause" (p. 692). Emotional reactions may include such manifestations of grief as "feelings of anger, guilt, anxiety and numbness . . . [and] mood swings that vary in intensity" (p. 692).

It can be intimidating for some nurses to undertake a ministry to the bereaved; it might seem like a pastoral minister might need the "wisdom of Solomon" to know what to do or say when visiting with parishioners who are grieving, especially those grieving the most traumatic losses, such as the loss of a child or young member of a family. In their book *Grief Ministry*, however, Williams and Sturzl (2001) advise that although a pastoral caregiver may have "fears" about an initial bereavement visit, he or she should "remember that those who mourn feel worse pain when they find that nobody cares enough to visit them when they are hurting" (p. 75). "What you say," they add "is not nearly as important as your presence" (p. 75).

If a parish nurse has been visiting a dying patient and his or her family prior to death, the nurse's attendance at the wake and/or funeral or memorial service is encouraged. Family members long remember those who attend these important rituals of bereavement, as well as those who do not. Another important role of the parish nurse may be to assist with the planning of a wake and a funeral and possibly coordinating volunteers to minister at a final service of remembrance. In speaking of the "ministry of consolation in death," Piil, De Grocco, and Cover (1997) suggest that the role of ministering to the bereaved family "belongs to all who have been baptized in Christ" (p. 18).

Although a parish nurse ministering to bereaved families may well assist with planning of final religious rites and rituals, as with ministry to a dying parishioner, the nurse's bereavement ministry will most probably center on the activities of presence and listening. It is true that religious rituals can provide much support for bereaved families; as Kenneth Doka (1993) observes, "Faith, with its rituals and beliefs, can be a powerful elixir at times of loss. Its ritual can provide structure and succor. Its beliefs may offer comfort and conciliation" (p. 185). After the rituals of remembrance are over, however, most bereaved persons very much need to talk; to talk about their loved one who died, to talk about missing him or her, to talk about the pain of the loss. A parish nurse's role, as a representative of the bereaved person's faith community, is to listen, to care and to bring the love and the consolation of the community and of Christ to the person who is grieving. If bereaved family members are open to such intervention, a parish nurse may pray with them, or share some comforting scripture. Arnold (1982) suggests that the Old Testament book of Psalms is a very helpful resource for those who are grieving (p. 162). As an example, he cites Psalm 22, which "opens with a cry for help . . . then . . . moves on [with] agonizing descriptions of illness, apparent moments of relief, and meditation on God's promises" (pp. 162–163). "Even when God's faithfulness is questioned," Arnold notes, the psalmist continues to "address . . . him. The expressions of pain seem to diminish and the expressions of hope increase until the psalm ends with a hymn of praise" (p. 163).

Parish nurses ministering to bereaved parishioners will have their own favorite scripture passages and prayers that may be particularly identified with their religious tradition. These may be supportive to the bereaved person at the time of a pastoral visit; they may also be recalled at a later date when the grieving parishioner is alone and in need of a comforting memory. Ultimately, parish nursing ministry to bereaved parish families must be approached and carried out, as suggested for all the ministries to suffering parishioners, directed by the gospel mandate of care and compassion for brothers and sisters in need and must be guided by the infinite wisdom and love of the Holy Spirit, "the comforter," whom Jesus sent to teach us all things.

After a church's ill and infirm population has been identified, the parish nurse must begin planning ministry visits; some of these visits can be delegated to other members of the health ministry team, as they feel comfortable and prepared to minister in a particular setting or situation. Many health ministry team members will be quite willing to visit older parishioners at home or in a nursing home; some nonnurse team

Table 8.4 PARISH HEALTH MINISTRY VISITS TO TERMINALLY ILL
PARISHIONERS AND BEREAVED FAMILY MEMBERS

1. Listen! Listen! Listen! Dying persons and bereaved family members very much need to talk to someone who cares.

2. Don't preach! Allow the Holy Spirit to do that through the ministry and caring of your visit.

3. Be gentle in response to anger (if manifested). As a representative of the Church, and of God, you might be faced with hostility related to a parishioner's pain.

4. Be present! Don't give up unless you are asked to leave. A dying person and a bereaved individual are both experiencing loss; they may need to work through frustrations and anger in the presence of a caring minister.

5. Pray at the beginning and end of the visit.

members may not, however, feel confident to minister in settings such as the hospital intensive care unit or the psychiatric unit. Nonmedical health ministers may also feel unprepared to minister to dying parishioners and their families. The parish nurse, as leader of the health ministry team, will need to assist parish volunteers in identifying the unique personal gifts and strengths that they bring to the program. Through the communal sharing of talents and abilities, a comprehensive and compassionate parish health ministry program can be created. Table 8.4 identifies some points to remember in making parish health ministry visits to terminally ill parishioners and bereaved family members (admittedly, the two concepts are different; nevertheless, a number of ministry issues are similar for visits to both parishioner populations).

References

Arnold, J. (1992). The voices of pediatrics: Walking with children and parents. In L. E. Holst (Ed.), *Hospital ministry: The role of the chaplain today* (pp. 93–106). New York: Crossroad.

Arnold, W. V. (1982). *Introduction to pastoral care.* Philadelphia: Westminster Press.

Berggren-Thomas, P., & Griggs, M. J. (1995). Spirituality in aging: Spiritual need or spiritual journey. *Journal of Gerontolgical Nursing, 21*(3), 5–10.

Boutell, K. A., & Bozeht, F. W. (1988). Nurses' assessment of patients' spirituality: Continuing education implications. *Journal of Continuing Education in Nursing, 21*(4), 72–76.

Burns, S. (1991). The spirituality of dying. *Health Progress, 72*(7), 48–52.

Carson, V. B. (1998). Spirituality. In J. M. Leahy & P. E. Kizilay (Eds.), *Foundations of nursing practice: A nursing process approach* (pp. 1074–1093). Philadelphia: W. B. Saunders.

Catholic Health Association of the United States. (1999). *Parish-based health services for aging persons*. St. Louis, MO: Author.

Clark, C. (1991). *A spirituality for active ministry*. Kansas City, MO: Sheed & Ward.

Clinebell, H. (1991). *Basic types of pastoral care and counseling: Resources for the ministry of healing and growth*. Nashville, TN: Abingdon Press.

Conrad, N. L. (1985). Spiritual support for the dying. *Nursing Clinics of North America, 20*(2), 415–426.

Derrickson, B. S. (1996). The spiritual work of the dying: A framework and case studies. *Hospice Journal, 11*(2), 11–30.

Doka, K. J. (1993). The spiritual crisis of bereavement. In K. J. Doka (Ed.), *Death and spirituality* (pp. 185–194). Amityville, NY: Baywood.

Elkin, M., & Miller, R. M. (1996). Facilitating grief work. In M. K. Elkin, A. G. Perry, & P. A. Potter (Eds.), *Nursing interventions and clinical skills* (pp. 691–696). St. Louis: Mosby.

Ellor, J. W., Thibault, J. M., Netting, F. E., & Carey, C. B. (1990). Wholistic theology as a conceptual foundation for services for the oldest old. In J. J. Seeber (Ed.), *Spiritual maturity in later years* (pp. 99–110). New York: Haworth Press.

Elsdon, R. (1995). Spiritual pain in dying people: The nurse's role. *Professional Nurse, 10*(10), 641–643.

Emeth, E. V., & Greenhut, J. H. (1991). *The wholeness handbook: Care of body, mind and spirit for optimal health*. New York: Continuum.

Fowler, J. (1981). *Stages of faith: The psychology of human development and the quest for meaning*. San Francisco: Harper San Francisco.

Georgesen, J., & Dungan, J. M. (1996). Managing spiritual distress in patients with advanced cancer pain. *Cancer Nursing, 19*(5), 376–383.

Gillman, J., Gable-Rodriguez, J., Sutherland, M., & Whitacre, J. H. (1996). Pastoral care in a critical care setting. *Critical Care Nursing Quarterly 19*(1), 10–20.

Grey, R. (1996). The psychospiritual care matrix: A new paradigm for hospice care giving. *American Journal of Hospice & Palliative Care, 13*(4), 19–25.

Halstead, H. L. (1995). Spirituality in the elderly. In M. Stanley & P. G. Beare (Eds.), *Gerontolgical nursing* (pp. 415–425). Philadelphia: F.A. Davis.

Heidish, M. (1997). *Who cares?: Simple ways you can reach out*. Notre Dame, IN: Ave Maria Press.

Hynes, M. R. (1989). *Ministry to the aging*. Collegeville, MN: Liturgical Press.

John, S. D. (1983). Assessing spiritual needs. In J. A. Shelly & S. D. John (Eds.), *Spiritual dimensions of mental health* (pp. 73–84). Downers Grove, IL: InterVarsity Press.

Kirkwood, N. A. (1998). *Pastoral care in hospitals*. Harrisburg, PA: Morehouse Publishing.

LeMone, P., & Burke, K. M. (1996). *Medical-surgical nursing: Critical thinking in client care*. New York: Addison-Wesley.

Livingstone, E. A. (1990). *The concise Oxford dictionary of the Christian Church*. New York: Oxford University Press.

Lubkin, I., & Payne, M. E. (1998). Family caregivers. In I. M. Lubkin with P. D. Larsen (Eds.), *Chronic illness: Impact and interventions* (pp. 258–282). Sudbury, MA: Jones and Bartlett.

Maltby, T. (1990). Pastoral care of the aging. In H. Hayes & C. J. van der Poel (Eds.), *Health care ministry: A handbook for chaplains* (pp. 98–104). Mahwah, NJ: Paulist Press.

McCulloch, C. M. (1997). How spirituality transforms the care of older persons. In M. S. Roach (Ed.), *Caring from the heart: The convergence of caring and spirituality* (pp. 135–147). Mahwah, NJ: Paulist Press.

Miller, K. C. (1995). *Ministry to the homebound: A 10 session training course.* San Jose, CA: Resource Publications Inc.

Muldoon, M. H., & King, J. N. (1991). A spirituality for the long haul: Response to chronic illness. *Journal of Religion and Health, 30*(2), 99–108.

O'Brien, M. E. (1983). *The courage to survive: The life career of the chronic dialyisis patient.* New York: Grune and Stratton.

O'Brien, M. E. (1989). *Anatomy of a nursing home: A new view of resident life.* Owings Mills, MD: National Health Publishing.

O'Brien, M. E. (1992). *Living with HIV: Experiment in courage.* Westport, CT: Auburn House.

O'Brien, M. E. (1995). *The AIDS challenge: Breaking through the boundaries.* Westport, CT: Auburn House.

O'Brien, M. E. (2001). *The nurse's calling: A Christian spirituality of caring for the sick.* Mahwah, NJ: Paulist Press.

O'Brien, M. E. (2003). *Spirituality in nursing: Standing on holy ground* (2nd ed.). Sudbury, MA: Jones and Bartlett.

Paprocki, J. (2000). *Renewing your ministry: Walking with Jesus in all that you do.* Notre Dame, IN: Ave Maria Press.

Piil, M. A., DeGrocco, J., & Cover, R. M. (1997). *A ministry of consolation: Involving your parish in the order of Christian funerals.* Collegeville, MN: Liturgical Press.

Post-White, J., Ceronsky, C., Kreitzer, M. J., Nickelson, K., Drew, D., Mackey, K. W., Koopmeiners, L., & Gutknecht, S. (1996). Hope, spirituality, sense of coherence and quality of life in patients with cancer. *Oncology Nursing Forum, 23*(10), 1571–1579.

Poyatos, F. (1999). *I was sick and you visited me: A spiritual guide for Catholics in hospital ministry.* Mahwah, NJ: Paulist Press.

Praill, D. (1995). Approaches to spiritual care. *Nursing Times, 91*(34), 55–57.

Reese, D. J., & Brown, D. R. (1997). Psychosocial and spiritual care in Hospice: Differences between nursing, social work, and clergy. *Hospice Journal, 12*(1), 29–41.

Roen, O. T. (1997). Senior health. In J. H. Swanson & M. A. Nies (Eds.), *Community health nursing: Promoting the health of aggregates* (2nd ed., pp. 347–386). Philadelphia: W. B. Saunders.

Sawyer, L. A. (1990). Mental health. In H. Hayes & C. J. van der Poel (Eds.), *Health care ministry: A handbook for chaplains* (pp. 93–97). Mahwah, NJ: Paulist Press.

Simmons, H. C., & Peters, M. A. (1996). *With God's oldest friends: Pastoral visiting in the nursing home.* Mahwah, NJ: Paulist Press.

Smithe, F. F. (1990). General health care ministry. In H. Hayes & C. J. van der Poel (Eds.), *Health care ministry: A handbook for chaplains* (pp. 114–127). Mahwah, NJ: Paulist Press.

Swift, H. C., & Rench, C. E. (1991). *Life, fulfillment, and joy in the sunset years.* Huntington, IN: Our Sunday Visitor Publishing.

Taylor, E. J. (2002). *Spiritual care: Nursing theory, research, and practice.* Upper Saddle River, NJ: Prentice Hall.

Toth, J. C. (1992). Faith in recovery: Spiritual support after an acute M.I. *Journal of Christian Nursing, 9*(4), 28–31.

Van der Poel, C. J. (1999). *Wholeness and holiness: A Christian response to human suffering, a theology of health care ministry.* Franklin, WI: Sheed & Ward.

Van Heukelem-Still, J. (1982). Assessing the spiritual needs of children and their families. In J. A. Shelly (Ed.), *The spiritual needs of children* (pp. 87–97). Downer's Grove, IL: InterVarsity Press.

Williams, D. R., & Sturzl, J. (2001). *Grief ministry: Helping others mourn.* San Jose, CA: Resource Publications.

Young, C. (1993). Spirituality and the chronically ill Christian elderly. *Geriatric Nursing, 14*(6), 298–303.

Zarek, C. (1990). Parish health care: Unique needs, special responses. In H. Hayes & C. J. van der Poel (Eds.), *Health care ministry: A handbook for chaplains* (pp. 105–113). Mahwah, NJ: Paulist Press.

CHAPTER 9

AN EXPERIMENT IN PARISH NURSING: THE GIFT OF FAITH IN CHRONIC ILLNESS

Those who wait for the Lord shall renew their strength, they shall mount up with wings like eagles.

—*Isaiah 40:31*

"With Eagle's Wings"

Lord God,
   The prophet Isaiah taught
us the value of hope; if we but
   hope in You *(Isaiah 40:31)*, we
will soar as with eagle's wings.
                    (Isaiah 40:31)

That seems such an easy lesson;
   only to hope . . . and all will
      be well.

But when the days are dark,
   Dear Lord; when we are
filled with sorrow and suffering,
   Isaiah's message seems a
distant echo; a muted bell
   tolling from afar.

Teach us, Lord God, to hope:
  to hope in illness and infirmity;
    to hope in pain and anger;
      to hope in hurt and
        frustration;
          to hope in anguish and
            despair.

Guide us to hope in You, O Lord,
  that we may indeed, one day,
    "soar as with eagle's wings"
      in the radiance of Your
        light and Your love.

D ata from clinical nursing practice and nursing and medical research reveal that sick persons, especially those with chronic illnesses, who demonstrate a spirit of faith and spiritual well-being, cope notably better with their conditions than those who do not (O'Brien, 2003a; 2003b; Koenig, 1999). Harold Koenig (1999), following extensive research on the relationship of religion/spirituality and health, found that "people with strong faith who suffer from physical illness have significantly better health outcomes than less religious people" (p. 24). Even when physical deficits increase, a deep personal faith and the support of one's church or faith community promote a sense of spiritual well-being and a positive quality of life reflected in hope and life satisfaction in the midst of suffering (O'Brien, 2001).

Previous research has also revealed that an individual's *spirituality* or *faith development* tends to deepen with age (Fowler, 1981); thus, some older, disabled persons are able to achieve a sense of spiritual well-being and positive quality of life related to their personal relationship to God and the transcendent reality of life. For many chronically ill persons, however, the situational stress of becoming marginalized from the living out of their spirituality, in terms of religious practice, can be very distressing.

The purpose of this parish nursing project, therefore, was to provide pastoral ministry to a population of chronically ill adults marginalized from practice of their faith because of illness and/or disability and who were desirous of spiritual/religious support. Project participants were evaluated in terms of the variables of spiritual well-being, hope, and life satisfaction, both prior to and following a period of parish nursing/health ministry intervention.

Study Aims

The aims of the project were twofold: (1) to test the effectiveness of a model of parish nursing/health ministry on spiritual well-being and quality of life among ill persons marginalized from practice of their faith; and (2) to explore the relationship between spiritual well-being and quality of life (operationalized in terms of hope and life satisfaction) in chronically ill persons. For a study participant distanced from his or her faith community, and/or desirous of additional spiritual support, pastoral care intervention to promote or increase spiritual well-being, and thus positive quality of life, was carried out by parish nurses and health ministers. Based on an initial assessment of each study participant's spiritual and religious needs and concerns, project staff, both parish nurses and health ministers, tailored the pastoral care intervention to the needs of the chronically ill individual.

Research Methodology

Project Staff

The project staff consisted of four parish nurses (including the principal investigator/project director) and two nonnurse parish health ministers who were currently serving as lay ministers in their parishes; the parish nurse/health minister staff roles primarily involved data collection and pastoral care intervention. Some parish nurses and health ministers assisted in accessing study participants. The staff also included as consultants two data analysts/transcriptionists to assist with data processing, a statistician, and two pastoral care consultants.

Sample

The parish nursing/health ministry intervention study sample consisted of 45 chronically ill adults, whose health conditions interfered with the usual or desired practice of their faith. Many project participants were completely marginalized from their former faith communities due to illness or disability; others were able to participate minimally in spiritual or religious practices, but not to the degree to which they had previously and/or to which they currently desired. Forty-nine patients were initially entered into the project; of these, the final assessment was not completed for four individuals (one project participant died, one moved out of state, and two became too cognitively impaired to continue participation in the project).

Study participants were identified initially through referrals from church pastors in a tristate area and their staff, both clergy and lay ministers; church pastors also directed the project staff to local nursing homes and assisted care facilities, where it was anticipated that parishioners and/or former parishioners might be found. Accessment of study participants proved challenging, though not impossible. The project team worked diligently with each of six pastors, as well as with a part-time chaplain for a nonsectarian nursing home. As described in an earlier chapter under the topic of "locating the ill and infirm of a parish" (Chapter 7), advertisements including the pastor's words of support of the project seeking referrals and placed in one church's parish bulletin for three or four weeks, yielded no response. Several study participants were found through personal contact with one of the church's lay ministers, however.

Overall, pastors were incredibly supportive of the project and welcomed parish nursing to their churches; the difficulty for them, also, was in locating parishioners or former parishioners that the pastors described as having "slipped through the cracks." One pastor was able to give the project staff several names, however, of disabled former parishioners who were, in his words, angry at God and at the Church; he suggested that we might succeed as parish nurses where he, as a clergyperson, was not welcome. This turned out to be the case, as is described later in this chapter.

Another pastor suggested that we approach a neighboring life care community. He reported that he believed several former parishioners were now living in this long-term care facility, but he did not have the time or the staff to seek them out. *Note*: It is important to point out here that nursing homes and life care or assisted care communities vary widely in type and frequency of spiritual and religious support for residents. Some religiously affiliated long-term care facilities employ a full-time director of pastoral care, who provides spiritual ministry to the residents, and who coordinates opportunities for residents from a variety of denominations or faith groups to attend services of their religious traditions. Other facilities consider spiritual and religious support as falling broadly under the aegis of "resident life," and pastoral ministry is left primarily to neighboring clergy who visit periodically and provide services as their schedules permit.

A health minister working with the pastor of a local church located only one homebound parishioner for the study; she was, however, able to identify a number of persons fitting the study criteria at a local assisted care community recommended by the pastor. In another instance of seeking to identify potential study participants, the project's principal investigator, a parish nurse, met with a pastor who regularly ministered at a local, nonreligiously affiliated nursing home. The pastor, who attempted to provide services weekly, though not always was able to, suggested approaching some of the nursing home's "roombound" residents, most of whom were not able to attend worship, even when it was offered. The nursing home administration was very supportive of the project staff talking with the residents; ultimately, seven roombound individuals living at this facility were accepted into the project.

Finally, through the combined efforts of the staff parish nurses and health ministers, 45 project participants were enrolled in and completed the study. These persons were from a tristate area; some were homebound individuals, others resided in nursing homes, life care communities, or assisted care facilities. The comments of a parish nurse (excerpted from a study report) describe her experience in locating study participants:

> A few of the clients I have been working with came from parishes in [a local area]. Others were residents of a nursing home; still others came from other areas [nearby]. I came across these persons in a most unusual way, much like the Lord destined it. I went to stay with some family friends for a weekend. I attended a Sunday [service] with the family and they invited the pastor of the parish home for dinner. I decided to tell him about the study. I did not think I would find clients in his area as it seems to be a young and affluent population. As it turns out, because of how affluent and young the population is, [the pastor] stated that he felt that oftentimes the older, more spiritually needy, were neglected by the church and he did not have the manpower to get to all of them, with how much his parish was growing. He suggested my calling an area nursing home; he knew that several former parishioners now lived there and he simply couldn't get to them. He also stated that he knew the home was not religiously affiliated and that the residents could use the ministry.
>
> [The pastor] also gave me the name of his younger brother who was the pastor of another parish and who I ended up working with. [His brother] knew also that he had several parishioners who fit into the project category. He was in a similar situation to his [pastor] brother, running a large, rapidly growing parish. There were some parishioners that he had not gotten to see in some time; and there were some other parishioners that he had, in fact, gotten to see but they were so angry and bitter that they had not responded. I agreed to go to see these [parishioners] as a "last ditch" effort. We both hoped and prayed that I would be able to reach them and connect with them in some way and make a difference; thankfully our prayers were answered!

A parish health minister accessed several study participants through contact with a nonreligiously affiliated nursing home recommended by one of the pastors mentioned earlier. A detailed explanation of the project was required by appropriate officials of the facility prior to any resident being approached; after review of the study protocol, however, permission was given. Assistance from the nursing home Recreation

Department staff was then forthcoming; staff members suggested which patients they felt could talk, understand, and be able to answer questions posed to them and which residents might desire and benefit from pastoral ministry. The staff accompanied the parish health minister on initial visits to meet the residents identified as potential study participants. The residents approached agreed to participate in the study; the parish health minister commented, however, that the time for her pastoral visits had to be scheduled around the residents' busy schedules of nursing home activities. She observed: "I started to bring Communion with me as often as possible. I noticed that the patients always had time to take Communion, and would be willing to give up their activities to meet with me. We usually closed our talks with a prayer and a hug."

Staff Training

The project staff (described earlier), other than the principal investigator/project director, consisted of three parish nurses with a variety of pastoral care and community health nursing backgrounds and two parish health ministers, who were lay Eucharistic ministers at their parishes and were trained in visiting and interacting with ill or disabled parishioners. All staff members were oriented to the background, aims, and methodology of the study by the principal investigator (PI). The PI is trained in pastoral ministry as well as spiritual direction and has been commissioned as a parish nurse. Staff members who had not previously participated in such research or pastoral intervention were accompanied by a senior team member on a first parishioner visit. The PI kept in touch with staff through personal meetings, phone calls, mail, and/or e-mail during the course of the data collection and intervention to answer questions and discuss staff or study participant issues and concerns.

Study Instruments

After appropriate informed consent procedures had been carried out, the trained parish nurses and health ministers conducted an initial assessment of spiritual well-being and quality of life (hope and life satisfaction) using four instruments: (1) the *Spiritual Assessment Scale*, a 21-item Likert-type scale, which measures spiritual well-being overall and, in three subscales, the concepts of *personal faith*, *religious practice*, and *spiritual contentment* (O'Brien 2003b, pp. 65–66); (2) the *Spiritual Well-Being Interview Guide*, a 15-item qualitative tool exploring, in narrative data responses, the concepts of personal faith, religious practice, and spiritual contentment (O'Brien, 1999); (3) the *Miller Hope Scale*, a 15-item quantitative tool that measures the concept of hope in light of such issues as the meaning of life and attitudes toward the future (the scale was abbreviated for a more fragile population with permission of the author, Dr. Judith Miller [Miller & Powers, 1988]); and (4) the *Life Satisfaction Index-Z*, a 13-item quantitative tool designed to measure satisfaction with life for an older population (Wood, Wylie, & Sheafor, 1969).

Procedure

The study was conducted over the course of one year. Following the baseline data assessment of spiritual well-being and quality of life, a plan of pastoral care intervention was designed and carried out for all project participants. The study protocol suggested a spiritual ministry intervention of three or more pastoral visits, to be conducted over approximately six weeks to three months, to be followed by a final assessment of spiritual well-being and quality of life. Most study participants received five or more visits from the parish nurse or health minister; some staff members made phone calls in between visits and sent notes to project participants with whom they were working. Several staff members reported keeping in touch with those to whom they ministered after the study was completed. The ministry was tailored to the chronically ill study participants' spiritual/religious needs and concerns; physical and psychosocial needs and abilities or disabilities were considered as well. Devotional materials were distributed, as desired, to study participants to assist them in reconnecting with their faith or in strengthening spiritual well-being; these included such articles as large-print Bibles, crucifixes, rosaries, religious books and prayer books, religious statues and pictures, and religious music tapes. If study participants were willing, those not currently affiliated with a church were referred to a nearby faith community prior to the conclusion of the study.

Because of the diversity of spiritual needs and concerns among study participants, as well as myriad individual physical deficits and disabilities, the parish nursing and health ministry visits varied greatly in terms of process and content; this was expected, for, as with any pastoral caregiving, the minister cannot always plan precisely what interaction the Holy Spirit may guide during a parishioner visit. Nevertheless, significant findings both quantitative and qualitative reveal the impact of the parish nursing/health ministry intervention on project participants.

Data Analysis

Quantitative data analysis was carried out using parametric procedures for both correlational and pre-post intervention data: Pearson's r; multiple regression analysis; paired t-test. Qualitative data were content analyzed to identify and describe common dominant themes that emerged idiosyncratic to the data.

Instrument Reliability.   Reliability scores, using the Cronbach's alpha procedure, were calculated on all study tools as follows (all statistics were calculated for study tools at time 1 [T1] prior to parish nursing/health ministry intervention and time 2 [T2] following intervention): Spiritual Assessment Scale—total scale (spiritual well-being): T1 0.94, T2 0.92; subscales of personal faith—T1 0.95, T2 0.94; religious practice— T1 0.86, T2 0.76; spiritual contentment—T1 0.77, T2 0.87. Miller Hope Scale reliability scores were T1 94, and T2 95; and Life Satisfaction Inventory-Z reliability scores were T1 0.70 and T2 0.64.

Quantitative Study Findings

Because of the diversity of ministry activities carried out by project parish nurses and health ministers, and the creative strategies employed in the ministry visits, after a summary overview of quantitative study findings, case study examples derived directly from project staff reports, in the parish nurse's own words, are presented. Following the presentation of case studies, dominant themes reflective of study participants' spiritual well-being, derived from analysis of qualitative data, are identified and described.

Demographic Profile of Study Participants

The project participants in the study the Gift of Faith in Chronic Illness consisted of 45 Roman Catholic persons marginalized from practice of their faith due to illness or disability. Twenty-nine percent of the population were male; 71 percent were female. Over half of the sample group had at least a high school education. In terms of racial identity, 78 percent were Caucasian and 13 percent African American; two percent each were Asian, Hispanic, and Native American. Over 50 percent of the study participants reported attending church only once a month or less; while 47 percent of the group stated that they attended church weekly or more often. These numbers are misleading in terms of attendance at religious services of the individual's own religious tradition, however. That is, a significant number—approximately two thirds of the study participants—resided in nursing homes, life care communities, or assisted care facilities; these study participants included in their responses to the item measuring church attendance attending whatever worship services were available at the facility, which might be Bible study sessions or nondenominational services.

Quantitative Changes following Parish Nursing/Health Ministry Intervention

There were significant positive increases in individual item mean scores for data elicited from all major study tools following parish nursing/health ministry intervention; that is, from time 1 to time 2 data collection periods. (Time 1—initial data collection on spiritual well-being and quality of life [hope and life satisfaction] prior to intervention; time 2—final assessment following the parish nursing/health ministry intervention.) For the Spiritual Assessment Scale, time 1 item mean scores ranged from 3.55 to 4.80; and at time 2, mean scores ranged from 4.23 to 4.91. For Miller Hope Scale items, scores ranged from 2.80 to 3.55 at time 1, and from 2.98 to 3.70 at time 2; and Life Satisfaction Inventory-Z item mean scores ranged from 1.38 to 1.95 at time 1, and from 1.42 to 1.98 at time 2.

Overall Scale Mean Score Changes from Time 1 to Time 2.   Mean scale and subscale scores for all study instruments increased from time 1 to time 2; findings are as follows: *Spiritual Assessment Scale* (spiritual well-being): time 1 = 91.84 to time 2 = 97.27; *personal faith subscale*: time 1 = 31.69 to time 2 = 33.29; *religious practice subscale*: time 1 = 29.64 to time 2 = 31.71; and *spiritual contentment subscale*: time 1 = 30. 51 to time 2 = 32.27. The *Miller Hope Scale* mean scale score increased from time 1 = 48.91 to time 2 = 51.18; and the *Life Satisfaction Index-Z* scale means increased from time 1 = 21.64 to time 2 = 22.38.

As noted by the study's statistician consultant, this project population had a high sense of spiritual well-being and positive quality of life (hope and life satisfaction) at the initiation of the research (time 1 data collection); there were, nonetheless, significant increases in study variables following the parish nursing intervention as the preceding findings demonstrate and as revealed by analysis of the paired t-test data.

Paired t-tests were computed for all scales. There were statistically significant differences; that is, positive increases on all three instruments: the Spiritual Assessment Scale overall (t 0.44 = 5.23, p 0.0005); the three subscales for personal faith (t 0.44 = 3.86, p 0.0005), religious practice (t 0.44 = 3.41, p 0.001), and spiritual contentment (t 0.44 = 4.80, p 0.0005) ; the Miller Hope Scale (t 0.44 = 2.68, p 0.010); and the Life Satisfaction Inventory-Z (t 0.44 = 2.12, p 0.040). In sum, following the parish nursing/health ministry intervention, the study participants had a greater sense of spiritual well-being, more hope, and a higher degree of life satisfaction than at the initiation of the study.

Relationships among Major Study Concepts.   Finally, a correlation matrix was calculated, using the Pearson's r statistic, among major study variables: spiritual well-being, personal faith, religious practice, spiritual contentment, hope, and life satisfaction. Significant correlations of the Spiritual Assessment Scale subscales with the total scale score at times 1 and 2 indicate that the personal faith subscale correlates highest (0.94; 0.91), followed by the religious practice subscale (0.93; 0.82), and the spiritual contentment subscale (0.83; 0.84). The Spiritual Assessment Scale significantly correlates with the Miller Hope Scale (0.70; 0.65) and the Life Satisfaction Index-Z (0.41; 0.35) at times 1 and 2, although the correlations with the Miller Hope Scale are higher. Test-retest correlations of the same scale at times 1 and 2 indicate that the Spiritual Assessment Scale is the most consistent (0.83), followed by the Miller Hope Scale (0.76) and the Life Satisfaction Index-Z (0.58).

Multiple regression analysis also revealed that spiritual well-being was a predictor of hope and life satisfaction. The multiple regression analysis indicated that after controlling for the demographic variables of race and frequency of church attendance, spiritual well-being significantly predicts hope and accounts for 20 percent of the variance at time 1 and 23 percent of the variance at time 2. While controlling for church attendance did not impact spiritual well-being's ability to predict life satisfaction at time 1, after controlling for race, spiritual well-being was found to significantly predict life satisfaction and accounts for 9 percent of the variance at time 2.

Descriptive Data Elicited on Individual Scale Items

Study participants' responses demonstrated increasingly more positive attitudes on many individual scale items following the parish nursing/health ministry intervention; these findings are also of relevance for the parish nursing community. Some example items include the following:

Spiritual Assessment Scale items: Item 10, satisfaction in engaging in religiously motivated activities: $n = 17$ (that is, 17 study participants scored higher on this item at time 2 than at time 1). Item 18, confidence in the forgiveness of God: $n = 15$. Item 19, no longer being angry at God for "bad things" happening: $n = 15$. Item 14, being helped to communicate with God through reading and meditation: $n = 14$. Item 9, being strengthened by pariticipation in worship services: $n = 12$.

Other Spiritual Assessment Scale items on which positive changes were demonstrated following the parish nursing/health ministry intervention included: item 5, God's interest in one's life; item 12, receiving support from a spiritual companion; item 13, importance of personal prayer; item 16, feeling closer to God; item 6, trusting in God's care; item 4, receiving strength from spiritual beliefs; item 11, support of family and friends regarding spiritual beliefs; and item 15, denial of pain associated with spiritual beliefs.

Miller Hope Scale item changes following pastoral ministry intervention included these: Item 1, positive attitude toward life: $n = 15$. Item 9, feeling valued for who one is: $n = 12$. Item 2, ability to set goals: $n = 11$. Item 3, life having meaning: $n = 11$. Item 10, looking forward to things one enjoys: $n = 11$. Item 4, energy to do what is important: $n = 10$. Item 6, being positive about the future: $n = 10$.

Other key Miller Hope Scale items that demonstrated notable changes were item 8, feeling hopeful; item 13, feeling loved; and item 14, finding meaning in life events.

Life Satisfaction Inventory-Z items that changed were: Item 10, getting most of the things one wanted in life: $n = 10$. Item 3, this not being the dreariest time in one's life: $n = 8$. Item 7, doing interesting things: $n = 8$. Item 9, making plans for the future: $n = 8$.

In summarizing the key findings from descriptive analysis of quantitative data in terms of conceptual changes facilitated through the parish nursing/health ministry intervention, three central themes emerge, which were described as *confidence in God*, *religiosity*, and *sacredness of life*.

Confidence in God.   Project participants' responses identifying trust in God's care for one and in his forgiveness, denial of pain associated with spiritual beliefs, and no longer being angry at God for losses or sufferings led to a theme of "confidence" in God. While it is true that a number of study participants identified positively with this concept at the time of initial interview, a significant number did not, but changed their opinions following the pastoral ministry intervention carried out by parish nurses and health ministers.

Religiosity.   The concept of religiosity, or active practice of one's faith, was notably changed for many study participants after pastoral ministry, as demonstrated by the over-time changes, from negative at time 1 to positive at time 2, on such items as satisfaction with religious activities, communicating with God through spiritual reading and meditation, being strengthened by participation in worship services, receiving support from a spiritual companion, and the importance of personal prayer.

Sacredness of Life.   The concept of a study participant's personal respect for the sacredness of his or her own life was evidenced by positive changes from time 1 to time 2 on such items as finding spiritual meaning in life, the ability to set desired life goals, having a positive attitude toward the future, being able to do interesting things, and, most especially, the attitude of feeling valued and loved as a member of God's human family.

It is believed that the interventions of the parish nurses and health ministers supported and contributed significantly to the preceding changes. This conclusion is explored further in the following discussion describing analysis of the qualitative data collected during the course of the study.

Qualitative Study Findings

Even to your old age I am He, even when you turn gray I will carry you. I have made, and I will bear; I will carry and I will save [you].

—Isaiah 46:4

Because each of the 45 study participants who completed the study, was, as noted earlier, unique in terms of physical, cognitive, and spiritual needs, the spiritual ministry provided by the parish nurse and health ministers, sometimes including such activities as health counseling, advocacy, education, and referral, was also unique. Thus, to flesh out the basic qualitative data obtained through responses to items on the Spiritual Well-Being Interview Guide, case studies describing the project participants and their ministry experiences were developed. The project staff varied somewhat in the amount of detail describing their interventions reported; however, every effort was made by the principal investigator to expand these data through discussions with the staff parish nurses and health ministers. Whenever available, project staff members' own words, describing study participants' spiritual needs and the minister's attempt to meet these, are included. The data were derived from tape-recorded patient–caregiver interactions, as well as from handwritten staff members' journal notes relating anecdotes describing health-related spiritual needs and spiritual care. To maintain confidentiality of project data, pseudonyms are employed in referring to all project staff and participants.

Following the presentation of 15 sample case studies (parish nursing intervention with 11 women and four men) exploring study participants' needs and concerns and parish nursing interventions carried out, five conceptual themes derived from content analysis of the qualitative data are described; these themes reflecting spiritual attitudes and behaviors important to study participants and supported and strengthened by the parish nursing/health ministry interventions include: *reverence, faithfulness, religiousness, devotion,* and *contemplation.*

The Case Studies

| Case Study 1. | Study Participant: Mr. O'Connell |

Project Parish Nurse: Anne Marie

Demographic Profile.   Mr. O'Connell is a 76-year-old widower with one daughter. He is Roman Catholic, Caucasian, and a high school graduate whose career had been in sales. Mr. O'Connell lives in a nursing home and has multiple medical diagnoses, including osteoarthritis, osteoporosis, and a compression fracture of the spine. He requires the assistance of a walker to ambulate, and sitting is difficult because of his spinal injury. He takes a multiplicity of medications. Mr. O'Connell attends worship services (Mass) only "two or three times a year," when, he stated, "my daughter [who lives some distance away] takes me."

Spiritual Profile.   Mr. O'Connell reported that one of the most important things in his life had been going to church, but now he rarely goes. The closest Catholic Church to Mr. O'Connell's facility (this church is attended by the parish nurse visiting him) was not aware of Mr. O'Connell's unmet spiritual needs. Mr. O'Connell also reported that he loved to say the rosary but that his was broken. He had asked someone in the family to get him a new one, but "they are busy and have not had a chance to get to it." He would like to have a rosary, he said, but "nothing fancy." Mr. O'Connell's parish nurse, Anne Marie, prayed with him, got him a black rosary, had it blessed, and brought it to him. Mr. O'Connell was grateful. He said: "I don't know what I can do to repay you for your kindness." Anne Marie, who had sat and listened and prayed with Mr. O'Connell on a number of occasions, replied that he could say a prayer for our project. "I can do that!" he said with enthusiasm.

Parish Nursing Notes.   "Mr. O'Connell stated that he was very pleased that a nurse would take time to come see him. He asked many questions about what a 'parish nurse' is and the services provided. One important [spiritual] thing he misses is being able to go to church and to Mass. Because of his back and his disease he rarely goes now. He told me how he would like to sit in church and say his rosary. He showed me his old rosary beads that have broken.

"The visit made the patient upbeat," Anne Marie added; "he stated that religion [Catholicism] was the most important thing in his life. He was able to complete the spiritual assessment without much difficulty. . . . [He] felt comfortable about his answers and about discussing his beliefs with me. . . . The first visited ended with [Mr. O'Connell] stating that he was very appreciative of my visit and was looking forward to my next visit." (All of Anne Marie's visits ended with a prayer with the study participant.)

Anne Marie described a second visit: Mr. O'Connell "was very talkative today about his family and the lessons he had learned during his life." Many personal stories were shared, and then he said: "'You don't realize how many things you have to live through. Gosh! I am sorry. I am going on and on and you are a busy person. I have never told anyone about what I just told you! I don't know what made me do that. I didn't mean to bore you.'" Anne Marie assured Mr. O'Connell that she "did not find any of his stories or conversation boring at all"; she added: "I felt flattered that you could talk to me about different things." Anne Marie added: "We ended our visit with a prayer and a hand squeeze. I told the [study participant] that I would return next week. He stated that he would look forward to it."

In notes describing several more parish nursing visits, Anne Marie reported continuing to pray, listen to, and talk with Mr. O'Connell, sometimes including some teaching and advice about coping with his physical problems as well as discussing spiritual issues. She also arranged to have Mr. O'Connell receive a subscription to a religious newspaper that he liked very much, but had not seen in many years, and made a referral to the local Catholic parish for continued ministry after the study concluded. In approximately six visits, including some in-between phone calls and notes, Anne Marie fulfilled many of the identified parish nursing roles of *spiritual companion* (*integrator of faith and health*), *counselor*, *educator*, *advocate*, and *referral agent*.

Anne Marie concluded her parish nursing notes with the following summary: "At the time 2 spiritual assessment [the last study participant visit] I saw that 12 responses to the questions [scale items] had changed positively since the initial assessment [time 1]. I think these are due to the visits I made and the gifts of the new rosary and religious newspaper subscription. *This program has definitely had a positive effect on this [study participant]!*"

Positive Changes in Quantitative Data Elicited in Interviews with Mr. O'Connell (Time 1 to Time 2).   Mr. O'Connell's responses to quantitative tools changed positively on the following items following parish nursing intervention:

> *Spiritual Assessment Scale (SAS) items: 14) meditation and spiritual reading; 15) spiritual pain; 16) alienation; 19) anger.*
>
> *Miller Hope Scale (MHS) items: 5) enthusiasm; 7) resilience; 9) self-worth; 10) enjoyment of life; 11) endurance; 12) fulfillment; 13) love.*
>
> *Life Satisfaction Index-Z (LSI) items: 1) satisfaction in later years.*

Parish Nurse's Final Assessment.   "SAS item 14: [Mr. O'Connell feels that] meditation has increased because he has been saying the rosary more frequently because he has a new rosary." SAS item 19: Mr. O'Connell "is more resolved that things we consider 'bad' oftentimes are the things that shape us into who we are." MHS item 7: "Since [Mr. O.] has shared some of the hard times in his life with me, he states he strongly agrees that he can now handle problems." MHS item 9: "After spending time with the client, he states that he feels more strongly valued for who he is." MHS item 13: (Mr. O'Connell) "feels more significant to other people at the nursing home because of the interest of this program. Having a parish nurse visit and bring him a new rosary makes him feel that he is important and loved." And, LSI item 1: Mr. O. reported to Anne Marie that "some things are better now; he is able to offer prayers and suffering for the good of all."

In summary, this case study example, as do those that follow, speaks for itself in documenting the importance of parish nursing and health ministry, especially for those who are isolated, disabled, and marginalized from practice of their faith. All project participants expressed much appreciation to the nurses and health ministers who visited them both at home and in long-term care facilities. And, importantly, the parish nurses and health ministers themselves verbalized deep gratitude for the gift of their ministry, in living out the gospel message of caring and compassion for those in need.

Case Study 2.   Study Participant: Mrs. McGlothlin

Project Parish Nurse: Anne Marie

Demographic Profile.   Mrs. McGlothlin is a 78-year-old married woman whose spouse is living but who currently resides in a nursing home because of her disability. She is Caucasian, a convert to Roman Catholicism, a high school graduate, and has been a homemaker most of her adult life. Mrs. McGlothlin has multiple diagnoses, including such conditions as congestive heart failure, deafness, vertigo, and peripheral edema; she takes many medications and her gait is unsteady.

Spiritual Profile.   Mrs. McGlothlin is able to attend Mass only occasionally but spoke about how important her faith is to her. However, she has no family locally to visit her or take her to Mass. She does always receive Communion when someone from a church comes to the facility. Mrs. McGlothlin would like support in the practice of her faith but communication is difficult because of her deafness; some conversation needs to be written.

Parish Nursing Notes.   On an initial visit to Mrs. McGlothlin, "all communication was handwritten" to explain the project. Mrs. M. stated that she "did not need any devotional items except a rosary but that she *liked the parish nurse's visits 'very much'*! She seemed confortable to write and discuss many things about her life. She appeared pleased that I would return next week to visit. At the end of the visit, [Mrs. M.] hugged me and kissed me. [My plan] is to continue to visit and pray with [Mrs. M.] and to try and find her some [spiritual] reading material and a rosary."

Anne Marie called Mrs. M. several times prior to the next visit. On the second visit, the parish nurse reported: "Mrs. McGlothin was happy to see me. She stated 'I have missed you very much. I like you to visit me. We can talk about God and everything.' She stated that she was the 'last of her clan' and that she had no family left to visit her or to take her to Mass [she does have some friends who come to visit but they do not seem to be supportive of her faith practices]." At the end of this visit, Mrs. M. hugged the parish nurse and said "I love you!"

Because Mrs. McGlothlin's vision is better than her hearing, Anne Marie sent her a religious greeting card for the Thanksgiving holiday. "Mrs. McGlothlin does not ask for things; she is very frugal and states that she can 'make do with what she has.' She does, however, state that she really enjoys my visits." On a third visit, the project parish nurse brought Mrs. M. a rosary.

In a summary statement about her parish nursing intervention with Mrs. McGlothlin, Anne Marie observed that Mrs. M. had moved into a nonsectarian nursing home only three days prior to entering our study; Mrs. M. expressed anxiety that nursing home staff or other patients might "ridicule her for her faith practices." The nurse commented that the study's spiritual assessment and intervention seemed to validate the value, importance, and respect for her faith tradition and practices.

Positive Changes in Quantitative Data Elicited in Interviews with Mrs. McGlothlin. Mrs. McGlothlin's responses to quantitative tools changed positively on the following items following parish nursing intervention.

> SAS items: 12) spiritual support; 15) spiritual pain.
> MHS items: 2) goal setting; 6) hopefulness; 9) self-worth.

Parish Nurse's Final Assessment.   Anne Marie wrote that Mrs. M. had four important improvements on her second spiritual assessment (time 2); she had, at time 1, demonstrated a positive sense of spiritual well-being, as she is a "strongly religious person." "Mrs. M. stated that the parish nurse's visits have been very important to her. She 'feels good' that [the funding agency] has supported this spirituality assessment." Changes in Mrs. McGlothlin's spiritual well-being following the spiritual care intervention of her parish nurse are especially related to "receiving comfort and support from a spiritual companion" and "not feeling ridiculed for her religious beliefs." Mrs. M. "feels she is adjusting better and feeling more comfortable in the nursing home environment; she is now feeling valued for who she is 'even though she has had to move from her home into the assisted care facility.'"

Case Study 3.	Study Participant: Mrs. Quinn

Project Parish Nurse: Anne Marie

Demographic Profile.   Mrs. Quinn is an 86-year-old widow, with one daughter; she currently resides in a nursing home. She is Catholic, Caucasian, a high school graduate, and for some years worked as a nurse's aide. Mrs. Quinn has multiple diagnoses, including chronic obstructive pulmonary disease, asthma, and osteoporosis. She takes many medications and does not ambulate well.

Spiritual Profile.   Mrs. Quinn reports that she only attends Mass two or three times a year. Mrs. Quinn has not been receiving any pastoral care. At a first visit, Mrs. Quinn told her parish nurse, Anne Marie, that she had asked a family member to look for her Bible and rosary, which had not been brought to the nursing home with her when she was admitted; so far, she has not received them and some time has passed since her request. She explained that her family members were no longer interested in practicing their faith, so the request for religious articles was, in her perception, not important to them. She added: "I am old and sick and who knows what will happen!"

Parish Nursing Notes.   "In the past six months Mrs. Quinn has sold her 'beautiful home,' was packed up and brought [several states away] to this nursing home. [Mrs. Quinn] verbalized to me that she misses her home and her friends; it was a hardship to 'give up everything there' [her former home]. Mrs. Quinn had many questions about the state of her health. I suggested that she write down the questions and concerns that she has and then show the list to the doctor when she saw him next. I also reviewed with her some things to make the [nursing home] staff aware of her state.

"Mrs. Quinn was 'anxious to do the spiritual assessment' . . . [she] stated that she didn't feel that she was 'religious enough,' 'like other people.' I asked her how and when she prays. She stated that she says at least one rosary a day and prays in between, off and on during the day. She became tearful when I questioned her about growing older and if she felt this was a good period in her life. She cried and said: 'No, I'm sick and I'm stuck in this place for the rest of my life!'" Anne Marie added: "I decided to end the questioning at this time due to the patient being visibly upset" (the assessment was completed at the next parish nursing meeting).

Anne Marie continued: "I asked [Mrs. Quinn] what I could do or maybe bring to her that would make her feel better or closer to God. She said she really didn't know right now but started telling me about how all her important 'religious items are packed away somewhere,' especially her large-print Bible. The client was more comfortable when we ended the visit with a prayer; I told her that I would be back next week to check on her." Anne Marie added: "I decided on a pastoral care plan to do weekly/bi-weekly visits to Mrs. Quinn and to purchase a large-print Bible for her."

On a second visit, Anne Marie brought Mrs. Quinn both a large-print Bible and a rosary. Mrs. Quinn put her face in her hands and cried. She said: "I can't believe anybody could care that much about me." She said: "I don't understand why someone who doesn't know me would provide this beautiful Bible; it is so nice. I'm going to read it all the time. I have missed my Bible so. Thank you, thank you. You are so wonderful to bring me this." Anne Marie concluded by talking to Mrs. Quinn about God's love for her and told her: "There are people in the world who care about you and it was important for them to provide this Bible for you; they are instruments of God." Anne Marie then recorded her own gratitude for being able to participate in the study as a parish nurse, in this opportunity to bring Jesus' love to those in need, to, as Saint Theresa of Avila taught, to be His hands, His feet, and His eyes to His frail ones."

After giving Mrs. Quinn the large-print Bible, Anne Marie observed: "I had not expected such an emotional response. I thought she would be pleased; however, her words and actions moved me so deeply, *I too cried!*" The nurse concluded her report of the pastoral visit note with the comment: "The client was by this time emotionally and physically fatigued so I decided it was time for me to leave. We hugged and kissed. I told [Mrs. Quinn] I would call and plan another visit next week or so. She stated: '*That will make me happy.*'"

On a next visit, Mrs. Quinn spent some time expressing concern about an adult child who was "raised Catholic" but who no longer practices the faith: "You know, it makes me very sad but my [child] is [an adult] and I can't do anything about it" (she became tearful). The visit ended with a prayer and an assurance that the parish nurse would continue to visit and would call her to set up the next meeting. The parish nurse made a follow-up call to check on Mrs. Quinn's physical, emotional, and spiritual states. Mrs. Quinn "stated that she was doing some better and that she had been doing a little reading in her Bible; she still was very pleased about the new Bible." Anne Marie also mailed the patient a note and a holy card.

Positive Changes in Quantitative Data Elicited in Interviews with Mrs. Quinn. Mrs. Quinn's responses to quantitative tools changed positively on the following items:

> *SAS items: 1) belief in God; 4) strength; 5) guardianship; 6) trust;*
> *8) church membership; 9) worship; 10) religious activities; 12) spiritual*
> *support; 13) prayer; 14) reading and meditation; 19) anger.*

> *MHS items: 1) optimism; 3) meaning in life; 4) energy; 10) enjoyment;*
> *11) endurance.*

Life Satisfaction Inventory-Z (LSI) items: 6) boredom; 7) stimulation;
    8) satisfaction; 9) anticipation; 10) failure; 12) acceptance;
    13) pessimism.

Parish Nurse's Final Assessment. These positive changes in individual questionnaire items followed ministry by the parish nurse:

SAS item 9: "Client states that it now gives her more strength when she can attend Mass or receive Communion." SAS item 10: "Client now realizes the importance of praying for others and offering up her suffering." SAS item 12: "Client is now supported by visits from Eucharistic ministers from the Church, the parish nurse visits, and the spiritual care program." MHS item 1: "Client states that her illness can be used in a positive manner for herself as well as for others." MHS item 3: Mrs. Quinn "feels that she does make a contribution through prayer and meeting and visiting with others." MHS item 7: "She is still nervous but is trying to do better." LSI (overall): The parish nurse noted that at the initial assessment Mrs. Quinn was too upset to respond to some of these items (she did respond at a later visit); now she is able to respond without distress.

In summary, Anne Marie wrote that Mrs. Quinn "has improved on 17+ items on questionnaire. I feel that is a very positive thing. I think that part of the improvement came from the visits I made and the significance of receiving a new Bible. These combined seemed to improve the client's self-worth."

Case Study 4.   **Study Participant: Mrs. O'Connor**

Project Parish Nurse: Teresa

Demographic Data.   Mrs. O'Connor is a 90-year-old Caucasian, Roman Catholic widow who currently resides with her sister. She attended high school and worked as a homemaker most of her adult life. Mrs. O'Connor currently suffers from fibromyalgia, diverticulitis, and depressive disorder. She has impaired mobility related to chronic pain and is taking multiple medications.

Spiritual Profile. Mrs. O'Connor is depressed about her physical condition and the state of her life and is somewhat angry at God because of this. She was, however, very open to meeting with Teresa, a parish nurse, to discuss the state of her spiritual well-being and her relationship to the Church. She had not received the sacraments in some time.

Parish Nursing Notes. "I was very nervous for my first visit with Mrs. O'Connor. I had been warned by her family that know her to be feisty, withdrawn, and very angry with God. They were elated that I was coming in; hoping that I would be able to reach her and alleviate some of the pain and anguish that she was feeling daily. I was not so sure of myself . . . all I could do was pray and ask God and the Holy Spirit to guide me, and to just allow me to be an instrument for Them.

"I entered her home, and yes, I did find a woman who was very bitter and upset, but I did not find the fear within myself. I felt totally at peace, and we sat down and began. Mrs. O'Connor has suffered for many years with everything from chronic depressive episodes and panic attack to fibromyalgia. I found a woman suffering through incredible physical, emotional, and spiritual pain every day and not ever finding peace or solace in anything.

"I opened our discussion with Psalm 90 and a prayer to the Holy Spirit to guide us in our interactions and discussions together. She was not excited about the prayer, but was open to the idea. That set the tone for the afternoon, and I realized what a wonderful, strong woman I was sitting next to. She had amazing stories of all that she had been through. Sadly, intertwined in all of this was how and why she drifted away from God and the Church. She disclosed that she had not seen a priest in over three years, and that she felt more separated and isolated than ever. I talked to her about possibly receiving the sacrament of the sick and she immediately denounced the idea: 'There is no way that could help. Nobody can help me. I try to pray, but I don't think that God ever listens, so that makes it hard.' She also told me that her son has been pushing her to move to a Catholic nursing home. Mrs. O'Connor was not happy with this at all and does not want to leave her home. If she does, *she does not want to live in a place where Catholicism will be pressed and imposed upon her.*

"Though it was hard to hear of all the pain that Mrs. O'Connor has endured in her life, we connected in a very real way, and I knew that I could reach her . . . it would just take a little time. She did not immediately request any spiritual aids [devotional materials]; however, I have a feeling that come our second visit, I will be able to better see what her needs are and what kind of progress she is making on a spiritual level. I asked Mrs. O'Connor if she would be willing to pray a novena to Saint Jude with me every day for the next nine days. She agreed. We offered the novena up for her pain and her discernment in her relationship with God and future living plans. We closed our interaction by starting the novena together, and with a recitation of the Our Father. I left her with one of my favorite scripture verses to think about: 'I have told you this so that you might have peace in me. In the world you will have trouble, but take courage, I have conquered the world' (John 16:33). I left feeling confident that I had gotten into her heart, and that I would be successful in my ministry with her; however, I was not prepared for the profound change that I saw on my second visit.

"I returned to Mrs. O'Connor roughly two weeks later not knowing what to expect. I was afraid of what I might find, and what state she might be in. She greeted me with a warm hug and told me how excited she was to see her 'kindred spirit.' I nearly cried because in many ways I had felt the same way. She opened us in prayer, and we began our discussion. We talked about all that had transpired during our time apart. I found the most wonderful changes in this woman. She had said the novena all the way through the ninth day as had I, and I think that Saint Jude did in fact intercede with many blessings for us both.

"Mrs. O'Connor had reflected on all that we had talked about in my first visit. I again asked her about the anointing, and she said that she thought that might be something that she needs in order to be at peace, and feel at ease as she enters into the last stage of her life. She asked me if I might be able to arrange it, and I told her that I would. She also asked me if she might be able to receive the sacrament of Reconciliation, as it has burdened her heart for years that she never gave an accurate, whole-hearted, 'good' confession. I explained that it was generally offered prior to an anointing so that this too should not be a problem. We spoke about forms of prayer, and I learned that Mrs. O'Connor at one time had a beautiful and deep relationship with the Blessed Mother. She would really like to start praying the rosary daily again, but she could not find the stamina to do it. So I suggested a rosary tape, and her face lit up. Then she remembered that she had one, we found it together and prayed the rosary together right there with my beads that I always have with me. She expressed that she might like a single decade of beads so that she could continue with the prayers on a regular basis. She also expressed that she would like to read her scripture again, but that she just could not read her Bible anymore. I told her that I could get her a giant-print Bible as well.

"Mrs. O'Connor was by no means content with everything and the world was not suddenly perfect. However, in those two weeks, remarkable things happened to her and she was more at ease, and at least open to seeing what comfort and strength God could bring her. She was ready to slowly return to Him, and in a word had hope. We closed by reciting the Memorare together, as it is a favorite of both Mrs. O'Connor and myself. I also left her with another quote from scripture for her to reflect on. She told me how much she loved it the first time, and how it was a reminder of not only God and me, but that every time she felt down she just looked at it and thought of it. 'Therefore gird up the loins of your mind, live soberly, and set your hopes completely on the grace to be brought to you at the revelation of Jesus Christ' (1 Peter 1:13). I left this interaction with tears of happiness and joy in my eyes, amazed with the power of God and the Holy Spirit as I knew it was not me but Them who had helped Mrs.

O'Connor so much. I was merely an instrument, and I was so happy that I had helped to bring her some peace and started her back on her journey towards God.

"On my third visit with Mrs. O'Connor we began in prayer and discussed her life and her relationship with God. She noted feeling more at peace, and even feeling less pain since beginning to restore her prayer life. We talked about mantras and some simple meditation techniques that might further aid her in her ability to fight through the pain peacefully. Mrs. O'Connor had truly become a very different person in a relatively short period of time. I thought of the woman that I saw when I initially visited her, and I looked at the person sitting in front of me. There was life in her, she had more drive and energy in her ADLs [activities of daily living], was taking much better care of herself, and was in a word at peace. She did not seem nervous or edgy like she had in the past. In her own words, she was free.

"As we continued to talk she also told me that she thought she was ready for something like the nursing home and that she wanted to try it out. She was going to arrange to stay there for a few days on a trial basis. In watching and listening to Mrs. O'Connor, I saw that she had let go, surrendered, and left everything to God. She said, 'it feels marvelous.' We ended the day in prayer to the Holy Spirit for continued guidance and support in both of our lives. I left her with a joyful quote from the Gospel of Luke: 'Nevertheless, do not rejoice because the spirits are subject to you, but rejoice because your names are written in heaven' (Luke 10:20)."

Final visit: "Mrs. O'Connor has made tremendous improvement since I began seeing her. *She is now residing at the Catholic nursing home.* She seems much happier and is much more open and talkative since we began seeing each other. We opened this final session with a prayer to Saint Patrick, as we are both Irish, and his feast day is tomorrow. We saw it as fitting and appropriate. Mrs. O'Connor is very proud of her Irish heritage, so I thought that it would be good for her in that respect.

"Mrs. O'Connor was very interested in what I had been doing, and I filled her in minimally, as I felt that she and our journey together should be the focus of conversation, not me individually. So we began talking about her new home. It was very clear to me that she was much more at peace with life and particularly with God than she had been previously. She met with one of the priests I referred her to and received the sacraments of reconciliation and anointing of the sick. I think that this helped her tremendously. She had wanted to make that confession for a long time, and this really allowed her to be more peaceful. It has just been so long since she has had access to clergy or any kind of religious services that it [guilt] was very burdensome.

"She stated that she had more energy now, because she did not have to do as much for herself. I think that for someone like herself, always in chronic pain, that this is a very good thing. She is still very self-sufficient, but is given aid in the ADLs where she really had needed it before and did not have it. She also states [that she is] having fewer bad days and in less pain over all. She also has more convenient access to medical care. This has also contributed to her improvement.

"Spiritually, Mrs. O'Connor is much stronger and more content than I have ever seen her. When I began seeing her, she was skeptical of letting me pray under the same roof that she was in. Now she is leading us in prayer, or at least saying them with me. She is also praying the rosary daily, now that she had beads and people to do it with. She also states that she has been attending Mass three to four times per week, now that she has access to worship services. When I began seeing Mrs. O'Connor, she had not even seen a priest in over three years, so it has been amazing to see the transformation in her. She also said that she truly felt like God was with her, and she 'was really glad to have Him back batting for the home team.'

"It was a wonderful final visit with Mrs. O'Connor. She has benefited tremendously from this study, as it allowed her to have faith enough to make the move into this new living environment which has been one of the greatest things to happen to her in a long time. She attributes the rebirth of her hope and faith to 'me' [the study] as it allowed her to feel and remember all that she had forgotten. She got tears in her eyes, and told me that she could never repay me. We closed in prayer of thanksgiving, and we promised to keep in touch."

Positive Changes in Quantitative Interview Data

SAS items: 1) belief in God; 5) guardianship; 6) trust; 7) self-confidence; 8) church membership; 9) worship; 10) religious activities; 13) prayer; 14) reading and meditation; 19) anger.

MHS items: 4) energy; 8) confidence; 12) fulfillment; 15) trust.

LSI items: 2) breaks.

Case Study 5.   Project Participant: Mrs. Noone

Project Parish Nurse: Teresa

Demographic Data.   Mrs. Noone is a 91-year-old Roman Catholic, Caucasian widow who resides at home. She has arthritis and chronic back pain. Mrs. Noone is a retired schoolteacher who completed a high school education.

Spiritual Profile.   Mrs. Noone does have faith in God, but she has suffered some significant losses in her life and has not resolved them or come to peace with them before the Lord. She tries to pray but only attends Mass two to three times a year at present.

Parish Nursing Notes.   "I opened my first interaction with Mrs. Noone with a prayer and an excerpt from Psalm 51. After introducing myself and telling her a little about what I was doing, we reflected on the psalm and how it was relevant to everyday life. We talked about her faith and spirituality; where she was on her journey and where she would like to go. I found that, compared to many others, Mrs. Noone had a great outlook and was full of hope and faith. Although she cannot attend Mass on a weekly basis, she has tried to maintain an active prayer life, and I think this helps her be at peace.

"I noticed a beautifully framed print of the poem 'Footprints' on her dresser, so I asked her about it. Mrs. Noone loves that poem and uses it as a source of strength. She and I talked about it for a while: what it meant, how it makes us feel, and where she could apply it in her life. It was through this conversation that she began to feel comfortable discussing her physical pain with me. Mrs. Noone suffers daily with chronic back pain, arthritis, and fibromyalgia. She is also in remission from malignant melanoma and has edematous side effects related to the surgery endured for treatment of the cancer. She talked about how it is only through God and His intercession that she continues to press on every day. She then got very emotional and disclosed the fact that she had lost her husband and two children in a car accident 20 years ago. She admits that she has never been at peace with God about this.

"We then talked at length about God's providence. She wanted to know what I thought about it. I feel that this conversation stemmed from some of the pain that she still feels related to losing much of her family so tragically. She stated that God's divine providence was something that she had always wanted to believe in, but that she felt in essence it turned her away from God. She felt that believing in His providence meant that her God was someone who willed for her to feel this pain and tragedy and that He 'wants' bad things to happen to us. I did not know how to react at first. I do not think that I had ever thought of it that way, but I offered her the lesson learned in John 16:33: 'I have told you this so that you might have peace in me. In the world you will have trouble, but take courage, I have conquered the world.' I also offered her my perspective on the matter, and I told her that I thought that God's providence and His intention in the bad things is the strength that we pull from it. The ability to become a better, stronger, wiser person through times of trouble is something that has always comforted me. It helped her to hear a new perspective on the matter, and if nothing else I know that it was thought-provoking in her and was something that she could and would think about. We closed with the prayer of Saint Patrick, as Mrs. Noone is very proud of her Irish heritage and that is one of her favorite prayers. There was nothing in the way of spiritual or devotional material that she stated she needed, and I decided to wait until after our second visit to see if she might change her mind.

"I opened my second visit with Mrs. Noone with Jeremiah 18:1–6, as the story of the Master Potter is one that I have always loved, and I knew that Mrs. Noone would as well. We talked about the meaning behind the passage, and how truly great God is for all His works. She told me about a few of her life events that she knew were only because of God's work and 'molding.' She talked about how these were some of the most important times in her life, and they were some of the greatest examples of God's influence in her life.

"On this day, Mrs. Noone really wanted to talk about meditation. She really felt that this is something that she would like to use to deepen her prayer life, but she just didn't know how. She noted that it was something that her sister had been trying recently, too, and she really wanted to learn. She thought that it might do her a world of good. We talked of a few of the different forms of meditation that I knew of. I even talked her through a guided meditation. We talked about some simple mantras that might be helpful; I also told her that I would look into some of my resources here since I have only been exploring meditation as a form of prayer for a little over a year.

"These two topics took up a little over an hour and we closed with a reading from the book of Revelations that she likes along with an Our Father. She wanted to read the passage, and I noted how much she struggled in reading it. I asked her if having a large-print Bible would in fact help her, and she admitted that it probably would a great deal, as the tiny print keeps her away from reading Scripture.

"I opened our third interaction by playing the song 'On Eagle's Wings,' and we talked about the song for a while and some of the other songs that remind her of God's greatness, gentleness, and love. Music was an area that I could tell right away that Mrs. Noone was passionate about, and she loved talking about her favorite worship songs. I gave her the Bible and large-print prayer books that I had obtained, and she was very happy with them. She was very appreciative, and I could tell that those small tokens really meant a great deal to her. I also gave her a few things that I had found on the Internet related to meditation, and I told her what one of my favorite priests had to say on the issue when I asked him about it.

"Mrs. Noone and I talked more about the role of God in our illnesses and daily pains, and she was especially interested in my take on the matter. She did not know if I believed what I preached, so to speak, or if I was just giving her 'fluff' to try and make her feel better. I do not generally like to go into my own story, unless I think that it is going to be to the benefit of the client. In this case I truly thought it was, so I told her. She was so relieved and I could see happy to know that in essence she was not alone, and that I truly did understand much of what she was feeling and going through. It was also comforting to know that I lived through the pain, but that I was, in her words, 'spiritually there in a big way.' I think that this really helped our whole relationship; I just knew that Mrs. Noone was uncomfortable with some aspect of my presence. This is what it was. Her conversation with me from that point on was much more free and open.

"She talked about trying some of the simple meditation techniques in the time that I was gone and how she really felt that it had helped her some. She also stated that she was excited and intrigued at the new information regarding the topic. She then disclosed even more about her past and where she had been, and how all of those circumstances affected her relationship with God in some way. We had a great conversation, and closed in simple prayer to the Blessed Mother asking for her intercession in our lives.

"Mrs. Noone has been much more challenging to work with than some of the other clients simply because she had a much stronger faith, a much stronger prayer life. In many ways she has been easier to work with because she had a strong faith, but it forced me to be more creative and innovative. it also was a blessing for me in that her inquisitiveness allowed me to deepen my own faith and try new forms of prayer that I was not as familiar with.

"Mrs. Noone has a deep love for the Lord and as I found out in this, our final visit, a special relationship with the Lord as the Good Shepherd. We opened our session with the Disciple's Prayer. Mrs. Noone started a very deep discussion and we talked about what we both thought it meant to truly be a disciple of Christ and how we each try to live out this role in our lives on a daily basis. We then talked about people we knew who inspire us to be disciples of Christ, and how amazing and blessed their works are.

"Mrs. Noone went on to tell me of how much she has enjoyed expanding her prayer life by incorporating meditation into it. Over the time that I have been seeing her, she has really worked at becoming more comfortable in this form of prayer and has pulled from it many benefits. She states that she is less anxious, and has a greater ability to 'let go and let God' when hard things come up in life.

"She also mentioned that she has once again been able to pull strength from Scripture. She had stopped reading and reflecting upon the Bible because the print was too small in her older one. She had done much annotating of and reflection in the form of journal entries since receiving the new large-print Bible.

"She talked about things that she was looking forward to and how much she was anticipating Easter, as she gets to see her great-grandchildren then. Mrs. Noone seems even more positive and upbeat than she had been. She states that the drastic improvements in her sister's spiritual life have helped her and inspired her as well lately. She also enjoys the fact that they can have conversations about God and faith once again, something that means a great deal to Mrs. Noone and unfortunately something that she has done without for a long time. She has found a driver, as well, to get some help in transportation so that she might be able to attend Mass more frequently. Mrs. Noone is an intriguing person with much to offer, and I am very happy to see that she is finding ways to slowly share herself with more and more people. We closed with recitation of the Memorare, and a short guided meditation that she had acquired on cassette tape. We left, promising to keep each other in prayer and to see each other again."

Positive Changes in Quantitative Interview Data

SAS items: 2) peace; 3) confidence; 4) strength; 5) guardianship; 6) trust; 8) church membership; 9) worship; 10) religious activities; 11) social support; 12) spiritual support; 13) prayer; 14) reading and meditation; 17) fear; 18) unforgiveness; 19) anger.

MHS items: 1) optimism; 2) breaks; 4) energy; 5) enthusiasm; 6) hopefulness; 8) confidence; 9) self-worth; 10) enjoyment; 11) endurance; 12) fulfillment; 13) love; 14) meaning in life events.

LSI items: 1) promise; 7) stimulation; 9) anticipation.

Case Study 6.   Project Participant: Mrs. O'Donnell

Project Parish Nurse: Teresa

Demographic Data.   Mrs. O'Donnell is a 55-year-old Caucasian, married Roman Catholic who lives with her husband but is homebound. She is college educated and a former teacher. Mrs. O'Donnell has severe osteoarthritis and insulin-dependent diabetes. She has loss of sight also. She attends Mass less than once a month.

Spiritual Profile.   Mrs. O'Donnell misses being able to get out to her church but has deep faith in God. She also greatly wishes that there were more priests (for home ministry) but is also philosophical about the situation and about her personal life. She was very enthusiastic about participating in our parish nursing project and receiving visits from a parish nurse.

Parish Nursing Notes.   "Mrs. O'Donnell is going to be a joy to work with. She suffers from diabetes and chronic arthritis, but she has a wonderful and deep faith for the Lord. Her parish has only one priest and is dominated by younger adults. Because she is homebound, she misses her contact with church and wishes that there were more priests, but she accepts the situation as it is. She says that the lack of contact has caused her to question her faith and sometimes wonder if God is listening to her. She feels badly about this and is so excited that I will be coming to visit her.

"Mrs. O'Donnell did not want to talk about us; she just wanted to talk about God. So we dove right in and opened our session with the prayer for light. Mrs. O'Donnell told me about how her faith in the Lord had been tested quite a bit lately since she doesn't have any spiritual stimulation, but also because her daughter is sick with cancer. Then she began a conversation about Sister Briege McKenna. She wanted to know if I was familiar with Sister Briege and her works. I was so excited! I have read some of her writing and was inspired by her book *Miracles Do Happen* when I was sick. We talked extensively about how God works through His people, and how they can be such an inspiration and comfort to so many. I always find it amazing how those people are able to serve the Lord day-in and day-out without tiring. Mrs. O'Donnell feels they are angels on earth and that God blesses us greatly by sending them to people like us. I agree with that, but I also think that they are beautiful examples of how we, as Christians, should try and live. Mrs. O'Donnell summed it up with 'He puts 'em where we need 'em.'

"This was really all that we talked about [on the first visit]. I asked Mrs. O'Donnell if there was anything that she could use to help her to practice her faith and enhance her prayer life some. She asked for a statue of the Blessed Mother and a rosary with large beads, as the diabetes is affecting her sight. She hopes to have surgery to stop the progression of blindness and remains hopeful that it will be successful. We closed our session with the Peace Prayer of Saint Francis.

"On our second visit, Mrs. O'Donnell seemed a little more down than she had before. Her daughter was not doing well and they had all just learned that she had 'mets' to different body sites. There was no stopping the progression, and her daughter's prognosis was not good. Mrs. O'Donnell had the surgery to stop the progression of her blindness. It had been successful. Mrs. O'Donnell will not regain any of the sight that she has lost, but she can adapt and make behavioral changes with where her vision is now. She was very distraught over the news that her daughter had given her, though.

The one very positive thing that came from all of this was that she had been able to rely on God through the painful news of her daughter's condition. She had relied on her prayer life and faith in God; she had been able to pull some strength and comfort from this. I was very encouraged by this. She was even more excited when I gave her the statue and rosary that I had gotten for her. I had also picked up a small leaflet of common prayers that was printed with giant print. I thought that might be something that she could use. She was very excited and touched by the gifts.

"We had a long conversation about accepting trials and pain in our lives with grace. Ever trying to keep the big picture in perspective is important. She talked about how hard it was for her to see her daughter in pain, and she talked about how she hoped that her daughter's husband would be able to take good care of her grandchildren after her daughter passes on. We talked about the importance of being able to leave those cares and fears to God, as He is the one that can take care of our needs. There is nothing that Mrs. O'Donnell can do to save her daughter or to help her family, outside of praying. They are far away, and she is not in the physical capacity to take care of them herself. She would like to get out to see her daughter, but she will most likely need to be accompanied in order to do this.

"After talking about her daughter for quite a while, Mrs. O'Donnell admitted to the fact that she wasn't feeling well herself and that her arthritis had been particularly painful during the past week. She was just very glad that she had been able to pray and truly felt confident that God was watching over her and doing all He could. She was having trouble accepting the fact that she was going to have to watch her daughter die before she herself was called, but that at the same time she was praying that God's will be done in all areas of her life. She feels that this is the only way to find peace.

"I was a little down about our conversation, but I was also very proud of Mrs. O'Donnell for the way that she was handling things, and how she had found recourse to God. We closed with the prayer in affliction, and I promised to keep her, her daughter, and the entire situation in prayer.

"Our third visit was much better, and I am starting to see some significant changes in Mrs. O'Donnell. She is still excited about her prayer life and is constantly relying on God and the saints to help her through her troubles. Her daughter's health continues to deteriorate, but she has a greater acceptance of this now. She was able to go and see her daughter; another local family member took her.

"We opened in prayer, asking the Lord that we might all respond to what He is gently calling us to, and to alleviate the suffering of Mrs. O'Donnell's daughter. She then just really wanted to talk about what it was like to see her daughter so frail and hurting so much. She recalled very specific and vivid details about things that she had seen and how much she knew this was tearing her family apart. She hoped that she would be able to hold the family together. At the same time, though, she said that she would have to let God do it, because she couldn't be everything for everyone and take care of herself. She was too weak.

"Then Mrs. O'Donnell asked me for something that hadn't been asked of me. She really wanted to read the daily readings and asked if I had any idea what they were. I had them on a [brochure], so we read them and talked about them. It was amazing because the two readings really spoke to her situation and brought her a lot of comfort. We talked for quite a while about what was being said and how we could both apply the lessons to our lives. Then she talked about her prayer life. She said that it had been going very well, and she told me some of the things she had been doing, and that she was also trying to incorporate a daily rosary to the Blessed Mother for her daughter. We closed our session with the Memorare, and I left.

"On our final visit, Mrs. O'Donnell had totally surrendered herself and all of the intentions in her heart to the Lord. It was clear that she was on her way to doing this before, but she hadn't been able to completely let go. She had made a comment about how much easier life is when it is all up to God, and she didn't need to worry about it working itself out anymore. She opened us with a prayer of thanksgiving from the heart. It was so beautiful to hear those words coming from her, as she had been struggling so much.

"I mentioned how much happier she looked, and she lit up with a huge smile. Then she told me all about the evening that she gave up. She described it as being in a wrestling match with the Lord. She said that she felt arrogant for thinking that she was even worthy to be in the ring with Him. I told her not to worry, as I know of many people who had been there at least one time or another . . . it is more a question of how many rounds it takes before you realize that you are in over your head. She described it as having the weight of the world taken off of her shoulders. She just told God to take her physical pain, the pain she felt for her daughter, and her daughter's situation and do with it as He will, because He is the Lord and Savior and knows what is best. I thought this was beautiful, and I was really glad that she had been able to do that.

"We talked about her daughter for a little while. She was still alive and hanging in there, so to speak, but is now bedbound. It has been a major period of adjustment for the husband of the daughter and her children. It has also been hard for the daughter herself because she has had to remove herself from so many roles that she was so familiar with. It was obvious that there were still many things running through Mrs. O'Donnell's heart, but she was able to talk about this much more freely this visit, and the works of God within her heart and soul were apparent. This was very nice to see, and it left me feeling more confident about this being our final visit. I had been concerned previously, because Mrs. O'Donnell does not have many people to talk to. Some people stop by to make sure that she is okay, but she doesn't feel like they take the time to really listen to her like they could . . . more like they are 'punching the ticket for visiting the old lady.' We closed with a prayer and a reading of Psalm 23. Mrs. O'Donnell will do well, she also has the phone number for the parish near her home if she gets into trouble again. I don't think that she will, though; she is now in good shape spiritually, and she is much stronger now!"

Positive Changes in Quantitative Interview Data

SAS items: 2) peace; 3) confidence; 4) strength; 5) guardianship; 6) trust; 11) social support; 13) prayer; 14) reading and meditation; 15) spiritual pain; 16) alienation; 17) fear; 19) anger; 20) loss of love; 21) hopelessness.

MHS items: 1) optimism; 8) confidence; 10) enjoyment.

LSI items: 1) promise; 3) dreariness; 7) stimulation.

Case Study 7. Project Participant: Mr. O'Leary

Project Parish Nurse: Teresa

Demographic Data.　Mr. O'Leary is a 67-year-old Caucasian man who is Roman Catholic and lives in a nursing home because of illnesses including kidney failure, severe diabetes, and hearing impairment; he is also currently undergoing maintenance hemodialysis treatment. Mr. O'Leary is divorced but has one daughter who visits him. Mr. O'Leary was a professional with a college education. He now attends church only about two to three times each year.

Spiritual Profile.　Mr. O'Leary had been offered some pastoral care by a local pastor but had refused; the pastor suggested that we try to work with him. Mr. O'Leary questions why God allows bad things, such as illness, to happen.

Parish Nursing Notes.　"Mr. O'Leary has end-stage renal disease (ESRD) and goes in for hemodialysis three times each week. He has many other complications and target organ damage as a result of juvenile onset diabetes that was left uncontrolled for several years. Mr. O'Leary has limited access to pastoral care, but has refused it. The pastor told me that I could go ahead and try, and if I had any luck in reaching Mr. O'Leary, to let him know how so that he could try and continue with the limited time that he had.

"I opened our session in prayer, that Mr. O'Leary might be open to what God was saying, and that our sessions might be helpful and useful. He talked for an hour about how God was great when things are going well, but that God was so distant when things weren't great. *Why did God let hardships come along? Why didn't God stop bad things in their tracks?* Those were the issues that Mr. O'Leary had. He talked for nearly an hour about these things. This was all that we really discussed. I felt the pain that Mr. O'Leary was expressing and only hoped that I could help some.

"As I was closing us in prayer, I left the client with John 16:33 and Ecclesiastes 3:1–12. He wanted to be close to God, but didn't understand why bad things happened and why there were times of struggle in our lives.

"I entered my second visit ready with the ever 'Footprints' sharing. Mr. O'Leary had taken the time to reflect upon the two biblical passages that I had given and was able to derive a lot from them. I asked him to describe their meaning to me. He talked about how there was in fact a time for many things, and that God intended life to be that way. Mr. O'Leary stated that the passages implied that times would not always be good but that God knew what He was doing.

"I read 'Footprints' and started a discussion about it. It was a very good thing that I started it, because I don't think that I said five words the rest of the hour! But Mr. O'Leary was heading in the right direction with his thought processes, so I let it go. He talked again about God's loving care and support in our hard times and how we each need to trust in His love and presence and that He wouldn't let us down. He also talked about how much better he was feeling but that he didn't know what to do from here. I had convinced him that the hard times were okay and didn't mean that God didn't care, but didn't know what else to do.

"We had a short talk about prayer and what that was and what it meant. I gave Mr. O'Leary some tips to get started with an active prayer life and told him that we would talk about it extensively during my next visit. He still did not want any devotional items, but I decided to wait and see for one more visit. We closed in prayer, and I assured Mr. O'Leary of my prayers between visits.

"Upon return for my third visit Mr. O'Leary was very down about his illness and the hemodialysis. He did not understand why he needed to endure that all of the time since he felt fine. I did a little diabetic teaching and tried to help him see that without the hemodialysis he would certainly feel less than fine!

"I opened in prayer, and he finished off the prayer, which I was happy to see. We dove right into the topic of prayer. He was intrigued, but did not see how it would help him. So we discussed some of the benefits that many people find in prayer. We talked about the peace and comfort that some people find. Mr. O'Leary brought up the fact that if God was so wonderful and omniscient, why do we need prayer? I talked a little about the human need to be helping a situation and to be doing all that one could. I also talked about it being a way to keep the communication lines open between God and a person. If someone is shut off, it is harder for God to speak to his or her heart. He was again intrigued, and I really seemed to be reaching him.

"We talked about meditation, formal prayers, and free praying. I also talked to Mr. O'Leary about being as individual as possible . . . these were merely suggestions. Prayer is such an individual thing, I don't think that there is a right way or a wrong way to do it. Many people feel that journaling is a wonderful form of prayer and that this might be something to try. We closed in prayer, and he was going to try some of these things. I decided to get him a small prayer book although he still had not requested anything.

"By the beginning of our final visit, I was beginning to see small changes in Mr. O'Leary. I was not as pleased with his progress as I had been with my other patients, but I was doing my best, and he was trying. He seemed to like the prayer book and I think that he will use it. I opened us in a simple prayer, and he told me that he wanted to talk about what it is that God wanted of us as humans. I told him that God didn't expect us to be perfect; that is why we have been given the sacraments. But I felt that God called us to live as closely to the image of Jesus as we could. He did not understand and wanted more. I didn't really know what to tell him outside of the message delivered by Matthew 25:31–46. I read this to him and we talked about it for a long time. All of the things that it entailed; all the different ways that we can go against God and not even realize it. It seemed to really reach him, and it was apparent that he had not thought of life from this perspective. I told him of the many amazing things that can be found within scripture and I encouraged him to read it in addition to keeping up with his prayers. He really wanted to try these things, but it was going to be a slow and working process. However, I could see that if he was diligent and applied himself to growing in God and His love, that he could. Our conversation took over an hour. Mr. O'Leary likes to talk and likes to analyze everything that is said. This contributed to the difficulty I had in working with him, but I think that he is on his way to great changes. Some of the improvements can already be seen. I pray that he keeps up with the forward progress.

"We closed in prayer and with a small scripture reading from Corinthians. I gave Mr. O'Leary my best wishes with his health and in his spiritual endeavors that he is currently undertaking. I reminded him to have faith, hope, and trust in God and to remember those two scripture passages that I had given if he ever started to feel distant again. (The local pastor will try to follow up with him now that he is beginning to pray.)"

Positive Changes in Quantitative Interview Data

SAS items: 4) strength; 5) guardianship; 6) trust; 7) self-confidence; 10) religious activities; 12) spiritual support; 19) anger.

MHS items: 1) optimism; 4) energy; 9) self-worth; 13) love.

LSI items: 9) anticipation.

Case Study 8.   Project Participant: Mrs. Scully

Project Parish Nurse: Teresa

Demographic Data. Mrs. Scully is a 73-year-old Roman Catholic, Caucasian widow who resides at home. She is suffering from Parkinson's disease and diabetes, which have left her an unsteady gait and peripheral neuropathies. She was a high school teacher with a bachelor's degree. She has a live-in nurse and a cook.

Spiritual Profile.   Mrs. Scully identifies as a Roman Catholic but states that she "never" goes to church. She does not have a sense of spiritual well-being and was somewhat hesitant about a parish nursing project at first (she had been referred by a local pastor). She did agree to meet with a project parish nurse, however.

Parish Nursing Notes.   "Mrs. Scully has been one of my harder clients to work with, as she has not only spiritual needs, but her physical and mental handicaps impede her ability to do a lot of the things that she would like to do. She has a live-in nurse and cook; this was deemed necessary as she would not follow an American Diabetic Association (ADA) diet on her own, and she also needs assistance with many of her activities of daily living (ADLs).

"The first visit was very difficult, as Mrs. Scully was very empty spiritually and was skeptical of me. She did not feel that I could possibly know anything about life. I opened our interaction with a very simple and quick prayer. I simply asked God to bless our time together and us. I also asked Him to allow Mrs. Scully to be open to His will in her life. We talked about God enough for me to get the spiritual assessment done, but

I knew that I was not going to be able to talk to her about God anymore for today. She needed to be more comfortable with me first. She was very broken and felt very far away from God. She did not believe that a loving God would allow all the painful things in her life to happen. She was very angry with Him and did not understand.

"We spent the rest of the afternoon just talking about ourselves. Things we liked, things we did not like, and what some of our favorite hobbies are. As it turns out, Mrs. Scully and I have a lot in common. This comforted her, and it also gave us many things to talk about. This allowed her to be more at ease with me, and I hope will allow her to be more receptive to what I was doing. During our time, I was able to help Mrs. Scully ambulate between rooms and help her do a few very simple things. This allowed her to see that I was a gentle and kind person and that I was not going to be judgmental or critical of her. She even told me how much better this made her feel about my being there.

"Our time was over with and I promised her my prayers and asked her to try and pray some, even if it was just a Hail Mary every now and then. She agreed, and I left, worried that I might not be able to help her, not really knowing what to do. I talked to one of the priests on campus about the interaction and asked for help in reaching her. He was able to give me some insight, and I prayed about it and remained hopeful that she would make progress.

"My second visit with Mrs. Scully was going to have to be short since she had to leave to see her cardiologist about 45 minutes after I got there. I had planned to spoil her with wonderful stories of God's love, healing, and forgiveness. I opened our interaction with a reading of 'Footprints.' She seemed to enjoy it and told me she hadn't heard that poem for 20 years. She just did not think that it applied to her anymore since she was so old and forgotten by God and society. I started a discussion with her and we talked about ways in which it applied to her more now than ever before.

"She was beginning to resist a little bit less. Then she asked me what I thought about God in relationship to all that had happened to her. So we talked about God's providence and His will in our lives. We talked about hardships and what we are meant to receive from those times of struggle. I told her a little bit about what I had been through physically, and in an odd way this was very comforting to Mrs. Scully. She thought that it might be worth trying; maybe God did care and He was listening. She just needed to start doing her part again.

"Mrs. Scully found an old single-decade rosary that her aunt had given her years ago and told me that she was going to try and say one decade each day until I came back. She made me promise to pray for her too. She left for her appointment and I left feeling much better about what had occurred. God had touched her heart and was slowly turning it back to Him. I am looking forward to our next visit, to see what surprises lie in wait for me. I just pray that God continues to work in her, and that she may once again fully realize God's presence in her life.

"Mrs. Scully was eager for our third visit. I thought that this was a great sign. She had not asked for anything, but I got her a rosary tape. It was apparent that there was some connection with the rosary, and I knew that she probably didn't have the stamina or energy to pray it alone. I thought that she might like it, and she was really touched. We opened this session together by reciting the Memorare.

"We had a wonderful talk about God's love and forgiveness. Mrs. Scully seemed very interested in coming fully back to God, but she was afraid that He would not forgive her for some of her wrongs, and then He might be angry with her leaving and doubting Him in the first place. She was very emotional, justifying her leaving and lack of faith on all of the pain and illness in her life. She has endured much pain and suffering. I learned thorough our interactions that her husband died of Parkinson's disease 20 years earlier. This was very hard for her to watch him suffer with, and now she knew what she would be going through. She resented God for that and was very angry with Him for allowing that to happen. However, she knew that her life was very empty without a spiritual component and was ready to reconcile her relationship with Him.

"After talking, she had decided that receiving the sacrament of reconciliation might really help her. I also suggested an anointing since she is suffering with so many ailments. She resisted for a moment, thinking that she was not worthy of this. I told her that she most certainly was, and she could receive absolution before the anointing. This made her feel a lot better, and I told her that I would arrange the anointing.

"She was going to use her rosary tape and was even going to get back into reading scripture on a daily basis. We closed our session in prayer, and I promised to be accompanied by a priest for our fourth visit together. I am very pleased with her progress. I think that there is still a long way to go, but she has taken several large steps toward God, and I hope that this might even help some of her physical suffering since she is more at peace with Him.

"I was accompanied for my final visit with Father Thomas, a priest from a local religious house of studies. He opened us in prayer and with a blessing on both of our lives and works. I left the room and allowed Mrs. Scully to have her confession with him and was then present for the anointing. The whole process did in fact bring a lot of peace to her and there was a calmness about her that had not been there previously.

"For the rest of the hour we had a wonderful conversation about prayer and the many different forms of prayer. Mrs. Scully had just in the past several weeks come to realize how individual prayer is and how one form may not suit another individual. She talked about some of the things that she had tried and the ones that did not work for her. She stated how much deeper her prayer life is now and how much inner peace that brings her. Father discussed his ways of praying, and I talked about my favorite forms of prayer. This gave her many ideas that she could try out to see if she liked any of them. Father and I also talked to her live-in nurse to see if she might be able to transport Mrs. Scully to church occasionally, as she expressed and interest in getting back to Mass sometime. She does not have the physical capabilities to go very often, but even every now and again would be beneficial to her.

"We closed with a prayer of thanksgiving for the many blessings that we have all received. I am very happy with the progress of Mrs. Scully. I hope that she is able to allow her faith to grow even more now, but I think that she has made phenomenal improvements over the past two months. She thanked me for everything that I had done as I was leaving and told me that I had really facilitated positive change in her life. I was so happy to hear this. Not only had she seen the changes within herself, but she knew that it was God working in her heart."

Positive Changes in Quantitative Interview Data

SAS items: 3) confidence; 4) strength; 5) guardianship; 8) church membership; 9) worship; 10) religious activities; 13) prayer; 14) reading and meditation; 16) alienation.

MHS items: 1) optimism; 3) meaning in life; 8) confidence; 9) self-worth.

Case Study 9.   Project Participant: Mrs. Daly

Project Parish Nurse: Teresa

Demographic Data.   Mrs. Daly is a 96-year-old Roman Catholic, Caucasian married woman who lives with her husband. She completed the 11th grade in school and worked for the government prior to retirement. She has chronic congestive heart failure and had a stroke (CVA), which has left her debilitated.

Spiritual Profile.   Mrs. Daly has suffered from some confusion following her stroke; however, her husband prays the Chaplet of Divine Mercy with her and reads scripture to her. She likes to watch the rosary on EWTN (Eternal Word Television Network).

Parish Nursing Notes.   "Mrs. Daly is going to be a little more difficult to work with than most of the other patients simply because she is losing her mental capabilities. She has recently suffered another CVA, and this has greatly impacted her. Her husband lives with her and takes care of her. However, she has great willpower and wants to overcome the complications that she has suffered due to the CVA and does have a drive to get better. She is working with many specialists and trying to regain as much function as possible.

"In my initial visit with Mrs. Daly, I am almost more concerned for the well-being of her husband. He waits on her hand and foot, but has absolutely no time for himself, and it is very plain to see that caring for her is very draining and exhausting for him. Her husband sat with her through the first pastoral interaction. Her husband had told me how much Mrs. Daly enjoys the daily chaplet, scripture reading, and rosary recitation on EWTN. So we opened with that as our prayer, and that also gave us something to talk about. We talked about the scripture reading and what Mrs. Daly got out of it. She can only talk about simple things and had a lot of difficulty even reflecting on this, although she did the best that she could. After a short talk of reflection, we talked about her family and all they meant to her. I found that she had a much easier time talking and formulating thoughts when the subject was things that she was very familiar with, like her siblings, children, grandchildren, and great-grandchildren. It was very easy to work God and his blessings in this conversation. It is very clear to me that Mrs. Daly has a devotion to the rosary, but that much beyond that is hard for her to do at this point.

"We closed in prayer, and I told her that I would return soon. She asked for a Miraculous Medal and some hymns to listen to. She thought that music might be a way that she could listen and think to herself about God. She could hear and comprehend questions very well, just has some trouble formulating and articulating responses. I also told her husband that he could leave if he wanted to while I was there. This meant the world to him. To just have an hour off every now and again to be alone and not have to worry about Mrs. Daly was really going to benefit him a great deal. He seemed appreciative and I really hope that this will help him to cope some. It has to be hard to watch the woman that you love and have lived with for so long deteriorate like this.

"On my second visit to Mrs. Daly, her husband promptly left after I got there; he had made plans to go out with some of his friends that he had not seen in a long time. They were all going bowling, and it was apparent that this meant a great deal to him. I got there right as the daily chaplet started, and I used that to open us. It was not until we finished that I realized how much Mrs. Daly had deteriorated between visits.

She was having a very hard time articulating any thoughts, even her name. She knew exactly who I was and it was apparent that she was happy to see me. She loved her medal and seemed pleased with the music that I had brought her.

"I found that we really had to communicate by my asking her yes and no questions. She could still very easily comprehend all that was going on around her; however, she could hardly speak and if she did, she had very loose associations and was having trouble remembering the entire thought that she had wanted to say. Essentially, I knew that Mrs. Daly was very sad and a little depressed about her current health situation, but that she remained devout and hopeful in God and His mercy. She faithfully watched and participated in her heart daily through the chaplet, reflection, and rosary on EWTN. She also was hopeful that the music would allow her to ponder her faith and allow her to focus on God and His mercy for a greater period of time each day.

"I closed us with a prayer, and I promised to say a novena to Saint Clare for the healing of her condition. I hoped that even if she did not recover, the progression could be slowed. Her husband appreciated this and thanked me for his afternoon off. I am happy with the enthusiasm, positive outlook, and zest for life that Mrs. Daly continues to show, amidst this slow and progressing deterioration. Her husband remains strong. I hope that he asks for help if caring for her gets to be too much. I told him not to hesitate and told him where he could go to get assistance.

"A follow-up visit with Mrs. Daly was heartbreaking. She could not articulate anything and did not have the same positive outlook as she previously had. She just did not appear interested in much of anything. Her husband remained around because he was very worried about her. We turned on the EWTN rosary program, but she fell asleep shortly into it. I talked to her husband about how long she had been like this, and how she had been previous days. He told me very innocently that this was all very sudden, but that she had fallen earlier that morning and he had given her aspirin to alleviate a headache. He said that this had all happened that day, and that she could no longer stay awake through anything. I had a fairly good idea of what was going on, and I told her husband that I really thought she needed medical attention and we should call an ambulance. He agreed, so I called 911 and stayed with Mrs. Daly until the paramedics arrived. I held her had and prayed while we waited. Her husband went with her to the hospital, and she slipped into a coma en route. She had a massive brain hemorrhage, and the coma is most likely irreversible, but only time will tell. I continue to pray that God's will be done and that she not suffer any more than she has to. She and her husband have been through so much, but many of the doctors are saying that Mrs. Daly is nearing the end. Her husband has signed a do-not-resuscitate (DNR) order. With the last report from her husband, her temperature was extremely high and they think that she may be getting a little septic. They have told her husband that she may only have a few days left to live." Mrs. Daly did go to the Lord several days following the writing of this final note by her parish health minister.

Positive Changes in Quantitative Interview Data

SAS items: 1) belief in God; 2) peace; 3) confidence; 4) strength; 5) guardianship; 6) trust; 7) self-confidence; 8) church membership; 9) worship; 10) religious activities; 12) spiritual support; 14) reading and meditation; 15) spiritual pain; 16) alienation; 17) fear; 18) unforgiveness; 19) anger; 20) loss of love.

MHS items: 2) goal setting; 5) enthusiasm; 6) hopefulness; 7) resilience.

Case Study 10.   Project Participant: Mrs. McAuley

Project Parish Nurse: Teresa

Demographic Data.   Mrs. McAuley is an 81-year-old Roman Catholic, Caucasian married woman who resides in her home. She has a doctorate in the biological sciences and worked in the field of animal husbandry during her career. She currently suffers from both bipolar disease and Alzheimer's disease.

Spiritual Profile.   Mrs. McAuley self-identified as Catholic but admitted that she only attended Mass two to three times each year and had some difficulties with the Church and with prayer. She was, however, quite amenable to participating in the OSVI project and enhancing her personal spiritual well-being.

Parish Nursing Notes.   "Mrs. McAuley is a very happy, hopeful, and uplifting woman. I could tell from our first few minutes together that something prevented her from having a full relationship with God. Something was holding her back, and she clearly felt badly about it, but was not comfortable about talking to me about it right away. That was fine and is very understandable. I began by talking a tiny bit about myself, just so that she would be more comfortable and know that I was there for her, and that I truly cared about her and facilitating her relationship with God.

"I asked her if she would like to begin in prayer with me, and she told me very cordially to just go ahead on my own and that she would listen. *She did not feel right praying.* I just did not understand, she was such an upbeat and happy person that loved to talk about everything, her past, where she had been, and where she was going. So I carefully selected a special prayer. It is one that I would generally find fairly morbid to open an interaction with anyone and even more so to open my first interaction with someone. However, I decided that I had to take a risk or we were never going to leave the topics of her time in England and how much we both loved Stonehenge. The prayer is about uncovering hidden wounds and learning to accept those wounds as blessings from God, because of the lessons and strength that we can pull from our trials.

I gambled, and it worked. She disclosed to me how much she loved God and how many wonderful things He had done for her over the years. However, she perpetually felt guilty for not being able to attend church services very often. Because of this, Mrs. McAuley felt very guilty about even praying, like she was no longer worthy. She also knows that she has been blessed with relatively good health. She struggles with arthritis and some decreased mobility related to this. However, other than this she is in very good shape physically and is very well controlled with all other health-related issues. However, I quickly discovered that this in essence made her feel worse for not doing more for God or trying harder to get to Mass.

"It was so wonderful to see a person with so much spunk and zest for life, yet at the same time it was heartbreaking because she felt so unworthy of God. I was thinking of how to respond to her, and she asked me if I thought that she could still be looked at by God with favor. I told her that I felt that God never asked for more from us than trying to be the 'best we can, where we are, with what we have.' I also told her that I felt she could live a very full spiritual life from home. Prayer can be done anywhere, and I showed her how she could get special programming with EWTN and the daily chaplet program. She told me that she did not think she was ready to watch a Mass on TV and have that replace a normal celebration. I told her that was fine and that just taking baby steps back toward God through prayer would be an excellent place to start. We had a very nice conversation about the little things that could be done to enhance her spiritual life. She stated that she used to have a small statue of Saint Francis, but that it had broken. She talked about how much she had always liked Saint Francis and how he reminded her of herself! I knew that she would really like one, so I got a statue to take her on my second visit.

"We closed the session with scripture reading, and even within the short amount of time we spent together, she was more at ease with me, what I was trying to do, and with the idea of allowing God into her heart and life once again. I really look forward to working with Mrs. McAuley. I think that she has much to offer and has a wonderful attitude about everything else in her life. I find her very admirable, and I think that this study will really help her to improve her life even more.

"I returned to Mrs. McAuley about three weeks later. This is a lot longer than I would have liked to go without seeing her, but we had some scheduling conflicts. *She loved her statue of Saint Francis.* She dusted off the top of her dresser and placed it front and center. She had not asked for any devotional items, and this just really made her day. I also gave her a prayer card with Saint Francis on the front and the Peace Prayer on the back, so that she could have him with her always.

"The difference between these first two visits was absolutely amazing, but not entirely surprising. I thought that Mrs. McAuley would really take off and get a lot out of the visits because of her general outlook on life, and because it was obvious that there was a deep and profound faith and love of God in her. It was simply buried by needless guilt. She asked if she could open our discussion in prayer, and I told her that I would be delighted. She went to the bedroom and got a very old crumpled piece of paper. She told me that it was the prayer that her mother used to read to her everyday when she was young. It was a wonderful prayer to Saint Ann.

"We began talking about how beautiful it was when people find God in their lives and how special it is to be witness to amazing spiritual transformations in people. She told me beautiful stories of people that she had seen convert in her lifetime and how truly wonderful and awesome it was to watch people experiencing this. So then we started talking about how hard it is to keep the flame of faith lit even after the 'honeymoon' period is over. She brought up the example of young adults. Many are forced to practice and at least go through the motions with their upbringing, but how awesome it was if young people are able to hang onto that into their own adult lives.

"I found it interesting that she was so intrigued by this, so I asked her how she had initially hung onto her faith after the 'honeymoon.' She told me that God was just such an awesome and amazing presence to her that she surrendered her life and her being to Him. She totally trusted in Him and knew that He would take care of her in all her doings. She talked about how wonderful and 'freeing' this was. To just know that someone walks every step with you and cares about what direction life takes. She just felt so guilty that for the past several years she no longer felt that was true, as she was not fully participating and practicing her faith in her own eyes. She thought that this was something God would not look highly upon and that she had felt it meant she was not worthy of Him.

"This conversation took quite a while, and I could tell that Mrs. McAuley had talked herself into believing what she was telling me, although I could see that she did not *want* to believe it. I had a copy of one of my favorite songs in the car. The hymn of 'Love, Trust, Surrender.' It just repeats over and over, so I brought that into the house and I used that as a closing prayer. Mrs. McAuley had made a lot of progress and stated how much fuller her prayer life had been, but she was just clutching this guilt. We sat and listened to the hymn, and I could tell that it reached her heart. As I got up, I told her that it was never too late to love, trust, and surrender . . . and that it was certainly

okay to love, trust, and surrender again. She asked me if I really thought that someone of her age could do that. I told her absolutely and that I honestly felt it was one
of the most beautiful expressions of love for the Lord. Completely turning life over
to Him and trusting in His providence no matter what are not easy. I know that she
was very touched, and I am anxious to return to Mrs. McAuley. I am sure she will
have changed even more!

"My final visit with Mrs. McAuley brought some of the changes that I had expected
to find in her. There was a beautifully strong faith buried deep in her soul, and my
goal had been to help her recognize that once again. She had managed to get to Mass
twice since our last visit, and she had received the sacrament of reconciliation before
one of the services. This was great, and I was pleased at how self-actualized she had
been about it. We had not even discussed this, and I was *so* happy to see that she had
gone and done such a thing on her own. I knew that it had helped her a great deal
and had brought her a lot of peace and comfort one again.

"We opened our discussion for the afternoon by reciting together the Prayer of Saint
Francis that was on the back of the prayer card that I had given her. Mrs. McAuley
really directed the conversation on this afternoon by herself. She told me about all of
the things that she had been feeling and doing in relation to God and her prayer life.
She talked about how strong it made her and how much she gained from having it
back in her life. However, two of her most profound statements that really got me a
little choked up were (a) that she had been in contact with her family and was bringing all of them back to God, and also that (b) she knew how lucky she was to have
rekindled her faith life before she became severely debilitated later in life as she knew
that this would all help her cope and feel less pain all around. I thought it was fan-
tastic that she had been able to see these things and make these changes. I was very
pleased at how she had progressed and how self-directed she was about it.

"We talked about her favorite European vacation spots a little more, as she loves
Europe and brought it up, then we closed in a prayer of thanksgiving and parted ways.
I am really going to miss her spunk and influence in my life! Her faith has taken off
and I feel confident that she will remain fervent in that, as she can see the positive impact that it has in her life."

Positive Changes in Quantitative Interview Data

> *SAS items: 5) guardianship; 6) trust; 10) religious activities; 11) social
> support; 12) spiritual support; 13) prayer; 15) spiritual pain;
> 18) unforgiveness.*

> *MHS items: 3) meaning in life; 6) hopefulness; 10) enjoyment; 14) meaning
> in life events.*

Case Study 11.   Project Participant: Mr. McAleer

Project Parish Nurse: Teresa

Demographic Data.   Mr. McAleer is a 68-year-old Roman Catholic, Caucasian, widower who lives alone (his children take turns helping him). He completed an associate's degree in college and worked in skilled labor. Mr. McAleer suffers from diabetes and severe rheumatoid arthritis and has chronic pain and some deformities.

Spiritual Profile.   Mr. McAleer is Catholic by his own description; however, as a scientist, he has some questions related to his faith and to God's will in the world and perhaps in his life.

Parish Nursing Notes.   "Mr. McAleer is going to be a challenge to work with. He is a brilliant man who has put up with a major disability since his young adult years. He is very well educated and at first glance seemed to be someone who does everything he can to prove you wrong. Anything you say to him must be backed up with evidence. He currently suffers from severe diabetes and chronic arthritis in his wrists, hands, and fingers.

"From a spiritual standpoint, Mr. McAleer believes that there is something greater than he is, but does not have faith and trust in God, as His presence has not been proven to him. He says that he feels this way because when he was diagnosed with diabetes he was assured that everything would be fine and that he would not incur problems if he was compliant with medications and dietary alterations. He has a severe case of diabetes and is in need of insulin injections several times daily. His vision is beginning to fail, and he is in the beginning stages of renal failure. He feels that the doctor could not prove things would be okay and, therefore, should never have told him that they would. How could he trust that God would be his strength and salvation? Nobody could ever prove that. Mr. McAleer also said that it is very hard to devote oneself to something that is not tangible, not seen, and therefore probably not there all of the time. His arthritis is crippling for him and has nearly left him totally incapacitated, as he does not have the use of his legs either. He has a brilliant mind and reads incessantly, constantly trying to broaden his horizons in all areas of published literature.

"It was very intriguing to me that he could say that he lost his faith in God because a doctor had misinformed him of this prognosis. I was glad that he knew what the root of his problem was, but at the same time it pained me to hear that he lost faith in God because of a mistake of the human condition. Granted, he had been hurt by the loss of the use of his legs, later by diabetes, and even later by this arthritis. He had been led astray by many in his life and this has had profound consequences upon his life. He has lost the ability to trust and feels if something is to be done he must do it himself, otherwise things probably will not be accomplished. In losing the ability to trust and have faith in people, he also lost trust, faith, hope, and love in God.

"I wanted to slowly allow him to regain faith and trust in the Lord. With a couple other clients who were greatly lacking in trust, I had left a biblical quote for them to think about and reflect upon. I decided to try this with Mr. McAleer. I could tell that he wanted to believe and that he wanted to have peace, but he did not think that was possible without proof. My hope was that God would work in him and that he would get proof enough through the great works of the Lord. I gave him Psalm 38:18–23 to reflect before my next visit. I felt this was appropriate, as this passage acknowledges that things aren't perfect and that bad things can and do happen. However, through all of this God can be the salvation of the world; one simply has to be open to this influence within one's life. I incorporated this passage into a closing prayer, and he promised that he would try to understand it; I hoped that this in turn would bring him comfort.

"Upon returning for a second visit, I found Mr. McAleer a little more open to talking about his spirituality. He was not yet ready to discuss his religion and religious beliefs, but spirituality was a start nonetheless. I have found that for the clients lacking in trust, 'Footprints' is an excellent reading. It paints such a beautiful image that nobody can deny. It is comforting, and I decided to try this with Mr. McAleer as well. Then suddenly I found myself talking once again about God's providence and will in our lives. This seems to be a common spiritual issue encountered by all of the chronically ill clients that I have worked with. I also think that questioning God and wondering why He allows bad things to happen in our lives is legitimate and can be expected. My hope is that through conversation and sharing of mutual experiences, they will all begin to see the greatness, the strength, and the blessing that these trials can bring them. I hope for nothing less of this client. However, as in most parts of our interactions, I have had to work much harder to convince him.

"Mr. McAleer wanted to feel God again and wanted to believe, but he had not been convinced that He was there and that He cared. I obtained a book when I was sick that was titled *He Is There and He Is Not Silent*. I had it with me, and I gave it to Mr. McAleer to read before my next visit. We also talked about some simple meditation techniques since he told me that he wouldn't pray because that had to mean that one was 'nuts,' 'just sitting there talking to themselves.' I knew that he would not pray just yet, and that meditation was probably more his style. He did guided meditations already for relaxation, so was to a degree familiar with the style and was comfortable with it. He promised to read the book and try to meditate, as long as I prayed for him.

I told him that I absolutely would every day, for his comfort, healing, and peace in his heart.

"Our third visit brought many surprises to me. I saw many changes within Mr. McAleer. He would not admit that anything great had happened or that he had changed at all, but it wouldn't be like his personality to admit that God was winning just yet. However, some of the things that I noticed were he was much more well groomed, there was less of an edge to his demeanor and personality, there was a sense of tranquility and peace about him, a Bible had snuck out onto his coffee table, and there was more order to everything about the house. I saw these to be very positive signs of change in the right direction.

"We opened in prayer with an Our Father. Mr. McAleer did not resist like he had in the past. He started talking about love. As it turns out, he had lost his ability to love long ago as well. He felt worthy of love, but did not feel that he received any and therefore found it difficult to give any. He had his heart broken long ago, and I do not think that it was ever given a chance to heal. This was another reason that he stated he had drifted from God. There was no way that anyone or any God could possibly love him unconditionally because of his appearance and all he had been through. He felt that he would just be a burden to anyone. This took quite a while, and he eventually asked me what I felt love was, and how God acted through that. I simply summed it up with 1 Corinthians 13:4–13 and that God is love. I believe that with a passion and with all my heart and life. I told him that unfortunately we cannot always trust all human beings, as he had learned. However, God is constant, steady, always there, and always loving. You cannot go wrong with Him if you put your faith and trust in Him.

"He seemed to accept this as a plausible answer and was willing to at least consider it. I also used the analogy with him that God can write straight with crooked lines. As humans, we tend to take the crooked lines, think we can fix things, and make an even bigger mess. God, however, takes the huge mess and can make a line, straight as an arrow, from our heart to His. Mr. McAleer lit up, that had really touched him. . . . I really feel that this is something that might help him to rediscover all that he is missing and allow him to find some peace. Throughout our conversation, he was much more receptive than in previous encounters and he was really trying. He had even purchased a book on meditation from Amazon.com and was using that to enhance his prayer life. I do not feel that I have been as effective with him as I have with the other clients, but I know that I am making a positive difference. Mr. McAleer is starting to make significant changes with his life, and that will allow him to live a longer, happier, and fuller life in the long run. We closed in prayer, and I look forward to our final visit to see what further progress has been made.

"On my final visit with Mr. McAleer, we sat and talked for quite a while. He had been working hard on different meditation techniques, and he chose to open us in prayer. I felt that this was a sign of significant forward progress since I had started working with him. I still saw all of the positive changes in him and his environment; however, I noticed a few other things as well. Mr. McAleer was now initiating conversation about God and telling me about all that he had been doing, instead of my trying to pry for any information or feeling about it.

"He began a conversation with me about the strength and inspiration that he had been able to gain from the written Word. He was once again learning to have God play a more central role in his life and to turn to God with his fears and frustrations. He also was more willing to accept the fact that God may in fact be around, and that may be the reason that the positive good things in his life had occurred. It was a totally different outlook on life than he had previously had, and I was very glad to see it.

"Mr. McAleer has also stated that his pain has been decreased and that he has a greater ability to function and use his hands since discovering his faith once again. This was absolutely astounding and tremendous to me. It was true as well. I feared for a second that he may have just been telling me what I wanted to hear, but I could see in watching him that this was in fact so. We talked for quite a while, and I closed us in prayer, thanking God for our time together and for the positive changes in Mr. McAleer.

"There is no doubt in my mind that Mr. McAleer made tremendous progress and that he benefited greatly from our meetings; however, the greatest lesson in my interactions with him was for me. I was so down on myself for not being able to reach him and feeling as though I was of no use for him. I did not feel that he had progressed as much as some of the other clients, and this really bothered me. It took until this afternoon when I saw him for the final time for me to once again remember that I merely allow myself to be used by God as a facilitator. I think that this is something that is very important never to forget when doing work like this. The changes will come, and God is just as present, he may just use another port of entry; in this case the silent recesses of Mr. McAleer's heart."

Positive Changes in Quantitative Interview Data

SAS tems: 2) peace; 3) confidence; 5) guardianship; 6) trust; 8) church membership; 9) worship; 10) religious activities; 13) prayer; 16) alienation; 17) fear; 18) unforgiveness.

MHS items:1) optimism; 4) energy; 6) hopefulness; 10) enjoyment; 14) meaning in life events.

LSI items: 6) boredom; 9) anticipation.

Case Study 12. Project Participant: Miss Erin Kelly

Project Parish Nurse: Anne Marie

Demographic Profile.   Erin Kelly is a 35-year-old woman who attended college for two years prior to an automobile accident in which she suffered brain damage. She is Roman Catholic, Caucasian, and lives at a nursing home. She is quadriplegic, has short-term memory loss, speech impairment, contractions of her hands and feet, and suffers from convulsions. Ms. Kelly is on multiple medications, and she is able to attend Mass about once a month with much assistance. Her parents were very enthusiastic about the parish nursing study including Erin in our project, although it was recognized that they would have to assist with answering standardized questions related to her spiritual well-being. Based on the parents' request, Ms. Kelly was included as a project participant in the study.

Spiritual Profile.   Although Ms. Kelly is somewhat cognitively impaired, her parish nurse noted, "Erin is able to say all her prayers, word for word, but at the same time cannot remember what day it is or what she ate an hour ago. Erin can also recite the entire Mass. She will say it along with the priest offering Mass and is very proud of herself." Her nurse added: "The most striking characteristic about this client is that she is always smiling, especially if someone initiates any communication with her. I introduced myself as a parish nurse. She smiled and laughed and appeared that she understood in her own fashion. She wanted a hug, moving her upper extremities away from her body as best she could. I told [Erin] I wanted to visit with her at different times. I stated, 'We can pray together, color pictures of the Blessed Mother and of Jesus.' I asked her if she would like that. [Erin] moved her upper body back and forth, smiled and laughed, and put her hands together [like clapping]."

   "I explained to [Erin] that I would return again to visit. She put her head down on my shoulder when I hugged her good-bye. She said : 'I love you.'" The nurse added: "[Erin] shines and is the picture of unconditional love to me and I think to everyone who comes into her presence. Erin is usually able to go to Mass once a month at the nursing home and receives communion if a Eucharistic minister comes and prays with her family.

Erin's Parents.   Anne Marie met and talked with Erin's parents: "I explained who and what I was about and also explained the plan for spiritual assessment, intervention and pastoral visits. [Erin's] parents stated that they were very excited about the study and that they felt the needs of their daughter would be seen and met through this program. They explained her handicaps and initially were concerned that I would not visit with her because of these; but I reassured them that I felt [Erin] and I would find a common ground to relate to each other. [Erin's] mother stated that her daughter enjoyed being with other people and 'she loves everyone; she is love.' She added: 'I think that's why [Erin] is like she is, to show others what love is.'

"[Erin's] mother became tearful; then she took my hand and thanked me for taking the time to visit her daughter." The parish nurse, herself a mother with two daughters, noted in parentheses: "This pulled on my heartstrings!"

"I told [Erin's] parents to feel free to call me at any time if they had any questions or just wanted to talk. [Erin's] dad stated that he wanted to see, read, and help fill in the spiritual assessment form from his perspective. I made plans to leave him the forms and decided that I would [also] do my own assessment; then review his and include both in the study."

Parish Nursing Notes.   Describing her first visit to Erin Kelly, Anne Marie reported: "Due to [Erin's] multiple medical problems, I decided not to ask the questions one after another. I thought this would be too difficult and frustrating to her. I approached the study in a different manner. I used observation of the study participant and then interacted with her to carry out the spiritual assessment [with the assistance of her father].

"[On my next visit] I took [Erin] a book titled *The Lord's Prayer*, illustrated by Tasha Tudor. The pictures are beautiful and appealing to younger people. Erin and I said the Our Father together slowly and looked at all the pictures and talked about the pictures. We talked about how wonderful and loving God is and all the wonderful things God has made. We talked about the religious pictures, palm, and rosary up on the wall of her room. She said: 'I love them' and that 'the Father loves and protects' her.

"[At a next minisitry visit] I visited with [Erin] a few minutes prior to Mass; she was in a dayroom waiting for Mass to begin. Erin was very excited about Mass being said at the nursing home and was the first to say 'Hi, Father' when Father arrived. (I attended Mass with Erin.) After Mass I visited with [Erin]. We talked about Mass.

I asked her if Mass was important to her. 'I love Mass,' she stated. 'I love you'; then she gave me a kiss."

"I thought to myself how amazing God is. Here is this young woman, who cannot remember what she ate this morning but recites Mass, receives Communion, and loves everyone. It is evident that God works through [Erin]. It is like God's light and love shines out to all who are in Erin's presence. Erin's shows us God's love is unconditional, loving all of us for who we are even with our faults and sins; to be in [Erin's] presence is to be in God's presence!"

Erin's parish nurse concluded a report of one of her visits with this note: "I pulled out a little tattoo with 'joy' written on it. She laughed and kissed the air which is a sign for me to bend over for her to kiss me. I said: 'Oh, [Erin], you give me joy like the word on your new tattoo.' She said: 'You too!' The visit ended with hugs and kisses and left me with a warm loving feeling in my heart with hopes that I could imitate [Erin's] unconditional love. I thank God and the Blessed Mother because Erin is really *the gift*, not I to her. I feel at peace and fulfilled after our visits.

"I plan to continue weekly or biweekly visits with Erin and then will do a final spiritual assessment in a month or two. I think she and I will grow spiritually from this relationship."

Final Assessment.   "The final assessment [spiritual assessment] went easier because I had made several visits and could communicate with Erin better than at the first visit. This study participant has really touched me in a special way. With all her handicaps she still manages to radiate love to all. Any small gift I bring to her makes her smile [book *The Lord's Prayer*, rosary, holy card]. I have really enjoyed interacting with [Erin]."

Positive Changes in Quantitative Interview Data

SAS items: *1) belief in God; 2) peace; 3) confidence; 4) strength;*
 5) guardianship; 6) trust; 7) self-confidence; 8) church membership;
 9) worship; 11) social support; 12) spiritual support; 13) prayer;
 14) reading and meditation.

MHS items: *11) endurance; 14) meaning in life events; 15) trust.*

LSI items: *2) breaks; 9) anticipation; 10) failure.*

Parish Nurse Comments on Over-Time Changes in Quantitative Interview Data.   The quantitative interview data reflecting Erin's spiritual assessments combines her father's comments and the parish nurse's questions to and observations of Erin. The parish nurse made many comments related to these questions both on initial assessment and final assessment; selected comments are presented here.

SAS item 1: Erin "has pictures in her room of the Trinity, Jesus, and the Blessed Mother." SAS item 2: "Client states, 'God loves me.'" SAS item 3: Nurse asked: "Does God watch over you?—'yes!'" SAS item 4: "Does believing in the Catholic Church and praying make you feel good?—'yes!'" SAS item 7: "Because of her family's involvement with [Erin] and their Catholic faith, I feel that Erin feels as good as she can in her state." SAS item 13: "Client able to say all her prayers once they are started by someone else [the accident did not affect this area of her brain]." SAS items 15 through 21: "I think by observing [Erin] and the wonderful support from her family that Erin doesn't feel any of the [distress] in questions 15 to 21, at least not in her 'world.'" MHS items 1, 3, 4, 7: "Erin is always smiling and happy; I think her goal or purpose in life is a perfect example of unconditional love; Erin participates in the activities offered at the nursing home [she has to depend on others, being totally paralyzed]; Erin does not appear to think she has any problems; she appears to accept things as they come." MHS items 8 through 11: "Watching staff and other residents interact with [Erin], they are always smiling and laughing." MHS items 14 through 15: "The accident has left [Erin] developmentally delayed. I think she lives day by day and in the moment." LSI items 4 and 5: "Just observing the love that emanates from [Erin], I would say 'agree' to both of these [happy and best years]."

Erin's spiritual assessment at T2 (final interview) appeared similar to that done at initial interview: "[Erin] thinks that she is 'lucky' because of all her family and all the people who come into contact with her and love her. I asked Erin 'Is this the best time of your life?' She said 'Yes.' Erin looks forward to the important things in her life, visits from family and friends."

Case Study 13.   Project Participant: Mr. Garvey

Project Parish Nurse: Anne Marie

Demographic Profile.   Mr. Garvey is an 83-year-old Roman Catholic who resides in a nursing home. He is Caucasian, married, and formerly owned his own business. Mr. Garvey attended business college. He currently has multiple illness conditions, including Alzheimer's disease (moderate to advanced stage), Parkinson's disease, and arthritis. His wife visits daily and provides him with much support.

Spiritual Profile.   Mr. Garvey's wife feels that her husband's church membership is still very important to him; it is difficult for him to verbalize his feelings. She does worry that her husband's spiritual needs are not being met because of his illness. She feels that Mr. Garvey would be strengthened by participating in Mass, but he has not attended church services for some time. Mrs. Garvey is also very worried that her husband has not received Communion in some time; it is very important to her that he receive the Eucharist. On an initial meeting with Mr. Garvey's parish nurse, Mrs. Garvey asked whether the nurse would accompany them to Mass; she agreed. Mrs. Garvey also agreed to assist him in responding to study questions.

Note: Parish nurse Anne Marie admitted her own fragility in this situation (the project had originally been designed for fully cognitively aware persons only):

> *On my first visit with Mr. Garvey, he would not converse with me or look at me. I felt overwhelmed with an impending sense of failure. I started praying right then. I knew that I would not be able to make Mr. Garvey do anything, least of all open his mouth to receive the Eucharist. "It's in Your hands, God, please help me; give me strength," I thought to myself. Every time I thought about Mrs. Garvey's wish to have her husband take Communion, I would say a prayer.*

The parish nurse continued her narrative:

> *Well, the big day arrived! I was on one side of the client and his wife was on the other. Mr. Garvey was quiet during the Mass. When Father came to give him Communion; Mr. Garvey seemed frightened and unsure. He would not open his mouth. Father said he would come back again after giving Communion to everyone else. Father broke the Host in half and with Mrs. Garvey's assistance, Mr. Garvey took the Host into his mouth. Mrs. Garvey cried; so did I!*

Parish Nursing Notes.   Anne Marie, the project parish nurse, made contact with Mr. Garvey: "Mr. Garvey was nonverbal initially then would speak short-word responses. I told him my name and that I am a nurse from the Church. He looked at me with a blank look. I told him that I would return again to check on him."

On a second visit, "I met Mr. G.'s spouse, who had come to assist her husband with lunch. She appeared pleased that a nurse would be interested in visiting her spouse and providing spiritual care. She expressed her concern about her husband's change mentally and physically. She became tearful talking about the progression of Alzheimer's disease. She stated that her spouse was very outgoing; 'he never knew a stranger.' Mr. G.'s spouse stated that her husband doesn't participate in Mass or other religious activities: 'I have only gotten him to take Communion one time. I would really like it if you could come to Mass with us, maybe that would help. Sometimes I don't know what to do.' I told Mrs. Garvey that I would contact her and I would plan to come to Mass next Friday to be there to assist her. She thanked me.

"[I plan to attend Mass next Friday with Mr. G. and spouse.] I left a phone message on Mr. G.'s spouse's phone that I would be attending Mass this Friday to be present to assist her with her husband.

"Mr. G.'s spouse phoned to talk about having me visit and assist during Mass this coming Friday. Mrs. Garvey expressed how difficult it has been for her to accept and at times deal with the Alzheimer's disease that her husband is diagnosed with. She repeated that this disease had changed her husband into the opposite person he used to be. She stated she had cared for the client at home for over two years. As the disease progressed, the symptoms of agitation, wondering, and confusion increased. She often only got minutes or an hour's sleep. She stated that her health began to fail and finally her children told her that she needed to place him in a program or nursing facility. She opted for the day program at a local church at first. Initially things went 'pretty good' but before too long the staff could not 'handle him.' At this point they place him in a skilled nursing home facility. She continued, 'He does know me and will talk in phrases. I do not know what I will do when and if he doesn't know me. I don't think I'll be able to deal with that.'

"I asked Mrs. Garvey if she had been to any Alzheimer's support groups or classes about the disease. She stated 'no' to both questions. She said that she had not gone to either because of spending time with her husband, and also she did not know how she would feel once she got there.

"Mrs. Garvey discussed how she felt that taking her husband to Mass was so important. Her biggest desire for both of them is the hope that he will participate and receive the Holy Eucharist.

On a fourth visit, "I did a follow-up spiritual assessment to the best of our ability. Mrs. Garvey was anxious today, and the fact that the staff had not gotten her husband up and ready for Mass made her distraught (PI/PD note: Often the reason disabled Catholic patients residing in nursing homes do not get to a weekly Mass, if one is offered, is because nursing home staff are either too busy [especially on weekends] or they do not consider it a priority to prepare patients [bathe, dress, and assist to wheelchair] for Mass attendance. This is especially true in a nonreligious-affiliated home, although it occurs in religiously affiliated facilities as well). Mrs. Garvey verbalized that the care her husband has been receiving in the last few months has not been up to her standards. 'Now you know why I come every day. If I didn't come, they would not feed him or maybe not even get him up. It upsets me so much.'

"I assisted Mr. G. and spouse to get him ready for Mass. We then went down to the activity room where they celebrate Mass. Mr. Garvey was quiet during the Mass.

When Father gave the client Communion, he seemed frightened and would not open his mouth. Father then returned after giving Communion to everyone else. Father broke the Host in half and with the client's wife's assistance, Mr. Garvey took the Host into his mouth. I was holding his right hand and Mrs. Garvey was holding his left hand. After her husband took Communion, Mrs. Garvey cried.

"(Parish Nursing Plan—Assist spouse with client at monthly Mass and support for spouse with client's progression of Alzheimer's. The spouse's biggest wish is for client to receive Holy Eucharist willingly.)

"We returned to Mr. G.'s room after Mass. Mrs. Garvey was concerned that she had touched the Host. 'I feel I may have done something wrong, but I just so wanted him to take Communion. I know he doesn't understand now, but if he was 'normal' he would want it.' Mrs. Garvey was still tearful, she thanked me for 'being on our side.' She said, 'I know that you being here has made a difference.' I told Mr. Garvey good-bye [holding his hand]. I winked at him and asked him if he would wink at me— and he did! Then he laughed. I was so surprised and touched since the client only interacts minimally with anyone. Mrs. Garvey stated, 'I'm surprised he did that.' I told client's wife to feel free to call me if she had any questions or even if she just needed to talk.

"After I returned home I called Father to talk to him in regard to the client. I told him that Mrs. Garvey was worried about having 'touched the Host' earlier at Mass. I asked him if he felt comfortable with this. Father stated that he considered Mr. Garvey's spouse as a Eucharistic minister: 'He will take Communion from his wife and not from me. It is more important that he receives Communion than not at all.' I told Father that I would let the client's spouse know this so that she would not worry.

"I called and Mrs. Garvey was not home, so I left her a message about the above information. Later in the evening, Mrs. Garvey called me back. She asked 'How did you know I was so worried about my touching the Host?' I told her that I observed how worried she appeared to be about it. 'I cannot thank you enough for calling me. You have really made me feel so much better about the situation. You are very kind and thoughtful. Thank you.' I told her that it was not a problem and that I was here to assist her however I could. I also told her never to feel that she was imposing in any way. 'It made me feel so much better that you came to help me at Mass. It means a lot to me and if my husband knew, like he used to, it would mean much to him also. I thank you for him too.'

"I just listened as she talked about their shattered hopes and dreams for this time in their life. It made me feel sad and how important it is to live each day to the fullest.

Then at the same time I am thinking to myself, 'Dear God, please guide me. I am here to do as you wish because I certainly cannot handle this on my own!' The sadness, disappointment, and unanswered questions of Mrs. Garvey squeezed my heart. I told her that I would plan to visit this week and I would see her and the client then and to call me if she needed anything.

"My plan for Mr. Garvey was:

1. Weekly to biweekly visits when spouse is present.

2. Attend Mass with Mr. G. and spouse to assist them.

3. Act as liaison between Mr. G., spouse, and the parish.

4. Work on education of spouse regarding Mr. G.'s disease process and prognosis (if spouse is agreeable).

5. Recommend/facilitate spouse's participation in support group/or individual who has experienced similar circumstances."

Final Spiritual Assessment.   "There have been 10 changes in the second assessment from the first assessment. One thing was that Mrs. Garvey and I are more comfortable with each other. Mrs. Garvey definitely feels better now that her husband will take Communion. She feels that this has helped her accept her husband's illness better and that she is not as worried about his soul as much as she had been. It has been a pleasure working with this couple."

Positive Changes in Quantitative Interview Data

SAS items: 1) belief in God; 2) peace; 3) confidence; 4) strength;
     5) confidence; 6) trust; 7) self-confidence; 8) church membership;
     17) fear.
MHS items: 10) enjoyment.

Case Study 14.   Project Participant: Mrs. Ahearn

Project Parish Nurse: Anne Marie

Demographic Profile.   Mrs. Ahearn is an 89-year-old widow who has one son and who currently resides in a nursing home. Mrs. Ahearn is Roman Catholic, Caucasian, attended business school, and is a retired secretary. She has multiple diagnoses, including osteoarthritis, hypertension, and hyperthyroidism and takes approximately 16 medications. She needs assistance transferring from bed to a chair. Mrs. Ahearn attends Mass about once a month at the nursing home.

Spiritual Profile. Mrs. Ahearn seemed to have a very strong spirituality on initial assessment but responded vaguely about attending the monthly Mass at her nursing home. When asked about Mass, she commented that she attended Mass "when she wasn't sick" and asked her OSVI parish nurse: "Could you come to Mass with me sometime; I would like that." The nurse noted: "I told [Mrs. Ahearn] I would be happy to come to Mass with her."

Note: A possible explanation for Mrs. Ahearn's somewhat cautious response about Mass attendance and her request that the parish nurse come with her may relate to a classic concern identified in the geriatric literature about elderly long-term care clients' fear of taking road trips—even a trip to a makeshift chapel in the facility, a dining room, or a game room may cause anxiety about a possible fall or inability to return to one's room quickly if not feeling well (see O'Brien, 1989).

Parish Nursing Notes. The parish nurse described her first visit to Mrs. Ahearn: "I explained to her who I was and explained about my visits. Mrs. A. stated she was glad to meet me. She talked about her multiple health problems. She stated: 'I have edema, arthritis, and I have to have someone get me into a chair. I'm not very steady and I'm afraid I may fall. That's why the girls help me.' We talked about health issues, then she talked about her family. I asked her if she was able to go to Mass once a month when they had it at the nursing home. She said she did go as long as she 'wasn't sick.' 'Could you come to Mass with me sometime?' she asked. 'I would like that.' I told her I would be happy to come to Mass with her. We visited a while longer. I left and told Mrs. A. I would plan to return in the next week or so to visit. She stated she looked forward to my visit.

On a second visit, "I assisted Mrs. A. to Mass—physically, she was tired but did not want to miss Mass. She refused for me to take her oxygen to the room. Once settled in the main room for Mass, she did okay.

"After Mass I assisted her back to her room and into bed. I visited with her for a while. She asked me to get Father to come to her room if I could. She said she wanted him to hear her confession. When I went to get him he had already left. Mrs. A. was disappointed; she said that she had not been to confession in a very long time and the priest rarely stayed after Mass.

"I asked her if she would like me to call Father and tell him she would like for him to come by and hear her confession. She was pleased with that arrangement. I made the follow-up phone call to Father—he stated he would go see Mrs. Ahearn tomorrow.

"On a third visit, Mrs. A. reported that Father did come to hear her confession. She was pleased by this. Mrs. A. declined any need for religious articles—has several rosary beads, Bible, books, etc.

"(I'll think about what I can bring to patient or will just visit—I think that is probably what Mrs. Ahearn will like the most.)

"On the next visit, I met with Mrs. A. for a shorter time; her family had recently visited, and she was upbeat today. She talked about how important her religion is her. We prayed together."

Final Assessment.   "There were minimal changes in the final spiritual assessment. I think that there were fewer changes at this time due to client's aging and her declining health. I think too at this time the aged look back on their life and realize that death is probably not far off. I think that this Mrs. Ahearn gets much consolation from her religion and family support."

Positive Changes in Quantitative Interview Data

SAS items: 10) prays for others; 12) support from priest, eucharistic ministers and parish nurse; 14) mostly meditates; eyes get tired easily; 15) spiritual pain; 16) alienation; 19) anger.

LSI items: 3) dreariness.

Case Study 15. Project Participant: Mrs. Brady

Project Parish Nurse: Anne Marie

Demographic Profile.   Mrs. Brady is an 83-year-old widow who had been married for 50 years. She is Roman Catholic, Caucasian, a high school graduate, a retired telephone operator and currently resides in a nursing home. Her multiple diagnoses include cancer, osteoporosis, atrial fibrillation, and hardness of hearing; she is also almost blind and can only transfer from bed to chair with assistance. Mrs. Brady had one son and takes approximately a dozen medications daily.

Spiritual Profile.   Mrs. Brady stated that her son is not a practicing Catholic but that she gets spiritual support from other Catholics in the nursing home. Due to her physical condition, she rarely attends worship services but does get consolation from the parish nurse's visits and from their praying together. Her important goals are occasionally getting to Mass (if one is offered at the nursing home), and praying for other patients and family. Mrs. Brady loves to pray the rosary.

Parish Nursing Notes.   The parish nurse "explained who I was and that I wanted to visit her to see if there was anything she needed. Mrs. B. is oriented to place and person but not time. She is cheerful and talkative. She talked about her different health problems. She stated that she has a lot of pain in her legs and knees from arthritis. She said that the staff has to help her up into a chair because she has trouble walking.

"I noticed during my visit there were no religious articles in her room. I asked her if she had a rosary and she said that she did. We talked about Mass being said once a month at the nursing home. She said that she would like me to come to Mass with her. She also said that she goes to all the Sunday services even though they are not Catholic. Then she said quietly to me, 'You know, God doesn't mind if I do that.' I smiled and said, 'Yes, I know.'

"Our visit was ended when the staff needed to walk with client. I told Mrs. Brady that I would return in the next week or so to visit again. She stated she would like that.

"On my second visit the initial spiritual assessment was done. Mrs. Brady is hard of hearing so it took some time and repetition too with the questions. Religion and faith are important to this client; she looks forward to all the church services they have at the nursing home. She is pretty open-minded and thinks it is more important that she attends any service they have than not to go to services [not of her Christian denomination].

"When asked what religious article could she use, she declined anything. She has several rosary beads and she is unable to read [macular degeneration], so a Bible or book even in large print would not be useful. She does enjoy visits and participating in Mass and other church services. I prayed with the patient.

"On the next visit Mrs. B. stated she enjoys people coming to visit her. She talked about her son and how important he is to her. It moves me how she raised her son (that is hard work, I know); then as people age and children grow up there seems to never be enough time to visit. It can really make you sad. After my visit with her, it makes me realize the importance of visiting family and friends because time is short."

Final spiritual assessment. "There were four changes in the second spiritual assessment. This was one of her better days. Again, Mrs. Brady declined any religious articles. I think, too, that this client has been frugal all her life. Elders don't want to ask for too much! When the assessment was done we visited for a while. She loves having some to talk to! We ended with prayer together."

Positive Changes in Quantitative Interview Data

> *SAS items: 12) spiritual support; 17) fear; 19) anger.*
>
> *MHS items: 2) goal setting; 9) self-worth.*

Note: Several individuals, such as Erin Kelly (case study 12), who is cognitively impaired, and Mr. Garvey (case study 13), suffering from moderately severe Alzheimer's disease, were included in the study at their family's request. Quantitative item responses for these individuals were coded employing a combination of the study participant's response, family comments, and the parish nurse's observations.

Qualitative Themes Emerging from Narrative Interview Data

Qualitative data elicited in open-ended interviews with project participants were content analyzed to identify dominant themes reflective of the population's overall spiritual well-being in chronic illness; these themes, related to concepts supported and encouraged during the parish nursing/health ministry interviews, have been labeled *reverence, faithfulness, religiousness, devotion,* and *contemplation.*

Faith-Based Coping in Chronic Illness

Reverence

> I came that they may have life, and have it abundantly.
> —*John 10:10*

The term *reverence* is derived from the Latin *reverentia* and is described as incorporating "profound respect mingled with love and awe as for a holy or exalted being" (Gove, P. B. [ed.], *Webster, Unabridged* 1967, p. 1942). Theological definitions of reverence tend to focus on the "honor and worship of God, and by extension, those persons and things that God has created" (O'Brien, 2001, p. 97). Reverence, as found among the project participants, included both reverence for God, as creator and Lord, as well as reverence for the sacredness of their own lives and the lives of those around them. Many project participants spoke of their gratitude to God for their lives and their families; they spoke also of their deep love and respect for the Lord.

Some comments reflecting individuals' expression of reverence include the following:

Mrs. Fitzgerald: "I am thankful to God when I wake up every morning. I am thankful . . . that I do have an understanding every day. . . . I pray to God every day. . . .

Each day you waken you know there is a God. When you see the sunlight, you know God was there through the night. I don't see how anybody could say there isn't a God."

Mrs. Dooley: "I have been with Him all my life. [Prayer] is automatic, just like eating every day. I just say my prayers, an Our Father and a Hail Mary; all the ones I like. . . . My faith makes the quality of my life stronger."

A parish health minister commented on one of her project participants: "Mrs. Sheehan began to cry as our interview progressed . . . the sharing of her deep love of Christ and her unshaking faith that God has His arm around her at all times brought the tears to her eyes."

Faithfulness

> Daughter, your faith has made you well.
> —*Luke 8:48*

Faith means belief or trust in someone or something. From a theological perspective, Dominican Mary Ann Fatula (1993) notes that "used in a Judaeo-Christian context, the word *faith* refers to a rich, multidimensional human stance that is inseparably God's gift and our own deepest actualization" (p. 379). Faith is also, she adds, the basis of our personal relationship with God, "on whose strength and absolute sureness we can literally stake our lives" (p. 379). Contemporary holistic nursing theories suggest that an individual's personal religious faith may provide strength to combat illness and to promote wellness (O'Brien, 2003b).

Some comments indicating the faith or faithfulness of project participants include the following:

A parish health minister's description of Mr. Malone: "He is a very devout and pious man. He never gets angry with God or questions His judgment. He accepts that whatever happens, just happens; he is in the habit of praying often. He is always certain to say his morning and evening prayers, as well as prayers before and after meals." The nurse added: "On one of my visits, he did not want to receive Communion because he had just had his lunch. He always insisted on saying an Act of Contrition before receiving Communion and he always insisted on his own sequence of prayers before we could continue with the prayers in my booklet."

A nurse also spoke of the faith of one of her patients, Mrs. Devlin: "Mrs. Devlin made it very clear that she had difficulty living in her facility because the [other residents] were so hopeless. She found few who shared her beliefs [faith]. There were virtually a small number of Catholics and those had sort of turned from God in the face of their debilitating health. Mrs. Devlin firmly believes that if they continued to pray and strengthen their faith, that they would not degenerate as quickly. In fact, her own illness, she believes, would have taken over totally had she not such a strong connection with God. . . . Mrs. Devlin," the nurse added, "prays for those around her 'whether they want it or not!'"

Three other examples of project participants' faith are those of Mrs. Doherty, who can't get to Mass often, even when there is one offered occasionally at her facility, and so she asked for a Sunday missal so that she could follow the Mass in her room; Mrs. Brady, who admitted that when there was no Sunday Mass at her nursing home, she attended whatever Christian service was being held, noting, "You know, God doesn't mind if I do that" (she also loves to pray the rosary by herself); and Mr. Convey, who was unable to attend Mass at all and who had no visitors until the parish nurse came, who was "so touched that he cried when the nurse brought him a large-print Bible and a rosary."

Religiousness

> And I tell you, you are Peter, and on this rock I will build my church.
> —*Matthew 16:18*

The term *religiousness* refers to a strong commitment to religious practice or the practice of one's denominational worship rituals and prayers. Although this study was carried out in conjunction with several churches, all denominations were Roman Catholic. While the project participants did consider themselves, and in fact labeled themselves, Catholic in terms of religious affiliation, a number admitted at initial interview that they were nonpracticing or at best minimally practicing Catholics. Those who described a state of being marginalized from practice of their faith, however, also expressed spiritual distress about this admission. Thus, the ultimate goal of this project was to nurture an individual in the practice of his or her faith; that is, Catholic religious practice and identity and/or, if appropriate, to assist the person in reconnecting with the Church. Although some project participants were indeed found to possess a strong personal religious faith, as revealed in both quantitative and qualitative data, a number of these were marginalized from faith practices because of their illness and/or disability. A few had become disillusioned with their faith or were "angry" at God because of the multiple losses they had experienced. At the conclusion of the pastoral care intervention, however, all project participants had deepened their faith, and spiritual well-being was notably enhanced. It was especially important for those who had distanced from their "religiousness" or religious practice to become reconnected to the Church. Two classic examples are described in the case study titled "Two Anointings" presented later in this chapter.

Overall, data revealed that the study participants' "religiosity," or Roman Catholic faith practice and identity, was very important to them, especially during times of illness and suffering, as some of the following comments illustrate:

Mrs. Sheehan: "I love my faith and I love God. He is always there for me. I believe that."

Mrs. Lonergan: "I really can't attend church; my church is far away and that is really hard. I think about being there and I feel like I am there." She added: "I'm a Catholic and I was raised in the Catholic Church. I had Confirmation; I sang in the choir. I used to love to go to Midnight Mass at Christmas." Mrs. Sheehan concluded: "I talk to God a lot in my prayers and I feel that He answers me and hears me. It makes me better. If I didn't have my faith to hang on to I would go crazy."

Mrs. Lynch: "I believe in God because I was brought up to believe in God. My mother made sure, bless her heart, that I went to church every Sunday. I got Confirmed . . . I have Communion and I just practice His ways in the Church." Mrs. Lynch added: "When I wasn't sick I went to church all Sundays and holy days . . . I really love church . . . I made novenas." She noted, however, "My church doesn't really know that I have been real sick because when I got sick . . . [I couldn't] go back home . . . at the hospital they weren't Catholic." Mrs. Lynch concluded: "If I didn't have my faith in God, I don't know what I would do."

Mrs. O'Connor's parish health minister comments: "When I began seeing [Mrs. O'Connor], she was skeptical of letting me pray under the same roof that she was in. Now she is leading us in prayer, or at least she is saying [prayers] with me. She is also praying the rosary daily, now that she has beads and people to do it with. [Mrs. O'Connor moved from her home to a Catholic nursing home during the project]. When I began seeing Mrs. O'Connor she had not even seen a priest in over three years, so it has been amazing to see the transformation in her. She also states that she has been attending Mass three to four times per week now that she has access to worship services." Mrs. O'Connor's parish nurse minister admitted: "Mrs. O'Connor has benefitted tremendously from this study, as it allowed her to have faith enough to make the move into this new living environment which has been one of the greatest things to happen to her in a long time. She attributes the rebirth of her hope and faith to 'me' [the study], as it allowed her to feel and remember all [about her faith] that she had forgotten. She got tears in her eyes and told me that she could never repay me. We closed with a prayer of thanksgiving."

Devotion

> I remember the devotion of your youth, your love as a bride, how you followed me in the wilderness in a land not sown.
>
> —*Jeremiah 2:2–3*

In a pastoral letter to his coworker Titus, Saint Paul wrote that certain directives for Christians must be insisted upon; the first of these was "that those who have believed in God be careful to devote themselves to good works" (Titus 3:8). For the follower of Jesus, *devotion* is identified as "the feeling side of Christian faith" (Dehne, 1990, p. 283). And contemporary psychologist and spiritual writer Benedict Groeschel (1997) describes devotion poetically as "the place where the word of God planted by the Divine sower of the parable takes root in the life and being of the believer" (p. 12).

Some comments describing the devotion of project participants include the following:

Mrs. Higgens: "If it wasn't for my [belief in God], that is what keeps me going. I feel terrible if I have to miss out on a day, because that makes my day, when I can get to church. It makes everything different . . . if I can go to church. I just feel at peace with God; it makes my day all the time." Mrs. Higgens added: "Of course I have the Sacred Heart picture, and if things get bad, I will just kneel down in front of it and automatically things will start to get better. I have certain prayers that I say every day; I say the rosary every day."

Mr. O'Connell admitted that although now he rarely goes to Mass, "one of the most important things in his life was going to church." He had asked for a rosary because his was broken and was so grateful to his parish nurse for bringing him a new one that he said: "I don't know what I can do to repay you for your kindness." He is now praying the rosary each day.

Mrs. Quinn was very distraught because her rosary and Bible were left behind when she was brought to a nursing home and no family member had been able to bring them to her. When her parish nurse brought her a new rosary and large-print Bible, she put her face in her hands and cried; she said: "I didn't know anybody could care that much about me."

Mrs. Flatley was a younger woman who was living in a nursing home because of advanced cancer. There were no religious symbols at all in her room or in the facility. She told her nurse that when she was at home, she had a small "shrine" to Our Lady and to the Sacred Heart, which she loved. When the nurse brought her a small statue of the Blessed Mother and one of the Sacred Heart, she held them to her heart, kissed them, and said how "beautiful" they were. She had the nurse help her create a small shrine on her dresser with the two statues so that she could see them and pray to Our Lady and to Jesus. The OSVI parish nurse also brought her a rosary; she kissed the Crucifix and kept holding it to her heart also.

Contemplation

> In the morning, while it was still very dark, he got up and went out to a deserted place, and there he prayed.
>
> —*Mark 1:35*

William Shannon (1993) explains that "in the history of spirituality the term *contemplation* has been given many meanings. What is basic," he asserts "is that it has to do with awareness of the presence of God apprehended not by thought but by love" (p. 209). To be contemplative, James Finley (2000) suggests, requires "learning to sit and be, to slow down and settle in the precious givenness of who we are right now, just the way we are" (p. 29). In many instances, Finley's suggestion reflects the life situation that, because of illness and disability related to the aging process, has been forced upon many of our project participants. In his book *Aging Without Apology*, Seymour (1995) cites a lovely quotation from a 150-year-old volume on aging that well describes the contemplative milieu of many elders: "Is your eyesight dimmer? Then the world is seen by you in cathedral light. Is your hearing duller? Then it is just as though you were always where loud voices and footsteps ought not to be heard . . . yes, for twilight and silence . . . old age makes us like daily dwellers in the house of the Lord" (p. 100).

The following comments and anecdotes describe the contemplative posture that has been adopted by a number of the project participants:

Mrs. Conrad: "God is my all; I don't have anyone to talk to but God. I know God listens." (Mrs. Conrad lives alone in her own home and says the rosary all the time.)

Mrs. McDonald: "God is always with me."

Mrs. O'Boyle: Belief in God "is my life. Even if I don't go to church every day, I know He is here."

Mr. Hogan: "I have faith in God. I look at the trees; I sit and look at these beautiful trees and see a bird or a butterfly or anything and that is all part of me that is God. When I look at my little grandchild or babies, it is all God. My trust in God as far as the activities of my life . . . I just have faith that God is going to protect me all the time." Mr. Hogan added: "If you believe in God, you've got to feel comfortable within yourself. And you have to believe that others are made in the image of God and Jesus and you have got to feel comfortable with those people . . . He said: 'love your fellow man.'"

Mrs. Burns: "I feel that I can talk to Him [God] and that He listens to me and sometimes He answers me. Sometimes I fuss with Him. I'll say: 'Dear God, why do I have this terrible pain? . . . I feel like I have a personal relationship with Him." Mrs. Burns added: "I don't think I would be around if I didn't believe in God. I think I would have given up a long time ago. My faith in God allows me to fight back all the time." She stated that she had not seen a priest since the summer and "this is almost coming into Christmas" but, she asserted: "I've got my rosary and . . . my holy cards and my Bible and sometimes I just talk to Him. Especially when I'm mad with Him, I tell Him about it. The only things I fuss with Him about is when I hurt real bad. I fuss with Him and ask Him to take it away." Mrs. Burns concluded her comments: "If I didn't have faith in God, I don't think I'd have any quality of life. I'm not even sure I would still be here. . . . I just don't think I could get along if I didn't have faith."

Mrs. Donovan: "I am Catholic but I don't go to church anymore. My relationship with God is strengthened by my personal prayer. I just turn off the TV and say the rosary. I talk to Him. God would do anything for you if you have faith in Him." Mrs. Donovan added:

"I feel at peace with God. I talk to Him. That is all that prayer is; giving your heart to God. That is what I think it is anyway! I sit here and I say, 'Here I am, Dear Lord; here is the trouble I have today. I just want You to try and listen. I know you are so busy but please find time to listen to me. That is the way I talk to God. I call that prayer."

While the previously identified project participants may not fit the category of "contemplative" as understood in a Carthusian or Cistercian monastery, many elders do live lives of contemplation in the world. Nursing home residents can often be observed going to a chapel just to "sit with God" or "be with Him," in their words; to be silent in the presence of the Lord; to love Him. This activity would indeed seem to qualify as contemplation.

In summary, the five qualitative themes, *reverence, faithfulness, religiousness, devotion*, and *contemplation*, are concepts used to broadly categorize the important dimensions of spiritual well-being that emerged in open-ended interviews with 45 chronically ill persons; all project participants were marginalized from practice of their faith due to illness and/or disability. While the concepts might be greatly expanded and clarified in future work, findings from the present effort provide important data to assist parish nurses and parish health ministers in planning services for parishioners marginalized from the larger congregation because of health deficits.

Religious Ritual: Two Anointings

The Parish Nurse's Experience

One of the staff parish nurses described how blessed she felt to be involved with and present for the anointings, the administration of the sacrament of the sick, for two of her project participants. The following is her account of the conferring of the sacraments to Mrs. O'Connor and Mrs. Scully:

"I saw within my first few interactions with two of the clients that they could potentially benefit a great deal by receiving the sacraments, particularly the sacrament of reconciliation and the sacrament of the sick. I knew how much the sacraments had helped me when I was ill; and I hoped that it could do something similar for the study participants. I then had to find priests that were willing and able to celebrate these sacraments for the clients. I found priests who were very willing and welcomed the opportunity.

"Mrs. O'Connor was seen by a local priest. I did my best to try and prepare her for the sacrament. I explained what it entailed and the significance behind the sacrament. I also suggested several ways in which it might help and that although she may not experience a physical healing as a result of the anointing, there is certainly a spiritual healing that takes place, and this can help in coping with the physical ailments all the more.

"As the date of the anointing approached, Mrs. O'Connor realized that she was holding on to a lot of 'baggage' and that she needed to surrender all these anxieties and fears to the Lord. She was hoping that the anointing would help to bring her a heightened sense of peace so this could be accomplished. I felt she was ready and that she was very eager to receive the sacrament. I was very pleased with this, as three months prior, when I first met Mrs. O'Connor, she was nearly doubting the existence of God. In that span of time she had moved to a Catholic nursing home, began attending daily Masses, gone to confession, and was now ready for her anointing.

"Father accompanied me to the residence and we went to see Mrs. O'Connor together. She had recently celebrated her 91st birthday, so I started an 'icebreaker' sort of conversation about the festivities. Although Father is one of the warmest, most caring individuals one could ever meet, and he easily assimilated into the situation, Mrs. O'Connor was still a little nervous and talked quite a bit at first. Within five minutes she was showing Father every picture of her great-grandchildren that she had with pride, and she was much more comfortable.

"After a few minutes, Father proceeded with the anointing. Father explained the sacrament to her again, and then proceeded. We prayed together and had lovely readings from the Psalms and the Gospel of Matthew. Mrs. O'Connor was so serene and tranquil through the whole thing; there was an amazing, peaceful presence in the room, and as Father anointed her head and her hands, she just had a look of relief and peace on her face that shone brightly through a beautiful half-hidden smile. We left fairly soon after the service, but two things were certain: the Holy Spirit was present in that room, and all three of us had been touched in a special and holy way that day. It was such an awe-inspiring experience that I came home and wrote down the memories in my journal. I knew that Mrs. O'Connor had gotten a great deal out of the anointing, and the next time I saw her, she was just beaming and had wonderful things to say; how much more she had been able to deal with since the anointing.

"Mrs. Scully was the other study participant that I had been working with who was to receive the sacrament of reconciliation and the sacrament of the sick. A priest who was visiting at a local religious house of studies for the year accompanied me to see her. I truly felt that Mrs. Scully was ready for this day; however, part of me still worried about her reception of Father. I had absolutely nothing to fear and should have been more trusting of the Lord's grace. It was great and they hit if off beautifully.

"Mrs. Scully had expressed to me several times and in several different ways, that there were many things for which she was afraid she was not worthy of God's forgiveness; that she did not feel He would forgive her. It was very important that she went to confession for her own peace of mind. I left Mrs. Scully alone and went into the kitchen to talk to her nurse while Father heard her confession. After quite a while Father came to get me. I was glad that her confession had taken so long, to really allow her to express all of the things that she was feeling. Father had not rushed her. That did her a world of good and she was much more peaceful even before the anointing.

"Father performed the anointing in a traditional style. I think this was excellent for Mrs. Scully, as simplicity and tradition are definitely two things that she likes a lot. I believe that the sacrament brought a lot of healing to her soul. She stated that she felt 'as light as a feather' and that the burden of the world was off her shoulders. She also stated that she had the 'glassy, transparent, elated in the love of God feeling.' She said that 'she had not felt that way in 50 years!'

"I spoke to Mrs. Scully over the phone after this day and she had even gotten to Mass twice with the assistance of her live-in nurse. I am very pleased with the progress Mrs. Scully had made and am very glad that I had the opportunity of ministering to her. I am grateful to the priest who went with me to help a stranger. This was a great lesson for me. That was a great act of love and faith in Christ.

"Although both anointings were performed in slightly different ways and in different settings, the effect was great and profound in both clients. I do not think that I could have asked for a better match in priests either. Both priests had a different style and personality that matched perfectly with Mrs. O'Connor and Mrs. Scully and this only served to enhance the experience as far as I could tell. Both women's spiritual lives were enhanced as a result of the celebration of the sacraments, and they are both wonderful examples of how much good spiritual ministry can do. Their lives were both transformed, rediscovered, and ignited in a spiritual sense as a result of this project."

The Chaplain's Experience

The study's principal investigator interviewed the chaplain who anointed Mrs. O'Connor to explore his perceptions of the parish nursing role in ministry to the homebound, expecially to those marginalized from practice of their faith. Father noted that he felt that the parish nurse who was working with Mrs. O'Connor had truly "prepared the way" for him to do the anointing, as Mrs. O'Connor had been "angry with God" prior to the parish nursing intervention. The chaplain described his ministry experience:

"[Mrs. O'Connor] was very mentally clear—a very bright woman but very physically disabled. She had experienced some suffering in her life and I'm not sure if she felt that God had abandoned her or the Church had abandoned her, but she received me very, very graciously and I think, in part because of Teresa [her parish nurse], because Teresa had set the stage; she had introduced the notion of having the anointing of the sick.

"It seemed very natural and I was sort of surprised because Teresa did say that she had some issues, a kind of a coolness about the practice of her faith and when I went in it was pretty surprising how smooth the sharing went. I didn't want to overwhelm her right off the bat. She had pictures of her family that she wanted to share and so we sort of had a conversation. She showed no signs of discomfort in my presence and so after about 10 or 15 minutes of sharing, talking, I asked her if she wanted to be anointed and she was very welcoming to the idea.

"I explained to her at the beginning, as I usual do, that oftentimes when we get sick, when we suffer, we feel like God is very, very far away and I think more than a physical healing is that emotional and spiritual healing of the wound of a mind that is suffering can often be healed. God assures us that He is here; His touch is here. And that is the spiritual healing that I find most powerful in the sacrament of anointing. And even in that laying on of hands, there is a certain stillness, a very tangibleness of the sacrament, that is an assurance to the person that God hasn't forgotten them. And you could also say that the Church hasn't forgotten them and has a powerful witness. There is an avenue to 'come home' that might not have been sought out before. Family members, I think, oftentimes, aren't there, and it doesn't sound like Mrs. O'Connor's family is really too present to the faith.

"Before an anointing I always try to link where the person is in their own suffering with the presence of God, the tangibleness of the sacrament, that Jesus walked the earth and healed. The gift of the power of Jesus' touch is so present in the power of the Church, through the sacrament.

"In visiting nursing homes as a parish priest, oftentimes if I was praying over a person in one bed, someone else would hear the prayer and if I would ask a person in the next bed if they would like a prayer (either a non-Catholic or someone not practicing their faith), if I would say, 'Would you like a prayer?' they would say, 'Oh, yes!' And I felt blessed just to be drawn into those situations and just open to the spirit.

"There is the notion with the theology of anointing that even if one has committed some sins, their sins are forgiven in the receiving of the sacrament. Many times in those situations I'll ask if someone wants to go to confession before the sacrament of anointing (Mrs. O'Connor had gone to confession). Sometimes they don't want to; that's alright because sometimes I think the sacrament of anointing takes them another step in Christ's healing that opens them up to a deeper healing that then they want to confess. So it can be another channel into something more deeply into the heart of the Church. So it goes from the human contact and the touch, the sacrament of anointing and oftentimes it will lead someone back into practicing their faith, and then coming to confession and the Eucharist; anointing can be a turning point."

Parish Nursing Roles

With the exception of the role of coordinator of volunteer activities, parish nurses involved with the study project were found to engage in all of the other identified parish nurse role behaviors: *spiritual companion (integrator of faith and health)*, *health advocate*, *health educator*, *health consultant (referral agent)*, and *health counselor*. Some examples include the following.

Spiritual Companion (Integrator of Faith and Health)
An excellent example of the spiritual companion ministry role is that operationalized in the pastoral care provided to Mrs. O'Connor by her parish nurse/health minister. Mrs. O'Connor entered the study angry at God and not having seen a priest in over

three years; she completed the project by receiving the sacraments of Reconciliation and Anointing of the Sick. After the first three weeks with the project, Mrs. O'Connor's parish nurse/health minister (a nurse but not yet formally trained as a parish nurse) wrote: "Mrs. O'Connor [is] by no means content with everything and the world [is] not suddenly perfect. However, in [these] three weeks remarkable things happened to her and she [is] more at ease, and at least open to seeing what comfort and strength God [can] bring her. She [is] ready to slowly return to Him."

Health Advocate

The parish nurse practitioner working with Mrs. Conrad served as her advocate. She often listened to her health concerns and helped her to verbalize her needs and anxieties. She also made suggestions, for example: "One day [Mrs. Conrad] had a bad cold, so I made her a cup of tea and asked her if she had taken her medication. I also asked her to call her doctor to schedule a flu shot." The nurse added: "Because Mrs. Conrad's severe congestive heart failure interfered with her going to church, at one point I called a nurse from her church to arrange to get her driven to church for a special affair."

Health Educator

Although a number of the parish nurse/health ministers working on the project admitted to doing some health teaching during their visits, the focus of the project was first and foremost the role of spiritual companion; thus, most discussion revolved around the relationship between religious faith and health/illness issues. One documented example of the health educator role is that contained in the report of the nurse working with Mr. O'Leary, an end-stage renal disease patient:

"Upon return for my third visit, Mr. O'Leary was very down about his illness and the hemodialysis. He did not understand why he needed to endure that all of the time since he felt fine. I did a little diabetic teaching and tried to help him see that without hemodialysis he would certainly feel less than fine!"

Health Consultant (Referral Agent)

Mrs. Daly's parish nurse played an important role in referring her for hospital care in an emergency situation: "My final visit with Mrs. Daly was heartbreaking. She could not articulate anything and did not have the same positive outlook as she previously had. She just did not appear interested in much of anything . . . her husband . . . was very worried about her . . . he told me very innocently that this was all very sudden, but that she had fallen earlier that morning and he had given her an aspirin to alleviate a headache. . . . I told her husband that I really thought she needed medical attention and that he should call an ambulance. He agreed, so I called 911 and stayed with Mrs. Daly until the paramedics arrived. Her husband went with her to the hospital and she slipped into a coma en route; she had a massive brain hemorrhage."

Health Counselor

An example of the concept of the parish nurse as counselor is described by Mrs. Noone's nurse: "I noticed a beautifully framed print of the poem 'Footprints' on her dresser, so I asked her about it. Mrs. Noone loves that poem and uses it as a source of strength. She and I talked about it for a while, what it meant and how it made us feel, and where she could apply it in her life. It was through this conversation that she began to feel comfortable discussing her physical pain with me."

Summary and Conclusions

The study An Experiment in Parish Nursing: The Gift of Faith in Chronic Illness provided important and heretofore nonexistent data on the concerns and needs of chronically ill Christians, whose disease or disability has prevented them from embracing the fullness of practice of their religious faith. Study data were also collected describing the creative and innovative parish nurse/health minister interventions employed in the pastoral care dimension of the project. Analysis of both quantitative and qualitative data revealed that the intervention provided by parish nurses and parish health ministers resulted in positive increases in the variables of spiritual well-being, including the concepts of personal faith, religious practice, and spiritual contentment, as well as in hope and life satisfaction among project participants.

The parish nursing intervention study findings provide important support for the practice of parish nursing and the development of parish health ministry programs among contemporary faith communities. Study data identify numerous models for parish nurses' ministry, especially for pastoral care with those marginalized from practice of their faith because of illness or disability.

In sum, the project the Gift of Faith in Chronic Illness was a blessing and a "gift" to both study participants and research project staff.

References

Dehne, C. (1990). Devotion and devotions. In J. Komonchak, M. Collins, & D. Lane (Eds.), *The new dictionary of theology* (pp. 283–288). Collegeville, MN: Liturgical Press.

Fatula, M. A. (1993). Faith. In M. Downey (Ed.), *The new dictionary of Catholic spirituality* (pp. 379–390). Collegeville, MN: Liturgical Press.

Finley, J. (2000). *The contemplative heart.* Notre Dame, IN: Sorin Books.

Fowler, J. W. (1981). *Stages of faith: The psychology of human development and the quest for meaning.* San Francisco: HarperSanFrancisco.

Groeschel, B. (1997). Introduction. In B. Groeschel & J. Monti (Eds.), *In the presence of our Lord* (pp. 12–16). Huntington, IN: Our Sunday Visitor Publishing.

Gove, P. B. (Ed.). (1967). Reverence. In *Webster's third new international dictionary, unabridged* (p. 1942). Springfield, MA: G. & C. Merriam Company.

Koenig, H. G. (1999). *The healing power of faith: Science explores medicine's last great frontier.* New York: Simon and Schuster.

Miller, J., & Powers, M. (1988). Development of an instrument to measure hope. *Nursing Research, 37*(1), 6–10.

O'Brien, M. E. (1989). *Anatomy of a nursing home: A new view of resident life.* Owings Mills, MD: National Health Publishing.

O'Brien, M. E. (1999, June 30). *The gift of faith in chronic illness: An experiment in parish nursing.* Unpublished Report submitted to Our Sunday Visitor Institute.

O'Brien, M. E. (2001). *The nurse's calling: A Christian spirituality of caring for the sick.* Mahwah, NJ: Paulist Press.

O'Brien, M. E. (2003a). *Prayer in nursing: The spirituality of compassionate caregiving.* Sudbury, MA: Jones and Bartlett.

O'Brien, M. E. (2003b). *Spirituality in nursing: Standing on holy ground* (2nd ed.). Sudbury, MA: Jones and Bartlett.

Seymour, R. E. (1995). *Aging without apology: Living your senior years with integrity and faith.* Valley Forge, PA: Judson Press.

Shannon, W. H. (1993). Contemplation, contemplative prayer. In M. Downey (Ed.), *The new dictionary of Catholic spirituality* (pp. 209–214). Collegeville, MN: Liturgical Press.

Wood, V., Wylie, M., & Sheafor, B. (1969). An analysis of a short self-report measure of life satisfaction. *Journal of Gerontology, 24*(2), 465–469.

CHAPTER 10

PARISH NURSING MINISTRY IN CONTEMPORARY CONGREGATIONS: THE LIVED EXPERIENCE

We have this treasure in clay jars, so that it may be made clear that this extraordinary power belongs to God and does not come from us.

—2 Corinthians 4:7

"We Hold This Treasure"

Dear Lord Jesus,
   Help us never to forget the
"treasure" we hold *(2 Cor. 4:7)*;
The "treasure" which graces
   our earthen vessels with
      Your compassion and
         Your care.

Bless our earthen vesselness,
that we may be instruments
of Your "surpassing
power" *(2 Cor. 4:7)*:

to teach the insecure;
to counsel the confused;
to advise the anxious;
to advocate for the
helpless; and
to bring the light of
Your loving Spirit
to those who
suffer.

During the past decade, I have talked with many practicing parish nurses about the spirituality of their calling, as well as about their ministry experiences in a variety of Christian churches. There are many commonalities in the parish nurses' stories, especially in regard to vocations of service within their respective congregations. The majority of the nurses I spoke with were carrying out their parish health ministries as volunteers; the few who were in part-time paid positions admitted to including numerous hours of unpaid service in their parish nursing activities.

Parish nursing is a calling; a spiritual calling to be concerned about the hungry, the thirsty, the unclothed, the lonely, the sick, and the isolated, especially those within one's own faith community. The call is rooted in the gospel message of Jesus. In evaluating their spiritual callings, virtually all of the parish nurses I have met agreed with the theology presented in Paul's second letter to the Corinthians (4:7). That is, they recognized that their nursing ministry was an instrument of the healing mission of the Lord; that they were simply "earthen vessels," called to be used to reflect His light and His love to those who were ill and infirm.

Within the gospel call to caring, to parish nursing, there is, nonetheless, embedded a very real and very practical ministry of service to the sick. And while the parish nurses' gospel-oriented reflections on their spiritual calling possess many similarities, the anecdotes describing the carrying out of parish nursing activities are unique and varied. Thus, to gain a better understanding of the "lived experience" of parish nursing in the twenty-first century, I solicited the "stories" of three practicing parish nurses, each of whom differed in age, parish nursing education, and Christian denomination in which they ministered. To broaden the vision of parish nursing for the future, I also obtained the perceptions and experiences of five nurses ministering to homeless persons under the sponsorship of a local Christian church. Although the latter nurses were not formally trained as parish nurses, they carry out a similar kind of gospel-oriented nursing ministry, with Jesus' mandate to care for the poor and the sick as the underlying framework for their caregving.

Parish Nursing Ministry in a Lutheran Congregation

Mary is a single, baccalaureate-prepared, 27-year-old nurse who works part-time in a hospital and attends graduate school; she received her parish nursing education through a hospital-affiliated two-hour evening introduction to parish nursing course. Mary has been serving for five years as a parish nurse in her Lutheran congregation; she is assisted by another nurse in the parish who follows her leadership. Mary commented that the hospital parish nursing program, where she received her parish nursing education, served in an advisory capacity as her congregation's ministry was getting started; she said, "They actually came and worked with us." The hospital program staff are still available to advise the church. Currently, Mary works approximately two or three hours each week as a volunteer parish nurse for her congregation; she recently told me, however, that the church's Social Ministry Board is now "working on developing a plan" to include hiring a parish nurse in a 10-hours-per-week paid position.

Mary described parish nursing, which she admitted was still evolving, in her Lutheran congregation of approximately 200 parishioners; she began with an overview of her parish:

"I love my parish; it is multicultural and not too big. We have two Sunday services, an early service at 8:15 A.M. and a late service at 11 o'clock; so there are, a lot of times, two distinct groups. I have been a member of that church all my life (it's actually the church that my grandparents belonged to) and am very thankful to have the church because they have been very supportive over the years. I find the parish nursing program [important] in that because I am trained as a nurse, this is a way that I can give back to my church community. Our congregation is mostly elderly; very few young adults. When I turned 18 and looked around and saw that I was probably the only young adult, I was really ready to leave because I didn't feel like [the church] was meeting my needs, but [Mary described a personal life stressor] . . . it was really God . . . my family and the church who brought me through, so now any way I can give back I am willing."

Mary then explained that she was not quite sure how the parish nursing program began over five years ago, but she remembered that some parishioners had heard of a hospital program to assist parishes get started: "As a new graduate in my church, I think one of the other nurses brought it [parish nursing] up; I mean, people in the church have always been caring people, and [the nurse] said that this is something that is a very new area that churches have started to work in." The program was started in the Lutheran church with Pastor Granger Westberg in the late 70s or early 80s. Mary and another nurse then attended the "Introduction to Parish Nursing" seminar presented by a neighboring hospital whose staff would serve as advisors to beginning parish nurse programs. Mary commented that the hospital parish nursing staff advised that a parish health needs assessment be done; she confessed that because of limited parish nursing personnel in her congregation that suggestion had not yet been carried out. She was, however, hoping to have a nursing student come and assist with the process; "then," she commented, "we can substantiate why we are doing what we are doing."

Mary identified the volunteer group that has been coordinated to assist the two parish nurses: "We call our group the 'Wellness Committee' because we don't want people to think it's just for nurses; we want the whole congregation to participate; anyone who wants to work with the parish nurse program. That committee is headed by me, only by default, because there isn't anyone else to take it on. We have about five or six nurses in the congregation; we don't have a physician, but when we had our first [Wellness] committee meeting, we did have people not in the health field come because they were interested."

Mary continued: "It's been more of an issue keeping [volunteers] involved. We need to have a plan for training. That is something we would like to do in the future; to have people come in and be CPR certified, to have a training program that if there is a medical emergency [people would know] who is going to do what . . . to make sure that everything flows smoothly and that we call [EMS] as soon as possible and that type of thing." Mary explained the importance of this: "Five or six months ago we had two different situations where we had two members of the congregation, on two different Sundays, pass out during church because of medical conditions. We alerted EMS and they actually came into the sanctuary and this really alerted the congregation that things can happen no matter where you are, and to [the need for] parish nursing."

Mary next described the parish nursing activities in which she and her companion parish nurse had been engaged recently. Mary now practices parish nursing according to the ANA-published *Scope and Standards of Parish Nursing Practice*; this document did not yet exist when her congregation's program began.

"We maintain blood pressure screens four times a year, after our services on a Sunday morning"; this she noted was important because of the many elders in the congregation. "When we have blood pressure screenings, we regularly do about 15 to 20 blood pressures each Sunday that we do screening but we are not really catching everybody. . . . We've tried different places. We can't have it outside the church because it is too loud when people are coming out, but if we are hidden away in a classroom, nobody comes because they don't know where to find us." Mary admitted that the parish nurses are still searching for the best location for BP screenings and may increase the frequency of screenings.

Another activity of the parish nurses is to coordinate the presentation of educational and wellness programs for the congregation. Some of the programs Mary described were "Body and Soul Aerobics," "which is a program that has been ongoing for a year and a half"; "First Place," "a weight management program"; a "Lions Club Vision Screening Program"; and "Eight Weeks to Wellness." When discussing the initiation of programs, Mary commented that some of the older parishioners have concerns about liability, which she notes is a source of stress because the parish nurses "need the involvement of other people from the congregation." Mary added that the pastor is very supportive of the parish nursing effort, as is the congregation's Social Ministry Board.

Mary continued to describe her parish nursing activities: "[After the blood pressure screening] any time we find that someone has an elevated blood pressure we are going to double-check it, follow up with the parishioner, do patient education on how important it is to have their blood pressure checked, and if they do have high blood pressure, we educate them about their medications. [We encourage parishioners] to keep taking [their medications] as their physician ordered or if they have questions for us; we [also] encourage them to talk to their physician. A lot of [parish nursing] is health education. I have a lot of people, because they know you are a parish nurse, they will come up and ask lots of different questions. For example: 'How do I access this?' Or, 'I have a friend who was just diagnosed with this, where can I go for help?' So, it's a lot of referral and linking of services."

Mary also identified assisting parishioners who become ill during services as part of her role: "Just this past Sunday, when we were doing blood pressure screening, we had an 80-year-old member who was helping to serve lunch become dizzy and nauseated. It was a hands-on assisting her with that situation. In her case it wasn't life-threatening, but being able to assist whoever needs helping."

"Sometimes," Mary concluded, "[parish nursing] is helping [parishioners] understand, helping them phrase what they need to ask the physician on something they have been concerned about, encouraging them to call the physician, giving them tips on how best to get in touch with the physician, or encouraging them, that 'yes,' that would be a situation that you call because some people are very afraid; they don't want their physician to feel like they are bothering him. [We tell parishioners] if you have a question or you're not sure [about something], it's best to clarify it and seek guidance." Mary also mentioned an issue that is raised in an earlier chapter of this book, that of a parish nurse ministering within her own faith community. Mary again affirmed that she felt it was both appropriate and beneficial to both nurse and parishioner for the nurse to minister in her own congregation; she did point out, however, that sometimes confidentiality is a concern: "I have difficulty in that every time something happens [to a parishioner], other people think that they can come to me and I can give them information but . . . [there is] patient confidentiality. Because I am part of the church community, and they feel comfortable with me, they think they can come to me, but I need to maintain confidentiality. I can't share [parishioners' health-related] information with others. . . . A lot of times [the questions are] out of love and concern, but I still can't share that information."

Mary explained that her church does have a Stephen ministry program to counsel and advise parishioners who are in crisis or experiencing extremely stressful life events, and in an informal needs assessment, it was suggested that the church might consider purchasing an AED (automatic external defibrillator) now that shopping malls and airlines have them. One of the church's nurse practitioners raised questions about liability, however, and Mary noted: "We know we would have to be trained to use it correctly and have someone be responsible for it."

As to plans for the future, Mary admitted that presently the church's parish nursing effort is all volunteer: "We don't have a lot of workforce at this point." But, as noted earlier, the congregation is now considering a plan to hire a 10-hour-a-week paid parish nurse. Mary added that she would also like to begin to bring in lecturers, for example, a physician and a nutritionist to speak about such conditions such as high blood pressure and diabetes. "Right now," she concluded, "we [parish nurses] don't have office hours, or a 'hotline' for parishioners to call, so a lot of discussion has to be done while I am taking a blood pressure, or if I am following up with someone [about an illness]."

Finally, Mary admitted, that because her church's parish nursing program has grown slowly, although she feels that it "has grown a lot in the last couple of years," she has not had much experience of visiting and praying with parishioners in their homes; she anticipates such activities in the future. Mary concluded her thoughts with describing the "most important" dimension of parish nursing, that of the parish nurse's personal spirituality:

"I think that the most important thing in parish nursing is having a personal relationship with Christ, His word, daily reading of the Bible, praying . . . this has been the most beneficial for me. Really seeking God's guidance in every area of my life and knowing that when I put it into His hands He is going to direct me on how He wants me to handle a situation or where He wants me to go, what He wants me to do today. He is going to bring different things into my life. God is in control, definitely, and [I need] to maintain that focus. And then, out of that, comes the love to serve; the willingness to see others where their needs are, and to be able to help them. It's not on my own that I am able to do this; it's because of God that I am able to do this!"

Parish Nursing Ministry in an Episcopal Congregation

Sarah is a 54-year-old master's-prepared nurse practitioner who is married with three children, and who serves in a paid, part-time position for a metropolitan Episcopal church. Sarah has never formally taken a course in parish nursing, although she participated in an elective graduate-level course in spirituality and care of the sick; she also practices according to the directives included in the *Scope and Standards* of *Parish Nursing Practice*. Sarah has been ministering to a congregation of approximately 485 active members for approximately one year; she is presently the church's only parish nurse and has a service commitment of approximately 20 hours per week. Sarah admits that her parish nursing ministries often run over the usually scheduled part-time hours.

In describing her parish nursing ministry in the Episcopal church, Sarah began with an explanation of how the parish nursing program was initiated:

"In my congregation, a parishioner died and left a financial gift to the church to care for the ill and the shut-ins of the parish. An elderly woman in the parish, a retired nurse, had researched the concept of parish nursing; she had done a lot of reading, a lot of research about parish nursing. Some of the parishioners had already become Stephen ministers, and they were also supportive. They wanted someone to organize the parish into having a Health Ministry Team.

"After the retired nurse parishioner contacted me, the first thing to do was to talk to the pastor; he was very favorable. He saw parish nursing as innovative and new and necessary. The pastor is the most important supporter because he gives the ministry credibility. The pastor introduced me on a Sunday, during the service. I came up to the front of the church and said a little bit about myself. The pastor was very much an advocate; I think without his support there would have been many more barriers.

"I was given a column in the parish bulletin every month to write about topics on health promotion and the importance of prayer and health. Another big support was the retired nurse who had the vision to begin parish nursing and a health ministry team. The congregation's vision was for a 20-hour-per-week nurse. The nurse advocate and the vestry set up a Parish Nursing Oversight Committee. The committee not only oversees the work of the parish nurse but also the entire health ministry program.

"The congregation did not want me to just do Sunday blood pressure screening, but they wanted me to visit shut-ins and keep them connected to the parish. My primary role is to visit the ill, to bring the church to them. This involves both a physical needs assessment and a spiritual needs assessment during visits to parishioners in their homes, in nursing homes, or in the hospital. I bring the prayer that is included in the parish bulletin, read the Bible with parishioners, talk to them, and listen to them; to see what they want and need."

Sarah gave an example of one parishioner's need: "A parishioner called me very early—I had barely started [the ministry]—to tell me that her husband had fallen and broken his back. She wanted me to see him and give advice. They weren't comfortable with his treatment. So I visited the couple, went over the medications with him and assured them that they were appropriate. The patient's wife also said that her husband was not really being compliant with what the doctor wanted him to do and she wanted me to reinforce his therapy directives as a 'nurse from the church.'" Here Sarah interjected: "Coming as a 'nurse from the church' gives you a kind of authority!"

Sarah continued describing her parish nursing ministries: "I have an office in the church, and I stock it with a lot of health promotion materials; pamphlets that people can come in and pick up. I have regular office hours but very few people drop in; a lot of the work was getting phone calls. I do a lot of 'drop-in' visits to shut-ins in their homes or in nursing homes, or in the hospital. I thought that was a good way to begin a relationship with individual church members who I did not know well. This is also a way to keep them connected to the church. I had personal cards made; I always leave them."

Sarah reported: "I have been very well received and at times my ministry is more to the family, if a person is very ill or dying; they are the people I work with. Sometimes it was connecting a parishioner or their families with someone who can bring food or provide home care. Often it is a lot of 'hand holding' and supporting and listening and praying with people. In cases of terminally ill parishioners, it is helping them understand and accept the meaning of death; just being a presence of God and of the Church. The most rewarding part of the job is the response you get from ill parishioners and from their families."

Sarah added: "There are other areas to my job also. The congregation's youth minister asked me to talk to the youth; the parents wanted someone to talk to the youth about drugs and alcohol. I also worked with volunteers in the church to set up a Health Ministry team: a psychiatrist, two nurses from the parish nursing oversight group, and other laypeople. We ended up adding two physicians, but we don't really talk medical talk at our meetings. We talk about how to care; how to bring people into the church community; how to make calling visits. I've had four workshops during the past year: one on listening skills, one on bereavement, one on communication, and one was on loss and death and dying. We tried to find ways to get people into the workshops."

Another activity that Sarah took on during her past year's parish nursing visits was the delivering of greeting cards made by the church Sunday school classes: "each card had the parishioner's name and a personal note, and I took them with me on my visits. I also went to the Sunday school classes and talked to them about how Jesus visited the sick."

Sarah described her schedule: "Some weeks I do less and other weeks I work much more than the 20 hours a week. I didn't do an official needs assessment of the parish but I did do a role assessment of the parish nurse's role after my first four months (it was sort of a needs assessment for the parish). One thing I found was a need for lung cancer education; seven parishioners had died of lung cancer that year. Also, we needed a program of education on how to prevent falls in the home. Most parishioners do not want to leave their homes to go to a nursing home; they would almost rather die. So, to maintain safety in their homes is one of my goals; to support their desires and needs but to be safe. I've been seeing a 94-year-old woman and I've finally got home care to come in, which she resisted for a long time. I had to help her see how to manage in her own home.

"I also go to doctor's visits with parishioners if they don't have family, to advocate for them. It was amazing to me to see how many of the elderly have nobody; they are alone! The idea is how to connect them. Some other things I do are ministry to new parents: bringing a sippy cup for new babies with the parish logo on the side, bonding the family and child with the congregation. I send developmental pamphlets to new mothers; they may know that information but it's another connection to their spiritual home in the parish. I've also taken parishioners grocery shopping and helped an elderly woman clean out her house filled with papers and magazines; we did a lot of reminiscing as we worked. I also monitor blood pressures in parishioners' homes.

"The pastor asked me, one day, to see a woman who was not answering her phone or her door. I arrived to find her writhing in pain and holding her stomach; she said she just wanted to die. After assessment, I felt the problem was psychological; the woman felt useless, a burden, and had planned suicide. We [her daughter and I] got her admitted to a psych unit for six weeks and on medications, set her up with meals-on-wheels, and now she is okay."

Sarah evaluated her role, after a year of parish nursing: "I felt my role was not a physical caring role; that occurred almost as a sideline to my parish nursing. The community health nurse goes in as a task-oriented person; she goes in to do a dressing and she leaves. I would spend a couple of hours just talking and listening to people; otherwise, I would never be able to give what you're there to give and the person wouldn't be open to receive it. You're there to give the spiritual caring, and parish nursing gives you the opening to do it."

At this point in the interview, I asked Sarah why she had chosen to engage in parish nursing. She explained: "I've been a nurse a long time and I've worked in many settings, but I think many [sick] people don't really need physical care; you see how people love some of the older physicians, one of the big things they do is give people time. This is a way to give spiritual care; to minister to the spirit. I love my work! Parish nursing is evolving. The gospel message is a personal support; reading the Bible was something concrete I could do with people. It was also an entre to assess their needs and find solutions. Having God as a goal, meaning in life and connectedness to God, gives me great freedom as a nurse. It gives me no fear in talking about death; about people planning for death.

"As a matter of fact," Sarah continued, "one of the things the parish wants me to work on is advance directives and power of attorney; families want this also. One way I bring this up with terminally ill parishioners is by asking if they would like to read the Bible together, and do they have a favorite verse? Then I ask how they feel about their life right now; do they want to pray about it? These are very basic questions and most people are very willing to talk. I also see some younger people who have a lot of pain and suffering from things like mastectomies or back surgeries, and some of the pain is related to fear, fear of the unknown, and we talk about it and bring in God to kind of smooth over the fear of the unknown; in a sense that's not a road that the community health nurse goes down, but the parish nurse does.

"In contemporary society, parish nursing and parish health ministry are very needed because the healthcare system is not being well utilized; it's partly lack of access and partly lack of knowledge. One of the parish nurse's roles is to do education and make referrals, to advise people how to use the existing system, to utilize the system wisely. Our parish also has a little 'Give and Get' program for medical equipment; maintaining that was part of my role. If a parishioner died, their family gave us things like commodes, wheelchairs, walkers, crutches, canes, and bath stools. It was a whole other way of accessing medical supplies needed for care."

Sarah concluded her comments with the thought: "This job is never boring! It's often surprising, stimulating; you never know what you're going to run into, but you also know that you can handle it because the bottom line is the spiritual connectedness of the ministry and of the patient to God and to the church."

Parish Nursing Ministry in a Roman Catholic Congregation

Elizabeth is a 74-year-old, retired, master's-prepared adult nurse practitioner, married with grown children and grandchildren, who found herself in the unfamiliar situation of having free time on her hands. She began to read about nurses who were volunteering in a variety of ways within a church setting and decided to discuss possibilities with a member of her church's pastoral team. It was agreed they would work together in exploring the possibilities for organizing this new ministry for their Roman Catholic parish of about 2700 families.

Elizabeth reported: "We got off to a slow start for a number of reasons, and for a while I thought my co-organizer was no longer interested. Then, one day, she called and suggested we begin to look around at what other churches and hospitals were doing and things began to move. We began by putting a notice in the church bulletin asking for interested volunteers to explore the possibilities for 'parish nursing' and set a date for our first meeting. About 18 women attended, not everyone a nurse."

The "opportunity to combine service in a truly holistic manner: body, mind, and spirit, was a major reason" for Elizabeth's interest in parish nursing: "Through most of my years in health care, my personal moral values, the spiritual side of my life, took a back seat to the physical and mental needs of those who came to me for help. The fact that in parish nursing I would be not just allowed to include the Spirit in my relationships with patients, but encouraged to do so, was very motivating and exciting."

At the same time, Elizabeth reported that "communicating" her vision of parish nursing "based upon [her] early career in public health was not easy in terms of achieving a commitment from the first volunteers. Over the next several months of biweekly meetings, the number [of church volunteers] dropped to 10 or 12.

"However," Elizabeth noted: "we did get some things done during that time. We wrote a mission statement. That helped us define, in very general terms, who we were, what we hoped to do, and how we would do it. This became the centerpiece of a brochure the group developed that enlarged upon each of these areas in more specific ways, what we would do and what we would not do. We had no intention of duplicating services already in place, but would act mainly as a referral source. It all began to sound like what the health system is now calling 'case management.' This document also gave information about getting in touch with us and was printed with a simple design and a motto, 'Turn to your neighbor,' the holy words of Mother Teresa."

To "enhance her understanding of the scope of parish health nursing," Elizabeth enrolled in a three-day continuing education certificate program in parish nursing. As time went on, she observed, she was able to arrange a series of lectures for her parish health ministry group, presented by the outreach department of a local hospital with connections to the Catholic diocese. Elizabeth added: "Last year I attended a week-long seminar sponsored by a national organization, Nurses Christian Fellowship. It was a residential program, very intense and spiritual. Just what the doctor ordered to provide me with resources, not just of information, but of people with experiences the same as mine so that I would not feel alone, while at the same time different from mine so that I would know where to turn if I needed some help."

Elizabeth continued: "It's now been five years since I first talked to the member of the pastoral team and almost three years since our first meeting. I must say one of the first things we did after I began attending some of the orientation sessions was to change the name of our service from 'Parish Health Nursing' to 'Parish Health Ministry.' That helped explain the unique focus of the services we provide; although, for those of us who are nurses, it does not completely relieve us of our professional obligations 'to do no harm.' However, we were able to include nonnurse members, one of whom became our secretary and kept wonderful minutes and circulated them so we now have a rather complete record of how we got started and have kept going. Other members who are not nurses include a veterinarian who will visit, at no charge, housebound parishioners with animals that need professional attention. We also have a physician who will answer general questions about medical conditions and how they are managed in medical practice. He does not give specific advice, however, and is not expected to."

Elizabeth went on to say, "It seems as if it's been slow going, but as I look back, we've done a fair number of things, not necessarily because we planned to do them at the beginning, but because we've responded to various needs and situations that have presented themselves over time. And that's the interesting part of this ministry. If you stop to think about it, you can see how the Holy Spirit has been working with us all the time. At the beginning, the pastoral minister wanted a group that could assist when visits to the homebound to give Communion revealed problems beyond the knowledge and experience of the Eucharistic minister. I wanted to be of service in this regard and could draw on my public health and clinical expertise to answer questions and refer to appropriate resources, sort of be a bridge between the patient and the person or agency that could help. Not everyone felt comfortable in this role; the other group members continued to be unsure regarding what they would feel comfortable doing."

Elizabeth and the health ministry group soon learned that the cornerstone of getting their parish health ministry program going was blood pressure screening: "So now that is offered monthly, and four or five of the group willingly take turns assisting because blood pressure screening is universally accepted as a low-risk service. One member volunteered to accept this as her project so I don't have to be present every time."

She continued: "Recently, we have had several parishioners become ill during a church service. There's not been an official plan for responding to this sort of situation up until now, and so another parish health minister volunteered to update the first-aid kit, talk to the First Aid Squad across the street about how we should proceed in emergencies, and make contact with the ushers' group who are, really, responsible for order during church events. This service of ours was not planned in advance. It is evolving in response to a need and the responder is someone who has come forward because it is something that she is familiar with and is interested in developing. These are just two examples of the value of waiting, with patience, to let the 'child' of Parish Health Ministry grow in age and grace with the help of the Holy Spirit, not insisting on what should be done, but allowing people of good will to find their own ways."

Meanwhile, Elizabeth has been making the parish nursing home visits and reports that she truly enjoys them: "There are not many, but when the requests come and I enter the lives of these wonderful people, I find, as is often the case, I receive more than I give. One homebound parishioner is computer savvy and we keep in touch regularly that way. She is pretty stable at the moment and so we have moved from discussing her problems to what books she's reading at the moment and her satisfaction with the local library volunteer who delivers them. This also gives me a resource to share with others who must remain at home but have a similar interest in reading. Another call for help came from an elderly gentleman who needed assistance changing the dressings on his feet. The visiting nurse was helping, but insurance coverage was nearly exhausted. I visited and planned, with the visiting nurse, how to contact family members and a neighbor, as well as a nurse from [a local] guild to provide instruction in the procedure and put together a schedule."

Elizabeth admits there are times when she "becomes discouraged, the phone does-n't ring, the church bulletin notices are postponed due to more urgent information filling the limited space, and so on." Then, she remembers that patience has never been one of her virtues and she turns to prayer and the sacraments. She remarks, "I find that I really receive support from attending daily Mass, receiving Communion, and listening to the readings of the scripture that, on a day-to-day basis, have continuity and tell powerful stories. It is at these times that I get ideas about what to say to pa-tients when I visit them, like, 'You do have options, you can choose, you know. You can suffer alone, or you can suffer with Jesus, for Him, as He did for you. That might give you a different and more positive perspective. You might then not feel so alone and helpless.'"

Elizabeth observed, however, "Sometimes I have to be careful not to be too direc-tive, as one might be in a busy hospital. The other day I visited a parishioner whose husband recently died and who is really reclusively grieving and seemed depressed. My inclination at first was to say, 'Now, this is what you really should do,' but then I realized that my role in this setting is mainly to listen and then say, 'What do you think you should do next? . . . I'm here to make some suggestions when you'd like to hear them.' I also, before I leave, offer to pray with the person I'm visiting, often sug-gesting they say the prayer for us. I'm continually inspired by the words that come forth spontaneously and fervently, without hesitation."

Speaking of the difficulty in finding parishioners who would benefit from the serv-ices of a parish health minister, Elizabeth described a rich resource for referrals as be-ing "other parishioners who become case finders," but added: "I always ask permission to visit, through the referral person or over the phone to the individual who might be in need." "The parish health ministry group," Elizabeth continued, "is beginning to grow, extending its services wider and wider, and is becoming a cohesive group. Frequent use of e-mail, with the setup of a group list, has improved communication among the members and is a vehicle for the sharing of prayers, through getting them to check their e-mail regularly"; this was a surprising challenge for Elizabeth, who checks hers repeatedly throughout the day! Elizabeth also consults nurse practitioner colleagues through an advanced practice listserv and another listserv that was created at the end of the weeklong parish nursing seminar she attended. Both of these resources have provided "answers made rich with information based on experience."

"Not much has been done in regard to program planning," Elizabeth admitted, "but recently a nurse with a master's degree in health education joined the group and is en-thusiastically developing a parish survey of need from which programs can follow. Other important support has been provided by the township public health nurses who helped us set up our first blood pressure screening day. They also, during last year's flu season preparations, offered to visit any homebound parishioner and administer both flu and pneumonia vaccine, at no charge. When I made phone rounds to offer this service, I included an offer to visit and thus added several new people to my list.

"The local diocese is becoming very interested in parish nursing," according to Elizabeth, who feels "this will have a positive impact on the church's parish health ministry: "Parish nursing orientation programs are being scheduled throughout the region and a diocesan committee has been organized to look at ways of practice and delivering services, always remembering the wide variation in the makeup and needs of each parish. However, I'm a little concerned about standardization and the setting of rules and regulations, that sort of thing," commented Elizabeth. "I've sort of had enough of that and am enjoying the informality of the relationship I have with those I visit, always within a professional framework of course, sticking to our mission statement and brochure, but not with a laptop or a pen and a Medicare form in my hand. That's not how the 'Good Samaritan' did it, right?"

Finally, Elizabeth concluded the description of her vision and experiences of parish nursing and parish health ministry by repeating the importance of nourishing one's own spiritual health through prayer, the sacraments, the relationships with colleagues and parishioners, and faith in the guidance of the Holy Spirit. She believes "this will build a spiritual bank account within yourself upon which you can draw and then spend on behalf of those who call upon you for help."

Parish Nursing Ministry to the Homeless

In order to broaden the discussion of church-related nursing ministry, I also sought interviews with five nurses who carry out their nursing ministry under the aegis of a Christian church-sponsored recovery facility for the homeless located in a large East Coast metropolitan area. Although these nurses are not formally trained as parish nurses, they engage in a similar kind of Christian nursing ministry, undergirded by the framework of the gospel message of Jesus to care for those in need.

A member of the recovery facility's nursing community described the program this way: "Patients are referred from local hospitals, clinics, shelters, and medical outreach projects. They suffer from an array of illnesses and injuries including fractures, hypertension, cardiac disease, diabetes, foot and leg ulcers, HIV and AIDS, respiratory illnesses, and cancer. Almost all of the patients have more than one medical problem and/or other conditions such as mental illness or substance abuse." She added:

"Homelessness itself is a significant risk factor for development of illnesses and decreased life expectancy."

The nurse continued: "[The facility] provides an opportunity for homeless men and women to heal and to address the issues that may have led to their homelessness. Patients receive 24-hour medical and nursing care . . . pastoral care, addiction counseling, and other supportive services. Through this multifaceted program, [the facility] treats the whole person, not just their physical maladies. [The facility] is staffed by . . . full-time employees [and] full-time volunteers. Many of the staff members live right at [the facility], building a community of empathy and friendship with those who are wounded in body and spirit. . . . It is our general goal that patients will leave [the facility] with a new sense of hope and dignity and will come to know the healing power of the 'waters of life.'"

Four full-time staff nurse employees of the facility and one full-time volunteer nurse shared perceptions of their nursing ministry with homeless people as follows.

Martha is a 68-year-old, master's-prepared nurse who has served as a nursing administrator at the homeless recovery facility for the past 13 years. Martha observed: "From its beginning, integral to [the facility] has been the presence of a live-in faith community. All participate in the patient care ministry in some way. Eight years ago . . . I became part of the . . . faith community. Our varied faith traditions include Mennonite, Methodist, Church of the Savior, and Catholic. As we journey together in ministry we pledge the following: to care for the poor, to create Christian community with homeless persons, to take time for prayer and scripture reflection, and to be present to our own suffering and healing, supporting each other in the process."

Martha continued: "These ministry commitments, while challenging and exhilarating, sometimes even heartbreaking, provide an extraordinary experience of community. My [family] supports and affirms me in this ministry. The homeless sick have helped me to continue a process, which is both growth and diminishment. Our preferential choice on behalf of the poor springs from the Gospel itself. To me, this experience relates deeply to the . . . concept of [a] spirituality of peace, with its component parts: contemplation, diversity, right relationships, interdependence, action for justice, and ministry at the margins. The call to continue this ministry and this exploration is strong and vibrant. I feel privileged to be here."

Cathy, a 23-year-old bachelor of science in nursing graduate, is a full-time volunteer at the homeless recovery facility and has been serving there in nursing ministry for the past eight months. Cathy shared the fact that in college she had been involved in a number of service projects, such as providing support on a Native American reservation in the Midwest, and it was during this time that she began to consider "giving a year of service to others." Cathy continued: "My position [at the facility] . . . has taught me more about real life than all my classes combined. I have learned how to deal with confrontation, suicide attempts, domestic violence, and alcohol poisoning, just to name a few."

Cathy described some other experiences at the homeless recovery facility: "I have had many opportunities for personal growth and exposure to medical conditions not seen in traditional medical/nursing settings. We have had several admissions this winter of individuals with frostbite. One woman arrived at our door at 7 A.M. on a cold, wet Saturday morning. She could barely walk because her feet were numb, having spent the night in a bus shelter. I was grateful to be part of an organization that responded immediately to her need. Then, this past week a 64-year-old man was retrieved by the outreach van from under a bridge. He is schizophrenic and has rectal cancer with metastasis to his liver. We are presently transporting him to daily radiation therapy and chemotherapy appointments at a city hospital."

Cathy concluded her comments: "Many patients come here . . . fearful and withdrawn, hoarding food from the dining room, [as] they did when they were on the streets and didn't know when their next meal might be. Slowly, the experience of being cared for and loved in a way that some of them have never experienced brings about a change. I have learned to redefine 'success.' Years of deprivation don't get transformed overnight. It is important to remember what a gift each life that passes through [the facility] is. I am cognizant that the healing that takes place here is not so much a measure of nursing competence, but of unconditional acceptance and love. This could not occur without the deep spiritual presence afforded us at [the facility]."

Tim, a 27-year-old baccalaureate-degree nurse, has served as a full-time staff nurse at the homeless recovery facility for the past four years. Tim explained that because of some early childhood illness, he was led to consider nursing as a career; he added: "Perhaps because of my illness . . . I am aware of the sacredness of life. The interconnectedness of health and spiritual well-being has always been part of my awareness since a young age. I chose the nursing profession as an outgrowth of my positive experiences with caregivers. It was also a deliberate choice to be able to minister to others."

Tim described his work at the facility: "For several years I worked in a hospital setting. Largely, I could not spend even five minutes with my patients because of other demands, such as IVs, charting, etc. At [the facility] this is different. The medical and spiritual aspects of the patient are attended to. I am able to provide high-quality nursing care to complicated patients and also be present to them. Because the length of stay for these individuals is greater than a month, I have the opportunity to get to know their stories; their resilience amazes me."

Tim concluded: "I have always relied on the three Fs for support: faith, family, and friends. In this setting, my coworkers provide a community of people with shared vision for health care, as well as a Gospel-based view for justice and ministry at the margins."

Agnes, a 52-year-old associate-degree staff nurse, has been ministering at the homeless recovery facility for the past four years. Agnes described her path to the facility: "My husband and I have been socially active since college. Our faith journey together, responding to God's call in our lives, brought us from coast to coast with several different job opportunities. My husband . . . worked extensively with homeless issues. During this time, I made a decision to return to school and pursue a nursing degree. This decision to become a nurse was as if God placed His hand directly on me to uncover secret gifts. At times in my life I have felt entombed in stone by fear and doubt. With my degree, I had concrete skills to offer. I am filled with gratitude for all that I have been exposed to at [the facility]. The patients' responses to my providing care for them have more to do with issues of respect and dignity than my expertise in wound care or knowledge of their illness."

Agnes added: "The spiritual dimension of this setting, evident in our daily interactions, as well as at the worship services, promotes wellness of the whole person. In my time here I have seen lives change as a result of their stay at [the facility]. However, I think it is I who has been transformed."

And, finally, Michael, a 51-year-old bachelor of science in nursing graduate, who has been a staff nurse at the homeless recovery facility for the past six years, admitted that for him the road to the facility had been "long and winding but never out of sight." Michael reported: "My father has been a paramedic for years and encouraged me to enroll in a nursing program. I have gratitude for his guidance in suggesting a profession so well suited to me. Seeking employment at [the facility] was a gut reaction to respond to my desire to help people least likely to get help. I have found my niche. When I leave the building, I always feel better than when I arrived. It is a good feeling to see these walking wounded develop positive images of themselves. I know they feel respected and honored here. Many of [the males] have manhood issues that I can relate to. I am impressed by their quiet dignity and courage."

Michael concluded: "I have always been aware of God's presence in my life, but never so tangibly as now in this nursing role."

Parish Nursing in the Twenty-First Century: A Prayer for the Third Millennium

From the time only a few decades ago when Pastor Granger Westberg rediscovered and reintroduced the concept of nurses serving under the aegis of their faith communities to provide holistic care for parishioners, parish nursing has blossomed in churches across the country. In a recent review of the literature, from 1991 to the present, I found approximately 257 articles dealing with some dimension of parish nursing. These articles, which discuss topics ranging from parish nursing as case management to anecdotal reports of parish nurses' personal experiences, tend to cluster in larger numbers in the years from 1997 on. From 1991 to 1996, anywhere from nine to 15 articles were published each year on the topic of parish nursing; beginning in 1997, the numbers of articles increased to close to 40 per year. One nursing periodical that has published a significant number of articles on parish nursing, beginning in 1989, is the *Journal of Christian Nursing* (*JCN*). Because of the volume of parish nursing publications that have appeared in the journal over the years, as well as the continued and currently burgeoning interest in the specialty, *JCN* editor Judy Shelly has recently published a collection of *JCN* parish nursing articles in a book titled *Nursing in the Church*; this collection constitutes an excellent reference source for nurses interested in reviewing early and recent journal articles on parish or congregational nursing.

Each year, more and more nurses from a variety of Christian denominations begin practicing the specialty of parish nursing. As noted in an earlier chapter, there is presently no formal credentialing exam for the parish nurse role; many parish nurses are supportive of such a mechanism being initiated through the American Nurses Association. Education for the specialty of parish nursing is currently offered primarily through continuing education courses, although some college- and university-affiliated programs exist that offer the option of obtaining academic credits for a parish nursing course.

Parish nurses, within a large number of churches, continue to practice under the mantle of volunteer ministry, rather than as paid church staff. The volunteer nature of the specialty practice is, however, beginning to change, as pastors and parishioners recognize the significant contributions parish nurses can make to the health and well-being of their congregations. Anecdotes presented throughout this book reveal the ever-increasing recognition of parish nurses by their clergy and church members. It is hoped that in the future every church will have at least one parish nurse and, at best, a fully functioning health ministry team to serve the needs of ill and infirm parishioners and to promote the health and wellness of all members of the congregation.

A Parish Nurse's Prayer for the Third Millennium

O Lord, Our God,
the world of this third millennium
   struggles with pain and suffering,
      the depth of which You,
         alone, truly know.
Guide us, as parish nurses, to use our
   chosen ministry to alleviate at least
a part of the anxiety,
      the fear,
         the insecurity,
            the sorrow,
               and the grief,
   with which so many of Your people
      are burdened.
Mentor us to be ministers of Your love
   and Your compassion
as we teach,
   as we counsel,
      as we advocate,
         as we advise,
            and as we attempt to bring
Your Blessed Presence to console
the spirits of those who are wounded.
We are gifted to be allowed to serve
   as ministers of Your gospel.
      Help us to be worthy.

References

Shelly, J. A. (Ed.). (2002). *Nursing in the Church*. Madison, WI: Nurses Christian Fellowship Press.

CARITAS CHRISTI HEALTH SYSTEM PARISH-BASED HEALTH MINISTRY "PARISH HEALTH ASSESSMENT PROFILE"

Health Assessment Profile (1)

Parish Name _____   Parish Leadership: _____
Address _____   Pastor _____
_____   Others _____
Telephone _____   Fax _____

Special Parish Health Needs: Please check (✓) those areas you identify as needs within the parish community:

Homebound Care (sacramental)
- ❑ Prayer
- ❑ Eucharistic ministry
- ❑ Pastoral visit
- ❑ Other

Homebound Care (daily living)
- ❑ Transportation
- ❑ Respite care (temporary rest for caregivers)
- ❑ Telephone (visit) call
- ❑ Friendly visit
- ❑ Shopping and simple household chores
- ❑ Yard work
- ❑ Other

Youth Wellness Programs ❑

Hospital Visitation Program ❑   **Nursing Home Visitation Program** ❑

I would like my parish community to provide the following:

Screenings	Yes	No
Blood Pressure	❑	❑
Cholesterol	❑	❑
Diabetes	❑	❑
Vision	❑	❑
Hearing	❑	❑
Parenting	❑	❑
Parkinson's	❑	❑
Other suggestions _____		

Support Groups	Yes	No
Grief/Loss	❑	❑
Caregivers	❑	❑
Alzheimer's	❑	❑
Weight Control	❑	❑
Elderly Concerns	❑	❑
Alcohol/Drugs	❑	❑
Other (specify) _____		

Health Education	Yes	No
Heart Disease	❑	❑
Blood Pressure Control	❑	❑
AIDS	❑	❑
Stress	❑	❑
Nutrition	❑	❑
Body/Mind Program	❑	❑
Prescription and Over-the-Counter Meds	❑	❑
Senior Housing and Nursing Homes	❑	❑

	Yes	No
Aging Issues	❑	❑
Medicare/Medicaid	❑	❑
Advanced Directives, Healthcare Agents	❑	❑
Loneliness and Depression	❑	❑
Health Issues for Women	❑	❑
Health Issues for Men	❑	❑
Other suggestions _____		

Parish Based Health Ministry (PBHM) of Caritas Christi

Health Health Assessment Profile (2)

This survey has been developed to assess the health needs of the parish in order to determine how we may best begin to meet the needs. Your input is very important in shaping the direction of this parish ministry. Please take a few minutes to complete this form.

Demographics:

Age: Under 20 __   21–29 __   30–39 __   40–49 __   50–59 __   60–69 __   70–79 __   80+ __

Gender: Male __   Female __

Marital Status: Single __   Married __   Divorced/Separated __   Widowed __

Children: Yes __   No __   If yes, how many? __

Ages of Children: _____

Health Needs and Services: Please check (✓) those areas that you find most helpful for the parish community:

❑ Eucharistic ministry
❑ Friendly visitors
❑ Transportation to hospitals, doctors, etc.
❑ Respite care (temporary rest for caregivers)
❑ Health screening (blood pressure, cholesterol, diabetes, etc.)
❑ Telephone health network
❑ Shopping and simple household chores
❑ Expectant and new mother
❑ Referral information (doctors, nursing homes, etc.)
❑ Other _____

Support Groups:

❑ Bereavement
❑ Parenting
❑ Alzheimer's
❑ Weight control
❑ Addictions (substance and others)
❑ Other

If you can consider (<u>even if only occasionally</u>) giving of your time and talent to our parish health ministry, please complete the following:

Name _____

Address _____

Telephone _____

Health Education: Please check (✓) the educational programs that you would be most interested in attending:

❑ Aging issues
❑ Medicare/Medicaid
❑ Advanced directives, healthcare proxy
❑ Loneliness and depression
❑ Health and spirituality
❑ Blood pressure control
❑ AIDS
❑ Stress
❑ Nutrition
❑ Body/Mind program
❑ Prescription and over-the-counter meds
❑ Senior housing and nursing homes
❑ Aging parents
❑ Health issues for women and/or men
❑ Environmental issues
❑ Other _____

Are there other areas of health (caring for mind, body, and spirit) that could be included?

_____

_____

Thank you for your cooperation.
Parish Health Ministry Team

Health Assessment Profile (3)

Maintaining good health has as much to do with issues of lifestyle, work satisfaction, social environment, relationships, and spirituality as it does with our physical condition. As God invites all of us to wholeness, to choose life, and live it to its fullness, health and faith are closely related.

Parish Name _____   Parish Leadership:

Address _____   Pastor _____

_____   Staff _____

Telephone _____   Staff _____

Fax _____   Staff _____

Number of Parishioners: Total _____   Active _____

1a. Does your parish have an active parish council?   ❏ Yes   ❏ No   **1b.** Would you see the role of the parish council as helpful to the parish-based health ministry?   ❏ Yes   ❏ No

2. What activities, groups, or ministries in your parish would you identify as health-related (e.g., bereavement ministry, visits to nursing homes, support groups, exercise classes)? Please identify.

_____

_____

3a. Do you have a parish school?   ❏ Yes   ❏ No   **3b.** Number of students _____

4. Does someone in your parish have coverage responsibility for a hospital?   ❏ Yes   ❏ No

Or a nursing home?   ❏ Yes   ❏ No

5. Please list health or social agencies within the local area that service parishioners.

Nursing homes _____

Hospitals _____

Health clinics _____

Social agencies _____

Other _____

6. Age distribution of parishioners (% estimate):
___% children   ___% young adults   ___% adults   ___% seniors

7a. What would you estimate to be the number of homebound (elderly and/or sick) in the parish? ___

7b. Are you presently able to minister to them on a regular basis?   ❏ Yes   ❏ No

8. Is there another population within the parish that you would identify as needing special attention as it relates to issues of healing or wellness? If so, please identify:

_____

_____

Health Assessment Profile (3 cont.)

9a. Does your parish have a core group of lay Eucharistic ministers?   ❑ Yes   ❑ No

9b. Do they bring Eucharist to the sick and homebound?   ❑ Yes   ❑ No

10. **Ethnic/racial background** (% estimate)

___ % African American

___ % Asian

___ % Hispanic

___ % White

___ % Others _____ _____

Education (% estimate)

___ % Some high school or less

___ % High school graduate

___ % College graduate

___ % Postgraduate or professional degree

11. Are many in the parish on public assistance?   ❑ Yes   ❑ No

12. Special parish health needs (**1 = little need to 5 = strong need**). Circle one in each area:

- Homebound care (sacramental/prayer)   1   2   3   4   5

- Homebound care (daily living)   1   2   3   4   5
  (e.g., transportation, meals, homemaking, referrals)

- Respite care (relief for caregivers)   1   2   3   4   5

- Support groups   1   2   3   4   5
  (e.g., chemical addiction, divorce, teen pregnancy)
  Identify _____

- Wellness programs   1   2   3   4   5
  (e.g., parenting, exercise, prayer, stress management, health screenings)
  Identify _____

- Social justice issues   1   2   3   4   5
  (e.g., hunger, homelessness, aging, racism, poverty, sexism)
  Identify _____

- Other needs: Identify _____

_____

ST. VINCENT'S MEDICAL CENTER "PARISH NURSE (ACTIVITY) REPORT" AND "NEWSLETTER SUBMISSION FORM"

Parish Nurse Program
St. Vincent's Medical Center
2800 Main Street • Bridgeport, CT 06606
Tel. (203) 576-5716 Fax. (203) 576-6499

PARISH: _____   MONTH/YEAR: _____

NURSE: _____   TOTAL # HOURS: _____

PARISH NURSE REPORT

I.   ACTIVITY: # OF PERSONS
    Blood Pressure Control (including screenings)   _____
    Health Counseling   _____
    Phone Contacts   _____
    Visits to:
        Homes   _____
        Hospitals   _____
        Nursing Homes   _____
    Referrals:
        Pastor   _____
        Hospital   _____
        Physician   _____
        Community Agency   _____
        Other: _____
    Health Programs (Health Fairs, Health Talks, etc.) _____
                            TOTAL   _____

II. OTHER ACTIVITIES:
    Health Display _____   Sunday Bulletin _____
    Meetings:
        Staff   _____
        Pastor   _____
        Community   _____

III. TOTAL # PERSONS CONTACTED   _____
    AGES: 0–19___   20–39 ___   40–59 ___   60+ ___

IV. FINANCES INCURRED: _____

V.   COMMENTS: _____
_____
_____
_____

Parish Nurse Program

St. Vincent's Medical Center
2800 Main Street • Bridgeport, CT 06606
Tel. (203) 576-5716 Fax. (203) 576-6499

Newsletter Submission Form

Date: _____

From: _____   Parish: _____

Phone: _____

Subject: _____

Article/Contents: _____

_____

_____

_____

_____

_____

_____

_____

_____

_____

_____

_____

_____

_____

_____

Please note that all articles/submissions will be edited as appropriate.

PRAYERS FOR PARISH NURSES

A Prayer for a Parishioner Preparing to Enter the Hospital

The Lord is my light and my salvation; whom shall I fear?
> —*Psalm 27:1*

Dear Lord,
    You know that this is an anxious time for [name],
        as [he/she] prepares to enter the hospital.
Hospitals are blessed places where healing and helping
    take place; but hospitals are also houses
        of the unknown,
            of things out of our control.
Remind [name], O Lord, that nothing is out of reach
    of Your ever present caring and compassion;
        that You are, indeed, [his/her] "life's refuge."
Help [name] to be comforted in the fact that [he/she]
    does not take this journey alone;
You are always at [his/her] side: guiding, protecting,
    supporting, strengthening, and loving.
Bless [name] with courage, strength, and peace that this
    hospitalization may provide a time of rest and
    restoration; that [he/she] may soon be gifted
    with the recovery which is Your gift
    and Your grace. Amen.

A Prayer for a Parishioner before Surgery

When you walk thought fire, you shall not be burned.
—*Isaiah 43:2*

Dear Lord Jesus,
None of us looks forward to surgery; the
anticipation itself may make us feel as if we are
about to "walk through fire"; and yet, surgery is
truly a precious and a healing gift,
with which You have graced our world, O Lord.
For it is sometimes only through this painful
"walk through fire" that our wounded bodies
may be made whole.
Bless the hands of [name]'s surgeon that they may
be instruments of Your healing and Your love.
Bless [name]'s spirit that [he/she] may be strong
and courageous as [he/she] takes on this new
challenge which You place before [him/her].
While [Name] knows that [he/she] is about to
"walk through fire," [he/she] trusts firmly in Your
caring commitment that, as promised in scripture,
[he/she] "shall not be burned." Amen.

A Prayer for a Sick Child Parishioner

People were bringing even infants to him that he might touch them. . . .
Jesus...called [the children] . . . and said . . . the kingdom of God belongs
[to them].

—Luke 18:15–17

Dear Lord Jesus,
You treasured children so much that You taught
our hearts should become like theirs if we would enter
the kingdom of heaven; and You would not allow
anyone to keep the children from You.
Be with [name], this beloved child of Yours, now in
[his/her] illness and suffering.
Gather [name] into Your caring arms during [his/her]
time of sickness and grant [him/her] the peace,
and the comfort,
and the rest
which You alone can give.
Let [name] know how much You love [him/her]
and that You suffer with [him/her] in [his/her] hurting.
Protect, bless, guard, and comfort [name] with the caring and
compassion which You alone can give. Amen.

A Prayer for a Parishioner Entering a Nursing Home

Do not worry about your life, what you will eat, or about your body and what you will wear.

—*Luke 12:22*

Dear Father in heaven,

[Name] is about to take a very important step in [his/her]

life journey; it is a transition that can be frightening, and yet it is

a transition that is also most blessed.

For, here, in the nursing home, the cares and worries

of the world are placed literally in Your hands.

Now it is time for [name] to enter into the contemplative phase

of [his/her] life; this is a grace which was not possible

in the midst of the busyness of [name]'s

former life commitments.

[Name]'s new ministry is now only to live in Your love and

Your light and to share these with those [he/she] meets

each day.

Bless [name] and grace [his/her] nursing home ministry of

presence with Your spirit of peace and prayerfulness.

Let [name] be to all [he/she] meets a beacon of Your love

and Your gentleness. Amen.

A Prayer for a Cognitively Impaired Parishioner

Nor height, nor depth . . . will be able to separate us from the love of God in Christ Jesus our Lord.

—Romans 8:3

Dear Father in heaven,
   You alone, who created us in Your image and likeness,
      can understand the illness that has taken away the
beautiful thoughts and feelings with which [name]'s human spirit
      was once gifted. This is a very painful thing for those of us
         who love [him/her]. And yet, we know that You do not reside
      in [name]'s mind, or even in [his/her] heart but rather in
         the depths of [name]'s soul;
      in a place where no illness which ravages the human body,
         no disease which destroys the human mind,
            can ever reach.
   Neither the heights of wisdom nor the depth of confusion
   can "separate" [name] from the love of Your Divine Son. Bless
[name] in the gentle mist of confusion which has become [his/her]
      earthly home. And take [name], one day, to [his/her]
heavenly home where, with the angels and saints, [he/she] will again be
   able to praise Your glory with the joy and the understanding
         that You alone can give. Amen.

A Prayer for an Unconscious Parishioner

O Lord, you have searched me and known me . . . you discern my thoughts from
far away.

—*Psalm 139:1–2*

Gentle Lord,
  You know that [name] is no longer able to pray for
[him/herself]. We do not know where [his/her] spirit now rests,
  but we trust that it is held tenderly in Your beloved hands.
[Name's] ability to speak words of prayer are not important to You,
  Lord God of life, for you "have probed" [him/her] and
    "You know" [him/her] both from near and "from afar."
[He/she] is Your beloved child and [his/her] name is written
  in the palm of Your hand.
Bless [name] with Your compassionate care and hold [him/her]
  close to Your loving heart during this time
    of fragility and weakness.
Let [name] hear Your voice in the stillness and silence of [his/her]
  immortal soul. Amen.

A Prayer for a Parishioner's Healing

I know the plans I have for you, says the Lord, plans for your welfare, and not for harm!

—Jeremiah 29:11

Dear Father in heaven,
    We pray now for healing for [name]. We pray that
[he/she] will be healed, in body and in spirit, from this illness
which has invaded [his/her] life. We pray for this physical
healing, Dear Lord, but only if it is Your blessed will.
You alone know what is needed for [name]'s life, for as taught
by the prophet Jeremiah, You "know well the plans"
You have in mind for [name]; "plans for [his/her]
welfare, not for [his/her] woe."
Thus, as we beg this healing, of [name]'s body or spirit, we ask also
"let us pray" in the precious words of Your Son, Our Lord Jesus:
"If it be possible let the chalice pass" from [name], yet not
[his/her] will but Thine be done. Amen.

A Prayer for a Parishioner's Strength in Suffering

My help comes from the Lord, who made heaven and earth.
—Psalm 121:1

Dearest Lord,
It's not easy for [name] to pray in the midst of
[his/her] suffering; sometimes the pain is overwhelming.
We beg You to become [name's] strength and help [him/her]
in the midst of these difficult days.
Wrap [him/her] in Your loving arms and cradle [his/her]
suffering soul in a blanket of Your tender care.
Breathe Your Blessed strength into [name]'s spirit, that
[he/she] may gain the courage to accept,
the courage to endure, and, at times,
even the courage to weep.
Make of [name]'s suffering a crucible within which
Your grace and Your beauty will shine forth
to all [he/she] meets, O God of
miracles and wonders. Amen.

A Prayer for a Parishioner's Acceptance of God's Will

Can I not do with you . . . as this potter has done? says the Lord. Just like the clay
in the potter's hand, so are you in my hand.

—*Jeremiah* 18:6

Dear Father in heaven,
    You asked the prophet Jeremiah if You could
do with him "as the potter has done." To remold him in
the image You would have him become. This is what
You are asking of [name].
But this is not an easy thing for [him/her] to accept,
    Dear Lord: to have [his/her] life plans dismantled,
    disorganized, or even destroyed,
that [he/she] may be remolded as Your will allows.
Bless [name] with Your courage,
    with Your strength, and
    with Your peace, in the midst of this time of
    challenge and suffering.
Help [name] to accept a plan that is not [his/hers].
    Be to [him/her] a refuge, where [he/she] might
    seek peaceful shelter until
    the storm has passed. Amen.

A Prayer of Thanksgiving for a Parishioner's Recovery from Illness

For now the winter is past, the rain is over and gone.
— *The Song of Songs 2:11*

Dear Lord Jesus,
    Thank you for the blessing of [name]'s recovery from
[his/her]illness. Let [him/her] rejoice in this precious springtime
    of Your love, for at last "the winter is past" and the
        "rains are over and gone."
    Bless [name] with the grace of gratitude for the gift of
        health and the gift of strength.
Guide [him/her] to use this treasure
        to share Your love and Your compassion
            in the ministry of Your gospel message
                to all [he/she] meets.
We praise You, O Lord, for Your care;
        we praise You, O Lord, for Your compassion;
            we praise You, O God of life and resurrection,
    for Your tender love and merciful heart. Amen.

A Prayer for a Terminally Ill Parishioner

Unless a grain of wheat falls into the earth and dies, it remains just a single grain; but if it dies, it bears much fruit.

—John 12:24

Dear Lord Jesus,
    You taught that the "grain of wheat must fall
        to the ground and die" in order to bear fruit;
    You, who came to know so intimately the lesson of
        that fallen "grain"! This is now the message
          which [name] has heard!
    Strengthen [him/her] with the courage which You
          alone can give.
    The "grain" of [name]'s earthly life is preparing
        to fall to the ground that [his/her] heart's legacy
          may bear fruit for generations to come.
    Let [name]'s falling be as gentle as an autumn leaf
        drifting slowly, rhythmically, tenderly, downward
        as it blankets the chilled earth with
          a splendid quilt of orange and red.
    Grace the world with the precious coverlet of [name]'s
        life and love, that [his/her] spirit may
          endure forever. Amen.

A Prayer for a Parishioner Beginning Hospice Care

Do not fear those who kill the body but cannot kill the soul.
                                        —*Matthew 10:28*

Dear Lord Jesus,
     [Name], your beloved [son/daughter], is about to
embark on [his/her] final journey to the blessed place
     which you promised to prepare for all of us.
The enemy of illness has ravaged the earthly body of [name]
     but [his/her] soul grows stronger and more beautiful
          each day.
As Saint Paul taught so many centuries ago, "even though
     our outer nature is wasting away,
          our inner nature is being renewed day by day" *(2 Corinthians 4:16).*
"For this," Paul added, "slight momentary affliction
     is preparing for us for an eternal weight of glory
          beyond all measure" *(17).*
Help [name] in this time of [his/her] life transition,
     to look, with Paul, "not what can be seen but
          what cannot be seen; for what can be seen is temporary,
               but what cannot be seen is eternal" *(18).* Amen.

A Prayer for Discontinuing a Parishioner's Life Support

For everything there is a season . . . a time to be born and a time to die."
                                                                    —*Ecclesiastes 3:1-2*

Dear Father in heaven,
        We are about to give our dear [name] into Your
tender and loving care.
        You know how hard it is for us to let go!
We have loved [name] in health and in illness;
        we have loved [name] in joy and sorrow;
                we have loved [name] in strength and suffering.
Our earthly world will never be the same without
[name]. But now it is time for [name]'s heavenly
        reward; now it is time for us to surrender
[him/her] into Your loving arms.
Bring [name] into the company of the angels and
saints; let [him/her] live forever in Your
        tender care, and let [name]'s memory live
        each day in the hearts of those
                who loved [him/her]. Amen.

(From O'Brien, 2003, *Prayer in Nursing*, reprinted with permission.)

A Prayer for a Parishioner Experiencing Grief or Loss

Blessed are those who mourn, for they will be comforted.
—Matthew 5:4

Dear Father,
You know that [name] is grieving deeply
right now. We know that you have promised comfort
to those who mourn, but sometimes it seems a long
time in coming.
Grant [name] peace and patience during this
time of loss and grieving.
Bless [him/her] with Your loving care and
compassion that [he/she] may face each day
supported by the tender awareness of Your
presence and Your love.
Help [name] to know that [he/she] is never
alone in [his/her] grieving but is
always accompanied by Your
Blessed Spirit of wisdom
and understanding.
Grace [name] with healing. Amen.

A Prayer for a Bereaved Parshioner

I am the resurrection and the life. Those who believe in me, even though they die, will live and everyone who lives and believes in me will never die.
                                    —*John 11:25–26*

Dearest Lord Jesus,
    [Name] has lost [his/her] beloved [spouse/parent/child];
no words can ease the pain of this terrible suffering.
[Name]'s only true comfort can come from You
alone, Lord God of life, and death,
who promised in Your own blessed
words: "I am the resurrection and the life;
whoever believes in me, even if he dies,
will live and whoever lives and
believes in me will never die."
Bless [name] with Your tender care and
comfort and help [him/her] to remember
Your promise;
that [his/her] beloved [name] is not dead,
but lives in glory in Your heavenly kingdom,
where one day [he/she] will be reunited
among the company
of the blessed. Amen.

SUBJECT INDEX

SCRIPTURE INDEX